Food and Environment
in Early and Medieval China

ENCOUNTERS WITH ASIA

Victor H. Mair, Series Editor

Encounters with Asia is an interdisciplinary series dedicated to the exploration of all the major regions and cultures of this vast continent. Its timeframe extends from the prehistoric to the contemporary; its geographic scope ranges from the Urals and the Caucasus to the Pacific. A particular focus of the series is the Silk Road in all of its ramifications: religion, art, music, medicine, science, trade, and so forth. Among the disciplines represented in this series are history, archeology, anthropology, ethnography, and linguistics. The series aims particularly to clarify the complex interrelationships among various peoples within Asia, and also with societies beyond Asia.

A complete list of books in the series
is available from the publisher.

FOOD AND ENVIRONMENT IN EARLY AND MEDIEVAL CHINA

E. N. ANDERSON

PENN

UNIVERSITY OF PENNSYLVANIA PRESS

PHILADELPHIA

Published by
University of Pennsylvania Press
Philadelphia, Pennsylvania 19104-4112
www.upenn.edu/pennpress

Printed in the United States of America on acid-free paper
10 9 8 7 6 5 4 3 2 1

Library of Congress Cataloging-in-Publication Data
ISBN 978-0-8122-4638-4

To the Silent Gardeners

"The tree of humanity forgets the labour of the silent gardeners who sheltered it from the cold, watered it in time of drought, shielded it against wild animals; but it preserves faithfully the names mercilessly cut into its bark."
> —Heinrich Heine, 1833, as quoted in Gross 1983: 323

This book is dedicated to the billions of ordinary people, almost all of them nameless and forgotten, who domesticated rice, developed bread wheat, invented brewing, created soy sauce, tamed the dog, and otherwise discovered our foods, domesticated our crops, invented our basic food processing techniques, and created our basic food production systems—while their leaders, the famous kings and premiers and generals, waged war and massacred. The ordinary people of history gave us life while the leaders gave us death. It is the ordinary creative farmers and gatherers and food technicians who have won immortality. Their names are lost, but their true glory is deathless.

"Let us now praise famous men. . . .
There be of them, that have left a name behind them, that their
    praises might be reported.
And some there be, which have no memorial; who are perished, as
    though they had never been; and are become as though they
    had never been born; and their children after them.
But these were merciful men, whose righteousness hath not been
    forgotten. . . .
Their seed shall remain for ever, and their glory shall not be
    blotted out."
> —Ecclesiasticus 44: 1, 8–13

CONTENTS

PREFACE

This book covers the development of the Chinese food system from earliest times into the Ming Dynasty. Most attention is devoted to recent work on predynastic China and on the Yuan Dynasty, since these are both key to the system and the subjects of recent major research. Considerations of space have made me leave most of Ming and all of Qing and postimperial China for other venues, but I provide conclusions about China's food system at the end of imperial times in the early twentieth century, as well as a few comparisons with recent times. For notes on later times, see my website postings "Ming and Qing: Population and Agriculture" on late imperial food and science, "China's Environmental Ruin" on contemporary mainland China, and "Chinese Food Updates" on contemporary food ethnography (www.krazykioti.com). These are works in progress, are not to be taken as final, and not to be cited without my permission.

This book owes everything to Victor Mair, who expressed interest in my work and helped and encouraged at every stage. I also owe an enormous debt to my lifelong coworker Paul Buell, and to many friends and helpers in the world of Asian food, especially those who kept contact and remained encouraging during my long years away from China studies—including Jacqueline Newman, Charles Perry, Françoise Sabban, and others. Many more recent friends and fellow scholars have also helped with the enterprise, including Sidney Cheung, David Knechtges, Zelda Liang, Nick Menzies, Tan Chee-Beng, Jianhua "Ayoe" Wang, and Sumei Yi. Peter Agree has served ably as editor, and I am deeply grateful to Alison Anderson and Gail Schmitt for extremely detailed and careful copy-editing. Thanks also for incredible experiences in a lost world, to Choi Kwok-tai and Cecilia Choi, and to Chow Hung-fai; and to Purevsuren Tsolmonjav for an intense and inspiring introduction to Mongolian life and environment. Finally, I am deeply grateful, as always, to my wife Barbara and our children, children-in-law, and grandchildren; they give me life itself.

USAGE

====

I use standard transcriptions of the relevant languages.

Herein, for western Asia and northern Africa, "Near East" applies to ancient and medieval times, "Middle East" to the modern zone so called. "West Asia" excludes North Africa but includes some borderlands such as the Caucasus. "West Asia and North Africa" would be far preferable to either of the former terms, for obvious reasons, but this is not the place to make the change.

Finally, one of the most consistent minor annoyances in East Asian studies is the stubborn insistence of historians and art historians on mistranslating Chinese and Japanese words for plants and animals. This is far worse for Japanese (where *tanuki*, the raccoon dog, becomes "badger," the *uguisu* bush-warbler becomes "nightingale," and so on) but bad enough in the case of Chinese. Especially annoying is the persistent mistranslation of *mei* as "plum." The plant is actually a species of apricot that is known in botany and in the nursery trade as the "flowering apricot." The problem would not be so bad if China did not have plums, but it does, and they are called *li*. Admittedly, "Oriental flowering apricot" is impossibly long for translations of poetry. Thus, herein, I follow some recent authors (such as James Hargett in Fan 2010) and simply use the Chinese word *mei*.

Somewhat farther from food, but important enough to be a problem here, are the absurd Victorianisms like "benevolence," "righteousness," and "caitiff" that still afflict Chinese translations and make good Chinese writing sound like stuffy Victorian nonsense. Also a problem is the old tendency to see ancient China as "feudal" and accordingly to use words like "marquis" and "earl" to translate Chinese titles that really mean something quite different. I shall try to avoid this, but some translations, such as "duke" for *gong*, are almost impossible to avoid.

Introduction

One adept at learning is like the king of Qi who, when
eating chicken, was satisfied only after he had eaten a
thousand feet: if he were still unsatisfied, there would always
be another chicken foot to eat.

—Lü Buwei 2000: 129

Assembling a Food System

Chinese food has swept the world. In general, "globalization," whatever else it
may be, has generally meant the spread of American popular culture. The
cultural forms that have "swum upstream," spreading worldwide in the teeth
of American advances, are thus of special interest. Among such cultural ways,
Chinese food has an almost unique place. Almost no town on earth is without
a Chinese restaurant of some kind. Chinese canned, frozen, and preserved
foods are available in shops from Nairobi to Quito. Chinese cookbooks
abound in every bookstore.

The credit for this belongs partly to the quality and diversity of the food,
partly to the industriousness and enterprise of Chinese farmers, food workers,
merchants, writers, and chefs. However, much of the credit also belongs to the
farmers and food entrepreneurs of the rest of the world and to the eclectic
Chinese innovators who drew on this global storehouse of ingredients, techniques, and knowledges.

In anthropological usage, a food system is a process for producing, distributing, and consuming food. It thus takes in agriculture, hunting, foraging,
environmental management, trade, marketing, and food preparation, as well
as consumption (see P. West 2012: 18–26 on anthropology of food).

The Chinese food system did not develop in isolation. It was, in fact,
formed from a diverse set of regional agricultures and cuisines, merging and
borrowing from each other and being themselves further influenced by foods

and foodways from every part of the earth. Many people are surprised to learn that such foods as chiles, peanuts, and potatoes were not indigenous to China, but rather Native American domesticates acquired by China in the last very few centuries. Much earlier, wheat, sheep, and dozens of other West Asian foods migrated across Central Asia to China.

The present book does not attempt to tell the whole story, let alone the story of China's contacts with the world. Excellent recent histories, including the *Cambridge History of China* and the newer but briefer Harvard series of histories of the great dynasties, cover the story. Some of the new Harvard histories, including Mark Lewis's history of Tang (2009) and Timothy Brooks's of Yuan and Ming (2010), are particularly good on China in its world-system context.

Instead of trying to do too much, this book centers on western Eurasian contacts and influences during the Yuan Dynasty—the Mongol Empire's Chinese phase. This book also provides dense coverage of all the events leading up to this period. I briefly consider the Ming, but have—in the interests of space—ended this book with the end of Ming, except for a final chapter that generalizes about China's food and environment in history.

Imperial China lasted 2,200 years, during which time the population grew from perhaps 40 million to 400 million. Assuming an average population of 100 million over that time, and three generations per century, perhaps as many as 300 billion individuals had to be fed. Famines were frequent, malnutrition common, and life expectancy short, but the accomplishment still stands as incredible. No other part of the world supported such a dense population for so long. Natural increase led to continual pushing the resource base hard. Serious famines occurred on the average of every other year. Yet most people, most of the time, managed to eat.

Admittedly, China had some rough periods. The time of the Three Kingdoms after the fall of Han, the period of Five Dynasties and Ten Kingdoms after Tang, the collapse of Ming in 1630–44, and other dynastic meltdowns were dreadful. But they were quickly resolved and did not lead to the long and profound dark ages that ended the Roman Empire, the lowland Maya civilization, or the great empires of Africa and Central Asia. China's natural endowments have much to do with this but obviously are not the main story. Other parts of the world were well endowed with resources but did not do so well.

China has a great deal of fertile soil and well distributed and abundant rainfall in much of the country and is well supplied with rivers. It has the greatest biodiversity of any temperate zone area; this biodiversity is concentrated in the southwest, because of the lush mountains and valleys there. Much of contemporary China is desert or barren high-altitude plateau, but most of these areas were not part of China until the Qing Dynasty. China has a great extent both north-south and east-west, allowing people, crops, and other plant and animal resources to migrate freely but also to take advantage of resources from different climate zones. Jared Diamond (1997) pointed out the disadvantages of having a long, narrow north-south country; it is hard to transfer crops around—they have to readapt to new climate zones. Climate change was frequent in Chinese history but had minimal effect, because of the north-south and east-west mobility noted above. If the climate turned warm and wet, as it did in Zhou and to some extent in Tang, people moved north and west. If the climate turned cold and dry, as it did in Ming, people moved south.

The one time this was ruinous was the Medieval Warm Period—but not because of climate. That period of astonishingly rapid and dramatic warming led to the Jurchen, Mongols, and other Central Asian nomadic groups being able to increase their human and livestock populations by stunning amounts and to spread and conquer. Genghis Khan was particularly good at parlaying good weather into world empire, but the successes of the Liao and Jin show he was not alone. Conversely, Song was weakened by disease, drought, local torrential rainfall, and other phenomena probably associated with the Medieval Warm Period. Climate is not destiny, but it can enable figures such as Genghis Khan. Otherwise, China dealt with the worldwide cooling of the early centuries CE and the much more dramatic cooling of the Little Ice Age, around 1400–1800 (Pages 2k Network 2013; they note that the Medieval Warm Period was rather weakly correlated across continents, but their charts (5) show it as strong everywhere, with dramatic warmth during 1000–1200 in Asia).

Another advantage, not often enough appreciated, is that China is centripetal. It seeks its center. The central part of the country is composed of the Yellow, Huai, and Yangzi valleys, a vast continuous area of fertile soil. In early historic times, this was an unbelievably lush landscape—swarming with game, covered by billions of fruit and nut trees and edible wild plants, and generally blessed with riches. China is bounded by rugged mountains and deserts that protect it from invasion—not enough to keep invaders out, but enough to prevent them from routinely devastating the landscape, as happened in eastern Europe.

The downside of this is that China is all too easy to centralize. Almost all historians now seem to agree that Europe's great natural advantage is the fact that it cannot be conquered and held as one single empire—at least, nobody has ever managed to do so (Lieberman 2009; Morris 2010). The central spine of mountains is surrounded by a set of detached, widely separated, very rich lands: the regions we know as France, Germany, Poland, Italy, Spain, and so on. The fact that nobody could centralize control over this disparate range of countries has led to a great deal of independence. In particular, in the critically important seventeenth century, when science, capitalism, imperialism, and liberal politics were all becoming major forces, the desperate attempts by autocrats to enforce their absolutism (P. Anderson 1974) were doomed to fail, because dissidents simply went to the next country.

China, unfortunately, could easily centralize, set up a dinosauric bureaucracy, and crack down on independent inquiry. This was done repeatedly: under Qin Shi Huang Di, Han Wu Di, and on down to Chairman Mao. The Warring States Period, of course, proves the point: China's great age of thought and philosophy was precisely when the country was divided into many small states, each seeking to attain an advantage over the others by getting the best experts on statecraft, war, and policy. The period of disunion from 300 to 589 was probably similar , but is poorly documented.

Why Study the Chinese Food System?

The world is now in desperate need of an intensive yet sustainable food production system. Such a system can be constructed on the basis of East Asian insights. For 10,000 years, East Asian peoples have been developing systems that often used resources in relatively sustainable and efficient ways, permitting extremely intensive and productive systems to survive over millennia. East Asian agriculture uses minimal land and resources for maximal production.

One key design feature of that agricultural system—arrived at by trial and error, not by deliberate plan—is the overall purpose of maximizing nutritional adequacy, not maximizing profit or starch or oil or any other single output. This objective has been accomplished by selecting strains of plants and animals that would produce maximum nutrients of all sorts, including vitamins and minerals, with minimum input. The result has been an agricultural system that maintains a great deal of biodiversity, both in the wild and in cultivated crops. Fields, gardens, managed semiwild lands, managed forests, and specialized agricultural landscapes are all part of this integrated system.

The system generally increased its food production capacity by intensifying the latter in place. This required a "biological" development strategy (Hayami and Ruttan 1985), in which more and more fertilizer, compost, and land improvement were used, and more and more crop species grown, over time. This requires a concomitant increase in skill and knowledge.

By contrast, the Western world has tended to rely on constantly expanding the range of cultivated landscape. The conquest of the New World and Australia was driven in great measure by the desperate need for more land. This was in large part because of concentration on animal husbandry—especially cattle and sheep—and on relatively low-yield grains, notably wheat and barley. The Chinese, typically, managed to develop high-yield wheat agriculture, and eventually the West did too, but expansion remained the key western developmental idea. Latin America, for instance, was, and continues to be, cleared of natural vegetation—and indigenous people—largely for cattle ranching.

There have been large pockets of intensive, and intensifying, agriculture in the West, for example, Italy throughout much of history, Moorish Andalucia, and northwestern Europe since the 1700s or earlier. China has had its extensive, expanding, low-yield zones, especially on the northwest frontier, where agriculture kept encroaching on the steppes, only to collapse and retreat when dry periods occurred. But the general difference was enough to make Chinese grain yields five times those in most of the West in the early twentieth century: about 2,500 kg/ha versus 500. Comparing, say, Denmark with northern Shaanxi would reverse those figures, but we are still contemplating a real and important difference. It matters for the future: the world has run out of agricultural land, and a collapse inward has begun as more and more land goes out of cultivation due to urbanization and erosion.

Especially intensive and sustainable has been the system that initially developed in southern China—long before it was "China" or "Chinese"—and spread widely throughout eastern Asia and Oceania. Rice paddy agriculture, highly fertilized vegetable plots, tree cropping, and intensive, dryland garden-fields are components. The principal domestic animals—pigs and chickens—did not require the vast expanses of grazing land required by cattle and sheep. Variants of the system exist from northern Japan to southern Indonesia. China has generally been the major site of innovation, but far from the only one.

Such hopeful and creative modern systems as polyculture carry these insights forward today. Traditional Chinese agriculture was far from perfect, but it was incomparably more efficient and environmentally sane than modern industrial agriculture—especially the form currently used in China itself.

The World-System Model

My analysis of the formation of this food system rests on a generalized world-system model. The idea of a world-system began with Immanuel Wallerstein (1976), who had a detailed and systematic theory of how such a system operates. At some point, a translocal or transnational network of exchange becomes so important that it is a real system—a bounded entity within which goods and information flow in large quantities and relatively freely, as opposed to sharply reduced flows outside the bounds of the system. Furthermore, in a system, everything is connected, directly or indirectly. Any fairly major event in the system influences every part of it. A human body is a system. So is the electrical wiring of my house. A world-system—or *oikumene*, to use an old Greek term—is a system of interacting polities that are closely linked by trade, communication, and information flow. The world has had local "world-systems" (or local polity systems, if you will) for a very long time (Chase-Dunn and Anderson 2005; Chase-Dunn et al. 2007). The major ones had joined into a single world-system by 1600.

Obviously, these definitions are vague and relative. There is no question that the world today is one system; a financial shock in Japan ruins companies in Germany and South Africa. There is no question that the world economy of 15,000 BCE was not a system. The flood of population from Asia into the Western Hemisphere around that time, and its dramatic increase there, did not affect the rest of the world one whit. In between, a great deal happened. Fairly arbitrary cutoffs have to be selected if one is writing histories; thus the invasion of Syria by Pharaoh Thutmose I around 1500 BCE is somewhat—but not entirely—arbitrarily set as the point at which the Egyptian system fused with the West Asian one into a single Near Eastern oikumene (Christopher Chase-Dunn, forthcoming).

The corresponding date for the Near East and East Asia has not been set. In formal world-systems theory, it probably did not occur until the nineteenth century, when the West could directly invade, dominate, and dictate terms. But this was only the end of a long process. The Mongols definitively united East and West in the 1200s, and no one could really say there were separate systems after that. Still earlier, West and East first came into violent contact in

751 CE, when the expanding Arab and Chinese Empires met and clashed at the Talas River in the dead center of Asia; the Arabs won, and Central Asia became Muslim. Far earlier came the fateful moment when wheat and barley reached China. No one knows the exact date, but it was apparently around 4,500 years ago. At some point a trader or farmer from somewhere that might later be called Afghanistan showed up at a compound in what would much later be called Shaanxi, and said "boy, have I got some seeds to show you!" Evidently this was a less memorable event than Thutmose's magnificent and grim war, but infinitely more important and meaningful in historic terms.

Shortly before this, around 3500 BCE, horse domestication permitted highly mobile steppe nomadism. The horse reached China by 1500, and west and east were well and truly united. The steppe became a vast freeway rather than a cold, hostile barrier. Today, in this world of air and ship transport, we have no concept of how important clear and unbarriered land routes were in earlier times. There was nothing to stop a rider from taking off at top speed in Beijing and galloping all the way to the Black Sea, changing horses as necessary. In fact, under the Mongols, the courier service did exactly that. Similarly, there was nothing in the American Great Plains to prevent the same institution arising: the Pony Express was copied directly from the Mongol post (Weatherford 2004) and had a brief but glorious "run" in 1860–61.

By the beginning of our Common Era, silk from China was already crossing Asia, to be exchanged for silver and other valuables. Not until the nineteenth century was the main route labeled the Silk Road (Hansen 2012), a term coined by geographer Ferdinand von Richtofen in 1877. The term is a good one, though there was no single road but rather a shifting set of caravan tracks through the desert. Also, all manner of goods flowed in both directions; silk was only the most famous and probably the most long-lasting as a trade staple. In any event, this great route was the most important long-range transnational pathway on earth for over a thousand years. Empires flowed along it, but more important were the foods and other ordinary goods—textiles included. The empires fell or faded, and even the names of many of them have been forgotten, but the domesticated crops and food-processing techniques are still with us, giving us life. Wheat and barley had already been crossing Asia on the ancestral routes that became the Silk Road, but later, horses and chariots, metallurgy, and countless other technological innovations came along the road or along the more northerly steppe routes. As David Christian pointed out (2000), it was a major belt of interface for pastoralists and settled people from the beginning, as well as a route linking West and East. The pastoralists often entered settled life by conquering Silk Road cities and settling down; at other times they worked, voluntarily or as slaves, for the cities and farms.

The other useful concept I take from world-systems theory is the idea that a world-system has a core (a core nation or small group of nations), some semiperipheral polities, and some peripheral ones. The core tends to dominate terms of trade and conquest, such that it keeps the other polities down. The peripheral polities are particularly disadvantaged by being politically and militarily weak and often are exploited for raw materials. Semiperipheral polities are potential rivals and often diligently develop themselves militarily so that they can loot or even conquer and take over the core.

These dynamics have played out time and again in East Asia. Whatever state or states ruled central north China has or have generally been the core. Siberia and parts of upland Southeast Asia were peripheral. In between were the fascinating semiperipheral states that rose and fell, especially in Central Asia: the Xiongnu, Turks, Tibetans, Mongols, and others. Many of these were cut down by Chinese rhetoric into "nomad" and "barbarian" states. As we shall see, they were far from merely that. Korea and Vietnam have also been semiperipheral throughout a good deal of China's history.

China was a core—usually the core—of East Asia until the nineteenth-century wars, in which China was brutally "semiperipheralized" in the unified world-system whose core became the Western European nations and, increasingly, the United States. Today we have seen the reemergence of Japan as a core nation and are watching China rapidly move into core status again. The world of the twenty-first century has multiple core areas.

The world-systems view takes advantage of the known facts of diffusion (Mair 2006). Humans are amazingly good at adopting each other's ideas. Some measure of this phenomenon occurred when Lewis and Clark contacted Native American tribes who had never been within hundreds of miles of a white person before and found them telling French folktales, reworked in local languages. The tales had spread from Quebec by word of mouth, through thousands of miles of trackless and unexplored country where no whites had ever been and where writing and literacy did not exist.

Similar spreads are numerous worldwide. If folktales can spread that fast, it is clearly no surprise to find, for example, that the bow and arrow spread from its invention in Africa about 50,000 years ago to the entire world (though some isolated areas still lacked it at the time of European expansion). Nor are we surprised to find early Indo-European loanwords in Chinese and ancient Thai loans in Korean.

A world-system theorist's teeth are set on edge by words like "hybridity" when they are applied to cultures. Cultures are not remotely like different species. There never was a time when cultures were pure, homogeneous, isolated, or essentialized. People have always been wildly creative and dynamic and, above all, open to any influences from any direction. People appropriate anything good they can get their hands and minds on. Cultures reflect this.

The Chinese had something like a world-system theory during the Warring States period, and to some extent afterward. Westerners are apt to think of the Chinese self-label Middle Kingdom (or Central Country) as mere vanity, but originally it seems to have meant "central states"—plural. The Warring States writers, or even earlier ones, saw that there were core states and peripheral ones. The latter were labeled with terms we now translate as "barbarians," but perhaps "peripheral peoples" would be a better translation. The Chinese even distinguished semiperipheral states—"cooked barbarians," those that had picked up Chinese culture or a good deal of it—from "raw barbarians," those without much Chinese culture. Snobbish, ethnocentric, and patronizing as this was, it displays awareness of the ideas underlying world-systems theory.

Today, however, core nations are defined by military and economic might, not by culture. The Chinese, by contrast, looked at culture as basic. This idea evolved into the Confucian theory that morality was key to politics, and politics to military and economic power. The counter-theories, based on a more sober awareness of military and economic influence, then became even more like world-system theory.

Recent studies are radically different from the old studies that portrayed China as a remote, unique, isolated, changeless civilization. Modern historical studies like those of Lewis (2006, 2009a, b), Mallory and Mair (2000), Tan (2009), and Wade and Sun (2010) and foodways studies like those brought together by Cheung and Tan (2007) emphasize the fact that from early times, China was involved in a huge, active network of trade and contact. The Chinese created a great civilization that has its own wonderful and fascinating features but is broadly parallel to other civilizations and went through the same stages as other civilizations: invention of agriculture, development of settled life, construction of great cities, development of law codes, and the rest.

Diffusion, Cultural Choice, and Chinese Distinctiveness

Those points are rather obvious, but they are worth stating because they stand in contrast to the old Orientalist view, still not uncommon in China studies. It holds that China is unique, homogeneous, and isolated and that its civilization cannot be compared with any other. Often it adds the idea that the Chinese live in a world of mystical correspondences, ancient texts, and changeless 2,500-year-old thoughts that are "not true philosophy" (whatever that may mean), rather than in a world where people concern themselves with food, clothing, and shelter and are quite willing to update or selectively reapply ancient guides.

Students of agriculture, metallurgy, and other "manual arts" have long recognized that China influenced, and was influenced by, other cultures; but students of medicine, political theory, philosophy, poetry, and other arts of the mind, including perceptions of the environment, still sometimes insist that China can be interpreted only on its own terms. They appear to believe the Chinese had not only different theories but different physical realities from the rest of humanity.

This belief in the uniqueness and changelessness of Chinese culture seems based, ultimately, on a Platonic view of the world. Plato held that we know only what is in our heads, and we can meditate to full knowledge of the Ideal. In contrast, his student Aristotle held that we must try to find out what we can about real, tangible things out there in the world. Western civilization has ever since been trying to deal with the difference between studying things of the mind and studying things that we can all see, touch, and discuss on the basis of the knowledge from those senses. Many people, especially in the humanities, prefer a broadly Platonic approach; they are more comfortable in a world of ideas. Others, especially in the hard sciences, are Aristotelian. The Chinese fail to make a huge distinction, and I have always followed them in this; I prefer to study both and to use both approaches in studying particular cultural matters.

Pointing out that China shared basic perceptions of agriculture with the West does not mean that they had the same crops or production systems. Pointing out that China shares much medical knowledge with the West does not mean Chinese medicine is merely some sort of variant of world medicine. The middle ground is the only tenable one: Chinese, like Westerners, responded to real-world conditions, but they responded in ways conditioned by the cultural and personal environments and knowledge systems they brought to the task.

Ultimately, however, agriculture has to produce food, and medicine has to provide at least some visible curing. Thus there is constant feedback from reality in both cases. Every society produces not one, but many, distinctive solutions, with different styles, perceptions, philosophies, and experiences. Wheat, maize, millet, and potatoes can all be starch staples. Beans, peas, cattle, pigs, and many other species can provide protein (contrary to myth, bean protein is not "incomplete").

In medicine, the body is basically the same everywhere, and malaria, dysentery, and smallpox vary only with the local microbial strains; but cultural understandings of the body, and above all the solutions people invent for their health problems, differ profoundly. Yet they are not in free variation; people want to be healed, and hence it is no surprise to find that the Chinese found many perfectly effective cures. *Qinghaosu (Artemisia annua)* cures malaria whether one is a traditional Chinese or a modern Brazilian. The difference between old China and modern Brazil lies not in the effect but in the perception: it determines whether one attributes the effects of the drug to its *qi* or to the toxic effect of artemisinin on *Plasmodium falciparum*. This is not a simple contrast of "error" and "truth," nor is it merely two different arbitrary cultural claims. It is a difference between an early, sincere, serious, well-thought-out scientific theory that is now in some ways inadequate, and a later serious, well-thought-out theory that is clearly more accurate but will no doubt prove inadequate in the future. We do well to respect all those who have seriously tried to understand these matters, and to understand their understandings as serious theorizing—not as some sort of random cultural noise or ignorant mysticism. Cultural arbitrariness of the sort alleged by postmodernists would never have let anyone find qinghaosu in the first place or observe its effects.

Kwang-chih Chang (2002a) pointed out that early China shared with Native American cultures a basic sense of continuity between humans and the rest of the cosmos—animals, plants, hills, stars. This was a concept that the Chinese themselves discussed with words like "harmony" (*he*) and "resonance." The West, in his view, committed itself to a rupture not only between people and nature but also between people and the gods. This he traces back to ancient Sumer (K.-c. Chang 2002). Chang rather exaggerates—I believe for effect—but the difference is real—and critically important. Any lingering doubts about the importance of the idea of continuity were removed when

Mao imported to China the quintessentially Western idea of struggling against nature. Within a few decades, China had devastated an environment that five millennia of imperfect but concerned management had at least partially preserved (E. Anderson 2012; Marks 2012).

Even this case, however, was not open-and-shut. The West is not wholly anti-nature, and China was certainly not environmentally perfect. The West has Celtic poetry, Renaissance botany, and the conservation movement to remind us of our intimate connections with nature. China has its love of the "heat and noise" (*renao*) of cities and its fear of wild beasts to balance the poetic love of "mountains and water" (*shanshui*) that define so much of its art. How much the very real difference prevails, and how and why it matters, is a question for serious investigation.

The Chinese fondness for continuity and the Western fondness for rupture, or dichotomy, is seen also in the west's Platonic/Aristotelian conflict and the Chinese lack of such a conflict. The Chinese never doubted that the world is important to know and that how we think of it is also important. Another example of continuity versus rupture is seen in religion. The Chinese and their neighbors have been relatively religiously tolerant compared to the West. The Chinese had many conflicts between Confucians and Daoists, Daoists and Buddhists, and the state and Islam; they also had to deal with millennial rebellions, the most clearly faith-driven being the Taipings. Still, it seems that China has nothing in its premodern history comparable to the Crusades, especially the Albigensian Crusade, the Fourth Crusade, and others that targeted "other" Christians rather than Muslims. China did not have anything quite like Europe's Wars of Religion or like the many sectarian conflicts within Islam. Many recent scholars have seen fascism and Communism religions (of a sort), which would add those ideologies to the pool of Western divisive ideas. Since 1800, the Chinese have become increasingly Westernized in these matters: the Muslim and Taiping rebellions of the nineteenth century had major religious components, and with Communism China adopted an exclusive dogma. The contrast with earlier dynasties is instructive.

Central Asian regimes were even more tolerant than the Chinese. The Khitans and Mongols of their golden era were dramatically tolerant. One can see a first documentation of this attitude in Cyrus's religious tolerance in ancient Persia; his dynasty came from Central Asia.

Related to the debate over China's uniqueness is a question of how much China is like the rest of the world. Chinese civilization does indeed broadly resemble civilizations elsewhere. This similarity can come from parallel invention—ancient Chinese farms and cities looked a lot like ancient Aztec ones—but more often it comes from actual borrowing. However, China is so obviously distinctive in many ways that one is always tempted to ignore such evidence of the unity of humankind.

The debate between those who see "a culture" as a unique, harmonious whole and those who see "culture" as complexly and contingently constructed is a very old one. Postmodernists often claim to have invented the latter view, but in fact it goes well back in social science. Deborah Tooker has provided a wonderfully concise list of the sins of old-time anthropology, as seen by today's postmodern anthropologists: "1) being too functionalist; 2) following a romantic Germanic notion of culture; 3) following a discipline-based rhetoric of holism in text construction . . . ; 4) biologizing culture by viewing it as organic; 5) imposing a coherent notion of culture that does not allow for contradictions and inconsistencies; 6) naturalizing culture and ignoring the fact that it must be socially produced; 7) exoticizing the other[s] by placing them out of time and space; 8) reinforcing indigenous systems of power inequalities by silencing alternative viewpoints (sometimes in collusion with colonialist interests) [this sin is actually more common among postmodernists than it was among the old-timers—ENA]; or 9) isolating indigenous cultures from historical forces and larger regional systems of power inequalities" (Tooker 2012: 38–39).

All these criticisms of old-time anthropology are well taken; they have much truth. (In fact, I was making them long before postmodernism was heard of.) But many old-timers succeeded in avoiding them, and many postmodernists do not. One might also counter that postmodern anthropologists often 1) deny any function to cultural ways, thus making them seem arbitrary and vapid; 2) forget that Herder (the "romantic German") was arguing for cultural tolerance and was the first known human being to do so with a full-scale logical argument; 3) ignore holism when it is there; 4) deny any biology in culture, even to alleging that people construct foodways with no attention to nutrition; 5) look only at contradictions and inconsistencies, ignoring real consensus; 6) unnaturalize culture by describing it as if it were mere arbitrary claims; 7) exoticize the others by maintaining that "indigenous" people had no power or resource conflicts; 8) focus only on external power imposition; 9) focus only on larger systems and never describing, or even showing any concern for, local cultures.

As always, truth is in the middle, but in this case it is not in some kind of missing middle ground, but rather in adopting all eighteen alternatives—but only to a reasonable degree. A functionalist explanation of eating with knife and fork is not historically adequate; people did fine before forks were adopted during the late Renaissance. But claiming that the fork has no function in modern eating would be insane.

Particularly important is getting a reasonable perspective on the last two items in the list. All societies have power inequalities (if only old versus young), and all have to deal with other societies who may push them around or who may push back when annoyed. There were indeed many anthropologists in the old days who ignored this point (though many did not), and many today who focus so exclusively on power that the people are reduced to cardboard-stereotype victims—reducing them to Agamben's "bare life" (1998) in description, when they are not in reality.

===

CHAPTER 1

Prehistoric Origins Across Eurasia

When freezing to death, face the wind and stand straight;
when starving to death, never bend.
(*dung si ying feng zhan, e si bu zheyao*)

—Chinese proverb

China Before Agriculture

China has been inhabited by humans for perhaps a million years. Here we speak, of course, of the geographical region now occupied (and overflowed) by the nation-state "China." The region is a compact, tightly defined one, bordered by mountains and deserts, but it had no name until the Qin Dynasty unified its inner, richer districts and gave a name that slowly became fixed on the whole land. Strictly speaking, then, applying the name "China" to prehistoric central East Asia is anachronistic (Standen 2011) but has a very long history, so I follow that usage.

During those million years, cold dry glacial periods alternated with warm wet interglacial ones. Primitive humans—*Homo erectus* and, later, little-known hominids similar to Neanderthals (*Homo sapiens neanderthalis*)—had to cope with these violent fluctuations. Their stone technology was sophisticated and diverse as early as 800,000 years ago (Gibbons 2000; Hotz 2000). Most technology then was evidently of wood or bamboo, and we have little evidence of it. They no doubt fed on anything they could find that would not poison them or outfight them. As we used to say in my youth in the rural United States, they "would eat anything that won't eat back faster." However, early claims of evidence for cannibalism in "Peking man" (*Homo erectus pekinensis*) have turned out to be wrong. The evidence for deliberate use of fire (accepted in Anderson 1988) has also been very strongly questioned by recent research (Weiner et al. 1998; Bar-Yosef and Wang 2012 provide a thorough recent review of the Chinese Paleolithic).

Modern humans—*Homo sapiens sapiens*—arrived before 30,000 years ago, introducing tools that were more varied, small-sized, and sophisticated (Liu et al. 2013). By 20,000 years ago, people were hunting mammals and birds and eating fruits and seeds across what is now China, leaving many sophisticated stone points, knives, grinding slabs (metates), and other tools for us to find. Among their foods were millets (already very important), beans, gourds, and tubers (notably yams) of genera that later produced domesticated species (2013). The yams may well have been used medicinally, as they were in later times.

Humans were also making pottery at that early date. By far the earliest pottery in the world has been found at Xianrendong Cave in Jiangxi, near the mouth of the Yangzi by Xiaohong Wu and collaborators (Shelach 2012; Xiaolong Wu et al. 2012; pottery that may be 17,000 years old has now turned up in Europe, Heritage Daily 2012). It was simple cooking ware. As the investigators point out, these findings somewhat demolish Gordon Childe's idea of a Neolithic Revolution (Childe 1954) that gave us pottery, ground stone, and agriculture all in one swoop a few thousand years ago. Pottery came later than agriculture in the Near East, but far earlier in eastern Asia. Ground stone was earlier everywhere.

In Japan, pottery was fairly common by 15,000–11,800 years ago and was used a great deal to make fish stews (Craig et al. 2013; it is tentatively reported by 16,000 BCE, Kuzmin 2008a). Pottery was also very early on the nearby Siberian mainland (13,000). Irina Zhuschchikhovskaya (1997; a wonderful name) found it at 11,000 BCE in the Amur Valley. By 11,300 it was well distributed across China (Jiang and Liu 2006; Kuzmin 2008a, b). It spread west through Siberia and Central Asia, reaching the Near East shortly after agriculture began, around 9000 BCE. Perhaps the Near East independently invented pottery (as the New World certainly did), but it looks to me more like a diffusion from east to west. It remains interesting that pottery came long before agriculture all over East Asia, while in West Asia and the New World, agriculture came first.

A Bit About Physical Ancestry

Humans are almost literally siblings beneath the epidermis. We are genetically so close that we are, in that sense, one big family.

Until the use of genetic tests on a large scale, we really could not say much about the complex population history of Eurasia. The mix of peoples was too great. With genetics to help, things have become somewhat clearer (see, e.g., Cochran and Harpending 2009; Diamond 2005b; J. Li et al. 2008). Broadly speaking, humans came out of northeast Africa, starting perhaps 100,000 years ago, and continuing, with a great deal of back and forth movement, usually in slow trickles. The earliest ornaments and other symbolic items first appear in Africa about 70,000 years ago.

In Eurasia, modern humans mixed with Neanderthals, so that modern Eurasians are about 2–7 percent Neanderthal (Africans mixed with their own equivalent neighbors). Also, as modern humans moved east, they encountered a mysterious, newly discovered form of human being. This form was first found as fragments in Denisova Cave, Russian Siberia, just northeast of Kazakhstan and not far from China and Mongolia (Dalton 2010; Gibbons 2011b; Krause et al. 2010; Reich et al. 2010). These are about equally distant genetically from Neanderthals and modern humans. Modern Melanesians and Aboriginal Australians are about 5 percent Denisovan, and at least some Southeast Asians show some mixing also. By normal biological rules, all these should be subspecies: modern humans being *Homo sapiens sapiens*, Neanderthals *Homo sapiens neanderthalis*, and Denisovans another subspecies not yet named. Neanderthals are usually termed a different species (*H. neanderthalis*), but that should be changed now that substantial mixing is recognized. In spite of mixing genetically, modern humans seem to have largely outcompeted these other types and replaced them.

At some point in the Near East, the local population sustained a couple of mutations that dramatically lightened their skin, eyes, and hair, allowing them to get more vitamin D, which is produced in the skin under the action of UV radiation in sunlight. Tropical populations everywhere remained dark-skinned. The melanin protects from the excessive UV light in the tropics (and thus from melanoma). Also, too much vitamin D is a bad thing; it is toxic in overdose. But dark skin is a huge disadvantage in the temperate-zone winter, guaranteeing vitamin D shortage unless you are taking supplements or eating industrial quantities of fish (as did the rather dark peoples indigenous to western North America). Too little vitamin D means not only poor bone growth—

rickets—but greatly increased susceptibility to multiple sclerosis and some cancers. So humans had to evolve light skin to cope with moving north. These mutations thus spread like wildfire, giving pale skin and often pale hair and eyes to people at the northwest end of the populated world. These are our modern "Europoids" or "Caucasians." The latter term has a rather charming origin: the physical anthropologist Blumenbach used it in regard to race because he thought the point of origin of a "race" would naturally have the most beautiful people of said race, and he thought the good people of the Caucasus were the most beautiful Europoids. One wonders how he came to these conclusions. Folklore among anthropologists holds that he was working with skulls and thought they had particularly lovely skulls. But he may also have been influenced by the reputation of the living population of the Caucasus.

Meanwhile, dark-skinned people spread through Arabia to India and onward to Southeast Asia and Oceania, where they sustained a whole range of other mutations—poorly known as of this writing. They reached Australia by 50,000–60,000 years ago. Better known is their career after they turned north in Southeast Asia (once past the Himalayan wall). Here they evolved light skin, but the mutation (one main one is known; there are evidently others to be considered) was a completely different one. It produced pale tan— "yellow"—skin instead of pale pinkish ("white"). It did not affect hair or eye color.

Later, farther north, further mutations gave northeastern Asians eyefolds, high cheekbones, padded cheeks, short noses, and nearly hairless faces. These are protective against cold; they reduce exposure of the face and its sensory organs. As the present writer, and any other bearded male who has been in really cold climates, know all too well, moisture freezes on mustaches and beards and becomes a real frostbite risk. Long noses are at risk of freezing.

With agriculture and settlement, northern and southeastern Asians spread out in all directions, leading to a wonderful mix in southern China. Typical extreme northeasterners survive on the very far north borders of China; fairly dark-skinned, short people survive in the far south. In between lies a vast gradient with a great deal of local diversity, variation, and remixing. The flow of people northward from Southeast Asia around 50,000 years ago was reversed about 8,000 years ago, and "China's march toward the tropics" (Wiens 1954) began. Meanwhile, in Siberia and central Asia, East Asians spread west and West Asians spread east. Siberia was an uninhabited void until sometime between 15,000 and 30,000 years ago. Central Asia became a meeting and blending ground where light-skinned, often red-haired or blond, Westerners met "yellow"-skinned and black-haired Easterners. At the dawn of history, most of central Asia was Western in general appearance. It is now substantially more Eastern-looking, thanks to massive migrations, especially of Turkic peoples. Afghanistan today is a wondrous mix of physical types—on a Kabul street or on a trip over the Hindu Kush, one can match individuals, as far as looks go, to Mongols, French, Arabs, or Chinese. To some extent this is still true in parts of Xinjiang, in spite of massive Chinese immigration during the last two millennia.

In India and South Asia, peoples from the Near East and Central Asia have been spreading down from the northwest for thousands of years, but the gradient from African to southeast Asian genetics is still quite visible in the southern part of the subcontinent (Reich et al. 2009).

It follows that standard racial terms are inadequate at best. The people of Europe do represent a fairly tight and genetically unified Caucasian or Europoid population, but they have mixed enthusiastically with everyone else along very broad contact zones. Also, their fondness for importing slaves and, more charitably, for welcoming immigrants has guaranteed that Europe itself is no homogeneous refuge. Similarly, in the East, vast migrations, largely but not only from north to south and northwest to southeast, have blended populations completely. Unsurprisingly, the differences in "intelligence" and "personality" that used to be claimed for different "races" disappear on inspection. Where people (of any origin) get an equal shake in the schools, they all perform pretty much the same. Given their long histories of mixing, this is no surprise.

Variation does not stop with visible adaptations. People evolved to tolerate milk in the West, but not in the East (see below). People throughout the Old World, but not the New, evolved some ability to survive common epidemic diseases—with the result that disease had more to do with conquering the Native Americans than superior armaments did (Diamond 1997). The differences that matter are not the trivial visible ones—which are mere simple adaptations to vitamin D intake, cold winters, and the like—but the invisible ones that convey resistance to smallpox, measles, plague, malaria, and so on. Southeast Asians widely share antimalarial adaptations; Chinese who ventured into that region usually died, in the old days. They often do today, as malaria evolves resistance to common drugs.

A final note of physical relevance to foodways and food anthropology is the existence of human taste abilities and taste preferences. Humans notoriously like meat, sweet, and fat—far too much for their own good, now that all those three things are easy to obtain. But humans also love a wide range of vegetable tastes, fruit flavors, and textures ranging from crisp to soft.

Humans everywhere also like certain spicy and herbal tastes (Billing and Sherman 1998). This might seem strange, since spices feel hot or even burning and are not major nutrition sources, but Billig and Sherman showed that most (if not all) of them are powerful antiseptic and antifungal agents and have other medicinal values. Many primates seek out such medicinal agents for food and for external application, and humans are clearly part of this pattern (E. Anderson 2005a). The Chinese fondness for things like peppers, cinnamon, rose, fennel, and other spices and herbs fits the world pattern perfectly, and the spiciness of much southern Chinese and Korean food tracks the high incidence of disease and contagion in these areas. Also, chiles are extremely rich in vitamins and minerals, and—like their Chinese relative the goji berry (*goujizi* or Chinese wolfthorn, *Lycium chinense*)—they take on a function as poor families' vitamin pills. Worldwide, chile consumption tracks rural population density, since both its antiseptic and its nutritional values tend to be recognized. It is commonly used as a food preservative in China as elsewhere.

One odd food preference is for mustard-family plants, including the Chinese cabbages and kales, cresses, mustards, and radishes. These plants are second only to chiles and wolfthorn, and in many cases even better than chiles, in nutritional value. The flavorful ingredients are glucosinolates, which the plant produces to kill insects but which are not only harmless to humans but beneficial—we have evolved not only tolerance to them but also the ability to benefit medically from them. Worldwide, many people are repelled by an extremely bitter taste caused by phenylthiosulfates in cabbage-family plants. However, about a third of people worldwide cannot taste the bitterness, because of a genetic difference (E. Anderson 2005a). The Chinese seem to be much more prone to like cabbage-family greens than Westerners are and thus must often be nontasters or mild tasters, but data on this are inadequate.

Yet another important aspect of taste in Asia is the recent discovery of the *umami* taste receptors. Previously, human taste had been considered to consist only of salt, sweet, sour, bitter, and—if it is counted a taste rather than a burning sensation—hotness or piquancy. Umami, which was not recognized by either Western or Eastern sages, was discovered only in recent decades. It is the savory taste of soy sauce and other ferments. It is found in some other products, largely as a fermentation product. In spite of not being identified earlier, it was extremely important in the development of East Asian food, since fermentation has been a major way of preparing and preserving food, and the umami taste has been a major goal of food preparation for gourmet taste (H. Huang 2000).

All these cases show the importance of the relationship between physical tasting ability and food culture. It is impossible to understand Chinese foodways without a solid awareness of these complex and detailed genetically guided human abilities.

A Bit About Languages

Languages spread from centers to far-flung regions. When modern humans came out of Africa, they brought languages with them, and some linguists claim to find commonalities in all world languages outside of southern Africa. The evidence is elusive, and so far unconvincing to most, but the human radiation was real, so linguistic relationships must have once been there.

Failing proto-world, there is considerable suggestive evidence that all or most of the northern Eurasian languages have some distant relationship (Pagel et al. 2013). "Nostratic phylum" has been proposed as the term for these northern Eurasian languages (and some North American ones) if they are indeed related. The resemblances could be due to borrowing across tens of thousands of years, because the steppes have been a highway since Neanderthal times. But there is no reason to reject common origin out of hand. Evidence may someday resolve the issue.

Today, the world's languages are grouped into a large number of families and combined in a somewhat smaller but still impressive number of phyla. Typical families are Germanic, Romance, and Sinitic (Chinese). Typical phyla are Indo-European, which includes most European languages and many Asian ones, and Tibeto-Burman, or Sino-Tibetan, which includes Chinese, Tibetan, Burman, and hundreds of related but extremely disparate languages in eastern and southern Asia. Many languages, including Basque, have no known relatives; Basque is its own tiny family and phylum.

A recent theory, developed from East Asian data, relates the spread of agriculture to the spread of language phyla. This theory was developed by Peter Bellwood to account for the dramatic spread of the Austronesian phylum (see Bellwood 2009, with critiques by other scholars appended). Beginning around 6,000 years ago, Austronesian speakers began to move outward from southeast China. They colonized Taiwan, evolving there into the so-called Taiwan Aborigines." This was only the beginning. Taking to the sea, the

Austronesians exploded over the vast realms of the Pacific and Indian Oceans. Today, somewhat closely related Austronesian languages are spoken from Madagascar to Hawaiʻi and from New Zealand to Micronesia. Wherever these people went, they took agriculture. Cognate words for chickens, coconuts, root crops, and dozens of other agricultural items and techniques are found all over their vast realm, indicating that the early Austronesians had all these things.

It occurred to Bellwood, and to other scholars, that other linguistic spreads might also be associated with agriculture. This has been the subject of much research, culminating in a volume edited by Bellwood and Colin Renfrew (2002). Independent genetic evidence confirms that many migrations occurred and that agriculture released spectacular demographic expansions. Agricultural peoples moved rapidly from the Near East through Europe and into Africa, expanding in numbers as they did so. Evidence from Europe, Southeast Asia, and western Africa confirms striking demographic expansions directly after the introduction of agriculture in these regions (Gignoux et al. 2011). Farmers multiplied fast and moved out to new lands. Local people were not wiped out but rather merged with the expanding farmers, leaving varying degrees of genetic admixture.

Of course, not all linguistic spreads were accompanied by farming. The Inuit, Athapaskans, and several other hunting peoples spread over thousands of miles without benefit of agriculture. Moreover, having agriculture does not guarantee spread; the Georgian-language speakers have probably had agriculture almost since it began, 11,000 years ago, but have remained confined to a tiny area in the Caucasus. Within eastern Asia, the Yao-Mian phylum has recently spread from southeast China into Southeast Asia, but before that it seems to have been narrowly confined to a small part of south China. The Miao-Hmong phylum started in northwest China, according to some Miao myths. It survives in central and south China, with recent radiation into northern Southeast Asia. It has certainly spread with agriculture but has never gained much territory.

But some groups do spread. Bellwood and others have made a very convincing case for the association of the Tibeto-Burman (Sino-Tibetan) language phylum with the spread of millet agriculture. The dates and geography make this seem reasonable. The Tibeto-Burman languages, including the ancestor of the Chinese languages of today, are about as different as you would expect if they branched off from each other 7,000 or 8,000 years ago. I find the association convincing, but it is controversial. G. Van Driem thinks the stock originated in Sichuan (van Driem 1999, 2002). Others (myself included) think it originated further north but then differentiated in Sichuan. Either way, the stock originated very close to the point of origin of millet agriculture.

The spread of the Thai-Kadai phylum is clearly associated with the spread of rice agriculture (Bellwood and Renfrew 2002). We know that Thai-Kadai languages diversified in, and probably spread from, the Yangzi Valley area, where rice was domesticated. Their routes of spread and the probable timing of the spread fit well with the spread of rice agriculture south and southwest. The Austronesian phylum was associated with rice agriculture early and has some very Thai-sounding words; it may be related to Thai-Kadai (P. Benedict 1975), or, more likely, it simply may have become connected with rice agriculture and a few loanwords in very early times. The Thai-Kadai languages branched from each other perhaps 6,000 years ago. Their speakers were, however, probably not the only rice-growers, and Hmong/Miao and Yao/Mien languages were in the right area then, too, and have been associated with the spread of rice by some scholars.

A significant fact is the spread of the Thai root for "chicken," *kai*. This word was borrowed into Chinese early, becoming *ji* in Mandarin but remaining *kai* in Cantonese. (The Cantonese language is likely the result of Thai speakers switching to Chinese in the Tang Dynasty and since. The Cantonese word for "chicken" is far from the only Thai-sounding word in that language.) Not stopping there, *kai* went on—increasingly distorted—into Korean, Japanese, the Central Asian languages, and thence into the Western world, eventually as far afield as Morocco (Blench 2007). It is awfully hard to escape the conclusion that the Thai peoples domesticated the chicken, which is native to south China and Southeast Asia. Borrowed words surely indicate borrowed chickens. Other local peoples in Southeast Asia, such as the Austronesians, have their own words for the bird, implying that they were aware of wild chickens before domestication.

Bellwood's correlation of advanced agriculture with the spread of the Austronesian languages in the islands east of Asia is no longer controversial. Millet reached Taiwan by 3,000–2500 BCE; a recent find revealed large amounts of foxtail millet and rice at Nan-kuan-li. This and related sites probably represent the ancestors of today's Austronesian-speaking "aborigines" of Taiwan, recently arrived from south China with seeds in hand (Tsang 2005). There is clear archaeological evidence for an explosive radiation of advanced farming and pottery-making people from south China to Taiwan and thence to the Philippines and the islands south and east—the lands inhabited by Austronesian peoples today (Bellwood 1997, 2002, 2005; Donohue and Denham 2010 dispute this, but Bellwood has a very effective answer in the commentary section of their article). However, subsequent profound changes in both language and agriculture took place when Austronesians mingled with Papuans in Melanesia (Paz 2002), with the result that Oceanic Austronesian agriculture looks much more Papuan than Chinese.

When we move to western Eurasia, however, we are in a very different situation. Bellwood and Renfrew hypothesized that the Indo-European (IE) phylum was present at the birth of agriculture in the Near East and spread along with it. This is certainly false. Agriculture in the Near East began at least 11,000 years ago, and the IE phylum is a very close-knit one. Suffice it to say that the Hittite for water is *wadar*. This and hundreds of other close pairs prove that IE cannot possibly have split up more than about 6,000 years ago. Languages change very fast, especially in the days before books, radio, and television. Languages diverge and differentiate faster than we once thought (Brown 2010), and this process probably happened even faster in preliterate times.

Moreover, we know that agriculture began in the dry Levantine back country. But the IE phylum has shared cognates for a whole host of cool-temperate plants and animals, including *laks* for salmon. (No, that word isn't of Jewish origin.) These biota firmly fix the IE origin somewhere between northeast Europe and the Caucasus—most likely in and around what is now the Ukraine. Conversely, IE significantly lacks words for dry Levantine commodities.

Also, there is plenty of evidence for pre-IE farmers in Europe. The surviving Basque language is the most obvious piece, but there are also the host of agricultural and rural words in Germanic that have no IE roots: "wheat," "sheep," "eel," "delve," "roe" (deer), "boar," and even "land," among others (Witzel 2006). Greek also borrowed from non-IE languages a whole host of agricultural and settlement words. Speakers of IE languages would hardly have borrowed such words from hunter-gatherers. Spreading in the other direction, IE speakers of the language ancestral to today's Iranic and north Indian (Sanskritic) languages borrowed a similar large range of words, including terms for camel, donkey, and brick as well as a whole host of religious terms (including names of gods, like Indra) and literary usages (Witzel 2006).

A recent hypothesis, based on virus epidemiology, has the IE languages originating in Anatolia and spreading with agriculture (Bouckaert et al. 2012). But again the timing is wrong; agriculture had already spread widely by the later, and more believable, timing they reconstruct, and one wonders what happened to the earlier propagators. Viruses do not make a very good model for humans.

What, then, accounts for the spread of the IE peoples? The traditional explanation was that they developed riding, horse traction, and horse-based warfare (chariots and, probably later, riding). This explanation has received a powerful boost lately from increasingly clear evidence that the horse was domesticated in Kazakhstan around 5,500 years ago (Anthony 2007; Harris 2010)—just east of the place and time reconstructed for the IE homeland. The horse was probably a food animal first. Only after domestication could it be milked and ridden. Anyone familiar with wild equines will know that they would not stand still for either process! Horses, unlike ruminant livestock, are neither stolid nor intellectually limited. They are high-strung, sensitive, extremely intelligent animals, and to this day it takes a tremendous amount of empathy and skill to work with them. Instead of dull servants like cows, they can become super-smart companions. In Mongolia, my wife saw small boys riding bareback, standing up, controlling the horses by pressure of feet. The horses went through the most amazing maneuvers, sensitive to every touch and knowing exactly what to do.

Breeding to maintain this level of intelligence while getting rid of the natural ferocity and cunning of wild equines was truly a piece of work. Domestication must have been a long process with a lot of mutual learning. The advantages of skilled horsemen include the military edge made famous by both ancient Greek and early Chinese authors but do not stop there; imagine the edge ancient horsemen had in herding, communications, trading, plowing, and just about every other mobile activity.

This theory has recently been supplemented by the idea that the IE peoples had the gene that allowed them to digest lactose as adults. In most humans, the enzyme that breaks down lactose—milk sugar—is not produced after age about six. After that, they suffer major intestinal discomfort if they consume much fresh dairy food over time. Among the world's milk-dependent peoples, however, mutant genes convey the ability to digest lactose throughout life. These genes are close to universal in Europe. They evolved quite separately among the herding peoples of East Africa (who actually have more genes for this trait than Europeans do). This is a recent development, known from many lines of evidence to be a product of dairy-dependent economics, and arose long after the beginning of agriculture.

The European gene is fairly common in the Near East but fades out rapidly in the rest of Asia. There—in Central and South Asia, in particular—people rely on lactose metabolism by *Lactobacillus* bacteria to make milk palatable. *Lactobacillus* breaks down lactose into lactic acid, not only making the food digestible but also preserving it (lactic acid is a strong preservative). *Lactobacillus* fermentation has thus proved very useful: it gives us yogurt, sourdough bread, pickles, sauerkraut, soy sauce, salami, and many other preserved foods. Asians, using this technology, did not need lactase. However, to carry out and maintain *Lactobacillus* fermentation requires a rather sophisticated lifestyle on the part of its users. It is not something that dates back to the dawn of farming.

Indo-Europeans were probably too mobile to maintain the sensitive, delicate cultures that give us yogurt and sourdough, so the mutant gene allowed the IE peoples to depend heavily on fresh milk products (Cochran and Harpending 2009). This may have given them a major competitive advantage as they took to nomadic herding. They could easily spread south and east into lands lacking the gene. I think this is quite probable, but evidently the pre-IE peoples in Europe also had the gene, since we know they were relying on cattle and sheep and doing at least some dairying.

The complex of riding and lactase allowed the IE peoples to depend on nomadic stockherding and to be superior at it. This allowed them to spread with lightning speed, which they evidently did, for their languages soon cropped up from the Atlantic to the frontiers of China.

Important to our history is one IE family in particular, the Indo-Iranian. The Iranic languages and the Sanskrit-derived languages of India are modern representatives of this early but compact branch. A number of sound shifts unite them and separate them from other IE families. Indo-Iranian speakers evidently nomadized east and south, eventually conquering and occupying vast realms from Iran to Bengal and from south Russia to westernmost China. In the process they assimilated many speakers of languages now lost. They have, in turn, lost most of their central Asian territory to Turkic languages—showing how fast languages can spread widely and then retreat. Most Turkic speakers today had ancestors who spoke IE tongues.

Bellwood and Renfrew also thought the Afroasiatic phylum—whose most visible representative is the Semitic family—might have developed along with agriculture and spread from the Near East. This, too, is impossible. The Afroasiatic center of diversity is Ethiopia, in or near which this language phylum certainly arose. The intrusion of one small branch, the Semitic family, into Asia is a relatively recent phenomenon, probably going back not much before their entrance to history, with the Babylonians. The original Afroasiatic speakers were certainly like modern Ethiopians physically and culturally.

So, who developed Near Eastern agriculture? The Sumerian language (and its possible relative Elamite) is in the right place at the right time. The Sumerians spread far and successfully into the best farmland before being conquered and linguistically assimilated by the Semites. Their art shows that they looked like modern Middle Eastern people—their genes have survived much better than their languages. My money is on the Sumerians.

We will have to deal with a few other language phyla in this book. The Uralic languages (Finnish, Hungarian, and relatives) arose near enough to IE to have exchanged ancient loanwords. The Austroasiatic phylum evidently arose in eastern India—that is its center of diversity and linguistic range. It spread east, possibly as recently as two or three thousand years ago. One branch is the Mon-Khmer family, which includes Khmer, Vietnamese, and many more obscure highland languages. Bellwood thought the Austroasiatic phylum began in China, but all evidence is against this; all evidence is consistent with an origin in east-central India. The Austroasiatic phylum probably spread with the rise of agriculture in India, about 6,000 years ago.

Finally, a fatefully important, putative phylum for Asian history is the Altaic, including the Turkic, Mongol, and Tungusic families. These three branches are very distantly related, if they are related at all. Much doubt has been cast on whether there really is an Altaic phylum. (It was once extended even farther, to include Korean and Japanese, but very few linguistic scholars accept this now, and evidence is overwhelmingly against it.) The Mongol languages show rather puzzling similarities not only to Turkic but also to Uralic and IE languages, ranging from such startling word resemblances as *minii* "mine," to the Mongol noun case system's similarities to Russian and Finnish (as opposed to Turkic, which structures these things differently). However, these similarities are notably lacking in pattern, indicating that they are likely borrowed. Those not borrowed very possibly have an older common origin in the "Nostratic" universe. Mongol has three roots for "I, me" (*bi*, *min-*, and *na-*), and all of them sound like pronouns in various languages all over the world (cf. Yucatec Maya *in* "I, mine"). Is this evidence for Proto-World (as some maintain) or merely a result of these being extremely easy sounds for the human mouth to make? People tend to save energy when talking—"television" becomes "TV"—and the commonest words, especially those much used by children, naturally become short and simple.

The Turks and Mongols certainly nomadized, camped, and fought side by side for thousands of years. They also lived near Uralic peoples, and had early contacts with the Tocharians and probably other Indo-Europeans. Mutual influence was inevitable. The basic vocabularies of Mongolian and Turkic languages, however, do not show any believable relationship. No one can miss the similarities of English *one, two, three*, Latin *unum, duo, tres*, and Sanskrit *eka, dva, tri*, and there are hundreds of other such sets of cognates, even for quite complex concepts (Celtic *ri*, Latin *rex*, Sanskrit *raja*, . . .), in Indo-European. But try to find any similarities between (Khalkha) Mongolian *neg, khoyor, gurvan* and Turkish *bir, iki, üç*, "one, two, three." The basic vocabulary words in the Mongol and Turkic languages are usually very different—unless they are so similar that they must be recent borrowings. On the other hand, there are some very deep and basic cognates, including the word for milk. The word for water is close—*su* in Turkic, *us* in modern Mongol—but Chinese is similar too (*shui* from earlier *söi* or *swu*). Perhaps we are looking at a very ancient common origin and a great deal of subsequent mutual influence. In any case, the idea that Turkic, Mongol, and Tungusic are related in an Altaic phylum seems extremely shaky, if not downright defunct (Vovin 2005).

Color words are as confusing as in English: just as English has half Germanic (blue, white) and half French (violet, purple), modern Mongol has basically Turkic loans for black, yellow, and deep blue, but utterly un-Turkic words for white, red, and gray, and even a thoroughly un-Turkic word for blue (now used for pale blue). The borrowing for deep blue is significant: it refers to the sacred blue of Heaven (medieval Turkic *gök*, Mongol *kök*, now *khokh*; the change from *k* to *kh* pronounced like the *ch* in German *ich* is standard in modern Khalkh Mongolian). The native word *tsenkher* refers basically to nonsacred blue. Anyone familiar with Mongolia will know the sky-blue silk scarfs wrapped around every venerable tree, rock, cairn, shrine, and other object (including the occasional telephone pole) that is sacred, fortunate, or deserving of spiritual respect. Borrowing the Turkic word for the sacred color may indicate respect for Turkic cultural forms in the early medieval period, when the Gök Turkic Empire ruled Mongolia and much of Central Asia.

The Altaic phylum, or cluster, bears the name of the Altai Mountains, where it supposedly originated. If it did not originate there, at least the Turkic languages apparently did. All these languages come from the cold steppes and forests of high Central Asia. The Altaic peoples emerge into history fairly late but were obviously active much earlier, having quickly acquired nomadic herding and riding, presumably from Indo-Europeans.

The Altaic peoples have shown a truly astonishing ability to build huge empires. The Mongol Empire is only the most conspicuous of many. Turkic, though not the other languages, has shown a monumental ability to flourish at the expense of local languages. Millions of square miles of formerly IE and other languages' territory are now Turkic speaking. There are parts of Turkey that in historic times have switched from Hittite to Phrygian to Greek to Turkish—yet archaeology reveals no change in the people themselves. They were and are genetically the same lineages. They switched languages according to who had most recently conquered them.

Similar, if less complicated, language shifts are almost universal in Central Asian history, as elsewhere. Conquered peoples usually pick up the languages of their conquerors, but if the conquerors are few in number, the reverse takes place. In China, the spread of Chinese languages within historic times has led to linguistic absorption of many Thai, Miao, Yao-Mian, Austronesian, and others. Often, these older languages leave traces. Cantonese, in particular, seems to have begun as a form of Tang Dynasty Chinese spoken by Thai people; its tone system, much of its vocabulary (remember *kai*), and other traits reflect the massive linguistic acculturation of the Zhuang and other Thai-related minorities in historic times. This sort of linguistic acculturation guarantees that any language phylum is going to include languages spoken by very diverse peoples.

It is certain that the Chinese languages proper have expanded with the Chinese state. The core of geographic China became Chinese speaking by the Shang Dynasty. The state of Chu, in and around what is now Hunan, seems to have originally spoken various Thai-Kadai languages. It became Chinese speaking in the latter part of the first millennium BCE—first among the elite, later—slowly—among all. With the spread of the Chinese-speaking groups, several very different languages developed: Cantonese, Shanghainese (Wu), Hakka, two or more Fujianese languages, Gan, Xiang, and so on. These have often been miscalled dialects for political reasons: political leaders have generally promoted the dominant and by far the most widely spoken language, Mandarin or Guoyu ("National Language"). A dialect is, correctly, a subvariant of a language—not a language in its own right. Guoyu is now rapidly replacing local languages and their (actual) dialects. This is, demonstrably, a huge loss to local cultures, literature, the arts, and free expression.

As with the term "China" in its geographical sense, referring to the inhabitants of the region as "the Chinese" or "the Chinese people" before the Qin Dynasty is technically wrong. I try to avoid it but obviously do not always succeed. From Qin on, there is the problem of whether one is using "the Chinese" to mean the linguistic Chinese, or the people of the Chinese state, or the people of the geographical region called China. I usually try to stick with language, but consistency is simply impossible, if only because one must quote sources that use the term quite differently. The linguistic Chinese are now called the Han Chinese, from the Han Dynasty. However, many of the citizens of the Han empire were Tai, Yao, Miao, Vietnamese, Austronesian, Mongol, proto-Turkic, and so on and on. Some spoke languages now extinct and unclassified, like the language of the Xiongnu. So "Han" is as misleading a term as "Chinese." However, it is established, and I cannot escape it.

The Origins of Agriculture

After humans managed to do without agriculture for around 150,000 years, they suddenly invented it in at least five places (perhaps more) almost at once. These were quite independent inventions. "Agriculture" is defined as food production based on domesticates, that is, plants and animals significantly changed by human selection from any wild ancestors. The selection can be deliberate or accidental, but it is usually deliberate. (Claims that inventing agriculture was an accidental or semi-accidental process are simply not credible; Asouti and Fuller 2013. The most accessible and accurate critique of theories of agriculture is Barker 2006. See also E. Anderson 2011.)

Long ago, V. Gordon Childe (1954) famously wrote of three key revolutions in human history: Neolithic, Urban, and Industrial. The Industrial does not concern us in this book, and the Urban will be treated later. As to the Neolithic: Childe followed the archaeology of his day in thinking that agriculture, pottery, settled life, and ground stone tools all developed together as part of one complex. This was suggested by the archaeology of the time. It has turned out to be wrong. Ground stone, pottery, and settled life all came earlier (and in that order). Pottery developed in East Asia at least 20,000 years ago and independently in the New World considerably later. Settled village life and ground stone tool technology have both been independently invented many times in many areas. Agriculture did ultimately revolutionize human society, but only very slowly.

Agriculture developed first in the Near East, specifically the interior Levant somewhere between south-central Turkey and central Palestine. Then agriculture was invented at least once and probably twice in China. Subsequent inventions occurred in central Mexico, highland and lowland South

America (probably as separate events), New Guinea, and possibly the Mississippi Valley and western Africa.

Wheat and barley were both domesticated in the Middle East. Barley may have been independently domesticated in a few spots (D. Harris 2010: 75). The earliest wheat domesticates were two species: einkorn (*Triticum monococcum*, or *T. urartu* var. *monococcum*), native to Turkey, the Caucasus, and the Fertile Crescent. The development of einkorn wheat centered on the Karachadağ (Black Mountain) in southeast Turkey but may have been domesticated over a much wider zone (Asouti and Fuller 2013; D. Harris 2010: 77). This species hybridized—naturally or through human selection—with the grass *Aegilops speltoides* to produce emmer, *T. turgidum* var. *dicoccum*, a wholly unnatural plant. Both were domesticated in southern Turkey and the western Fertile Crescent, with innovations likely occurring at various points and diffusing.

Einkorn is almost extinct today, but emmer remains a popular crop in parts of the Middle East, and especially in Italy, where it is known as *farro*. Thriving in cold wet mountain conditions that bread wheats hate, it remains common in the high Apennines. It also makes a superior porridge and good pasta. Much more important is a selected variety of it, durum wheat (*Triticum durum*). This is not really a species—simply a form of emmer with extremely hard grains. It is the ideal pasta grain, allowing good al dente preparation. It is largely confined to the Italian world and to the northern Great Plains of North America, which have ideal conditions for growing it and therefore grow most of the world supply. But it reached China early: it is described in the fourteenth-century *Yinshan Zhengyao* and was found uncommonly but quite widely in North China by J. L. Buck (1937) in the early twentieth century.

The real action, however, took place when emmer crossed with another *Aegilops*, *A. tauschii*, in northern Iran or the Azerbaijan region around 6000 BCE. Somewhere just southwest of the Caspian Sea, about 8,000 years ago, a woman noticed that her bread was astonishingly good. It was miraculously light and fluffy, as though the gods had inspired it to rise. Consistently, the bread made of grain from one part of her family field produced bread like this. No one else had anything so good. She and her husband thanked the gods, then carefully selected the grain from that part of the field, and saved it for seed. As neighbors and relatives learned of it, the new high-quality seed spread more and more rapidly. Eventually it took over the world: bread wheat is now the most commonly grown plant on earth and the staple food of billions of people.

Eight thousand years later and many thousand miles away, a laboratory team learned that the local wheat had crossed with a wild grass, a local form of goat-face grass (*Aegilops tauschii*). From that grass, the local wheat obtained a gene for a form of gluten that allows the dough to trap carbon dioxide bubbles more effectively than regular gluten. The result is light, fluffy bread.

No one knows the name of the discoverer, but we can be sure that it was a woman: baking was a woman's job then as now in that area. She benefited humanity more, I believe, than all the kings and generals of history.

This (slightly fictionalized) event produced bread wheat. It is nicknamed "BAD wheat" by geneticists because the genomes are respectively labeled A for the female ancestor (*T. urartu*), and B and D for the successive *Aegilops* inputs. A possible separate hybridization of the same species produced spelt, which makes better porridge but worse bread. This was not the end—other wheats have been developed but they are local and need not detain us here.

Many other domesticates come from the Fertile Crescent, and much activity seems to center on the aforementioned Karachadağ, where chickpeas are native and where some strains of barley may have originated. The oldest known cultivation so far, however, is in Syria and Jordan, where agriculture goes back to 9500 BCE or earlier.

Dogs were domesticated about the same time, or even earlier (recent claims have them going back to 30,000 years ago). They were presumably the earliest domesticated animal, but we know surprisingly little about their origin. They first show up in ritual burials (touchingly including children buried with puppies) from the earliest agricultural levels. Sheep and goats were domesticated not long after, and somewhat later came cattle and pigs. Cattle certainly, and pigs almost certainly, were independently domesticated in several different places. We know this for cattle because the domesticate strains are radically different forms. The Indian zebu is not even the same species as the Near Eastern cow, and hybridizing them was a modern scientific triumph. The traditional East Africa cow (the Ankole) is different from both.

Contrary to older ideas of progress, stockherding came well after farming, not before. The ancient Greeks thought herding was lower on the human scale than farming and so must have come earlier. They saddled history with this latter illusion, dispelled only by modern archaeology. Snobbism never makes good theory.

This is not the place to get deeply into theories of agriculture, but suffice it to say that all the classic theories are wrong. Most of them depend on the idea that people were primitive savages who wandered around at the mercy of nature until some genius noticed that seeds grew into plants. Of course, everyone has known the latter for hundreds of thousands of years. Agriculture was about choosing to sow, not about learning that seeds grew into plants. Other theorists assume people invented agriculture because they "needed food," but Carl Sauer (1952) proved long ago that people would have to be settled, knowledgeable, and aware of diverse and rich resources before they took up farming. Desperate people don't have time to invent. As the Chinese proverb says: "When you are thirsty, it's too late to dig a well."

The really revolutionary new finds are recent discoveries of large settlements just before agriculture began. The huge ceremonial site of Göbekli Tepe in Turkey is only 60 km from the Karachadağ (Mann 2011 provides stunning photos). In Jordan, a large, well-to-do, architecturally sophisticated village with a huge and beautiful assembly hall arose just *before* agriculture began (Mithen et al. 2011; this is the same Steven Mithen who delightfully holds that humans sang or at least chanted before they talked [Mithen 2006], an idea originally stemming from Giambattista Vico [1999, orig. ca. 1740]. I love the idea, but alas it is unprovable.) The villagers were eating well from game and wild plants. Clearly, settled, well-fed life *preceded* agriculture.

Therefore, fairly recently, some scholars have argued that agriculture was invented not to prevent starvation but to allow people to have a large supply of favorite foods at hand for convenience, defense, and trade. Perhaps, in light of the striking architecture in Göbekli Tepe and Jordan, ceremonies required copious supplies (Hayden 2001; Mann 2011). I would bet on trade as the major driver. It provides an incentive to have lots of food close to the village to be ready at hand and also protected from raids.

Very soon after the domestication of wheat and barley, chickpeas, lentils, and other legume crops were domesticated in the Near East. Beans were early in China, Mexico, Peru, and other ancient centers of farming, also. Their easily available protein makes them desirable crops to go along with the grains, which provide bulk calories and B vitamins but not enough protein for an easy living. The other great source of protein, animal husbandry, soon followed, with sheep and goats in the Near East, pigs and chickens in China. Then, not much later, or perhaps even earlier, came vegetables and herbs; they do not preserve well archaeologically, so we know less about them. Among the fascinating mysteries of science are the origin points of our common fruit trees. The peach and mei are native to China, probably the northwest and center, respectively. The apricot can only be localized to Central Asia somewhere. The walnut, hazelnut, almond, quince, domestic grape, and several other species center on the Caucasus and the mountains of eastern Turkey and northern

Iran and could have been domesticated anywhere in that region (or near it). The pistachio is native to the mountains of Iran and neighboring countries. Various species of pears and cherries were domesticated in both West and East Asia. One rare case of actual localization is the apple: genetics has pinpointed the domestic apple to the mountains of southeastern Kazakhstan, significantly close to the city of Alma Ata, whose name means "father of apples" (or "apple camp").

Humans worldwide tend to domesticate the same kinds of fruit trees and other plants and animals. Different but closely related species of cherries were independently domesticated in Turkey, China, and Mexico thousands of years ago. Plums, chestnuts, and several other fruit and nut trees show similar patterns. The domestication of the mallard duck in the Old World (probably China) is paralleled by the domestication of the muscovy duck in South America. Pigs were, according to at least one genetic study, independently domesticated several times. And so it goes—through grains, squashes, and many other groups of plants.

CHAPTER 2

China's Early Agriculture

The Dawn of Domesticated Grain

In China, at the same time, men and women were domesticating rice and millets, developing the first farming systems, and probably experimenting with other early farming activities. Soon afterward, in the Americas, men and women domesticated maize, potatoes, chiles, llamas. . . . The list goes on.

In the early and hopeful days of Chinese communism, Mao Zedong and his henchmen paid some lip service to "the Chinese people" and their "creativity." However little they may have meant it—Mao's own real hero was Qin Shi Huang Di, of whom more anon—it did make some people think, for a while. Alas, history and anthropology have returned to their more usual role of remembering only the famous names. Recent history books rehearse the old Imperial litany of hapless monarchs captive to their eunuchs and merciless generals decimating provinces. This is a pity. The ordinary people not only survived, but, year after year, dynasty after dynasty, fed the predatory elites. At best, this activity brought them peace, progress, and some prosperity. More often, it brought them more robbery and violence.

The great discoveries of history are those made by nameless farmers, craftspeople, cooks, and workers of every sort. Yet, also, from early times, China actually had government-sponsored agricultural experiments, manuals, extension services, and statistics. Unlike the West, it had an ideology favoring agriculture.

Archaeology, and a strikingly large amount of textual and documentary material, can now give us better images of ordinary life in old China. The present book cannot ignore elites, but I will attempt to move the balance a bit—to bring to consciousness the now silent millions who gave so much.

Early Farming in China

Immediately before agriculture, the people of what is now northern China were living on acorns, wild yams, wild grass seeds, and wild beans, as well as game and fish. The plants have been identified from starch grains on grinding stones (Liu 2012). Ropes, nets, and woven fabrics were presumably present; they are documented in nearby Russia from comparably early periods, up to 9,400–8,400 years ago (Kuzmin et al. 2012).

Agriculture began in two separate locations in China with two quite different crops. This might have been two different domestication events, or two local manifestations of an earlier, single event. Evidence at present points to the former conclusion, but we really do not know. The two locations were in the dry Yellow River drainage of the north and the moist, warm Yangzi drainage of the south (on Neolithic and early urban China, see Liu and Chen 2012; Underhill 2013). In the former, millets were the domesticates. "Millet" is a catchall term for any grain with small seeds—significantly smaller than those of wheat. There are a good half dozen millets in China, not very closely related to each other. Foxtail millet (*Setaria italica*) was probably domesticated first, being a better grain all round, but panic, or broomcorn, millet (*Panicum miliaceum*) was almost or quite as early. Both are well adapted to the dry, summer-hot, winter-cold north. Broomcorn millet spread rapidly west across the steppes, reaching Europe by 4000 BCE. In China, it was never adopted far from the dry northern interior. Foxtail did not spread west till much later; preferring more rain and warmth, it moved south instead, becoming important throughout China in later millennia. It eventually became a minor but significant grain in the uplands of Southeast Asia and locally in Central Asia and Europe.

In north China, agriculture began by 8000 BCE, possibly before 9000 (see, e.g., Crawford and Shen 1998; Higham and Lu 1998; Liu 2004; Liu and Chen 2012). Foxtail millet was domesticated by 8000–7500 BCE (K.-c. Chang 1999: 44–45; Liu 2004; X. Liu et al. 2009; T. Lu 2005; see Sagart et al. 2005, passim; Yan 2002; Zhao 2011). The early center of foxtail millet agriculture is a large area, from the Wei River Valley down the Yellow River and then south into the Huai River drainage.

Domesticated broomcorn millet may go back to 8500 BCE, but the finds are not securely attested (Zhao 2011). It was domesticated in northern China or Central Asia, somewhere between the Aral Sea and the Tian Shan. Genetic comparison of existing strains seems to pinpoint domestication there, and this seems logical given the early appearance of the grain in both China and Europe (Kimata 2012 and pers. comm.). Along the Yellow River, the Cishan culture may have been growing *Panicum miliaceum* as early as 8300 BP (around 6500 BCE; Bettinger et al. 2010: 703; Zhao 2011).

"Panic" is just the Latin root for "millet"—it has nothing to do with the Greek word for extreme fear. (The latter came from the god Pan; he keeps people away from his favorite spots by giving them an irrational terror when they go there.) Millet is a pretty obvious thing to domesticate; in pre-Columbian times, a foxtail millet was briefly domesticated in Mexico, and *P. sonorum* was independently domesticated on the Lower Colorado River. Interestingly, foxtail millet was replaced by maize in Mexico around 3000–2000 BCE, and then in China in the nineteenth and twentieth centuries CE. Also, several related (but different) millets were independently domesticated in Africa and India.

New data show that agriculture may even have been earlier than that. Starch grains on pots and grinding stones show extensive use, implying cultivation and some dependence, by 9500–9000 BCE at Nanzhuang tou, and 9500–7000 at Donghulin (Xiaoyan Yang et al. 2012). If this evidence means what it seems to mean, agriculture was at least as early in north-central China as in the Near East.

For this time period and later, Ian Morris, in his "big history," *Why the West Rules . . . For Now*, provides a chart purporting to show that the Near East was always earlier than China is every advance except pottery and "rich grave goods" (Morris 2010: 130; he thinks the reason pottery came earlier in the East was that the Easterners boiled food more). Unfortunately, much of this is at best speculative (including the boiling). Leaving aside some errors, the whole chart depends on the luck of the excavation. Archaeology is far more developed in the Near East. Moreover, China's archaeology is handicapped by the intensive occupation of the landscape. It is good for the residents that China's first real city—Zhengzhou—persists today as a flourishing metropolis, far bigger than it was in 1500 BCE, but it certainly does not help archaeologists! The Near East was ahead in many things, but the domestication of plants may not have been one of them.

Both kinds of millets were widespread and basic to many local cultures by 6000 BCE. The Peiligang culture, in the upper Huai drainage, flourished in 7000–5000 BCE and, along with Cishan, "signals the emergence of food production and ritual complexity in the region" (Liu et al. 2010: 816–17). However, much of the food of the Peiligang people comprised acorns, as shown by abundant acorn starch grains in their well-made grinding stones (Liu 2012; Liu et al. 2010). Acorns are still somewhat widely used in China; in ancient Zhejiang they were made into an acorn jelly (Liu et al. 2010: 830), evidently similar to that which remains a common food in Korea today. In any case, in Peiligang the acorns and wild yams of an earlier age were suddenly and dramatically supplemented (but not replaced!) by great quantities of domesticated millet and rice (Liu 2012). The Peiligang and other early cultures had small settlements, 1–8 ha in size. Agriculture reached Inner Mongolia by around 6000 BCE (Xinglongwa culture; Shelach et al. 2011). Here and elsewhere, tree crops were so important in those days that Li Liu suspects deliberate tree management—resource husbandry—as in ancient California (Liu and Chen 2012: 265–67).

Around 5500 BCE, people, pigs, and dogs in central north China suddenly shifted toward eating a lot more millet. One way we know is that their bones all show markers of subsistence on plants that use the C_4 pathway of carbon metabolism (Barton et al. 2008; Jing and Campbell 2009). (C_4 is found largely among tropical grasses. Most other plants use the C_3 pathway.) In this area, the only common C_4 plants are millets, so this is evidence for reliance on agriculture. Wild plants and other cultigens in the area are C_3. The only other important C_4 plant in China is maize, which did not reach China until the sixteenth or seventeenth century CE. Jing and Campbell (2009: 101) report a very odd case of two skeletons showing a C_3 diet among the many showing C_4. Were these strangers? Hunter-gatherers from the uplands? Migrants from rice regions to the south?

At Dadiwan, we have the unique advantage of an almost continuous record of 80,000 years. Dadiwan is in the dry loess plateau lands (around 20" annual rainfall) of the Wei River drainage, northwest of Xi'an, but the climate was wetter during at least some of the Neolithic period. The site shows millet agriculture appearing slowly from 5500 BCE and intensifying between 5000 and 4000 into full Neolithic (Bettinger et al. 2010). Most of the loess plateaus of interior China were grassy or brushy, with sagebrush steppes and wild jujube scrub. These dominated on level lands. On loess soil, rainwater seeps in quickly and deeply, leaving the surface both dry and fire prone. In areas as dry as this, grass takes over. The steeper slopes were brushy, because water ran off too fast to allow much tree growth. (In addition to cited sources, I have my own observations of the loess plateaus to go by, as well as careful scanning of satellite photographs. For magnificent photographs of Chinese Neolithic sites and objects, see Yan 2002; Zhang Zhongpei 2002.)

However, the vast loess plateau is broken by many valleys and ravines and by higher hills and mountains. These were, and sometimes still are, densely forested. At Dadiwan (which has an archaeological record from 6000 to 1800 BCE) and nearby Xishanping, there is a good record of pollen and charcoal from 3200 to 2200. It reveals that the area had surprisingly diverse and rich forests, dominated by maple, elm, oak, and similar trees (Liu et al. 2013). Hazelnuts, chestnuts, wild cherries, and acorns from the oaks would have provided food. Most of these were probably on the hill and mountain ranges. Spruce and birch were common higher on the ranges, indicating cool moist conditions there. A wetter climate had also allowed warm-temperate plants like bamboo and sweetgum to flourish in the valleys, now totally farmed. Today, any area not too steep to be terraced is now used intensively for agriculture. This area is now cold and dry.

Rice (*Oryza sativa*) was domesticated somewhere in or near the Yangzi River drainage. Theories of Southeast Asian or Indian origin and of multiple sites of domestication have now been disproved; recent archaeology and genetic analysis (Molina et al. 2011) suggest that domestication was a single event that occurred in central China around 6000–7000 BCE.

Rice was cultivated and very possibly domesticated by around 8000 BCE (K.-c. Chang 1999: 46; Jiang and Liu 2006, earliest site, Shangshan in Zhejiang; Liu 2004; T. Lu 2005, 2011; MacNeish and Libby 1995; Yan 2002). Crawford (2006), Zhao (2011), and many others doubt domestication by this early date, finding certainty only by 6500 BCE, but Kuzmin (2008a) has definite evidence for it by 7000 BCE. It is now clear that China, specifically the Yangzi Valley and environs, was the place of origin of domesticated rice and of rice agriculture, though rice was quite early in the Yellow River drainage also (Liu and Chen 2012). A recent paper by Xuehui Huang et al. (2012) maintains that rice was domesticated in the Pearl River drainage, but their collections of wild rice (*Oryza rufipogon*, the known ancestor of *O. sativa*) were all from south China; there is so little purely wild rice in the Yangzi Valley that they apparently could not find any to sample. Genetics confirms that rice was first cultivated there and spread from there throughout China, then Korea and Southeast Asia, and finally South Asia and—in historic times—the rest of the world (Molina et al. 2011).

From earliest times, rice was divided into *japonica* and *indica* varieties; these are different enough that they are difficult to cross. They show up as clearly different by 5000 BCE or soon after. Xuehui Huang et al. (2012) found that *japonica* was the original domesticate and think that *indica* developed by outcrossing to local varieties in Southeast and, later, South Asia. However, they may very well have been different wild types from different areas, since they are so different that it is hard to imagine them differentiating by 5000 BCE under cultivation; rice cultivation was very new at the time. Again one may suppose that the crossing took place earlier and farther north, somewhere in the Yangzi area. Others think these varieties may have been separate even before domestication. Japonica rices have shorter grains that cook up rather sticky; Japanese rice, derived from Chinese japonicas, is typical. Indica rices have longer grains that cook drier, like most Chinese and Indian rices. Some rices, also, already had the now-common genetic variant of the starch amylose that makes them cook up sticky. (This is mistakenly called glutinous in some sources; "glutinous," in reference to grain, should be confined to grain that has actual gluten in it. Wheat has it; rice does not.)

At Jiahu in the Huai Valley, almost in the exact center of today's China, rice was grown abundantly by 7000–6000 BCE (Zhang Chi and Hung 2013; the village was occupied until 5800). Since this village is apparently not in the natural range of rice, the plant must have been cultivated—unless it did range there in those warmer, wetter times. Jiahu rice still looks rather wild botanically (Cohen 2011) but has some morphological indications of domestication (Zhang Chi and Hung 2013). The inhabitants ate little or no millet (as shown by lack of C_4 indications in their bones). Game and fish, plus wild foods including acorns, water caltrops (*Trapa*, mistakenly reported as "water chestnuts" in most English-language literature), and wild soybeans, and domestic dogs and pigs filled out the food supply. There are many similar sites in the area.

From early Neolithic times, the Chinese were known to drink fermented beverage made of rice, honey, and grape and hawthorn fruit, as evidenced by unmistakable lees on pots from 7000–6600 BCE at Jiahu. Patrick McGovern, dean of oeno-archaeologists, has examined and analyzed these (Khamsi 2004; McGovern 2009 and pers. comm.; Zhang Juzhong and Lee 2005). This is as early as any cultivated rice in the world, if the rice was cultivated (it may well not have been). It seems that the Chinese started brewing as soon as they had domesticated grain. The drink itself has been reconstructed by McGovern in collaboration with Dogfish Head Brewery, which sells it under the name of Chateau Jiahu. It is possibly not the finest taste experience in the beer world, and thus is not widely sold, but it is at least sometimes available after almost 9,000 years (McGovern 2009 and pers. comm., plus my personal experience with a goodly amount of it).

The people of Jiahu made flutes of crane bones; many have been recovered, some still playable (Liu and Chen 2012; Zhang Juzhong and Lee 2005). Cranes are sacred in much of East Asia to this day, and one can assume the flutes were used in shamanistic or other religious rites. These flutes are the earliest known multinote musical instruments, and indicate a complex, sensitive use of biotic resources, as well as probable reverence for cranes, much venerated in historic times.

Dorian Fuller and collaborators (2009) looked at rice grains to see if they came from easily shattering heads as opposed to nonshattering ones. People domesticating a grain will naturally select for nonshattering heads; the shattering ones fall apart and the grain is lost, so nonshattering heads are a sign of domestication. In most of the Yangzi area, there was a slow transition from shattering to nonshattering, between about 7000 and 5000 BCE. Domesticated rice was common, widespread, and varied by 5000, or at least not long after that, though some areas lagged behind (e.g., Tianluoshan, Zheng, et al. 2010). Recent finds indicate early paddy fields by 4000 (Zheng et al. 2010).

Rice needs a good deal of phosphorus. This nutrient is often trapped in tight chemical bonds in the warm and wet areas of the world and is thus unavailable to plants. Some rice varieties get around this problem by growing more roots with more phosphorus-absorptive capacity. A gene for such roots has been discovered by Rico Gamuyao and associates (2012) in an Indian rice variety, Kasalath. This gene could almost literally save the world. Phosphate fertilizers are getting expensive as phosphate rock mines are depleted. The world's rice baskets—notably south and central China, Southeast Asia, much of India, and the American South—have the least available phosphorus (Kochian 2012), and this rice gene, bred into commercial rices, could help feed countless people.

Rice agriculture spread southward beginning around 6000–4000 BCE, and a complex mosaic of farmers and foragers emerged in the center and south—to remain there for thousands of years (T. Lu 2011). The south remained rather thinly populated well into Han Dynasty times, and the coastal people were already specialized fishers, seafarers, and traders (Jiao 2013)—a lifestyle reminiscent of southern China's boat people in historic times. Farming was widespread, but clearly "population pressure" and the spread of intensive agriculture were not driving development; trade and seafaring were (Jiao 2013:609–10). Today, there are still foragers not far away, in northern Thailand and in Luzon; the foraging adjustment is often the best way to make use of mountain forests, where agriculture often remains impractical. So a mosaic of practices is expectable. The far southeast may not have had agriculture until 3000–2000, when it spread via interior and coastal routes (Chi and Hung 2012: 12); the usual mosaic continued.

Zhao Zhijun (2011) believes a third agricultural center might have existed in the south, based on root crops such as yams and taro. Domesticated rice made a sudden and dramatic appearance there a bit after 4000 BCE. Its rapid adoption implies that the region was agricultural already, and some rice root remains have turned up.

Similarities in styles of houses, pottery, burials, and other cultural matters prove that the northern and central centers, at least, formed one great network (Cohen 2011; we do not know about the root-growing south). New crops and products flowed freely around that ancient core of East Asian civilization. In *The Food of China* I postulated river-bottom land as the ideal place for early agriculture, but Liu et al. (2009) make a convincing case for domestication in low foothill and piedmont slope areas, where easily worked soil, good drainage, and safety from floods exist. I would bet on both.

The Later Neolithic

The emergent cultures like Peiligang were followed by such cultures as Yangshao, made famous in the 1920s for its exquisitely beautiful, large, colorful pottery vessels. They are very early, dating back to 5000 BCE. Yangshao, with settlements up to 25 ha by its middle phase, was centered on the middle Yellow River valley, but widely distributed, and closely related to similar cultures in the Wei Valley and elsewhere (Peterson and Shelach 2010, 2012). The Yangshao people lived largely on the two types of millet but had some rice—a good deal more of it than earlier northern cultures had. The Yangshao also had vegetables and fruits, many pigs and dogs, and a few other animals. (Yangshao is divided into an early phase, 5000–4000 BCE; a middle, 4000–3500; and a late, 3500–2800. See Zhang Zhongpei 2002.) This was followed by gray-to-black pottery generally designated as the Longshan Horizon, or Tradition, in central north China. It lasted until 1900 BCE, when more urban societies entered the picture.

The Yangshao site of Jiangzhai, near modern Xi'an, has been particularly well studied (Peterson and Shelach 2012; see photographs in Zhang Zhongpei 2002). In the early phase, a circle of houses surrounded a circular central plaza; the whole was protected by a ditch. The houses were divided into roughly five groups, each with several small houses around a larger one; this may indicate kinship groupings. Storage pits could have held enough millet to support hundreds of people. The site may have had around 400 people at any given time. Many households, however, seem to have had slender resources, possibly requiring support from others, or trading goods unseen in the record. Some of them at least probably specialized in pottery making; many well-made ceramics were found. A few copper objects turned up, some including zinc and thus "brass," but this is surely accidental—there happened to be some zinc naturally occurring in the copper. Other sites have copper and even bronze, but again as an accident of copper and tin occurring together in the ore (Zhang Zhongpei 2002). Still, the occurrence of copper technology in Yangshao times is impressive.

A dragon figure and a tiger figure, picked out in mussel shells stuck to the floor of a tomb about 5,600 years old, were discovered in Henan in 1987 (Da 1988; K.-c. Chang 1999: 51; Morris 2010: 126; see excellent photographs in K.-c. Chang 2002b: 130, Zhang Zhongpei 2002: 78). The tomb, broadly Yangshao in culture, is probably that of a shaman or similar officiant. His skeleton is flanked by the animals, the dragon on his right, the tiger on his left. (To this day, the dragon, being *yang*, goes on the right; the tiger, more *yin*, on the left.) In the same tomb is a shell design of "an animal with a dragon's head and a tiger's body. A deer is seated on the tiger's back, while on its head is a spider, and in front of it a ball . . . [and] a man riding on a dragon and a running tiger" (Zhang Zhongpei 2002: 77–78). The same tomb contained a Big Dipper design laid out in bones and other similar art. The dragon, tiger, and deer are still associated with soul travel (such numinous beings are called *jue* animals; Zhang Zhongpei 2002: 78). *Shaman* refers to an independent religious practitioner who engages in curing or helping rituals that involve sending his soul to the lands of gods and dead—or sometimes receives souls from there. The word comes from a Tungus language spoken on the borders of Manchuria and is actually first attested in documents from the Tungus-ruled Jin Dynasty in the 1100s CE. True shamans occur in traditional religion throughout East and Central Asia, and the term can be reasonably applied to similar traditional practitioners in indigenous societies of Siberia, native North America, and neighboring areas. The word is *not* correctly used as a general term for any religious practitioner in a traditional society. In this case, however, it seems highly likely that the man in ancient Henan was indeed a shaman.

Many complex farming cultures existed in China by 4000 BCE. Dates for first millet cultivation get progressively later as one leaves the interior loess lands in the Yellow River drainage. Similarly, dates for the first rice cultivation get progressively later as one leaves the Yangzi Valley. Reflecting this chronology, rice vocabularies from neighboring but only dubiously related languages show similarities all across East and Southeast Asia (Blench 2005). Japan got rice cultivation only by around 1000 (Kuzmin 2008a); large-scale, intensive cultivation spread, apparently from Korea, after 400.

Paddy agriculture in China is attested clearly by 2500 BCE (Crawford 2006) and must have been common before then. The rice of West Africa is a different species, independently domesticated about 2,000 years ago (Carney 2001). The "wild rice" of North America is neither wild nor rice; it is an aquatic grass (*Zizania aquatica* and/or *Z. latifolia*), cultivated also in China under the name *lu sun*, a name recently (and confusingly) used for asparagus.

Decades of failure to find Neolithic soybeans strengthened the case that the soybean came from the north in the Zhou Dynasty—as Chinese records say. Finally, however, Lee and associates (2008) have found earlier domesticated soybeans. A sequence of larger and larger soybeans—indicating deliberate breeding for size—emerged in 3000–2500 BCE in the Erlitou area of central China (where an early "Xia" city rose; see following chapter). Full domestication at around 1100–1000 occurred through north China and Korea (Crawford 2006; Lee 2007). Ping-ti Ho's classic case for derivation from the Jung barbarians—Shanrong, in today's usage—may still be fair enough (E. Anderson 1988). *Rong*, as now transcribed, was a general term for non-Chinese peoples north of the Chinese, and the northeast was the earliest center of diversity of soybeans, though centers of diversity elsewhere in China soon appeared (Lee et al. 2008). They were not called barbarians (*fan* or equivalent) in the early texts; calling them so was a later interpolation.

Archaeology has revealed a vast number of Neolithic cultures. Every part of China, as well as Korea (Nelson 1993), had a complex, sophisticated Neolithic tradition by 3000–2000 BCE. These peoples lived on grain, with many fruits, vegetables, fish, turtles, and domestic and wild animals. China was still game-rich, and deer were important. Even far-off New Guinea may have contributed: sugar cane may be a New Guinea domesticate, and it arrived in China very early. Bananas, a complex hybrid of two species (*Musa acuminata* × *Musa balbisiana*), come from somewhere in the Malaysia-Indonesia region, and recent studies suggest a date of 7000 years ago. They also came early to New Guinea (Rice 2005), where another species (*Musa fehi*) was also domesticated.

Vegetables and minor grain crops are not well attested early, but many were no doubt cultivated long ago (Crawford 2006). Buckwheat is first attested around 1500 BCE and was domesticated in west China, on or near the Tibetan cultural frontiers, possibly by 3000 (Ohnishi 1998).

A dramatic new find is a 4,000-year-old bowl of noodles, at Lajia in northwest China (H. Lu et al. 2005). The noodles were made from millet (both panic and foxtail) and were about 20 cm long; they were excellently preserved, in an overturned bowl that had become sealed by clay below and around it. They were probably extruded by being forced through holes in a plate and into boiling water—this being the traditional Chinese way of making noodles from low-gluten grains like millet. The history of noodles in the Western world is well known; they first occur around 200–400 CE. Perhaps they spread from China, but it seems much more likely they were independently invented. In any case, China has a clear and very long priority. However, noodles are not mentioned in Chinese writing till about 100 CE, in the Han Dynasty, by which time there had been other archaeological finds of them. Textual evidence for practical crafts is late and spotty in China.

The classic association of greater cultural complexity with a widening gap between rich and poor and between male and female is confirmed by recent studies of body size, as well as of grave goods in cemeteries. In particular, people tended to be somewhat less healthy as the Neolithic progressed; then, in the late Zhou Dynasty, males were notably taller and females smaller than in earlier times (Pechenkina and Ma 2008).

Magnificent photographs of most of the sites mentioned in this chapter are found in Allan 2002 and Yang Xiaoneng 1999.

Animals

Pigs soon became very important as a wealth item, with consumption of pork showing high status. Domesticated pigs are now reported by 7000 BCE (Lawler 2009), though this date is questioned. The possibility of their being domesticated in China, independently of the Near East, is still open (Larson et al. 2010).

By 6000 BCE, pigs were domesticated in China (and also, apparently independently, in West Asia) and being fed millet husks and waste (Jing and Flad 2002; Li Liu 2004). It is possible that they occurred even earlier; bones from 7000 may be those of domesticated swine (Cohen 2011). This is about as early as domestic pigs are also found in the Near East; they were independently domesticated in both places. This is not surprising. Pigs, like many animals, tame themselves if fed, and they are very good eating. People all over the world keep young wild pigs (and other wild game) today, especially if hunters kill a mother and young ones are left. The young are eaten when they grow big. This provides a good context for domestication. The most tranquil young may not be killed until they have bred, and thus tranquility and "domestic"-ness are selected. Tame pigs have had their brains reduced in size by a third, more than any other animal; they have been bred for docility, nonaggression, and sloth (Zeder 2012). They are still fairly intelligent as animals go, but nothing like a wild pig or peccary.

Early use and steady increase in importance of pigs is visible in the archaeological record. Significant pork-eating and the pattern of status consumption are clear by 3000 BCE (S.-O. Kim 1994). This set a pattern; the same is true today throughout China except in Muslim areas. However, it is much more evident in north China than in the Yangzi country. The latter had so much game and fish that these resources remained more important than domestic livestock until quite late, perhaps 2000 (Yuan et al. 2008). Fish were so important in the lower Yangzi area that people were buried with them. Perhaps this was food for the other world. Fish may have been sacred (as some still are in south China) or may have been totems or spirit companions. Domestic dogs have existed in China since around 8000 BCE (Liu and Chen 2012: 56)—at least as long as pigs and probably longer. In fact, the dog may be partly of Chinese origin—genetics is equivocal but does not rule out an East Asian input into the domestic dog. Chinese has two words for dog. An ordinary dog is *gou*. The other word is a classical stylish word, *guan*, "hound," an obvious Indo-European borrowing (Mair 1998) cognate with the English word. Mair thinks *gou* too may be IE (from Tocharian), but it seems to be older and indigenous, and I think it derives from the proto-Tibeto-Burman (= proto-Sino-Tibetan) form, which was something like **kwe*.

Dogs too suffered from the skull and tooth reduction that marks modern animals; compared to wolves, dogs have 30 percent less brain mass. The difference comes largely in the sensory, motor, and emotional areas of the brain; fierceness and extreme power have been bred out of them (Zeder 2012).

Meanwhile, sheep were domesticated around 8000 BCE in the Near East. Recent evidence suggests that domesticated sheep came from the Near East across Central Asia. It now seems highly unlikely that sheep were domesticated independently in China (contrary to earlier speculations, e.g., E. Anderson 1988). In China they may go back to 4000 (Liu 2004: 59), but probably only to 2500 (Jing and Campbell 2009). The sheep are of a species found all across Asia then and now (Jing and Campbell 2009), but domestic sheep appear to be directly descended from a Near Eastern subspecies; still, the question is not closed. They are found earlier in Central Asia than in China.

Goats, which are strictly Near Eastern in origin, did not appear in China till 2800 BCE (Liu 2004: 59). Cattle and other Near Eastern domesticates got to China even later (cattle by 2500; Jing and Campbell 2009). Magnificent longhorns like Texas longhorns are shown on bronze sculptures from the Dian culture in early medieval Yunnan (personal observation, Yunnan Provincial Museum). Other early animals include chickens, domesticated apparently in what is now southern China (B. West and Zhou 1988) by 4000 BCE or earlier (Liu 2004), almost certainly by Thai-speaking peoples (see above).

Water buffaloes, so essential to rice cultivation, were possibly domesticated as early as 5000 BCE (Olsen 1993) but probably not till much later, since early finds claimed to be domestic were actually wild (Liu 2004: 59). The buffaloes appear especially in the Hemudu area (lower Yangzi Valley), already a center of rice agriculture (as it still is). Water buffaloes were certainly domesticated by the dawn of empire in China—some 2000 years ago or earlier. They seem, however, to have been of an Indian variety, which, if true, means they were introduced already domesticated, from farther southwest (Liu and Chen 2012: 109–10).

Horses came only later and will be discussed below. Wild animals exploited in the early Neolithic include "sika deer, water buffalo, water deer, hare, cat, raccoon dog, tiger, and bear" (Liu 2004: 59), among others. All these are still eaten or used for medicine.

Around 7000 years ago, the Western world experienced a dramatic "secondary products revolution" (Sherratt 1981). This was the development in the Near East (rapidly spreading to Europe) of dairying, wool production, hide processing, and use of other products of domestic animals over and above meat and furred skins. China never took to dairying, but it did do a great deal with hides, hair, and bones; the early cities had bone workshops that reached considerable size.

Meanwhile in Central Asia . . . Another Neolithic

Central Asia consists of a series of ecological zones stretching across the Eurasian continent. The tundra and taiga of the far north give way to forest-steppe and then to steppes, which in turn gradually merge into deserts in the mid latitudes. The climate is extreme continental, with intensely cold winters and unbearably hot summers. High mountains, usually in ranges oriented east-west, dominate the distant landscapes. A particularly high knot extends from Tibet north through the Pamirs and Tianshan to the Altai; many peaks rise well over 20,000 feet. At the west and east ends, in Kazakhstan and China respectively, the steppes grade into farming areas. The deserts contain many linear oases, some very large, along the rivers that drain the high mountains. These linear oases have been the seats of great civilizations for the last two to two and a half millennia.

Westerners tend to imagine a vast grassland stretching for thousands of miles. The truth is more complex. The vast grasslands are in the northern, northwestern, and northeastern borderlands of Central Asia proper and are broken by low mountain ranges and rivers. The vast empty spaces without mountains, lakes, or rivers occupy almost all of Kazakhstan—the true steppe nation—and a great deal of Mongolia, Uzbekistan, and Turkmenistan, as well as neighboring countries. These areas are much drier, ranging from extremely dry grassland to waterless desert. Outside Kazakhstan and northern Turk-menistan, however, they are broken at fairly frequent intervals by large river or lake valleys that drain the snow ranges to the south and east. These valleys permit intensive agriculture.

Thus, the true picture of Central Asia is a rather coarse-grained mosaic. In the north and in the many mountain valleys and slopes of the east and south, there is good grazing, and here the famous nomads raised stock (Khaz-anov 1984; Vainstein 1980). In the river valleys, which are concentrated in the south, large-scale intensive agriculture is practiced today. An interesting fea-ture of this agriculture throughout history, but apparently not in prehistoric times, is the extreme importance of tree and vine cropping. Apricots, mulber-ries, grapes, melons, almonds (in the far south of the region—they cannot take cold), and other such crops have been staple foods, not just minor dessert items. This sort of cultivation has not fared well in recent decades (and no doubt at many times in the past), due to escalating wars and scorched-earth policies; trees do not regrow fast enough.

Civilization flourished here, especially after 500 BCE, reaching a climax in the centuries of the Silk Road. In between are vast deserts, almost worthless, providing major barriers to travel. The Takla Makan Desert of Chinese Cen-tral Asia is one of the world's driest, with virtually no rain. Major travel routes followed the rivers whenever possible, thus keeping relatively close to the southern fringes of the region. There was, however, also a great deal of contact across the northern approaches, where grassland and forest-steppe permitted nomadic and forest-based livelihood. North of that, subarctic forest eventually became used for specialized reindeer herding.

Agriculture spread to the western steppe-margins very early. At the opposite end of the steppes from China, the Tripolye and Cucuteni cultures, in modern Ukraine and Romania, built enormous towns with extremely elaborate and beautiful ceramics, at the same time as the Ubaid culture was developing rapidly toward urbanism in the Near East: roughly 5500–3000 BCE (Anthony 2007; Kohl 2007). The huge Tripolye and Cucuteni sites are not ancestral to any modern culture; they apparently were eclipsed by Indo-Europeans. They grew "emmer, einkorn, bread wheat, barley, peas, vetch, lentils, sheep, goats, cattle, pigs, buckwheat, millet (*P. miliaceum*), and both wild-type and domestic grapes" (Kohl 2007: 44). The Yamnaya cultural horizon, occurring in the same general area, may have involved early Indo-Europeans (Anthony 2007). Cities and writing arose in Mesopotamia and Egypt around 3200 BCE, indirectly influencing the steppes through trade.

Meanwhile, the first indications of contact with China are visible: panic millet turned up in Europe by 4000 BCE and was common by 5500 in the Linearbandkeramik and other cultures (Bellwood 2005: 21). (The Linearbandkeramik, or LBK, archaeological culture was the first agricultural manifestation in most of central Europe; it spread very rapidly from the east around 5500 BCE.) Millet probably spread from China, though domestication in Central Asia is also possible. It was a crop in Central Asia by 2200 (Frachetti 2012; Frachetti et al. 2010). A glass bead from the Near East at 2900 shows early contact in the other direction (Anthony 2007: 354).

However, it seems likely that there were far earlier contacts between East and West. Pottery spread through Siberia to the West. The earliest European pottery looks very much like the much earlier Chinese ware. Later, the similarities in shape, color, size, and design between Tripolye, early Mesopotamian, and Yangshao pottery styles are so striking that they have long been noted (e.g., Andersson 1934, 1943). While denied by excessively cautious scholars who note slight differences in the designs, these similarities are so numerous, striking, and close that to ignore them is pedantic.

Statuettes associated with trees and fertility, and stylistically close to Near Eastern analogues, appear around 3000 BCE. They may be connected with the cult of sacred trees that endures in Central Asia in spite of Islamic puritanism; ten-foot-thick plane trees, elms that ooze healing sap, and other wonderful trees are frequent and widely distributed there (Gorshunova 2012). Sacred trees are important to Uralic and Altaic peoples and to some settled Iranic-speakers. The cult is clearly continuous with Chinese reverence for trees; the same ideas and behaviors are visible.

Agriculture flourishes in Ukraine and in river valleys and montane out-wash fans throughout inner Asia, but full steppe conditions are impossible for agriculture. They are, however, ideal for herding the hardier kinds of stock: sheep, goats, and horses. The riverine zones along the Tarim, Syr Darya, Amu Darya, and other rivers were once among the most agriculturally productive tracts of land on earth—grain, forage crops, fruit trees, vegetables, and other crops (including early cotton) flourished. In recent decades, however, pollution, salt buildup in the soil, monocropping (especially cotton), urban sprawl, and other features of extremely bad land management have ruined much of the land.

The existence of extremely rich zones near vast tracts of nomadic herding country was an invitation for trouble. The steppe nomads could raise huge mobile forces and descend on the cities and farms, especially when warm and moist climatic periods allowed the nomads to increase both human and animal populations. Then the nomad leaders settle in the cities, succumb to luxury, lose their martial ability, and the whole cycle starts over again—as pointed out by the great Arab social scientist Ibn Khaldun in the fourteenth century.

This sequence is complicated by the fact that steppe nomads were never independent of settled people (Barfield 1989; Khazanov 1984). They required grain to supplement the products of their herds. They produced felt and wool goods but depended on settled people for other fabrics. They needed more metal than they could produce themselves. Metal goods—especially gold—became major wealth and show items. (Stock-herders who could produce all their own food and everyday goods existed in Arabia and Africa, but could not do so in Central Asia, where at least some grain, clothing, metal, and the like had to be bought.)

At the margins of the steppes, farming people encroached during warmer, moister periods. Since these are also the periods when steppe populations were increasing, tensions naturally arose. The infamous "barbarians" that harassed the Roman Empire rode out during such a time: the favorable climatic period in the early centuries of the Common Era. So did Mongol hordes during the Medieval Warm Period a few centuries later. Cold periods, by contrast, were deadly. Late winter and early spring storms dropped deep snow or, worse, ice over the young grass, starving the herds just when they needed feed the most. The old myth that "droughts" forced the nomads out on raids is long dead; droughts kept the nomads at home, scrabbling hard to survive, with no strength to raid. It was good times that made them raiders.

The steppe world began to take shape around 4000 BCE with the coming of livestock to Central Asia. Sheep and goats slowly spread from their homes in the hospitable, pleasant Near East out onto the desolate, cold steppe and desert lands. The real dawn of steppe power, however, was the domestication of the horse. It apparently took place around 3500 BCE in what is now Ukraine and Kazakhstan. Horses are first known as tamed livestock from the Botai culture of the Ukraine area, around 3500–3000 (not 4000, as previously reported). Horses were apparently domesticated only once, though herds recruited mares from local wild populations all over Eurasia (Achilli et al. 2012). The first secure evidence comes from the Botai culture in Kazakhstan (Anthony 2007; Frachetti 2008, 2012; Levine et al. 2003). The Botai people depended almost exclusively on horses for animal protein—not just the meat (of which they ate an enormous amount) but also the milk, as shown by residues in pots. Milking horses implies domestication.

No one knows when riding started—claims of bit wear on ancient horse teeth have not held up—but presumably it entered the picture about this time. By 3000 BCE, mounted riders seem to have been ranging widely over the steppes, and by 2000 the war chariot was a major part of warfare as far afield as the Near East. Horses and war chariots reached China around 1500. The Indo-Europeans were among those who took advantage of the horse and of livestock nomadism in general to radiate in all directions and build up large populations. It is tempting to associate the Botai with them, but the Botai are farther east than the presumed IE center in Ukraine. Perhaps the Indo-Europeans were already in the east, or perhaps the Botai people were ancestral Uralic or Altaic groups.

Horses were in China by the middle Shang Dynasty, 1400–1500 (Harris 2010: 82; Lawler 2009), but, so far, are not reported earlier. China is not good horse country; there is little good grazing, and, in historic times, there was little room to grow fodder. Much of China's lands are deficient in selenium, which horses need (May 2012). China always obtained its best horses from the steppes.

Local conditions—ecological and cultural—led to different emphases in different areas of China and Central Asia: sheep and goats dominated widely, and there were even cattle specialists in some relatively favorable areas, but the all-importance of the horse in Kazakhstan was slow to change (Frachetti 2012). The western, central, eastern, montane, and far eastern steppes all had different histories, political as well as ecological; nearness to great civilizations, isolation by mountain ranges, and ease of mobility all mattered.

When the steppe peoples entered Chinese history, their way of life was already ancient. It was, however, far more than nomadic herding. Central Asia, especially at the western and eastern ends, was a complex intermingling of steppe nomads, seminomadic groups with varying degrees of agriculture, settled riverine farmers using intensive irrigation, and dry-farmers taking advantage of every wet period to extend farming far out into dry lands—as pointed out by scholars such as Owen Lattimore (1940) long ago and many others since (e.g., Barfield 1989, 1993; Barthold 1968).

By 1500 BCE there were substantial farming settlements in the Zhunge'er (Junggar, Dzungarian) Basin, in what is now far northwest China. The people dry-farmed wheat, barley (naked barley was prominent), and foxtail millet. They had sophisticated pottery, similar to that from other parts of eastern Central Asia at the time (P. Jia et al. 2011) but quite different from the wares of China—at that time just entering the Shang Dynasty. No hints of their ethnic affiliation exist. The area is traditionally a haunt of "nomads," but these people were not nomadic. The widespread occurrence of early intensive farming in Central Asia, now established, has changed some historical speculation.

Other high cultures with distinctive art and architecture have been discovered in Central Asia (see Lawler 2009 for a quick overview). They share many broad patterns with the better-known early cultures of the Yellow River plain but are still distinctive. Data on these societies are only beginning to appear, and the instability of the region makes excavation difficult at best.

The early Chinese and Roman historians shared a tendency to overstate the nomadism and the dependence on stock as a way of differentiating the "Huns" and "Xiongnu" and other "barbarians" from "civilized" folk. In fact, every major stable Central Asian state or conquering horde had to depend on agriculture for a great deal of its food, clothing, and wealth (cf. Honeychurch and Amartuvshin 2006). The Xiongnu, for instance, held vast areas that were very dry but that were and are farmed, as well as several major riverine oasis-strips.

The Central Asian cultures have produced many mummies, preserved by the dry, cold climate. They show that most of the people there were of West Asian (some perhaps even European) background. Current genetic theory holds that the East Asian peoples are derived largely from groups that moved up very slowly from Southeast Asia. So their late radiation into Central Asia led to a meeting of quite different stocks when they encountered Caucasians spreading through Central Asia from the west. Many of the Central Asian mummy-wrapping textiles are wool woven in patterns similar to European ones; some are strikingly similar to Scottish plaids (Barber 1999; J. Mallory and Mair 2000). The earliest mummies date to 1800–1500 BCE. These people certainly include the ancestors of the Tocharians. (The Tocharoi of Greek history were in northern Afghanistan, whereas the people discussed here, the Twghry, occupied what is now Xinjiang. *Tocharoi* is a very reasonable Greek spelling of *Twghry*, so the mistake may simply be a minor misplacement by the Greek writers. See Hansen 2012: 73.) At least three Tocharian languages were spoken in this area in early historic times. The better known ones are usually called Tocharian A and B, but the more useful names Kuchean and Agnean are coming into use (Hansen 2012: 74). They are Indo-European, close enough to eastern European languages that their word for "fish" was "lox"! (Phonetically *laks*, *lakse*, or *laksi*.) And a modern Uyghur bread resembles the bagel (C. Robinson 1998). The Uyghur, a Turkic people, absorbed the Tocharians in early medieval times. Also well represented are people related to known Iranic groups. Probably most of the people of the ancient Tarim Basin and neighboring areas were Indo-Iranian. Turkic and Mongol speakers probably were established at the northern fringes.

The food attested was largely wheat and barley, with sheep, goats, cattle, horses, Bactrian camels, donkeys, and probably yaks to provide variety of dairy and meat stock. Some of the mummies, including the spectacular Beauty of Xiaohe (1800–1500 BCE), were buried with wheat grains; she also has a basket and winnowing fan to use in the afterlife. She was blonde and probably blue-eyed and came with mummified lice. More significant is the fact that she was buried with very European-looking fabrics, including woven wool goods that look like modern Scottish or northern European woolens. A baby was buried at about the same time, with similarly European clothing and a sheep-nipple baby bottle and goat-horn drinking cup. By Han times, grapes, apricots, melons, and other fruit were established. Apricots and wild grapes are probably native to the area, and apples have their home not far off in the mountains of Kazakhstan.

Horses and chariots had not entered the picture yet in eastern Central Asia, although they were established by this time in the western steppes. The delay is strange. If, as seems virtually certain, the Indo-Europeans and specifically the Indo-Aryans were in at the birth of horse-and-chariot culture, why were these not found among the Caucasians of east-central Asia? The grave goods and appearance of the mummies seem almost impossible to explain if they were not Indo-Europeans. Possibly the horse riders all moved south and west, to where there was more booty, leaving the East to foot travelers.

Tibet may have been settled by 30,000 years ago, though evidence is shaky. In any case, people entering around 6,000 years ago indicate the coming of agriculture and presumably animal husbandry (Brantingham and Xing 2006), at least to the lower margins of Tibet; the highlands were only seasonally occupied at best until somewhat later. There and in Central Asia, once again, complex cultures flourished by 1500–2000 BCE or earlier.

Soviet archaeological practice, including some of the best Soviet work, came to China in the early Communist period, before Mao broke with the USSR (Zhang Liangren 2011 gives a very detailed, and favorable, analysis of this phase). Then, after a long hiatus, Russian archaeology in Central Asia is now so important and pervasive that Chinese archaeologists are once again following Russian work closely. American and European influences dominated before 1949 (with some unfortunate colonialism intruding; Zhang Liangren 2011) and again in the 1980s and 1990s, under much more cooperative circumstances. A great deal of ongoing work is now done by mixed-national teams.

CHAPTER 3

The Origins of Chinese Civilization

Civilization?

Development from the Paleolithic through the Neolithic to the rise of early states, in China, shows a remarkably even progress. Local declines were balanced by local growth elsewhere. Village societies merged into larger-scale ones, and ultimately into the first states, showing a steady rise in complexity of settlement patterns and technology, a rise in the importance of cultivated crops and animals, and a slow, fairly steady spread of cultural developments from the Yellow River-Yangzi River axis to the rest of northern China and then to the south as well (see Liu and Chen 2012; Underhill 2013). Detailed local stories show fluctuation, but the wide view balances these out.

Civilization, as the word suggests, is defined by cities. When a settlement not only reaches a large size, but also has big public buildings—"monumental architecture"—and other evidence of social and political differentiation on a grand scale, we speak of a "city." In the Old World and North (but not South) America, cities were accompanied by writing. They showed evidence of complex political organization, and the first written documents are usually business and administrative materials, soon followed by law codes.

The first cities were Uruk and its neighbors in Mesopotamia and the early cities of the Nile Valley in Egypt. The first identifiable kings and dynasties appeared. The first written law codes, official temples and government-dictated religion, standing armies, and other attributes of civilization followed soon after. Whether or not there was a Neolithic Revolution, we can certainly speak of a true Urban Revolution. Interestingly, cities were clearly a completely separate invention in the New World, and there they were more or less independently developed in Mexico and in Peru, but everywhere they had the same traits and characteristics, except for the anomalous lack of writing in

Peru. So there is clearly something functionally necessary about the unity of traits that characterize these early urban formations.

It seems that cities and organized formal governments go together and that such governments necessarily have armies. The government monopolizes the legitimate use of force. This became Max Weber's definition of a state (see Weber 1946), and it would serve as a definition for civilization. When ordinary people cannot kill as they wish, but formal elites can call out the troops, a great divide is crossed. One remembers that the Marxist explanation for the rise of states is basically predatory: bands of warriors conquered large territories and had to deal with them—inventing formal administration for the purpose (Engels 1942).

It has been repeatedly pointed out (notably by Carneiro and commentators on him, 2012a, b, and Lieberman 2009) that early states did not effectively monopolize violence and that even later ones often failed. Semi-autonomous lords—from feudal subkings to landlords—could call on violence up to a point, and often even ordinary people had rights of self-defense, feud, and duel. But Weber has a real point, even if we must often "take the intention for the deed." From quite early, Chinese rulers realized that local autonomy could go only so far before being really threatening to the state. They thus tried to make sure that it did not get out of hand. Once the empire was established, they moved quickly to crush such autonomous power bases. The rulers were never wholly effective, but they did make it clear that they agreed with Weber in principle. Most important, states and cities arose at the central points or key control points of great trade networks. They also had to have large tracts of extremely fertile land around them, since early agriculture could not otherwise support urban-size settlements.

Moreover, cities and states usually (if not always) arose in areas where people could not easily escape, as Robert Carneiro pointed out (Carneiro 1970, 2012b). Very fertile tracts surrounded by hostile desert land (as in the Near East) or mountains (as in China and central Mexico) were ideal. (An interesting exception is the Olmec-Maya civilization of south Mexico.) Carneiro views warfare as critical: the victims had nowhere to run and were incorporated into the winners' polities. In areas with dispersed resources, states did not develop until forced to do so to deal with aggressive states formed in circumscribed areas. Even these "secondary," or "reflex," states tended to develop in relatively bounded areas.

China's early states, however, were not confined by the absolute boundary of a lifeless desert, as were Mesopotamia, Egypt, the Indus Valley, and the

Peruvian river valleys, or by the extremely high and rugged mountains that shut in the Mexican centers. In response to a thorough survey by Yi Jianping (2012) of the countless small local chiefdoms that moved toward statehood, Carneiro (2012a) notes that the states arose in the more circumscribed areas (the Wei Valley, the Yellow River where it enters the North China Plain, the Sichuan Basin; he could have added the Lower Yangzi Valley). But Carneiro has to admit that it appears that "resource concentration" was more important in this case than circumscription.

Trade was clearly critical. All the pristine states, and for that matter, all the well-studied secondary ones, arose at trade nodes, and the more important and focused the trade node, the earlier and more important the state. At the Valley of Mexico, Mesopotamia, and the western North China Plain, all the natural trade routes of entire continents or subcontinents come together. Conversely, beautifully circumscribed areas that were peripheral to all trade, such as the Colorado River, the Central Valley of California, and the lower Rhine (including its delta), had no early states—but such areas shot into major prominence when major trade reached them. This phenomenon is visible in China, with the progress of civilization from the Yellow and Yangzi Valleys to the Pearl and Red Rivers; these were peripheral to the early trade routes in the North China Plain and Yangzi lowlands and to the early agricultural sites. Only very much later did urbanization come to the even more isolated Manchurian valleys. The great Amur River has yet to achieve centrality.

The chiefdoms, or local complex societies, in the most favored localities did well in terms of wealth and population and could both get rich through trade and conquer the less favored ones. If circumscription was sufficient to make it impossible for the less favored to escape or to unite in a large oppositional force, the central social unit would become larger, wealthier, and more populous. It would then be forced, at some point, to develop a ruling elite, law code, and other trappings of a state; informal rule and simple kinship would simply not provide enough structure. Military organization and financing the military, in particular, would require central organization and some sort of ruling group.

All this leads to a necessity for the government to show off its wealth and power by having huge buildings, if only as defensive structures—but usually they are much more than that: they show off administrative power. Moreover, the government moves to control religion, ceremony, spectacle, great holidays, and other solidarity-building institutions. As the Marxists point out, a happy harmony prevails among the elite when the rulers, the army, and the priests are all in agreement. Even if there are dissident factions, they can unite around the goal of keeping the people docile and taxpaying. They can also insure that the elites will get most of the rapidly increasing wealth that urban civilization and trade bring to the city gates. One sees why a natural fence is needed to keep the people in.

The only thing that can disarrange this neat picture is a situation in which a marginal area produces better and better-organized fighters—such that the core's superior numbers are neutralized. China was to learn all about this, to its enormous cost, when the steppes became organized into chiefdoms and then into true states. (The rise of independent city-states dominating trade could also disrupt this situation but this never happened in China, though it was a continual experience in the Mediterranean and Southeast Asia.)

On the other hand, such governments do often succeed in delivering relative peace and order, so the people may not always want to escape. Complex, densely populated nonurban societies ("chiefdoms")—like many societies in Native America and Oceania 500 years ago—are particularly conflict-ridden. States slowly but surely reduced the incidence of violent death (Pinker 2011). And of course there is much to be said for the spectacle, excitement, and variety of urban life. The Chinese speak of the "heat and noise" (*renao*) of cities as a positive and desirable thing, however much romantic and rural Westerners may view urban heat and noise as mere pollutants. The Germans say, "city air makes people free." (Early German elites lived in the countryside on their estates, however, whereas Chinese elites generally preferred to live in the biggest cities they could find, making Chinese city air rather less free than the German form.)

Civilization, like agriculture in the Old World, appears first in the Near East and then about a thousand years later in China. With agriculture, we can safely assume independent invention, but this is not true of cities. It seems eminently possible that the idea of cities and civilization diffused across Central Asia to China (see Mair 2005—though this source deals mainly with later centuries). We know that bronze technology, horses and chariots, and funeral rites spread from west to east in early civilized times. This being the case, it seems likely that the whole idea of urbanization spread similarly. By 2000 BCE, when the first signs of civilization appear in China, cities and urban life were well established all the way from the entire Nile Valley to northern and central India and the western edges of Central Asia. Large, sophisticated towns flourished throughout much of Central Asia, though they were to vanish in the dark ages that afflicted much of the Western world in the few centuries just before and after 1000. (Climate was one reason—it turned colder and drier—but there were other poorly known factors.)

On the other hand, it seems fairly clear that the Chinese independently invented writing (on early Chinese writing, see Li Feng and Branner 2011). The Chinese would not have invented such a difficult and problematic system if they had had access to the cuneiform or alphabetic options that arose in the Near East. (I realize that this claim could earn me a charge of bias, but I cannot see how it could have been otherwise. The value of the Chinese writing system today is that it distinguishes the countless homonyms of Mandarin. Reconstructions show that the ancient Chinese did not have anything like the current problem in that regard.) Nor would their writing have shown such clear evidence of slow and organic development in place.

Chinese civilization arose in a core area in the western parts of the North China Plain and the adjacent Wei Valley. Until recently, it seemed to be a civilization that began in one area and spread in discrete rings outward, like the ripples from a stone cast in a pond. This neat scenario was early questioned by Wolfram Eberhard (one of my teachers). Today, we know Eberhard was right.

The people of the Yangzi Valley were as advanced as those on the North China Plain, if not more so, from earliest times onward. By 2000 BCE they had large towns and sophisticated art, similar to and culturally related to the proto-civilization of the North China Plain (Underhill and Habu 2006. Sichuan is also providing dramatic new finds that show a related but distinctive early civilization there (Bagley 2001). Urban-size sites extended from the far north to the Yangzi and inland to Chengdu by 2500–2000 BCE. Many had huge walls and large public buildings. Differentiated occupations, complex religion, and other features of civilization are attested all over north and central China. Shao Wangping (2002) believes that neither the view of a West Asian origin for Chinese civilization nor the view of Chinese culture as spreading from a point source on the Yellow River can be sustained any longer. However, Western inspiration for urbanization is not ruled out. The spread of writing (at least) from the central Yellow River area is clear.

Moreover, stunning recent finds in north and northeast China reveal utterly unexpected cultures there. The mysterious and controversial Hongshan culture (4500–3000 BCE) had intensive agriculture, as well as pig burials (Nelson 1994, 1995). It produced many large towns long before China had dynasties. "A huge ritual complex, about 8 by 10 km^2, was discovered at the late Hongshan period (ca. 3500–3000 BCE) site of Niuheliang in western Liaoning province. . . . It contains stone platforms interpreted as altars, stone foundations that could have been temples," sculptures, images, jewels, shamanic figures, "pig-dragons," and much more (Underhill and Habu 2006: 131). Perhaps more striking is a statuette of a woman with inset eyes of pale blue jade (Morris 2010: 126). She was presumably blue-eyed. (This does not necessarily mean the people of the town were blue-eyed. In Chinese folk belief, spirit beings were often white-eyed or blue-eyed.) She has been regarded as a "goddess," and the whole complex called a goddess temple. Hongshan declined (Liu and Chen 2012) and the great sites were no more, but the Liao valleys continued to be important cultural foci.

Although their monumental architecture is huge, the communities were small, perhaps a thousand people. The subsequent Xiajiadian culture created huge stone walls, evidently for defense (Shelach et al. 2011). Magnificent photographs of these finds are now available and show a site a great deal like a city (Zhang Zhongpei 2002: 79–80). If writing were present, no one would hesitate to call it one. However, no writing or anything comparable is associated with these sites. The Hongshan culture remains totally mysterious. Its people may have spoken ancestral Chinese, ancestral Korean, or some lost language. Could they be among the Rong? We will probably never know.

Similar monumental settlements are now being found in northwest China and Inner Mongolia. These finds appear to be greeted with enthusiasm by local people. In one recent case, a road was being built between the Inner Mongolian towns of Chifeng and Chaoyang. Construction turned up a large town 4,000 years old, with a huge wall and several major structures. The choice was made, all the way up from the local archaeologist to Beijing, to delay the road and save the buildings. The mayor of Chifeng gave his opinion in a line that should be circulated to all archaeology projects: "We, people of Chifeng, would rather travel to Chaoyang by donkey than destroy this site." The site was saved by building an underpass below it (Carver 2011: 714).

Moving back to the focal area on the central Yellow River: Taosi in Shanxi reached 3 square km—the size of a middling Classic Mayan city or small early Near Eastern one—by 2300 BCE or so. It was nearly abandoned by 1900, possibly because of a severe drying trend in this very dry part of China (Li Min 2012; Shao 2002). Taosi had perhaps 10,000 people and major architectural relics. Burials indicate stratification: "one in ten was bigger, but about one in a hundred (always male) was enormous. Some of the giant graves held two hundred offerings . . . [some including] clay or wood drums with crocodile [actually alligator] skins, large stone chimes, and an odd-looking copper bell. . . . About two thousand years later the *Rites of Zhou*, a Confucian hand-book on ceremonies, would still list all the instrument types . . . as appropriate for elite rituals" (Morris 2010: 204).

Other cities were comparably large. So far, scholars have been very cau-tious about calling them civilizations. This is partly because they all lack writ-ing, which first appeared with the Shang Dynasty in the Yellow River plain area by around 1300–1500 BCE. Signs on vessels before 2000 (see, e.g., photo-graphs in Shao 2002: 106 and K.-c. Chang 2002b: 133) are suggestive, but most of them clearly are tally marks rather than real characters (see, again, Li Feng and Branner 2011). Earlier writing will, however, probably turn up. The earli-est Shang writing has a well-developed look, implying some prior history. Fast-wheel pottery, a technically sophisticated craft, was locally known by this time (Shao 2002). Spectacular jade work was common; many through the centuries have held that Chinese civilization never equaled the quality of its precivilization jades (see Shao 2002 for spectacular photographs that might convince many more). Southeast Asia has produced nothing so large so early, but advanced cultures by 1500 BCE show that this area too was advancing almost in step with China.

In short, Chinese civilization was a diverse set of traditions from earliest times. Different language groups are certainly represented and surely include Thai as well as Sinitic; most scholars suspect that Miao (Hmong), Yao (Mien), Altaic, and other groups were also involved.

The Earliest Dynasties

According to historical tradition, China's first dynasty was the Xia, which ruled the very center of the Chinese world: the great bend area of the Yellow River as it turns from the mountains to cross the North China Plain. It was founded by the legendary Great Yu, who tamed the Yellow River floods and prepared the land for planting. He was so busy that, according to folklore, he passed his family door several times over many years without once going in. This later gave him a reputation for a lack of filial feeling, causing debates about how much serious business must take precedence over family ritual. The Xia supposedly ruled from 2205 to 1766 BCE, when they were conquered by the Shang, probably from farther east.

The last emperor of Xia became the prototype of the "bad last emperor," who lost the Mandate of Heaven—the legitimacy of his rule in the eyes of the people and the gods—by sinning. He supposedly had a meat forest—trees hung with drying meat—and a lake of ale (or "wine"—*jiu*, i.e., fermented grain drink). Supposedly he went swimming in it, and the courtiers drank from it like beasts. This exaggeration was cut down to size by Wang Chong (1907: 486–89) in the Later Han dynasty. Wang, a chronic skeptic, debunked this and other fantastic tales of heroic drunkards (including Confucius). But the lure of a sinful wish-fulfillment fantasy was too much for the Chinese historians, and the lake of wine remained—often, though, with a skeptical disclaimer. Stories of bad last emperors proliferated thereafter, providing excuses for their removal by subsequent conquering dynasts.

The existence of a Xia Dynasty continues to be debated, but there certainly was a major chiefdom or early civilization at that time and place. The main city site known so far is Erlitou, often identified as the capital of the Xia Dynasty. It was large and complex, with stunning art and monumental architecture including many large buildings and walls. It peaked at around 24,000 inhabitants (Liu and Chen 2012:270), and more in large suburbs. During Xia times (perhaps a bit earlier), bronze technology was introduced from the Near East (see, e.g., Sherratt 2006). The evidence for Near Eastern origin of Chinese bronzemaking is now overwhelming (Golas 1999), but the Chinese were quick learners. A huge bronze industry flourished at Erlitou, with copper being mined as much as a hundred miles away.

The site seems to have had all the trappings of civilization—except one: true writing. We have tallies, symbols, and possible ancestors of characters, but no real characters. Erlitou's art style spread all over the core area of what would later be China (Allan 2007). A dragon made of turquoise stones, arranged carefully, was found in a grave at Erlitou (Lawler 2009).

A fascinating speculation on Xia religion and behavior exists in the *Li Ji*, a Han Dynasty text. The Han writers (or Warring States writers they were copying) assumed: "At the first use of ceremonies, they began with meat and drink. They roasted millet and pieces of pork; they excavated the ground in the form of a jar, and scooped the water from it with their two hands . . . when one died, . . . they filled the mouth . . . with uncooked rice, and (set forth as offerings to him) packets of raw flesh" (Legge 2008: 216). The *Li Ji* goes on to reconstruct a whole prehistory, including ideas that the very earliest people knew no fire, ate their food raw, and lived in nests; later they invented fire, liquor, and other foods and took to extensive use of the liquor in ceremonies. These ancient times were considered a sort of golden age, rough and hard but natural and free from guile. Because of this, there were no crop failures or disasters, and heaven and earth produced dews and sweet wine (227). Acquaintance with neighboring peoples gave early writers a sense of what simpler, less civilized cultures might do or have done.

Other large and impressive towns existed in many parts of north China at the same time. Current thinking suggests a mosaic of chiefdoms throughout the region (see, e.g., Hui 2005; Loewe and Shaughnessy 1999). There may have been 10,000 (give or take many thousand!) small independent local societies, with the number shrinking to a couple of thousand states or near-states during Shang times and perhaps still 1,200 at the end of Western Zhou (K.-c. Chang 2002b: 126). They rapidly declined to the well-known couple of dozen Warring States after 500 BCE. K.-c. Chang (2002a, b) points out that the growth of polity size enlarged the work forces available to the rulers of the states that managed to grow. He maintains that productivity per worker did not increase much during this period (a debatable claim). Of course the elites in the loser states became part of that work force!

Shamanism flourished, and shamans obviously had great power, but exactly how much is hotly debated. Chang (2002a) also notes that Chinese civilization resembled Native American civilizations, and differed from West Asian (and later European) ones, in seeing continuity with nature and revering nature spirits and nature-related deities who were close to humans. They seem to have been psychologically as close as ancestors. As noted above, Chang felt that the East Asian–American universe was one of "continuity" between humans and the rest of the cosmos, divine or worldly. The West, to Chang, displays "rupture" between people and nature and between people and their remote heavenly gods (K.-c. Chang 2002: 193). This is supported by texts from Mesopotamia from the same time period: works like the *Epic of Gilgamesh* display a strong contrast between the civilized and the wild, with the latter being disliked and feared. This attitude runs through Western literature and philosophy from that time on and is indeed in dramatic contrast with China's cosmology.

The Shang Dynasty, in contrast to Xia, is now quite well known (K.-c. Chang 1980, 1983; Keightley 2000; Loewe and Shaughnessy 1999). It began around 1500 to 1600 BCE, not 1766 (as traditional histories recorded). It ruled the central Yellow River region, and its power seems to have extended well up and down stream, as well as west into the Wei Valley and north into the North China Plain. Shang was a brilliant but local civilization, centered on the great central plain of north China, depending on intensive agriculture and pig-raising. It seems to have begun its glory days by conquering the Erlitou polity;

it was probably a semiperipheral marcher state conquering the local core, thus beginning a pattern that was frequently repeated in northern China. The Shang people built a capital nearby at Yanshi but soon afterward moved the seat of government downriver to Zhengzhou, which grew to at least 25 square km (Lu Liancheng and Yan 2002: 152) with a population of around 104,000 (Liu and Chen 2012: 282), a huge size for an early city. The capital then moved again, finally settling at Anyang, where another huge city grew up.

The Shang world was a world of small city-states, and Shang may have been little more than a league of them (Keightley 2000; Lewis 2006, see esp. 137). However, in later times it was clearly a true state. It was probably a typical early Asian state: centered on the capital with the boundaries vague (Keightley 2000: 56–57)—what anthropologists call a galactic polity.

Anyang was twenty-four square kilometers in extent, making it forty-five times as large as any other settlement remotely close, so we are clearly dealing with a real capital of a real state (Li Feng 2008: 25). About 500 place names appear in the oracle bones. This happens to be about the number of place names known to the average person, worldwide; there seems to be something about the human brain that makes 500 places perhaps the highest easily learned number (Hunn 1990).

Excavation of Zhengzhou is handicapped by the fact that it is still a flourishing metropolis. Many cultural traits have lasted the entire 3,500 years since it was a capital. These begin with the intensive agriculture and pig raising but also include some startling details. When I visited Zhengzhou in 1978, I became fascinated with the ash-glazed high-fired brownware in the town market. Notable was a pottery kettle with three short, stubby legs, which was sold by the hundred. There were also cups and bowls. In the city's excellent Shang Dynasty museum, I found the same kettles, cups, and bowls—not merely similar, but almost identical. The oldest of these are the earliest known ash-glazed high-fired pottery in the world. The technique is simple; I have seen it done at traditional kilns. The potter, or his assistant, simply mixes ash, water, and some of the pottery clay. Then the potter gives the pot (already made and dried, but not fired) a quick whirl in this mix and then fires it. The ash fluxes the feldspar in the clay into a good glaze. The style and technique produced pots so cheap and serviceable that no one could improve on them over the centuries. Today's "sand pots" (made of sand-tempered clay) carry on the tradition and are essential for making good Chinese stews, because they distribute the heat smoothly and evenly, "sweat" a bit in cooking, and do not create the ruinous hot-spots and cold-spots of aluminum ware.

The Shang world depended on agriculture, which was already quite intensive and involved millets, wheat, barley, rice, vegetables, fruits, and domestic animals. Far from being a largely ceremonial or political site, the capital city was a major manufacturing and commercial hub; at least this was true of the final capital, Anyang (R. Campbell et al. 2011). Vast workshops made artifacts from bone (from cattle, deer, pig, and so on); these were evidently traded widely. Impressive bronze foundries produced thousands of tons of beautiful bronze work, including huge vessels. One wonders how people in such an early civilization could work with several tons of molten metal at a time. The industrial accident rate must have been horrific, and deforestation must have been extensive to produce the needed fuels. Very possibly, tracts of forest were reserved and selectively cut, as was done for later metalworking activities (Wagner 2008).

The Shang bureaucracy was complicated and lavish enough to include Many Dogs Officers, who took care of the hunting hounds. There were also Many Horses Officers (Keightley 1999: 280; 2000: 111–12). These officials are frequently mentioned in oracle bone inscriptions. There were cooks, supposedly including the legendary Yi Yin, cook to King Tang. (The latter, at least, was apparently real.) Yi Yin came as part of the entourage of the bride in a royal marriage and appeared carrying a bronze *ding*, a big three-legged meat-cooking dish (So 1992: 11). Thousands of dings survive (maybe one of them is Yi Yin's), and residue analysis confirms that they were for cooking meat. Yi's teachings on cooking appear in the records of Lü Buwei in the third century CE; alas for ancient lore, it is fairly clear from the third-century writing style that they are apocryphal (see the discussion of Warring States foodways below in "Later Zhou and the Warring States"). The ordinary people, meanwhile, ate mallows and onions—for which, Wang Chong reminds us, no gourmet cook is needed (1907: 69). (Mallows, the *Malva parviflora* complex, are humble herbs that were an extremely common food among the poor and ordinary folk in old China; they became a symbol of poverty and thus were shunned by later generations [E. Anderson 1988]. They are, however, quite good and are also among the most nutritious foods known to science. Wang refers to the fruits, a children's snack still popular in my youth in California, where they were known as "cheeses"—they look and taste like tiny green cheeses.)

Weather and pests were an endless problem. Wind was a constant and major concern; David Keightley, who did archaeological work in the area, says from experience that the Shang kings did not exaggerate: the wind is ferocious. Situated in a fertile and lush but climatically challenged part of China,

Shang could lurch from lavish abundance to desperate want and back to prosperity in quite short time ranges.

Time was critical: seasons and dates had to be coordinated for planting. The Chinese obsession with almanacs and calendars had begun, driven by the need to manage planting and harvest. I should correct here the common scholars' belief that the rulers had to prepare calendars for the stupid peasants. Evidently these scholars have never farmed. Farmers know perfectly well when to plant and harvest and have many ways of determining this. The calendars were, instead, for timing elite rituals. However, the farmers later got some imagined benefits: the calendars included predictions about the coming year's weather. Dawn and dusk were important, but night was a scary time to stay indoors; lamps do not exist in the archaeological record (Keightley 2000: 25), and burning straw or wood for light could go only so far.

Shang had quite powerful rulers, who had extensive authority. They constructed vast earthworks: walls, altars, building complexes. They were buried in enormous tombs, along with vast numbers of human and animal sacrifices. (Ian Morris, 2010: 213, has rather morbidly estimated that "a quarter of a million people" were sacrificed during the dynasty's long run. However, this number seems a bit high.) Kings became deified ancestors, requiring a hundred or so individuals to accompany them into the other world. Even larger sacrifices of both humans and horses were sometimes made. One king went out with 79 humans, 28 horses, a deer, and, most oddly, three monkeys (Lu Liancheng and Yan 2002: 161). One wonders why the simians. Guard dogs were also sacrificed in some cases, presumably to guard the dead in the afterlife.

As elsewhere, however (Bellah 2011: 213), human sacrifice ended after a few centuries. During Zhou, some human sacrificing continued, and animal sacrifices including dogs were frequent (Falkenhausen 2006: 181–82), but sacrifice rapidly diminished and finally died out. I think the old Marxian explanation is the best: kings simply could not afford the loss of labor power, whether human or animal.

Human sacrifice declined early enough that Confucius was unaware of it (though burials show it was still being done locally in his time). He was horrified that people sacrificed straw figures of people and animals, since it seemed too much like the real thing; he did not know that the real thing had indeed been the rule and was not altogether extinct in remote states even in his own time. Straw itself then gave way to pottery by Qin and Han times. This delights archaeologists, since we have wonderful pottery models—accurate and often artistically beautiful—of virtually everything a dead person could wish. Alas for archaeology, pottery gave way a few centuries later to paper models, which are still the rule in Chinese memorial rites. They are burned ritually, thus "sent to the sky," where they become the real thing in the world of the deceased.

In Shang, the king could order farmers to work collectively in the fields. Officers supervised (Keightley 1999: 279). In one storage pit, "444 stone sickles showing wear were discovered with gold leaves, stone sculpture, bronze ritual vessels, and jade artifacts. Such precious items would be found neither in the storage pit of an ordinary farmer nor in a stone workshop. The implements must have been stored there by a master" (C.-y. Hsu and Linduff 1988: 28). He was evidently a noble—either an administrator or an owner of an estate. The Shang used stone implements to conduct slash-and-burn agriculture in forests, as well as upland agriculture on grass and brush steppes. (Bronze is impractical for farming, though it was used for lack of anything better; it is expensive and brittle and does not hold an edge well.) The bottomlands especially were valued as fertile farmland. Ash, vegetable debris, and presumably dung restored soil fertility (C.-y. Hsu and Linduff 1988: 29).

Worship was directed especially at the high god Di ("heavenly king" or "thearch") or Shang Di. (This *shang* means "above" and has nothing to do with the dynastic name, which means "merchant." Legends related that it got this meaning because the Shang elite became merchants when the dynasty fell. There is no proof of this, but it is an intriguing idea.) The high god was known in Zhou as *Tian*, "Heaven."

Dead kings—along with earlier, otherwise forgotten ancestors—routinely caused trouble when their wants and needs were not met. One of the main jobs of shamans and diviners was to find out which ancestor had been offended when things went wrong. Anything from the living king's sickness to a drought or plague of locusts could be caused by shortchanging an ancestor when sacrifices were made. Therefore, many sacrifices were intended to keep the ancestors from punishing the living or to make up for previous slights that caused the ancestors to punish the living. This custom survives today, as among the Akha minority of the far south: "a man who had a stroke made the connection that his stroke was caused by not offering the correctly colored chicken at his ancestral offerings" (Tooker 2012: 38). In Shang, this practice not only provided excuses for state-building rituals but also trapped Shang in a round of destruction. Humans and wealth goods were sacrificed at an appalling rate.

The vast majority of written records of Shang are questions to the gods and ancestors, carved on scapular bones and turtle shells. The bones and shells were cracked by heat, the cracks being read as answers to the questions. Often the answers were then carved on the bones.

These oracle bones can provide a whole ethnography of Shang (Flad 2008; Keightley 2000, 2006). They show, most obviously, consumption of sheep, pigs, turtles, deer, and so on. The inscriptions are somewhat less clear. There is continuing controversy as to what they are "really" about. If all that mattered was the forecast, it would have been easier to write it down with a brush, as indeed the scribes sometimes did (Keightley 2006); why go to incredible effort and expense to carve it? Evidently something about state power and authority is involved. Showing off expensive evidences of ritual divination may have been the goal. Presumably there was a validating religious idea that only carved oracles were truly effective. The Shang gods, like so many gods worldwide, probably demanded that the worshipers show seriousness by diligent hard work.

Writing seems to have been invented—or just possibly diffused as a concept from the Near East—around the beginning of Shang. By the end of Shang, writing was highly developed, with ancestral forms of modern characters well standardized and widely used. Early characters were largely pictographic, but eventually someone got the bright idea of using a pictograph to write various nonpicturable words that sound the same. The linguist David Prager Branner (2011: 107f–117) has described what followed. A picture of a person swimming in a stream was used to write "to swim" (now pronounced *yong*) and then was also used to write "eternally" (also *yong*—evidently they were already homonyms in Zhou times). Very soon, such duplications became terribly confusing, and people began to write small classifying particles, now called radicals, next to the phonetic symbol. These radicals indicated broad classes of meaning. Thus the word "to swim" added some dots that look like drips—the radical for "water"—while the original "swim" character, without a radical, became the word for "eternally." This sort of marking reversal—with the original pictograph acquiring a radical while a derived word did not—was very common. It seemed logical; it is easier to mark "swimming" with "water" than to mark "eternally" with anything. Thus, similarly, the word for "ancestor," a picture of an ancestral tablet (not—in spite of a rampantly viral folktale—a phallus), came to mean a particle indicating "good" (among other things). Both are pronounced *zu*, but "good" remains a simple picture of a tablet, whereas the word for "ancestor" has acquired a radical used to mark terms referring to gods and the supernatural. Then the word "butcher's block," which is pronounced the same way, was written with the same tablet plus a little picture of two bamboo plants, the radical for "bamboo" objects (Branner 2011). The original picture of a tablet has become a "phonetic"—a graphic device that merely marks the sound. Through such extension by meaning and sound, any word can be written, and foreign words can be transliterated.

The vast majority of modern Chinese characters consist of a radical and a phonetic. Usually the phonetic supplies nothing but the pronunciation and has nothing to do with the meaning. The cute stories that Chinese love to tell about the appropriateness of the phonetic are mostly fiction—delightful, but fiction. However, there are some important exceptions: cases in which characters are genuine ideographs. The commonest is the character for "good" (*hao*), which shows a woman (*nu*) with a son (*zi*—no sound correspondence there). Another important case is the extension of *ren* "human person" to mean "humaneness." Originally they were the same word and character. Scribes added the character for "two" to the character for "person" when it meant "humaneness," because it was the way two people should act toward each other. "Person" is both the "phonetic" and the "radical" in this case, "two" being inserted purely to differentiate meaning. A still different type of evolution concerns the familiar *yin* and *yang*. These terms originally referred to the shady and sunny sides of a hill (the north and south slopes). Both use the "hill" radical. *Yin* combines it with the word for "shadow"—used as phonetic but clearly with an eye to the meaning. *Yang* similarly uses an old character for "sun" as a meaningful phonetic.

Possibly the most interesting of all the Shang graphs is a cross, each arm tipped with a bar. This is the original form of the character *wu*, meaning a shaman or spirit medium. In Shang times it meant the divine powers associated with the directions (Keightley 2000: 73ff.). Divinization of the directions is a concept shared with Native Americans and many other cultures. There may also be some graphic relationship with the turtle, whose shell and four limbs may have been a world symbol (Keightley 2000: 93); the cosmic turtle is another concept known from India to South America. *Wu*, anciently pronounced something like **mag*, may be cognate with "magus"—deriving from an ancient Indo-Iranian word for a magician, and, indeed, is the root of our English word (see Mallory and Mair 2000). However, its presence in Shang documents makes the link tentative, since there is not much evidence of contact at the time and since the root meaning was quite different.

Shang religion involved concern for weather and geographic features. The *Li Ji*, that thoughtful Han Dynasty political work masquerading as an ancient ceremonial text, expressed concisely some 3,000 years of Chinese reverence for nature: "Mountains, forests, streams, valleys, hillocks, mounds, can emit clouds and produce wind and rain, and [make one] see strange things, and are all called divine beings" (see Keightley 2000: 124, but I have retranslated). By Han, the old beliefs were subject to agnostic speculation, and seeing gods in the mists was not the literal Revelation it apparently was in Shang.

Keightley thinks the elite "may have been nature worshippers—or, more precisely, worshippers of certain Powers in nature—but they were unlikely to have been nature lovers" (2000: 116). I doubt this. Fear and awe of nature not only can accompany love for it; they can also even be the reason for love. Nature's powers are truly awesome, in the old sense of the word, and demand respect and reverence. Humans have their own powers and can mutually love and respect other beings, a common experience in cultures everywhere that are dependent on direct interaction with nonhuman forces. Even the emperors of Shang were tiny and helpless in the face of the overpowering natural forces around them, and they knew it. They probably loved the smiling faces of heavenly and chthonic forces as much as they feared their wrath. China's famous love for the natural environment was surely well initiated by this time.

One bit of evidence is the Shang kings' love of hunting, abundantly attested in the oracle-bone records. Hunting and love of nature go together (paradoxical as this may sound) and certainly goes along with the love of animals. Those Many Dogs Officers prove that it was clearly as true of Shang as it was of Tudor England: "There is a saying among hunters that he cannot be a gentleman which loveth not hawking and hunting, which I have heard old woodmen well allow as an approved sentence among them. The like saying is that he cannot be a gentleman which loveth not a dog" (*The Institucion of a Gentleman*, Humfrey Braham, 1568, quoted in Almond 2003: 33).

Very few animal species are shown in Shang art; about half of them are mythical, mostly various types of dragons. Of real animals, sheep and water buffaloes are notably important. Many birds are shown; most are highly stylized and unidentifiable (Keightley 2000: 109–11). The pig, by far the most common animal in archaeological finds, was apparently too plebeian to show. Pigs are shown in both Neolithic and (rarely!) Zhou Dynasty art but not in Shang. An interesting sidelight, however, is the character *jia* (household), a picture of a pig under a roof. David Keightley (2000: 111) believes that, far from showing typical living conditions, this probably started as a sacrificial pig under a temple roof. This is another case of a true ideograph rather than a simple radical-phonetic combination.

Shang's neighbor states were almost or as brilliant. These included the Zhou to the west, and later successors to the mysterious Hongshan and its heirs to the northeast, as well as splendid local cultures in the Yangzi Valley. We can no longer think of Shang as *the* ancient civilization of China, though Shang remains the major locus for writing.

Shang was conquered by Zhou, a major state in the Wei Valley. The traditional date was 1122 BCE, the actual one around 1050. Claims that the Zhou people were "barbarians"—that is, non-Chinese in culture—are not sustained by archaeology; they seem to have been thoroughly integrated into early Chinese civilization. On the other hand, the early textual material cannot be simply dismissed. It records many features that, to at least one modern scholar, Sanping Chen (2012), thoroughly confirm the old "barbarian" identification. In any case, Zhou was a semiperipheral marcher state geopolitically in relation to Shang's centrality in the Chinese world-system of the time. This then stands as an early example of a phenomenon that happened over and over in Chinese history: a semiperipheral (often originally peripheral) state rising in power, challenging the center, and often winning.

The Zhou had a capital in the twin cities of Feng and Hao, near modern Xi'an.

The early Zhou world was still one of city-states, in spite of the empire; it could not abolish, or even well control, the city-states (Lewis 2006). Only later did the Warring States succeed in truly centralizing government in their smaller realms.

The early Zhou Dynasty, like Shang, subsisted especially on millets. The mythical founder of the dynasty was Lord Millet (Hou Ji; *ji* was some kind of millet, probably panic, possibly foxtail). He was further mythologized as the minister of agriculture under the court of the God of Agriculture, Shen Nong (Liu An 2010: 402). It is typical of China that a god of agriculture would need a bureaucracy under him! Wheat and rice were also important, but wheat is rarely mentioned in Shang and early Zhou texts and oracle readings, whereas hundreds of mentions of millet occur (C.-y. Hsu and Linduff 1988: 346; this is also true of the later *Book of Songs*). Archaeology confirms the great importance of millets. Beans and hemp seeds added to the pot. The hemp was grown for fiber for cloth, but no one was going to waste the edible seeds. The value of the resin for drug uses—anesthetic, religious, and recreational—was no doubt known, as it certainly was later, but was rarely (if ever) regarded in China as anything very special.

Ceramic and bronze vessels of enormous size, beauty, and technical complexity abounded. The Shang Dynasty already had a spectacular material culture, including what many consider the most beautiful bronze vessels of all time. Zhou produced ones even larger, if not more beautiful. Residue analysis confirms that these held meat, alcoholic beverages, and grains. This analysis confirms at least some of the traditional Chinese claims about which type of vessel held which food. Vessels were used in banqueting (Falkenhausen 1999), and some at least saw long use before being buried with their lordly user; residues attest this. So they were not purely ritual (Li Feng 2008). One small bronze piece, now in San Francisco's Asian Art Museum, was cast at the orders of one Ran in honor of a victory by the Duke of Zhou, brother of the Zhou founder and regent for the founder's son and successor in the latter's youth (personal observation, helped by Berger 1994: 86 and pers. comm. of November 17, 2012). Ran paid a hundred strings of cowries for the work, showing that bronze vessels were rather routine and cheap items at the time. The duke later became enshrined as Confucius's ideal ruler, held to be perfect at moral administration. Having an actual item from his time that commemorates a battle described in early histories is truly a miracle.

A huge bone workshop turned up near the old capital, Feng-Hao: "tens of thousands of kilograms" of bone were found, "including bones of horses, pigs, dogs, deer, elephants, and tigers" and "more than 4,000 cow skeletons" (Lu Liancheng and Yan 2002: 186). Most of these would have been recycled from food waste, though probably not the tigers.

Li Feng's brilliant study *Landscape and Power in Early China* (2006) notes the advantages of the Wei River valley: closed and hard to enter, difficult to supply, and poorly connected to the rest of China. It is, however, surprisingly vulnerable to conquest from the north, because its major tributaries provide routes—challenging but not impassable for early armies—from the fairly fertile and easily held plateau country there. Central Asian regimes thus naturally tried to conquer and hold these plateaus and use them as a platform from which to strike at the heart of China. The Xiongnu were to master this strategy. Already, Western Zhou were having to fight off attackers from that direction and later found the task insupportable. The Western Zhou capital was ideal site for farming and communication, but the conquest routes from the north point like arrows at its heart. After a final epochal conquest, Zhou moved the capital east, becoming (naturally) Eastern Zhou.

This vast and open corridor to Central Asia has been greatly misunderstood and its importance underestimated. States like the Xiongnu are routinely called nomadic without any awareness that they controlled vast areas of rich and fertile (if often very dry) agricultural land just north of the Wei valley and that they could and did use this area as a platform for both the logistics and the actual routing of invasions.

Zhou had many contacts with the West. A review of art objects that are either Western-influenced or downright steppe-nomadic in inspiration and manufacture is found in Lothar von Falkenhausen's study of Zhou archaeology, *China in the Age of Confucius* (2006; see esp. 204ff.). A range of objects from iron knives to belt buckles show Central Asian provenance or influence. Particularly interesting are belt plaques that are very close in style to items from Scythian and related cultures of the central and western steppe worlds (Falkenausen 2006: 231). It is possible that the Qin people, whose descendants occupied Chang'an and later founded the Qin Dynasty, were immigrants from the steppe zone. How far their origins were from Chang'an we cannot say. At least some of the Scythian-type belt plaques were cast in Qin workshops. That source may indicate a steppe origin for Qin, but the evidence suggests, instead, an exoticist fondness for the art. The romance of the steppe nomad, not unknown in our own time, was certainly present in old China, and the Qin seem to have been somewhat barbarian-influenced Chinese who romanticized their neighbors' art.

In 771 BCE, Hao was conquered and Western Zhou humbled by the Quanrong people (cooperating with a rebellious Zhou tributary). *Quanrong* is rather insultingly translated "dog barbarians," but could equally well be translated "northern non-Chinese of the noble hound." Recall that *quan* is a literary word for a dog. (The insulting indigenous word *gou* is long famous in the compound *zou gou*, "walking dog" or "running dog," for a collaborator or sellout.)

The dynasty moved its capital east to Chengzhou, later renamed Luoyi and much later Luoyang, the Yangzi Valley. This cost them the security of the easily protected Wei valley but saved them from the worst of the steppe incursions and gave them better access to the Yellow River and the North China Plain. Many later dynasties were to go through the same evolution. Han followed Zhou in moving the capital from Hao (near Xi'an) to Luoyang. Unfortunately, this move had its costs. Luoyang has no natural defenses worthy of the name. It occupies a vulnerable open valley on a tributary of the Yellow River. Thus it was easily, and frequently, attacked.

Li Feng, in his great study of Zhou and later strategic geography, comments: "It is true that some of man's great achievements were attained by overcoming natural limits, but it is also the tendency of man to use geography in the most fa-vorable way" (2006: 159). Indeed, but as Zhou well knew, nothing is harder to find in this world than perfectly defensible sites that are also open to easy communi-cation and trade. Venice came closest; Bahrain and Sicily had their merits; but China had nothing remotely comparable and had to suffer. Through history, this meant an unstable, three-way tug-of-war between three regions. Xi'an was central and defensible but cut off. The central Yangzi from Luoyang to Hangzhou was perfect for communication but impossible to defend against a determined army. Beijing, already a local capital in Zhou times, was more defensible than Luoyang, more connected than Xi'an, but suboptimal on all counts. It is now—not for the first time—suffering from lack of water. The other two regions are on major rivers; Beijing has only a small stream.

A striking change took place around 850 BCE (Falkenhausen 2006: 43ff.). Arrays of vessels changed suddenly and dramatically. Also, not too much later, the animal and mythic-animal faces of Shang gave way to beautifully done bird representations and, soon after, to more geometric forms (Li Feng 2008: 37). This may have been because lineages tend to grow over time, and eventu-ally there are simply too many people to remember separately or worship with the same amount of display.

At this point, in modern times, lineages would split and families would consolidate their worship around their own remembered kin. Something sim-ilar seems to have happened in Zhou. Younger and distant kin get less atten-tion, with rites being redefined and reorganized to take this into account. However, the most striking change around 850 is a quite different one: the overwhelming importance of alcoholic liquor comes to a sudden and dead stop. Vessels identified by both textual and residue evidence as vessels for jiu (alcoholic drinks—beer or ale at this time) disappear almost completely. After 850, the vessels are almost strictly for meat and grain dishes. Lothar von Falkenhausen quotes a number of later—but still quite early—texts deploring drunkenness at solemn rites and suggests that reform may have come about because people succumbed too enthusiastically to very human temptations at rites that were supposed to be properly serious.

Early Zhou was still kin based and patrimonial, not a feudal society (Bel-lah 2011: 400) and not a true bureaucratic empire like later China. Zhou grad-ually developed a true bureaucratic organization, with the emperor managing it. He had to deal with local lords who had their own courts and small bureau-cracies and who were rather conditionally loyal (Li Feng 2008 gives a long and detailed explanation of this system).

A neat insight into the transition is given in the Guanzi material (Rickett 1965) and the *Zuojuan* annals. These show the machinations of the Zhou court and the local lords as the former tried to bring the latter into a routine and subservient relationship. The latter, naturally, tried to maintain their independence. Power shifted constantly. Much later, the brutal Qin and autocratic Han Dynasties broke the power of the local lords.

The term "feudal" is not well applied to China; the old Chinese term *fengjian*, usually translated thus, really means something quite different (Falkenhausen 2006: 246; Li Feng 2008). Nor were China's hierarchy of local elites much like the dukes, earls, and marshals of the West. China went from a patrimonial system (based on the king's royal family and relatives) to a bureaucratic one with specified titles under court control; there were local semi-autonomous lords with tributary relationships with the states, but such lords were on the frontiers or in remote areas. The Zhou lords were not independent estate holders trading service for patronage. There were local lords with serfs or serf-like dependents, but they progressively lost their independence from about 600 BCE onward. By Han times, large estates owned by elites still existed but were under state control; by Tang, even these had been cut down, though not totally eliminated.

A fascinating insight into the thinking of the time is the word *gong*, translated as "duke," because it does indeed indicate a high and quasi-autonomous lord; it literally means "common," as in "the common people." Apparently the *gong* was the governmental head of the common lands or the direct governor of the common people or both. (Recall that our word "duke" simply means "leader" etymologically.)

Bronze inscriptions give more insight into this (Falkenhausen 2006; Li Feng 2008; see Allan 2002 for many pictures of early Chinese objects). There were three key functionaries: the supervisors of land, of construction, and of horses (Li Feng 2008: 71ff.). The last was so important that it became a surname, Sima—quite literally, "overseer of the horse." (Chinese surnames, like English ones such as Smith and Fisher, are often derived from the occupation of an ancestor.) The supervisor of land was in charge of many environmental issues, from levees along the rivers to regulating and promoting farming. He oversaw supplying forage grass and forest and other products to the court and its appanages, as well as managing the hunting grounds. There were hierarchies of such supervisors; we read of them at the national level, but apparently military units and presumably local officials had their own supervisors. These or other officials took charge of marshes, orchards, pastures, and other natural and domestic biota (Li Feng 2008: 125ff.). There was sometimes a separate supervisor of marshes (313; the word here translated "marshes" actually means "bottom lands"—it includes drier river-bottom forests, swamps, and other riparian environments as well as marshes). There was still, as in Shang, a supervisor of dogs—mostly of hunting dogs but also those used for sacrifice.

A fascinating and important environmental note is buried in an obscure inscription from around 800 BCE. Lord Qiu cast a bronze vessel with a long inscription concerning a summary transcript of the king's proclamation rewarding Qiu for meritorious service. The king said: "I order you to assist Rong Dui in comprehensively managing the Inspectors of the Forest of the four directions so that the temple-palaces be supplied" (Falkenhausen 2011: 243; his translation). It is extremely striking to find that forestry management was already considered so important that an entire bureaucracy for it was designated by the king himself. More important still is that it was clearly about management for sustainable production: continuing supplies for the temple-palaces. The Japanese still manage sustainable supplies of large timbers for temple construction.

Another revealing note on a ritual bronze tells us that the king rewarded one Pengsheng (who had provided some horses) with fields that extended from a birch-pear grove on one side to "the mulberry trees in the Yu stream" on the other (Li Feng 2008: 17). This use of trees to mark boundaries is interesting; it must have caused nightmares to the surveyors when those groves disappeared over time.

In both Confucianism and Legalism, farmers were held to be nobler and more virtuous than merchants; farmers produce food and fiber, merchants merely transport things around—and make a vulgar profit to boot. Throughout Chinese history, this differential valuation remained in place. In fact, it surfaced anew in deadly fashion under Mao Zedong. Still, few principles in human history have been more thoroughly ignored in practice. Many literati and others did indeed try hard to remain virtuous, devoting their lives and families to farming or the service of the state, but China never lacked for merchants. Merchants often tried to rise socially by getting their children educated and—if possible—into government service, but this did not usually mean giving up the family business. In fact, government servants got involved deeply in trade, as readers of Chinese histories and novels know.

The people who were less urbanized—the famous "barbarians" of Western-language books on China—were a diverse lot. There is no one Chinese word for them. In the Zhou Dynasty, the Rong on the north, the Yi and Di on the west, the Wu in the east, the Yue to the southeast, and other culturally differ-ent peoples each had their own names. (Many other terms came into use later, including the familiar *fan* of modern times. The latter is found not only in the well-known Cantonese slur *faan kuai lou*, "foreign ghost person"—mistranslated as "foreign devil"—but also in many food terms.) Translating all those Zhou ethnic words as "barbarian," as is traditional in western-language sources, captures something of the superior attitude of the Zhou, but it both overtranslates the concept and undertranslates the reality. The Chinese had reason to use all those different terms; they were labeling regional cultural groupings.

The Zhou were surrounded by non-Chinese peoples. Some may have spo-ken other Tibeto-Burman languages, some probably spoke Altaic or Korean languages. On the south, Thai was certainly very commonly spoken—there are countless mutual loanwords. Other languages of Miao, Yao/Mien, and Austronesian stock were presumably not unknown, but in these cases we lack identifiable loanwords in Chinese.

Later Zhou and the Warring States

In later Zhou, China became more populous, grain became more basic to life, and game gradually moved out of the reach of ordinary people. By the rise of Han, only the elite and the remote mountain dwellers had much chance at anything bigger than a rabbit. Farming was basically in the hands of yeoman farmers, as it remained throughout most of Chinese history—as a result of government policy established in Warring States times. Huge estates worked by serfs and/or slaves were, however, well known. The Warring States period was a time of political and social complexity, and the continuum from slave and serf to freeman was apparently as complex as it was in feudal Europe a few centuries later—though by this time China was firmly bureaucratic, not feudal. The complexities usually had more to do with relations with the state than with local landlords. Merchants were numerous, wealthy, and far rang-ing.

Populations grew as bronze and later cast iron farming tools became com-mon. Cast iron entered the picture in Zhou and became common in Han. This development has long been known (E. Anderson 1988; Bray 1984) but de-serves mention, because it made such a difference. Iron quickly became cheaper and more serviceable, making it easy for ordinary people to do state-of-the-art farming with tough, serviceable, cheap hoes, plowshares, brush knives, and the like. Bronze makes good tools and weapons, but they are more expensive and less hard-wearing than iron.

States had a few million people. Qi, the most powerful state around 300 BCE, had quite a few million; the capital, Linzi, was the largest city in China at that time in population, although some cities had larger walled areas (Lewis 2006: 151). The populations of these states are uncertain but were well into hundreds of thousands, or even millions. The Qin Dynasty, after consolidating control over all China in 221, may have reached 40 million (Falkenhausen 2006: 405).

The pious, fearful treatment of the ancestors, a characteristic of Shang and early Zhou, was progressively replaced by a rather cursory treatment of them and a great deal more attention to the living. Texts, both contemporary inscriptions on bronze and later records of later Zhou ideology, indicate that religion was considered to represent society and keep the living together and teach them social rules, not so much to worship remote and obscure beings. This view anticipated the theory of Émile Durkheim (1995) by two millennia.

Tombs included tableaus that represented ordinary life, with the food, furniture, and even the (fewer) sacrificial victims arranged as if to show how life should be when carried on in an ordinary way in the other world (Falkenhausen 2006). We seem to be dealing not with frightening ancestors in a vague sky but rather with an afterlife almost like ordinary life here. This view is, mutatis mutandis, the approach and ideology of Chinese folk religion today, and we see its formative stages in Eastern Zhou tombs. The reforms of Shang Yang, the authoritarian consolidator of the state of Qin in the fourth century BCE, established the new view for all time. Funeral offerings were more concerned with making the dead comfortable in the next life than with pacifying lineages of ancestors (Falkenhausen 2006: 321–23). The tomb became "a microcosmic representation of the world of the living" (382). Moreover, it seems clear from Shang Yang's writings that he knew perfectly well that the real purpose of these rites was to bring the living together and show the living social order, whatever the dead may have thought.

Also evident in sacrifices from Eastern Zhou through the Warring States period is a shift in the class system. Western Zhou had a small and only somewhat differentiated elite. Eastern Zhou, and above all the Warring States period, had a definite class society in which a high-ranking elite ruled over a vast middle range consisting of noble-born but not very wealthy individuals (Falkenhausen 2006). This should not be confused with a middle class—it was a lower-ranking elite—but it certainly had many of the characteristics one associates with a middle class, including an earnest desire to rise through education, sophistication, and proper behavior. This was the class from which most of the philosophers came. It is no accident that the Chinese word for "gentleman," *junzi*, means "son of the non-royal nobility." (Comparisons have often been made to Spanish *hidalgo*, "son of somebody.") It evolved the way "gentleman" did in English: from a class marker to a compliment on one's civil behavior. In any case, the high elite got fancier and fancier tomb goods, the lower elite got rather little. At worst, the lower elites would sink into commoner status.

One important development in Zhou and Warring States was the linguistic form we call Classical Chinese. This was an extremely terse, even telegraphic, language. Grammar was shown by rigid word-ordering rules rather than by function words; few such words existed, and they were highly regular and formulaic in placement and use. Redundancy and bisyllabic words were even less evident. Nobody could actually speak such a language. We need redundancy, grammatical function words, and "fillers" (including "filled pauses") to give our hearers time to process what we are saying. Classical Chinese was a form of speedwriting, evidently developed for taking down court records and orders, in an age when everything had to be laboriously written on bamboo strips or carved into tortoise shells.

One proof of this is that actual verbatim speech, recorded (though still somewhat summarized) for example in the *Records of the Warring States*, has fairly normal human redundancy and grammar. But for 2500 years all scholars in China had to learn to read, think, and above all write in Classical Chinese. They learned to exploit its distinctive traits. In particular, the telegraphic form makes for ambiguity, and later poets learned to cultivate deliberate ambiguity and multiple implication.

In 690 BCE, Chu, in modern Hunan, developed a bureaucratic system with governors and high officials reporting to the ruler. In 594 the state of Lu remitted the labor that farmers owed to local feudal lords, thus effectively turning partial serfs into yeoman farmers. They had to pay taxes and could be liable for military service (Morris 2010: 251). This was one of the beginnings of China's evolution from quasi-feudal and slave labor systems to the overwhelming importance of free yeoman farmers.

China's cultivators have long been called peasants in the West, but in the strict sense, they were rarely peasants—at least not after the Warring States period (though the situation in Han is somewhat unclear). They may have been small-scale farmers, producing for their own subsistence a good deal of the time, but they were not usually in a separate, servile class, as European serfs and peasants were. "Peasant" is a term correctly used for farmers with fewer rights and privileges than full citizens. Chinese farmers were usually full citizens (though sometimes slaves; slavery persisted, diminishing in frequency, to the end of Imperial China). Serfdom apparently diminished after Han. The vast majority of Chinese farmers, and a greater and greater majority over time, were free yeoman farmers, not peasants.

The Warring States period, like China's subsequent period of disunion from 220 to 581 CE, resulted from a situation in which the normal heartland of conquest—the Wei River Valley—simply could not marshal enough resources to defeat the big, rich states south and east. This was partly the failure of Zhou and partly the rapid rise of those other states, as they borrowed civilized governmental forms in their resource-rich lands. Since the origins of Zhou, civilization had been spreading fast. The northern and central realms had huge, powerful, wealthy kingdoms. These were soon joined by expanding ones in the Yangzi valley, and then those farther south as the wave of civilization kept flowing outward. The Chinese world-system was expanding fast. By Han it had drawn in most of modern China, except the far west, and was culturally affecting Vietnam and Korea.

Thousands of Zhou and Warring States tombs have been excavated in the last few decades. These fill out knowledge of local traditions and of sacrifice rites. Standardization and quality control were well in place by this time, and indeed all the elements of mass production in specialized factory-type settings were in place (see, e.g., Barbieri-Low 2011: 374; Falkenhausen 2006). The same is true of the thousands of pottery figures used in tombs. The famous pottery army of Qin Shi Huang Di shows a complicated production process including management by master craftspersons. Some of the latter were women (Barbieri-Low 2011: 379), a fact rather surprising to those who believe the stereotypes about Chinese women in imperial times. The pottery soldiers were mass produced but then given individual faces, clothing details, and weapon characteristics by highly skilled masters.

Recent work on the *Zhou Li*—theoretically the government manual of the Zhou Dynasty but actually a Han reconstruction—promises to add to our understanding of food and nutrition. It was the *Zhou Li* that first established nutrition as the highest branch of medicine. The *Zhou Li* claims that the court had—along with shamans, dream interpreters, and so on—special officers in charge of aromatic plants, wines, chickens, and other food items. The idealized Zhou court should have two court nutritionists overseeing all. They were the most important medical officials in Zhou. A proper court should also have 152 feast masters, supervising some 70 butchers, 128 cooks for the inner court, 128 more for the outer offices and functions, 62 assistant cooks, 335 masters of the royal domain who (among other things) oversaw collecting the foodstuffs, 62 game hunters, 24 turtle catchers, 28 meat driers, 110 butlers, 340 winemakers, 170 other beverage makers, 94 icehouse attendants, 31 people to manage serving baskets, 61 meat picklers, 62 other picklers, and 62 salt makers—some 2,263, or 55 percent of the 4,133 officers of the royal household (Knechtges 1986: 49). Of course, it is more than doubtful that the Zhou ever had anything close to so many. One finds it hard to believe that they had any specialized turtle catchers, let alone 24. Still, these figures confirm historical testimony that feasting was extremely important, being, among other things, owed to the ancestors (K.-c. Chang 1977).

Food in those days was, as always in China, based on boiled grain. The relish eaten with it ran heavily to *geng*, stews and thick soups. The poor ate vegetable geng, with pigweed or lambsquarters (*li, Chenopodium* spp.) a particular marker of poverty food; Confucius was reduced to it in his poorer days (Sterckx 2011: 15–16). A "meal of plain vegetables" became symbolic of rustic virtue. Of course, the geng of the rich involved various kinds of meat, fish, game, and turtles. Status was clearly shown by food: "In the retinue of the Lord of Mengchang, 'Senior Retainers ate meat, Regular Retainers ate fish, Junior Retainers ate vegetables'" (A. Meyer 2011: 79, quoting a fragment preserved in later works). One hopes that the suffering juniors got occasional meat!

With Zhou, we first find occasion to refer to the superb and encyclopedic history of Chinese food technology by H. T. Huang (2000), one of the greatest food historians. This book, the life work of Dr. Huang, sets a new standard for Chinese food research. Although it begins with the Neolithic, it really comes into its own with Zhou food. Among other things, Huang identifies the ritual vessels and shows some of the superb archaeological relics.

Roel Sterckx has recently taken up the task of seriously considering Warring States and Han food. He points out in *The Animal and the Daemon in Early China* (2002) that different regions had different animals, people, and customs and there seemed to be a mystic resonance here. His book *Food, Sacrifice and Sagehood in Early China* (2011; and see Sterckx 2005 and Lo 2005) goes into great detail not only about the food itself but also about the meanings it had during a time when rites and rituals changed from being genuine religious practices to being political gestures—no doubt having some sacred functions, but also serving to show off wealth, bond courtiers together, train the young in their obligations, and allow ritualists and organizers of ceremonies full play.

These sociological functions led Confucius and his followers to see rituals as critically important not only to statecraft but also to personal development. The proper gentleman (*junzi*) is trained in self-control and develops self-respect and a properly thoughtful, considerate, mindful attitude from following rituals to the letter, as the great founders of Zhou did in ancient times. Thus food took on a mystical importance: religiously important as sacrifice to the gods and ancestors, politically important as marker of status and solidarity, and personally important as part of a regimen of personal training and improvement. As I pointed out (E. Anderson 1988), this prevented puritanism from getting a foothold in China. That sour and mean philosophy was not without advocates (such as Mozi), but reverence for elders and ancestors meant that they had to be given the best of everything, and puritanism could not survive that imperative. It is a strange fact about humans that excuses for innocent enjoyment always seem necessary; puritanism is rampantly persuasive otherwise. It was to surface again in China when Buddhism became influential and became one of the reasons that Confucians condemned Buddhists for not caring about ancestors.

Sterckx provides a meticulous and fascinating account of the food of the era. A highly varied and complex cuisine (even including things like wolf's breast; Sterckx 2011: 17) is attested in the records. In general, it is confirmed by food residues in cooking vessels. The five flavors—the four of Western food studies, plus hot spiciness—were well organized and balanced in cooking. (There is now known to be yet another flavor, umami—the savoriness of fermented soy products. The Chinese did not pick up on this one because they did not yet have soy ferments; those came in late Warring States or Han times. Hotness is not a flavor but a feeling; the various chemicals in question actually stimulate the heat receptors, or the pain receptors, in the mouth.) The five flavors distinguished by Chinese thought were associated with the many other "fives" of Chinese correspondence theory. These were well described in countless sources, most of which date back to the Yellow Emperor's Classic, of Han Dynasty vintage (see below).

Food preservation became a major need and an important art. Preservation included not only salting, drying, smoking, pickling, and so on, but also icing; snow and ice were collected in winter and stored in pits under insulating material. (Many Americans did the same within my memory).

Literature, including the *Li Ji* (Chapter 6), attests the technique later used for "beggars' chicken"—baking an animal in clay without removing the fur or feathers, which would stick to the clay and come off by themselves. "Fragments of a Han gastronomic treatise recovered in 1999 from the tomb of Wu Ying ... include recipes for boiled deer, boiled lamb, and boiled horse" (Sterckx 2011: 16). Sterckx does not find much else about eating horses, but several famous stories mention eating them, and frequent careful directions to avoid the liver indicate that the rest of the horse was a popular thing to eat. Horse liver was believed to be poisonous. I suspect that the liver accumulated toxins from vegetation the horses ate.

An enormously complex etiquette governed eating, feasting, and foodways. Norbert Elias's "civilizing mission" had already been completed long ago, except for those "barbarians." Barbarians, of course, ate as barbarians do—at least according to Chinese records. In fact, of course, those records reflect biased stereotypes rather than reality. The Chinese began to use the term "raw barbarians" for those who had not learned Chinese cultural behavior; those who had were "cooked barbarians." The raw were the ones who supposedly ate their food raw; the civilized ones cooked it (Sterckx 2011: 20–21). Of course it is highly doubtful whether anyone really ate food raw. Grain and meat would not be very digestible, and raw pork would be downright dangerous. The point is that the more civilized the ethnic groups were, the more they ate like the Chinese of the central plains. The distinction between "raw" and "cooked" barbarians persisted in government records throughout the history of imperial China.

Sterckx provides a wonderful account. One can go to the *Li Ji* and *Zhou Li* for more; the rules go on and on, and the slightest infringement could get a servant killed or a lord assassinated. Confucius and his disciples and followers, known as *ru*, often made their living as ritual experts, planning and overseeing great rituals for local courts. Death and mourning had their own rules; the three-year mourning period for a parent involved moving from near fasting to an eventual full return to normal life. A large number of odd beliefs about food presage the ones that still exist in Chinese society. Avoidances, magical beliefs, and other ideas were current, including the idea that eating a rabbit's kneecap could doom you to having your kneecap cut off in punishment (Sterckx 2011: 23).

One point made by Sterckx concerns Zhuangzi's famous parable of the expert butcher. The butcher could keep his knife sharp forever by cutting only between the joints, where there was no resistance (anyone used to cutting up chickens is familiar with this concept). Zhuangzi has him advising the lord to govern accordingly—with a minimum of effort and bloodshed. But the brilliant and outspoken statesman Jia Yi (201–169 BCE)—martyred for his "fearless speech" in the early Han Dynasty—put a new spin on this recommendation by maintaining that even the best butcher could not cut up big thighbones and hipbones without a hatchet and axe, and thus the emperor should deal with restive feudal lords by the direct approach (Sterckx 2011: 53). Unfortunately, the emperor took the advice all too much to heart; Jia was later executed himself.

Then as now, meat could be boiled, roasted, grilled, or left raw. Sacrifices were eventually buried and hidden, supposedly, but surely people ate the meat, as they did at other times in history. Many spirits, then as now, preferred sacrifices of raw meat, often with the hair still on. Sterckx argues that such spirits liked things pure and tasteless, but in modern China the spirits that prefer raw and hairy meat are often wild, savage, and intimidating spirits.

Spirits in Zhou and Han times liked their water pure and cold; it was called "dark mysterious liquor" (Sterckx 2011: 89ff.). Sometimes moonlight was reflected into it by mirrors. The cosmological history of the times associated the Xia Dynasty with bright pure water, the Shang with unfermented grain drink (presumably a sort of near-beer), the Zhou with fermented ale (92). As now, spirits had varied taste in ales, waters, and liquors in general, but, unlike today, they never got tea; it had not yet come to China. Of course, since the spirits got only the qi of the offerings while the humans got the material remains, this led to a serious danger of drunkenness, discussed and condemned at great length in documents quoted by Sterckx (101ff.). Recall Lothar von Falkhenhausen's observations (see above) on the reduced numbers of wine vessels in late Western Zhou.

The documents go into incredible detail on the sacrifices and the construction of altars. An altar could be desacralized: "'When a state has ceased to exist, its altar of the soil is roofed above and fenced with wood below to indicate that its connection with Heaven and Earth has been cut off'" (Sterckx 2011: 117, quoting Wang Chong, ca. 1 CE).

Such sacrifices were a major economic activity. We read of offerings of "nearly 3,000 sheep and boar" at one time, of "more than 12,000 specialists . . . to oversee . . . more than 24,000 offerings" at another, and 37,000 shrines constructed in one year around 1 BCE (Sterckx 2011: 134). Of course, this created a huge demand, both for meat and for ru. The Chinese economists of the time—who were perfectly aware of Keynesian theory long before John Maynard Keynes himself—celebrated the major stimulant effect it had on the economy. A huge pottery workshop in Chang'an, the Han capital city (now Xi'an), could turn out 8,000 sacrificial figurines at one time (Sterckx 2011: 146). Even the humble bulrush supported a major industry, since it was used to manufacture mats and also strainers for ale (156). These were "*jing* reeds," described as having three ribs running the length of the stem, that is, bulrushes. The accounts tell us that demand for them led to a huge flow of wealth into the otherwise impoverished marsh districts and to an increase in economic activity generally, all described in terms that would delight Keynes and his recent followers. Ancient Chinese economists were no fools.

Sterckx is struck by the enormous range of sensory appeals. He is well aware, of course, that the sacrifices were accompanied by equally dramatic music, dance, incense, visual display, and everything else to dazzle the senses—as is still the case in Chinese religion. The object was (and is) to delight the spirits, who have even broader tastes than real humans, delighting in plain water and raw meat as much as in stews and roasts.

One slight problem with Sterckx's analysis is that he translates *jiu* as "ale" or "wine" indifferently—sometimes both in the same sentence. He knows that jiu is, technically, ale (often flavored with fruit or aromatic herbs). But the traditional idiomatic translation as "wine" often intrudes.

In Eastern Zhou, the most notable culinary story is apocryphal. According to legend, Duke Huan had a cook, Yi Ya, who was so superb a cook that the duke became too biased in his favor, showering him with gifts. Yi even killed his own son and cooked him for the duke, as a variation on the usual cuisine (A. Liu 2010: 324). This enabled Yi to fight for months for control of the dukedom after Duke Huan died, preventing Duke Huan from even getting a proper burial (A. Liu 2010: 260; So 1992: 14 provides a folkloric version). Even those who discounted such tall tales often regarded Yi as a mess maker in many senses, including interfering with the natural flavors of things. Even so, he became the symbol of great cuisine in China, and his name still crops up in that capacity.

We have noted above the even more tenuous existence of an ancient chef named Yi Yin. (Do Yi Ya and Yi Yin imply that there was a real association of cooking with the Yi lineage?) Much is recorded of him—all of it many centuries after his purported life span. In the Annals of the State of Lu (*The Annals of Lü Buwei*, Lü Buwei 2000), Yi Yin told King Tang: "Water is the first ingredient. . . . Fire serves as the regulator." It removes the raw flavors of things—the rankness of carnivorous animals' meat, the fishiness of aquatic food, and the fetidness of herbivores. In cooking, "one must use the sweet, sour, bitter, acrid, and salty" in subtle variations. "The transformation within the cauldron is quintessential, marvelous, extremely fine, and delicate." Food should be "cooked but not mushy, sweet but not cloying, sour but not excessively so, salty but not deadening, acrid but not caustic, mild but not bland, rich with fats but not greasy" (Lü Buwei 2000: 309). Note that the concern with fives, so obsessive in the Han Dynasty, is here as well, proving that the passage comes from Han times or at most the late Warring States, not actually from the ancient days of King Tang.

This good advice is followed a list of the finest delicacies, as retailed by Yi Yin to his king. The delicacies are almost all imaginary: "the lips of the human-faced ape; the feet of the *huanhuan* bird; . . . phoenix eggs, . . . the 'flying fish,' which is shaped like a carp with wings and usually flies nightly from the Western Sea to the Eastern Sea," and so on (Sterckx 2011: 72; see Lü Buwei 2000: 310–11 for the full list). These beings sound like the imaginary people and animals in *Classic of Mountains and Seas* (*Shan Hai Jing*, Birrell 1999), a somewhat later work of fantastic geography (see Lewis 2006; Sterckx 2002). The latter book recounts visions seen by shamans during soul travel. They sound very much like accounts received from shamans in modern ethnographic studies (see, e.g., Humphrey 1996). Yi Yin even mentions mythical steeds that could run fast enough to obtain these delicacies. They must have been fine mounts indeed, since many of the realms where these delicacies exist are purely imaginary. So Yi Yin and his favorite foods may all have been the inventions of storytellers or shamans. However, a few believable items, including tangerines from the Yangzi and pomelos from Yunmeng, are listed. Yi Yin lists animal foods, fish, plants, seasonings (including vinegar made from a sturgeon—a most unlikely concoction), grains, waters, and fruits.

Yi Yin also began a trend that lasts to this day in Chinese food books: evaluating not only foods but also waters. This is not so strange at it seems to modern readers. China's waters are all too often polluted, muddy, sulfurous, or otherwise awful. Good water was, and still is, something that had to be sought out. Mineral waters with delightful taste or curative properties were known early on and highly valued.

Yi Yin uses all this culinary lore as a lead-in to instruct the ruler in statecraft—among other things, the advice that Tang should conquer widely so that he could get all those delicacies. More sensible, and more in tune with traditional Chinese thought, was his counsel to Tang that before you gain control of the world "you must first gain control over your own person" (Lü Buwei 2000: 102). Also, just as one ox can provide meat for deep-frying, roasting, grilling, or smoking (Sterckx 2011: 74), so the Way (the Dao—the proper Way of living and ruling) can be used for many purposes. Note that stir-frying is not in this list. It is not mentioned or evidenced in any pre-Han sources.

Poems help us interpret the data. The Book of Songs is well known. Also, a major collection of songs from the lands of Chu contains several laments for the dead in which the mourners attempt to call a man's soul back. (Sometimes a man or woman was simply in a coma and then revived—hence the attempts. This practice of trying to call back the soul continues; I have seen it done.) The mourners lure the soul with promises of good living, including food. I quote from Arthur Waley's translation, more free than accurate, but giving the "flavor" of the poem:

Where pies are cooked of millet and water-grain,
Guests watch the steaming bowls
And sniff the pungency of peppered herbs.
The cunning cook adds slices of bird-flesh,
Pigeon and yellow-heron and black-crane.
They taste the badger-stew.
O Soul come back to feed on foods you love!

Next are brought
Fresh turtle, and sweet chicken cooked in cheese
Pressed by men of Ch'u.
And pickled suckling-pig
And flesh of whelps floating in liver-sauce
With salad of minced radishes in brine;
All served with the hot spice of southernwood
The land of Wu supplies . . .
  (Waley 1946: 37–38; compare the different translations in K.-c. Chang
  1977: 32–33; H. Huang 2000: 94–95; Knechtges 1986: 54–57; Sukhu 2012)

Interesting in this poem (but one has to read all the translations to learn it) is the use not only of Chinese "pepper" (*Zanthoxylum* spp., flower or brown pepper, actually a citrus relative) but also of smartweed (*Polygonum hydropiper, P. odoratum*, and relatives) and wormwood (*Artemisia* spp.) as flavorings. These were common in China before chile peppers replaced them in the last 400 years. Smartweed was also mentioned as a food in the *Huainanzi* (A. Liu 2010: 566; original around 120 BCE) as an important plant for a household to raise to flavor millet and rice. Rarely used in China today, it survives as a very common, important spice in Vietnam (*rau ram, P. odoratum*). *Artemisia*, either fresh or dried and powdered, survives as a common flavoring in Korea.

Qu Yuan, putative author of the best of the Chu songs, mentioned many obscure plants, often known only from his writings. (He may have been fictional or may not have written the songs [Sukhu 2012]; on the other hand, somebody had to have written them, and Qu is as good a candidate as any.) I have not tried to analyze these plant names because their identification is uncertain. One, *shu ma*, literally "sparse hemp," may just possibly be soma or haoma, the famous Indo-Iranic indulgent (Zhang He 2011). Soma, if it was anything, was probably marijuana and/or *Peganum harmala* (bush-rue). That would fit with the word *ma*, which means hemp, that is, marijuana. (The idea that soma was made from fly agaric mushrooms, which is still widely cited in secondary literature, has long been disproved.)

Qin, later to conquer all China, seems to have been a state of a marginal people, perhaps recently civilized in earlier Zhou times. Among finds in Qin state was a bronze vessel, found in a tomb, half full of liquid and bones and "turned murky green by verdigris" (Ma 2010): an ancient stew, almost certainly geng, which is very often referred to in Zhou sources. Another vessel held possible jiu (ale). A nearby tomb had broken cow ribs, evidently used for food.

Qin documents note seasonal prescriptions and countless detailed rules. If the oxen are in good condition at the end of the year, "the Overseer of Agriculture is granted a bottle of wine and a bundle of dried meat" and the cattle keepers are also rewarded. If three or more rat holes were found in a granary, officials were fined; "three mouse holes are equal to one rat hole" (Lewis 2007: 109, quoting Qin sources). Any lingering doubts that China had truly perfected bureaucracy are dispelled by the pervasiveness of such micromanagement!

All central northern China was thoroughly sinicized by this time. The people of Qin may well have been "barbarians" long before, but they were thoroughly Zhou in civilization, culture, and language by the time they entered the historical record. In another area, the people of Zhongshan made beautiful bronze work showing winged and horned animals that are similar to Near Eastern images of the time, but the style is Zhou and the iconography grades into purely Zhou designs, so any influence from the West is indirect (see Falkenhausen 2006: 260ff.; in spite of his skepticism, the ultimate West Asian inspiration of this style is impossible to ignore, but it had certainly been sinicized by the time it got to Zhongshan). The huge state of Chu, in what is now Hubei, Hunan, and neighboring areas, had a spectacular and flashy culture that has always looked "non-Chinese" in certain ways, but—as the songs cited above prove—it was thoroughly Chinese in language and culture at the elite levels. It certainly included some Thai speakers, however. There are still some in the area, preserving ancient variants of the language family. Many scholars have believed over time that the majority of the people were ancestral Thai. This seems highly probable, even though there is no evidence.

More clearly different were the pastoral and semipastoral groups on the north and northwest frontiers of the Warring States. A detailed recent study of a major cemetery at Majiayuan (in modern Gansu, but at the edge of Qin in Warring States times) has revealed a culture clearly not Han Chinese (Xiaolong Wu 2013). The tombs contained many typical Qin artifacts and many Qin-type items but also many objects—including spectacular and beautiful goldwork—typical of the steppes. The independent Yanglang people to the west were more Central Asian in their artistic tastes, indicating a major influence from Qin conquest or pressure. The Yanglang and Majiayuan sites appear to represent groups of the Rong people.

The elite burials thus reveal a cultural mix: the local culture was evidently already a blend, but also, like elites in Central Asian cultures before and after, elite individuals accumulated wealth and prestige goods from their trading networks. The lead excavator, Xiaolong Wu, refers to this as "cultural hybridity," but doing so considerably stretches a term that is problematical enough in its modern application (originally to English-influenced cultural ways in India). Cultures are not biological species. They are not pure and isolated. They are, in fact, not things at all—they are analytical abstractions, categories created by historians and anthropologists. They do not and cannot hybridize. What actually happens is that people naturally adopt anything they like and find useful, especially—of course—from the other people around them. Thus it is inevitable that trading and nomadizing societies will pick up all kinds of items, especially luxury goods and ideas about luxury, from everyone in their trading network. (Wu may also have too easily assumed that the Majiayuan elites felt "subaltern"; they seem to have been a proud, independent lot.)

More clearly alien were the Yue and their neighbors in the southeast from the Yangzi delta on southward (Falkenhausen 2006: 271ff.). They had a striking local culture that was quite different from Zhou. Their well-made, high-fired stoneware, which is probably ancestral to porcelain, is in the same general style, but distinctive enough to qualify as a different cultural formation. Yue fell to Chu in 307 BCE.

Farther afield, the regional cultures of what is now south China were even more different, as were the cultures of Central Asia. Korea, however was greatly enough influenced by China to have a dynasty started by local elites from China. Whether they spoke a language related to Chinese or to Korean is unknown, but they used Chinese for court purposes.

Recent findings in Central Asia show major resurgent activity there, from about 500 BCE. The "dark age" that began around 1500 BCE was definitely over. Population and towns rapidly grew. Around 500 a major irrigation system made urban life possible in a presently uninhabited desert in Afghanistan; Achaemenid pottery dates the settlement and gives at least some indication of who did the work (Lawler 2012).

Early Mongolia used copper with some arsenic content to make a sort of bronze; sophisticated tin-lead bronze appears only in the Xiongnu period, evidently due to influence from Qin and Han (Park et al. 2011).

Conclusion

In the development of Chinese food production, distribution, and consumption, the early civilizations and especially the Warring States period stand as absolutely critical. It was during these times that China's basic food system developed. The division between the wheat-and-millet north and rice-based south became established. Most of the critically important foods were known.

Vitally important in all this was the division of China into many competing states and statelets. Each tried to overcome the others, not only militarily but also economically and politically. Such rivalry led to the rapid competitive development of many agricultural systems and many political and philosophical ideologies that gave serious consideration to agriculture, often privileging it as the noblest and most important activity (after governing, of course!).

Food consumption was firmly set in a pattern of feasting, including the provision of the finest of foods and drinks for the ancestors and other revered beings in other realms. Puritanism was firmly equated with disrespect and rudeness toward one's elders and ancestors and thus chased more or less definitively from the Chinese scene.

CHAPTER 4

The Development of Chinese Sustainability During Zhou and Han

Ideology and Behavior

The most dramatic single document in Chinese environmental history is Mencius's famous parable of the "Ox Mountain":

> There was a time when the trees were luxuriant on the Ox Mountain. As it is on the outskirts of a great metropolis, the trees are constantly lopped by axes. Is it any wonder that they are no longer fine? With the respite they get in the day and in the night, and the moistening by the rain and dew, there is certainly no lack of new shoots coming out, but then the cattle and sheep come to graze upon the mountain. That is why it is as bald as it is. People, seeing only its baldness, tend to think that it never had any trees. But can this possibly be the nature of a mountain? Can what is in man be completely lacking in moral inclinations? A man's letting go of his true heart is like the case of the trees and the axes. (Mencius 1970: 164–65; the word translated "man" actually means "person": Mencius is referring to all genders)

China's philosophy, cosmology, and views of morality and nature were set in the late Warring States period and have endured surprisingly well. In the following section, I will describe the concepts of cosmos, morality, and knowledge as they were outlined at that time and during the Han Dynasty, and make some notes on continuities. Of course the last two or three centuries have seen vast changes in all aspects of Chinese thought, but I am not concerned with those in the present book; I am dealing with principles of environmental management that persisted, mutatis mutandis, over centuries.

Moral rules and governmental regulations to protect forests, game, and other natural resources were established early (Girardot et al. 2001; Tucker and Berthrong 1998; Vermeer 1998). Of course, such mandates indicate both that the Chinese were quite well aware of major problems and that they were doing something about them. Confucians in particular were concerned about conservation. Confucius himself taught and modeled conservationist practices such as sparing breeding females when hunting (see many quotes and discussions in Tucker and Berthrong 1998). He did not shoot sitting ducks. Mencius's parable above should be seen in this light.

Confucians were concerned with the actual details of government, and these included many conservation measures. Mencius's story of Ox Mountain, written in the fourth century BCE, shows the exceptional ecological sophistication of ancient China and the extraordinary psychological sophistication of Mencius. He is, for one thing, quite aware that a forest is an ecosystem. It is a group of interlocking adaptations, all dependent on each other and on the soil in which they grow. He is quite aware of how humans degrade such a system. He goes on to draw a thoroughly appropriate parallel, describing how people are naturally social. People are innately prone to do what is socially good or appropriate to the environment and to each other. Yet they are easily corrupted by bad teaching, bad company, and bad circumstances. Like Ox Mountain, they are degraded by ill-considered human actions. Mencius's highly insightful psychology still needs serious consideration, since it accords perfectly with modern findings; the usual textbook line that Mencius thinks people are "good" does not even begin to elucidate this view (see E. Anderson 2007).

There were many other extremely perceptive comments on the environment from China's dynastic times (Vermeer 1998). Mencius's famous critic Xunzi (fl. ca. 298–238 BCE), though he disagreed about human goodness (see below), agreed on conservation. He provided an entire policy of sustainable exploitation of natural animal populations (Xunzi 1999: 240–83).

One important ecological message of Mencius's story is that deforestation was already a common and obtrusive problem in the fourth century BCE and that people were concerned about it and were trying to stop it. This is the first time we encounter a theme that then continued for 2,400 years: the slow, erratic worsening of the environmental situation and the many measures taken to stop this. As Yi-fu Tuan (1968, 1969) emphasized long ago and Nicholas Menzies

(1994) has more recently demonstrated, China displays an inconsistent attitude toward the environment. Deforestation was deplored and reforestation constantly carried out, but the forests nevertheless slowly declined. Parks, sacred groves, gardens, public green spaces, and countless other means for preserving a green environment came and went. Much of the damage occurred during wars and rebellions (Menzies 1994), but much was simply the inevitable result of a great civilization, densely populated, doing quite well but never perfectly at the task of managing agricultural and ecological sustainability.

China conspicuously failed to save its forests (as Southeast Asia did) and to restore forests after damage as Japan did (Totman 1989). On the other hand, China never came even remotely close to the level of environmental damage in a short time that has characterized settler societies in the Americas. Like much of Europe, Chinese environmental management was a mixed bag (Tuan 1968)—bad enough to lead to increasing troubles over time, good enough to keep the system functioning as the population grew into the hundreds of millions.

The degree to which China, or rather China's local cultures, communities, and ethnic groups, succeeded at this task was revealed when Mao Zedong changed everything in the 1950s and declared a "struggle against nature." China's environment crashed; more damage has been done since 1950 than in the previous 5,000 years. Whole forests have been wiped out. Rivers have dried up. Millions of acres of grassland have been desertified. Much of this was done *before* technology had changed much, so it was not the result of more machines and poisons. It was the result of Mao's oft-stated policy "struggle against nature." Struggling against one's life support system is never a good idea. In this case it served one function: it proved the Chinese had been doing very well indeed for the preceding 5,000 years. They could have done far worse.

Agriculture, like medicine, was a genuine science from very early times. Whatever else the simplest and most ancient societies may or not have known, they always had to have a very great deal of practical knowledge about how to get food. Agriculture was from the first a scientific field. Anyone who did not know basic rules of ecology and agronomy and how to apply them in a variety of contexts did not survive. People may have had a range of religious and magical ideas about farming, but they had to have pragmatic, tested, wide-ranging knowledge.

With civilization came writing, and early Mesopotamian and Egyptian literature contains a great deal about farming. The Bible is a vast storehouse of knowledge about Near Eastern agriculture and herding. In ancient Greece, Xenophon portrayed no less a genius than Socrates discussing farming with an estate owner in a strikingly accurate and scientifically grounded farming manual, the *Oikonomos*. Our word "economics" comes from that title.

In China, agricultural lore is found in the Shang Dynasty oracle bone inscriptions and is well covered in Zhou literature. In the Han Dynasty came the world's first known agricultural extension manual, Fan Shengzhi's book (ca. 140 BCE). It describes case/control experimental field trials. These appear to be the first known case/control experiments in the world and were every bit as scientific as anything today (E. Anderson 1988; Bray 1984; Shih 1973).

In spite of the minor magical practices inevitable in peasant farming (and not unknown in modern agribusiness), Chinese agriculture remained highly rationalized. Agricultural handbooks and encyclopedias have demonstrated this since the Han Dynasty. The extreme sophistication of Chinese farming was described in a famous account, *Farmers of Forty Centuries* by F. H. King, in the early twentieth century (1911; many other early and laudatory accounts are cited in E. Anderson 1988 and Simoons 1991).

Food technology, too, was a formidable science. No one could possibly question its thoroughly rational, experimental, and fast-developing character after H. T. Huang's magisterial work documented it (2000). Chinese physics and chemistry may have stayed all too close to alchemy and ritual, but until the eighteenth or even nineteenth century, medicine and agriculture were as rational in China as in the West.

Dynastic collapses occurred when the government became overly bloated, corrupt, and distant from the people—"lost the mandate of Heaven," the people said. Often, proof of the loss of mandate came in the form of disasters such as floods, droughts, and plagues of locusts. Modern Americans call these events "natural" disasters or "acts of God" and fail to see them as related to human politics. However, the Chinese were right, and American folk wisdom is wrong.

Floods in old China resulted more from deforestation and failure to maintain dikes and levees than from an excess of rain. Locusts exploded when land mismanagement let them reproduce in masses. Droughts were less preventable, but government relief served to alleviate the problems when the government was strong. Nature may have sent the stresses—rain, drought, insects—but bad government was more involved than nature in the proximate causation of the actual problems. Instead of condemning the Chinese for "superstition" in seeing political judgments in "natural" problems, we should be learning from them. China's major dynasties lasted 200–300 years. Minor dynasties that controlled only part of the country rarely lasted a century. (Han theoretically lasted 400 years but was interrupted by coups and interregnal periods. See the many volumes of *The Cambridge History of China* and, for the period it covers, Frederick Mote's *Imperial China 900–1800*, 1999.)

Many scholars have published extensively on the more pragmatic aspects of China's traditional environmental management (see esp. Elvin 2004a; Elvin and Liu 1998; Marks 1998). Religion and ethics in relation to environmental management have also received much attention in recent years and are well covered (Callicott and Ames 1989; Waldau and Patton 2007). Recent volumes deal with the environmental philosophies of Confucianism and Daoism (Tucker and Berthrong 1998; Girardot et al. 2001). A companion volume on Buddhism (Tucker and Williams 1997) adds more East Asian data.These sources disclose a monumental environmental philosophy, applied to conservation, management, and environmental stewardship (E. Anderson 1988, 1996, 2001, 2007; E. Anderson and M. Anderson 1973; Anderson and Raphals 2007; Buell et al. 2010).

Whatever led to China's environmental problems over the millennia, it certainly was not philosophy, nor was it lack of science. It was, in fact, rising population and limited administrative scope and competence.

Cosmology

One must wonder why China's philosophical and religious ideologies maintained a strong relationship with, reverence for, and "connection" to nature, whereas the Western world developed its infamous attitudes of "dominion," "rupture," destruction, and waste. As Yi-fu Tuan (1969) pointed out, the contrast was less strong than many environmental writers seem to think, but it was real. China and the ancient West were both based on grain agriculture, dry-grown and irrigated. They both used the plow, had states that warred with each other, had commerce and trade, and developed centralized bureaucratic empires. They both developed philosophy and "world" religions at the same time, in the Axial Age. The parallels are close. Direct contact across Central Asia was evidently a reality long before the first historically attested contacts in the Han Dynasty (Morris 2010).

One proof of the early origins of China's deep concern for interactions with plants and animals is the *Book of Songs*, the folk and court song collection compiled by Confucius. It mentions more plants than the Bible does, even though the former is not as long as some of the individual books in the latter. Nature was richer in China, more productive, and less escapable. People relied heavily on wild resources and still do in some areas.

China's warring states were all culturally similar and all used Chinese, at least as an elite language. The highly analytical, isolating, nature-irrelevant world of Western thought was heavily concentrated among people who traded across major ethnic and ecological frontiers (Lerro 2000): the Phoenicians (who gave us the alphabet), the Greeks, the later Jews, the Syrians. Possibly their intercultural experiences made them more analytic and less attuned to local ecologies than the Chinese were. Possibly the rationality toward nature that the Chinese did develop came mostly from interstate zones. But these explanations remain conjectural.

The basic model of the universe was of a round heaven resting on a square earth. China was at the center of the latter. Barbarian realms lay around it, and the ocean circled all. The earth was oriented by the four directions and the center, and each of these five was marked by a sacred mountain. The earth, or at least China's central portion of it, sloped downward from west to east, causing rivers to run eastward. In heaven, *Tian*, were stars, sun, and moon, all with their effects on earthly affairs. The gods lived somewhere in the heavens or in sacred lands of the far and high west.

The energy of the cosmos flows as *qi* ("breath" or "spirit"). Qi includes also the subtle forces that are the dynamic shapers and movers behind the static landscape of mountains and plains. Currents of qi run through the landscape, just as they do in the human body. Human qi flow parallels that in the earth. Organs have their particular qi. Blocked, stagnant, deficient, or otherwise deranged qi is the major direct cause of sickness. Stagnant qi is pathological, but pooling qi can be beneficial, bringing good influences together at particular points.

Qi can be relatively yang or yin. In an alternate view, there are different qi's: yang qi's and yin qi's. Medical works are never quite clear as to whether qi is all one or a cover-term for many separate forces.

China may be the only traditional culture in which "male" and "female" are considered more or less accidents of a more basic set of forces, rather than basic aspects of the universe. Males are two-thirds yang in balance of forces, females two-thirds yin. This is, in fact, the ratio of androsterone hormones to estriol hormones in males and females, showing that the Chinese had a very good sense of reality. But yang and yin do not refer to maleness and femaleness. As noted above, they originally refer to the sunny and shady sides of a hill. In terms of qi, this means that yang qi is the energy seen in bright, dry, warm, golden-red influences, and yin qi is the energy of shady, moist, cool, dark influences. Males are thought to be more active and outgoing, while women have dark moist wombs.

According to early Daoist thought, which probably represents fairly widespread thinking, the Dao, the basic and original Way, gave birth to the Unity, which divided into yang and yin, whose interaction produced the Myriad Things. The yin dominated because the female accepts, engenders, and gives birth.

Whatever the Greeks may have thought about the literal role of their famous four elements in making up the world, the Chinese thought about the five Chinese elements as processes or influences. The five basic constructs of Chinese thought were traditionally called the Five Elements in English; a better term is Five Phases (Porkert 1974). The actual word translated by "element" or "phase," however, actually means "going" (*xing*), a term fitting well with Daoist phraseology. These xing are not components of a structure ("elements") but phases of a process. *Xing* can be, and often is, a synonym for *dao* in the literal sense of a street or road. In modern Chinese towns, *dao* tends to mean "road" (larger) and *xing*, "street" (smaller, local). So philosophers are constantly reminded of the literal meaning of these terms.

The xing transform into each other: water collects on metal, water nourishes wood, wood nourishes fire, fire produces earth (ash), earth produces metal. In reverse order, they disrupt each other: metal digs into earth, earth smothers fire, fire burns wood, trees (wood) suck up water, water rusts metal. They are connected to and defined by the five directions (including the center). Each of these had its sacred mountain.

They also appear in the five colors of the original Chinese color system: black, white, red, yellow, and green-blue, following a very widespread tendency in the world's languages to recognize those five as primary. They are the easiest colors for our eyes and brains to pick out. Like many languages, Chinese lumps green, blue, and light gray under one color term, *qing*. This can confuse translators. I recently read about a green fox in a Chinese poem. Of course it was a gray fox; the translator (I shall mercifully leave him nameless here) had mindlessly used the commonest meaning of *qing* instead of the obviously appropriate one. Modern Chinese has added blue, green, and purple, but only for dyes and dyed material, and the words originate from dyestuffs; the word for pure blue is simply the word for the indigo plant. Compare

English, with its use of flower names for late-recognized colors; pink, violet, mauve, and several other color names began as flower names.

The basic colors fit the well-known tendency of the human mind to be able to hold only five to seven items easily. There are also five tones in the Chinese musical scale and most other scales worldwide; again, the human mind at work. The West uses five- or seven-toned scales. Moreover, the human mind also recognizes four or five tastes, so the Chinese could easily see that as another fivefold ranking: sweet, sour, salt, bitter, and pungent.

The correlation of the five directions and five flavors is of interest to us here because it seems to refer to regional cooking styles. The center correlated with sweet, and central-eastern Chinese cooking is still notably sweeter than that of other areas. North goes with salt, and the north does have salt lakes and a salty cuisine. South goes with bitter, and southern Chinese food does make relatively more use of bitter greens and other vegetables. East goes with sour, and China's best vinegar comes from the central east; other correlations (especially when the center is left out) pair east with sweet, which may make more sense: eastern Chinese food has many sweets. West goes with pungent, and anyone who has had real Sichuan or Hunan food knows where that ascription comes from! West China's heat comes today from chiles, which were not introduced until the sixteenth or seventeenth century, but in Han, west China had brown or Sichuan peppers, smartweed, and many other spicy herbs and fruits. We know this from the Songs of the South mentioned above, which document Hunan's food in incredible detail.

The Han Dynasty began an orgy of systematizing everything under the five phases. The Han thinkers recognized five major bodily organs: kidneys, liver, heart, spleen, lungs—corresponding, in order, to water, wood, fire, earth, and metal. They recognized also five minor organs, five staple foods (various lists given), and five scents. Eventually there were five domestic animals, five favorite flowers, five favorite fruit trees, five favorite shade trees, and so on and on (see, e.g., Veith 2002: 21). Even the seasons were forced into the framework, in spite of their obvious "fourness" defined by equinoxes and solstices; the dog days of late summer were split off as a fifth season.

All these fives are dynamic fields created by the working out of qi. One might say the natural process that appears as "metal" also appears as whiteness, the west, bitter flavors, the large intestine, and so on. The idea is certainly not that the west or the large intestine was made of metal. The five major "organs" are not just the organs themselves but also the fields of physiological action they control, according to traditional Chinese physiology. In this system, qi and blood flow around the body in their proper vessels. It is the qi circulatory system that one pricks or rubs in acupuncture and acupressure. The acupuncture and acupressure points often correspond loosely to the nerve and tendon nodes of Western medicine. In medicine, health is maintained by keeping the qi of yang and yin, the five elements, the five tastes and smells, and above all the five major and five minor organ systems all balanced and circulating properly. Imbalance, disharmony, and stagnation beget sickness. The Mongols also developed a similar, more complex system (Bold 2009).

Chinese years are arranged in cycles of twelve animals, as almost everyone knows—many Anglo-Americans and Europeans now know their "birth animals." We all know that people born in the year of the dog are (supposedly) loyal, those of the year of the tiger are wild and fierce, and so forth. Less known is that these mesh with a cycle of phases that last ten years, two years per xing. The meshing produces the full sixty-year cycle of the Chinese calendar. The element of one's birth year influences one's birth animal. I am a metal snake, which means I should be a cold and hard sort of snake. By and large, people born in metal years will be relatively cold and hard; in water years, they will tend to "go with the flow"; in wood years, natural and warm (the feel of a wood-paneled room); in fire years, fiery (of course); in earth years, earthy and down to earth.

If one's personality does not fit one's year animal, one can blame the xing. One of my daughters is a tiger, but a gentler and easier soul would be hard to imagine. She was born in a wood year, so a Chinese astrologer would say her wood element dominates her tiger birth animal.

Neighboring cultures have adopted the Chinese animal-year system. The Mongol version is even more elaborate (Sanders and Bat-Ireedüi 1999). Vietnam substitutes a cat, rather recently introduced, for the rabbit. In Japan, people born in a fire horse year are believed to be so wild and unrestrained they are deadly. Rumor has it that in Japan many a doctor is paid under the table to backdate births that happen early in a fire horse year and postdate those that happen toward the end.

The fivefold system involved a great deal of forcing salient natural features into a rather rigid order. It climaxed in the Han Dynasty, began to give way to resurgent yin-yang cosmology in the following centuries, and slowly lost appeal except among tradition-conscious scholars. It remained the basis of *The Yellow Emperor's Inner Classic*, China's most famous medical work, and thus was never forgotten, but it gradually lost much of its cultural significance.

Poets mined it for images, antiquarians insisted on using it, but the practical traditional medicine I saw in East Asia in the 1960s and 1970s was based on quite other principles. Even in Han, the *Yellow Emperor* was unique in its obsession with fives; other texts, like the *Discourse on Fevers* (*Shanghan Lun*) and most of the texts recently found in Han tombs, are more empirical, if still far from modern biological theory. Today, except for the continuing fascination with birth animals, the old numerological system is more a curiosity than anything else.

Before and during Han, however, this cosmology developed into an extremely elaborate system by the yin-yang school of philosophers. This was a loose assemblage of thinkers that culminated with the synthesist Zou Yan (ca. 350–270 BCE) around 305–240 (Chang Chun-shu 2007a: 115) but developed largely in the Han Dynasty (Liu An 2010). They were a naturalistic group and fed into the rise of alchemy (Needham 1976: 12). These thinkers speculated on the basic cosmic principles, including heaven, earth, humanity, the yin and yang, and the five phases.

These correspondences, and other similarities and connections in the real world, were mediated by resonance. *Ganying*, resonance or responsiveness, was a key concept in Han thought. All things are linked by flow of qi; therefore, acting in way X in one realm has effect X in another. A related concept is *qiyun*, qi resonance; it is the concept that qi animates all things and that there can be some form of ganying between things that share some sort of qi. Similarity or parallelism could be taken to mean that there were real flows of qi, similarities in basic principle, or similarities in basic nature. An artist who truly captures the essence or spirit of a bird or tree or mountain has done more than portray it accurately; he has captured or called up its qi through qiyun.

Thus, doing things in one realm will affect other realms that are similar in spirit. Nurturing orphans nurtures crops; executing criminals would cut off the shoots and is best left till harvest is going on, or, better, finished.

Ganying makes sense of the analogies that are the basis of much philosophical discourse and argument in early China. Western readers tend to find these maddeningly ad hoc, illogical, and irrational. To modern Western philosophers, analogies seem a silly way to argue. To the ancient Chinese, however, good analogies were based on actual ganying—on real dynamic linkages of some sort. A useful contemporary analogy (!) is the entanglement of separated quarks in modern physics.

This was spelled out in many texts, but the "Ling Shu" (Spiritual Pivot) section of *The Yellow Emperor's Inner Classic* is clearest. This book is basically about acupuncture, but it discusses the theoretical basis of that medical modality at great length. The discussions reveal that acupuncture is about regulating the flow of blood and qi in the body. The terms used—flow, stagnation, overflow, overabundance, blocking, deficiency, turbidity, and so on—have little to do with anything biomedically verifiable but are exactly the terms used for irrigation in agriculture. Correcting problems of qi involves draining, supplementing deficiency, unblocking, and so on—point for point, what a water boss does to his canals. Clearly, the analogy of bodily dynamics with water dynamics is not a "mere" analogy, it is ganying. There are also many passages that equate governing a state with governing the body. Finally, the book ends in a sort of climax of applied resonance theory:

> Heaven is round. Earth is flat. Man's head is round and his feet are flat, making the correspondences and resonances. Heaven has the sun and moon. Man has two eyes. Earth has the nine regions. Man has the nine orifices. Heaven has wind and rain. Man has joy and anger. Heaven has thunder and lightning. Man has tones and sounds. Heaven has the four seasons. Man has the four limbs. . . . Heaven has winter and summer. Man has chills and fevers. Heaven has the ten days of the celestial stems. Man's hands have ten fingers. The earthly branches are twelve. Man's feet have ten toes, plus the penis and testicles make the correspondence. Women lack these latter two sections but can enwomb the human body [i.e., the female genitalia correspond to the male and thus make up twelve]. Heaven has yin and yang. Man has male and female. . . . Earth has high mountains. Man has shoulder and knee caps. Earth has deep valleys. Man has armpits and the crease of the knee. . . . Earth has grass and greens. Man has fine hairs. Heaven has day and night. Man has sleeping and waking. . . . Earth in the fourth month cannot produce grass. Man in later years does not produce children. (Wu Jing-Nuan 1993: 227; "Man" translates *ren*, "person of either sex"; note that women are specifically mentioned)

These correspondences may strain a modern reader's sense of reality, but it all makes logical sense in ancient Chinese terms. Humans naturally find patterns and seize on any similarities to construct patterned representations of this sort. This basic fact of human psychology was recognized by Plato and Aristotle and developed by Kant and many thinkers since. However, the correspondence system was extended beyond all reason and became enormously complex, rigid, and unwieldy. This circumstance unfortunately had a hugely limiting and constricting effect on China's thought after Han. The fivefold correspondences and the accompanying theories of resonance and mystic cosmological influence stifled more accurate science; they provided a convenient, time-hallowed, but ultimately sterile substitute. This body of theory was true science—it was not religious or magical, it was based on observation and logic, and it underlay much thinking and research—but, unlike modern science, it did not lead to further work and ultimate replacement by a better theory (T. Kuhn 1962). It simply continued.

In this view, the body was a microcosm of the universe, a center of health, and a place to nourish. Mark Lewis, in *The Construction of Space in Early China* (2006a: 13–76), describes early accounts of the body. The heart was the seat of mind, emotion, and control of the whole microcosm. Ritual nourished the mind, just as food and drink nourish the body. Energy flows included the famous qi, then becoming defined as a subtle breath cycling through bodily channels and divided into yang and yin energies. The soul was complex: the heavenly *hun* soul or fraction of the soul (it may already have had its own subcomponents, as it did later) was more yang. The *po* soul (or soul-fraction, again with components) was earthier and more yin and stayed with the body. In general, tombs and tomb writings indicate that the hun was expected to stay with the body as long as possible, at least up to decay, when it flew to heaven, or simply dispersed; the po soul always remained in the earth.

Natural energies manifested as odd or distinctive appearances; for instance, the brave man looked like a proper bully. Physiognomy was already a "science," albeit a very shaky one (Lewis 2006: 70); even the great Han skeptic Wang Chong (1907) believed in it.

In the more arcane schools of traditional Chinese thought, the entire earth was a macrocosm similar to the microcosm that was the human body (Stein 1990). Chinese farmers and fishers had only a vague idea of this, and educated people sometimes did not believe it, but in Daoism the idea is developed systematically (Schipper 1993). It is also developed systematically in medicine and physiology.

It follows reasonably enough from the foregoing discussion that China has no equivalent of the English word "supernatural." Communicating with the supramundane beings involved special techniques of sacrifice, ritual, and prayer but was otherwise like communicating with ordinary mortals.

Supramundanes—gods, ghosts, ancestors, disembodied forces, animal powers—must be contacted, today as in Zhou and Han, through burning incense at set points (shrines or temples), offering tea and wine in ritual ways, and sometimes performing other more expensive and serious rites. If necessary, they are invoked by special professionals who can go into trance and become possessed. In this case, one can actually talk to a supramundane being.

Shen—supranatural persons, as opposed to disembodied forces—have limited powers and need things from humans. They exchange what they can provide—health, fertility, good weather—for what we can provide: food, drink, incense, sacrifice goods. They also want entertainment and appreciate Chinese opera, which is performed for them on festival days. Supramundane beings include tree spirits, mountain spirits, weather and sky spirits, and locality spirits. Powerful impersonal forces, including cosmic qi and disembodied good and evil, are also involved.

Chinese lacks anything exactly equivalent to the English words and concepts "religion," "philosophy," and "cosmology." "Religion" is best translated by the verb-object construction *bai shen*, "worshiping divinities." The word frequently translated as "religion," *jiao*, means "organized body of teaching"— secular or religious. Purely secular philosophy that is organized into a real school, like philosophic Confucianism or Platonism, is a *jiao*. Chinese folk religion is not; it lacks a sacred text and an intellectual lineage. Separating religion from secular philosophy requires the use of a combination word like *zongjiao*, spiritual teachings.

Thus there is not the sharp opposition and separation of sacred and secular that occurs in the West. This disjunction was made part of Durkheim's widely used definition of religion (Durkheim 1995), which China thus calls into question. Philosophy in the ordinary sense of the word—serious thought about Big Questions—has always been common and well developed in China, but the highly technical, logical, analytic way of thinking that is the "philosophy" of Western world academic departments was only modestly developed in China (though it did exist; see Harbsmeier 1998). The Chinese always preferred to harness their sophisticated thinking to immediate political and social concerns. They rarely pursued the pure, abstract speculation beloved of Westerners, except when directly influenced by the alien philosophy of Buddhism. "Cosmology" is a looser term, but Chinese cosmology does not separate religion, philosophy, scientific speculation, and hardheaded factual observation and is close to what anthropologists call "worldview" (Kearney 1984).

Philosophy and Politics: Origins of Chinese Traditions

The Warring States period was China's Axial Age, in which philosophy flourished. (See Bellah 2011 for a fascinating and extremely perceptive comparison of Axial Age philosophic developments across Eurasia.) The great philosophies, or statecraft doctrines, that emerged from the period were Confucianism and Daoism, but there were many others—traditionally "a hundred schools," though this figure is probably an exaggeration.

These "schools" were only somewhat coherent and differentiated in the Warring States period; they were codified, given lineages, and otherwise systematized in the Han Dynasty. Han scholars were incorrigible synthesizers and systematizers and made these traditions into sharply defined *jia*, literally "households." In fact they mixed and merged happily in both Warring States and Han, defying the systematists. Similarly, the canonical books of these jia, assembled during Han, might not only be by many different authors, but also might include wildly different philosophies. This is notably true of the greatest Daoist work, the *Zhuangzi*, which includes a number of essays by primitivist, hyper-individualist, and other authors that were apparently included because Zhuang Zhou (the author of the core of the work) debated, refuted, or discussed them (Graham 1981, 1989). Master-disciple teaching situations are stressed in such works as Confucius's *Analects*. In fact, the Confucians may have invented the whole master-disciple idea (A. Meyer 2011: 58), though I doubt it, considering how universal it was in the ancient world. Most of the books of the time were assembled over a considerable period and intended for a wide readership. This readership even included the dead; texts were routinely buried with them.

The role of Confucianism in conservation has been briefly noted above (and much more elaborately in Tucker and Berthrong 1998). Daoism (see Girardot et al. 2001) is best known in the West from the uncompromising mysticism of Zhuang Zi and the anarchic sayings of Laozi, but in fact most Daoists (including Laozi—in modern, more accurate readings) were far more accommodating of government, rationality, economics, and materialism.

Zhuang Zi, the greatest and most ecologically conscious Daoist thinker, was said to be an orchard keeper at one point, and he admitted being an occasional poacher. A recent study provides a fascinating insight into Zhuang Zi's knowledge of agricultural technology. In one of his passages, he refers to "goblet words," *zhi yan*. These words are described in his usual mystical, paradoxical style. Even more paradoxical is the *zhi* itself. It is described as a vessel that tilted when empty, stood upright when half full, and tipped over when full. In a tour-de-force essay, Daniel Fried (2007) identified this vessel: it was an ancient form of irrigation pot that had handles suspended on ropes somewhat below the center of gravity of the vessel (which has a conical, pointed foot). So when filled it tipped over to irrigate the fields. Zhuang Zi's "goblet words" poured out naturally. Like the irrigation water, they grew the seeds of the ten thousand things. Ordinary words were sequential, coherent, logical, and therefore unproductive—they did not have the mystery and dark naturalness that grows creativity. Goblet words need not be spoken at all. Nonspeaking was, for Zhuang Zi, not only a way of speaking, but a particularly useful one. Early authors also referred to jade *zhi* being used by kings, and I would bet that these were drinking vessels made to tip over when set down, so that he who takes one up is forced to drain it dry (like the Greek *rhyton*).

Legalism was long viewed as a harsh, cruel, totalitarian school of thought. After the rise of Hitler, it seemed suspiciously similar to fascism. Arthur Waley saw it that way in his brilliant and influential *Three Ways of Thought in Ancient China* (1939), a book that introduced many of my generation to Chinese thought. Waley based his views on the work of the cynical and ruthless Han Feizi, the most extreme of the Legalist thinkers. Many others echoed him, and even more eclectic Confucian works could be guilty of cynical and brutal lines (e.g., Lü Buwei 2000: 176).

However, there were other, much less harsh Legalist thinkers. Shen Buhai, for instance, was more interested in "rectification of names," originally a Confucian point but elaborated by Shen (Creel 1974; see also Chang Chun-shu 2007a: 110). It involved creating a proper bureaucracy with each position defined and with every function and duty spelled out. Rewards and punishments were also codified and made consistent and regular. Shen and others advocated comprehensive codes of laws, applying to sovereign, yeoman, and slave alike, and enforced uniformly by bureaucrats who knew exactly what they could and could not do. Shen can thus stand as the inventor—to the best of modern knowledge—of organizational systems and thus of organizational research and systems theory. His work is one of the ancestors of modern business management and organizational theory (Creel 1974) and less directly so of computers and information technology.

Even more important was the major implication of the Legalist core value of consistent law. Little did Shang Yang or Shen Buhai foresee what they had created for the first and perhaps the only time in history: the idea that a state should be under the rule of law rather than the rule of individuals. This doctrine, which is basic to all modern democracies and even most totalitarian states, comes directly from Legalism. It was introduced to the West by Jesuit missionaries who returned from China in the seventeenth and eighteenth centuries, and they saw it as fitting in with many new ideas about the relative role of the king, the church, and law in the early modern state (on this, see Creel 1974). The full history remains to be written, and one must go back to the original Jesuit writings, such those of as Gaspar da Cruz, to get a sense of how the idea was transmitted. The concept was not completely unknown in the West, but the Jesuits stated it in an uncompromising, totalizing way that made it highly salient in the West—but that also exaggerated its effectiveness in the East.

"Legalism," after all, translates the Chinese term *fa jia*, "rule household." It was not really a school (or household), and *fa* means any set of rules, not just legal ones. The rules for producing good calligraphy or architecture are fa. So we are dealing with a set of thinkers who advocated, one way or another, the importance or supremacy of rules, methods, laws, or systems over individuals and individual mentality, and *also* over personalistic matters. The patrimonial state was giving way to the rationalized, bureaucratic one (in Max Weber's terms), and the Legalist philosophers worked out the implications of this change for rule of law, system-building, rational management, and environmental use. Their inventions in statecraft and systems management have vastly affected the modern world. The relative roles of China, Greece, Rome, Persia, and other ancient empires in developing state and environmental management systems have not been unpacked; it would be a fascinating history. China would clearly figure as a major contributor.

The Confucians, in contrast, idealized the rule of the good man—the sage-king—and, failing that, were willing to tolerate the rule of a bad man, hoping that he could change. (They were, however, never able to deal with rule by a woman; China's few reigning empresses have been execrated in Confucian scholarship.) This Confucian idea weakened the power of the Legalist principle of rule by law. However, the latter remained on the books, to influence the world in later centuries. Confucianism also advocated personalism and social ties above abstract bureaucratic principles; a son should defend his father even if criminal, a subject should be loyal to a bad lord, a wife should obey an irresponsible husband. This concept was generally modified by common sense and by other philosophic traditions in early times, but it became a serious problem for China, especially with the Neo-Confucianism of Zhu Xi in the Song Dynasty; Zhu presented not only the merciful and humanistic side of

Confucianism but also the hierarchic and personalist side, leading to conflicts and to very mixed assessments of Confucian tradition in recent decades.

The softer side of Legalism fused with the harder one of Daoism, producing a synthesis that remained influential although its texts and thinkers were forgotten (Pines 2009). The resultant formula for government requires some discussion, since it was really the dominant mode through most of Chinese history, in spite of lip-service to Confucianism, Buddhism, and harder path Legalism.

Recent archaeological research has uncovered many texts that show this fusion. (Robert Henricks, 1989, provides not only a vitally important translation of the *De-Dao Jing* but a particularly clear and available discussion). It survived as the more liberal tradition of empire: rule by law, with the sovereign as basically a head administrator, achieving Daoist "inaction" by being above petty concerns and sticking to high-level policy. Related was an emergent concept of loyalty to the state, its ritual structure, and its bureaucratic identity; this appears, for instance, in the earlier parts of the *Guanzi* (on which see below and A. Meyer 2011).

The Daoist ideal of the "uncarved block"—sitting like a block of wood—was interpreted not as a call for mindlessness, but rather as a call for the emperor to keep constant watch, be vigilant, and avoid picking favorites or trusting factions. He should stay strictly in the realm of high policy. The sovereign was supposed to rule with a light hand—punishing the guilty in no uncertain terms, but otherwise meddling as little as possible. There was a very conscious ideal of empowering the people rather than ordering them around. The emperor was to practice *wu wei*, literally "lacking action," but it was actually a policy of setting high policy and leaving details to bureaucrats (Pines 2009). Qin Shi Huang Di's disastrous attempt at one-man totalitarian rule resulted in future emperors following the more Daoist ideal, though to highly variable degrees. Many, such as Han Wu Di and the founder of Ming, went back to Qin Shi Huang Di's approach. Others were genuinely inactive. Most were somewhere in between. Not a few emperors across history managed to be both inactive and rapacious, and some of them claimed to be Daoist in the bargain.

China's imperial government could never raise enough revenue to be a micromanaging state. The government was also aware that high taxes discouraged enterprise, and thus it often lowered taxes to rates undreamed of even by American Republicans. Many emperors made a virtue of necessity doing rather little beyond ordering the bureaucracy, listening to advice, instituting major public works, and trying to maintain order. Thus the Warring States period began the tradition of a highly centralized autocratic empire, but one tempered by a strong sense that the emperor should not meddle; he should be above ordinary matters, leaving them to the intellectuals who staffed the administration (Pines 2009). All these aspects were to be developed much further under the Han.

As elsewhere, the philosophers came from what passed for a middle class. (By this time, something like a true middle class existed; we are no longer talking only about lower nobility.) They were advisors to kings and lords. They were thus minor functionaries with minor noble or official titles, wandering knights, successful craftspersons, religious officiants, wandering teachers, and simply clever people who got employed by lords to advise them. They often roved from court to court, seeking enlightened employers. Literacy was surprisingly widespread, and many ordinary craftspeople and specialists got into the ranks of thinkers and writers. Copious evidence shows that many craftspersons, serving people, women, and even soldiers could write (Yates 2011). Particularly astonishing are some soldiers' letters home that (almost miraculously) survived in a tomb; they indicate that even ordinary soldiers could have an appreciable degree of literacy (Yates 2011: 362; the letters sound a good deal like those from the front in World War II). This level of literacy—relatively high for a premodern society—is attested throughout Chinese history, and I found it among uneducated sailors and watermen in the 1960s. Many were self-taught; they had simply picked up the skill over time.

From these philosophical dialogues emerged a fairly integrated—if multifaceted—worldview that was holistic, cosmologically grounded, and dedicated to finding harmony with the Dao, and, later, with *li*, "principle." Obviously—from what has gone before—it was anything but homogeneous, but it has a certain unity if one contrasts it with the worldviews of, say, Greece, Rome, and India at the same time (see, e.g., Bellah 2011).

In comparison with Greece, for instance, this Chinese worldview involved a strong sense of nature, inner and outer; of flux and dynamism as opposed to stasis and frozen ideals; of harmony and resonance as opposed to conflict and sharp differences among things; of basic common principles and of flows of qi uniting the world rather than of detached essentialized entities; and many more fairly clear distinctions. Some Greeks, like Heraclitus, sound much more Chinese than Greek by this standard; one wonders if they were influenced by Eastern thought.

The Chinese worldview of pragmatic harmony and interpenetrating qi accompanied—and clearly was related to—the strong kinship and family orientation of Chinese society, so evident in Shang ancestor cults and in every aspect of Chinese life since. Modern writers have repeatedly commented on the holistic, socialized, harmony-seeking side of Chinese (and Japanese) culture, often contrasting it with American rational individualism. Indeed, enormous differences show up on every psychological test that has been provided (cf. Bond 1986; Kitayama and Cohen 2007; Nisbett 2003; Nisbett et al. 2001; X. Zhou et al. 2012), even though there are also many differences in degree within each group (Kitayama and Cohen 2007). It is notable that uncompromising individualism was found in early Chinese thought (Zhuangzi, notably), and rational analytic thought was common too (e.g., Mozi and Wang Chong), but from Han onward, the holistic, harmonic stream triumphed. One need think only of how many Chinese business names today contain the word *he*, "harmony."

However, a need to assert control over one's situation rather dramatically changes things. In modern psychological studies, the Chinese, when forced to assert control of a serious situation, act as analytically and independently as Americans (X. Zhou et al. 2012). Conversely, persistent failure to control a situation leads Americans to act more passively, approximating the Chinese (X. Zhou et al. 2012). It is clear from history that the same was true in ancient dynasties. The need to accommodate to family, village, and empire does seem to have made the Chinese holistic, and their philosophy encourages this; but it has been by no means an inescapable trap. It is, in fact, escaped when needed, as is proved by the countless rugged individualists in Chinese history—from Zhuangzi to the contemporary artist and political figure Ai Weiwei.

In the Warring States period, this need to accommodatealso led in the opposite direction: toward authoritarian policies of total control. This side of Legalism was developed in the highly pragmatic *realpolitik* of Xunzi (1999) and his followers, who held views strikingly similar to those later espoused by Thomas Hobbes. It became incorporated into Chinese thought from then on, as a hard-headed counterpoint to fuzzy Huang-Lao and cosmological thinking (Pines 2009).

Concepts of Nature

Like most societies, Chinese has no word for "nature" in the English-language sense. Words for "natural" conditions are often based on the root *zi*, "self." This

implies the spontaneous, naturally occurring selfhood of something or someone as opposed to learned or imposed changes. *Ziran* (originally something
like "self reality") has long been used to mean "spontaneous" and thus "natural" in the sense of "not deliberately made." Neologistic combinations like
ziranjie (lit. "self real territory") and *daziran* (lit. "great self real") now mean
"nature" or "the natural realm." *Tianran*, "heavenly spontaneous," was an old
term for "the natural world" as opposed to human-made landscapes and
items. Paolo Santangelo (1998: 621ff.) points out that this introduces a moral
note, since heaven's will was always considered to be a moral charge for humans (see also Lloyd 2007: 138–41). Another term important in these contexts
is *shen*, "spirit," which basically means a supernatural being but is extended in
more or less the same ways as the Latin/English word "spirit."

Many of these terms go back to, or are used in, Daoism. The Dao—the
great Way, or Flux, that is the "mother of the myriad things"—shows itself in
the word *ziran*. The uncarved block (*baopu*), the original being, can potentially be made into anything—or can simply evolve into anything. This is
much like certain deist concepts in the Western world, such as Spinoza's "eternal and infinite Being whom we call God or Nature" (Hadot 2006: 168).

Another set of terms is based on *sheng*, whose root meaning is "to be
born." This term is extended or used in various phrases that refer to anything
in its natural or original state. It can thus mean fresh as opposed to preserved,
raw as opposed to cooked, and so on. At some very early point, this word split
off—or assimilated—another word, *xing*. *Xing* is probably a verbal noun developed from *sheng*. *Xing* is written with the character for *sheng* plus the "heart
radical," a graphic particle used in many words to mark reference to inner
states and qualities. *Xing* means "inborn" (this is not the *xing* that means "go-
ings" or "phases"; the tones and characters are different). This *xing* means
"nature" or "natural" in the sense of one's innate natural tendencies, as in *ben
xing* "root nature," that is, "inborn nature." It is thus more of an essentialized,
abstract quality than a specific personal self (*zi*). For instance, Xunzi (1999:
199) saw it as selfish, unsocial, and in need of fixing and defined it: *ben xing*
"is what is impossible for me to create but which I can nonetheless transform."
Conversely, Mencius saw it as basically good, and his psychologically sophisticated view was known to every Chinese schoolchild for hundreds of years
through the classic children's primer *Three Character Classic* (probably by
Wang Yinglin, 1223–1296). This is a rhymed primer of three-character lines. It
begins: "People from birth have natures that are good at root; their natures are
similar to each other, but learned ways make them different from each other."

The Chinese, of course, is much more economically stated ("natures root good"). "Natures" is *xing* in both places. Every traditional Chinese child who had any education at all began his or her training by memorizing this rhyme. It had an enormous effect on the Chinese world.

As seen here, *xing* was the word used when classical Chinese writers contrasted "nature" and "nurture" (*jiao*—see below—or similar words). These words can also be combined with *ran* and other words in the cluster. Another word is *jing*, made up of the radical for grain and the character for "clear and pure," the result originally meaning clean and pure grain but evolving into a term for semen, and then on to a metaphoric extension as "the unadulterated essence of things or a state of mind concentrated on a single purpose" (Rickett 1998: 29). Closely related is *qing*, the same "clear and pure" with a spiritual rather than a grain radical and meaning "inner reality" (Rickett 1998: 82). These words may originally have been fairly interchangeable. The Han Dynasty *Comprehensive Discussions in the White Tiger Hall* (Tjan 1949: 565–66) defined *xing* as innate dispensations of the yang, and identified five basic innate moral senses (Tjan called them "instincts"): *ren* (humaneness), sense of the right, sense of ritual, wisdom, and truth to one's word (*xin*, defined on 566 as "sincerity"). *Qing* is defined here as emotion, the working of yin; joy, anger, grief, happiness, love, and hate are listed. This forms a very concise summary of late Han psychology.

Finally, plants, cats, stones, and mountains were not traditionally referred to in terms of nature or humanity but were the Myriad Things. (Like the Greek *myriad*, the Chinese *wan* literally means "ten thousand" but idiomatically means "a very large number.") They could be called "things that are born," but there was no word for them as "nature" in contrast with "people."

The nearest thing to a nature/human dichotomy was the sacred trinity of heaven (*tian*), earth (*di*), and humanity (*ren*). (*Ren* is translated "man" in the older literature, but it is a gender-neutral word, as was "man" in earlier English. Much of the endless garbage in the Western literature about Chinese sexism is based on not realizing this point.) Cats and trees were part of earth, clouds and flying dragons part of heaven, and humans mediated between the two. A key part of this was the emperor's major sacrificial rites at the Altar of Heaven and the Altar of Earth. These altars were always located in or near the capital and thus were rebuilt as the capitals shifted with the dynasties. The last imperial altars, dating from Ming and Qing times, survive today in Beijing.

The square Altar of Earth and the round Altar of Heaven were perhaps the most sacred altars of the old Chinese empire. Not only did the rites have to be done perfectly; the emperor had to have a properly humble and reverent mind. Any major disaster showed he had failed in this, and many emperors seem to have been quite sincere in their apologies and self-criticisms for failing in this regard when famine or plague struck.

The important thing to notice here is that there is *no* simple way in traditional Chinese to refer to nonhuman beings as opposed to the human realm. *Zi* and *xing* contrast the innate, human or not, with the acquired, human or not. The Myriad Things include people. As Kwang-chih Chang (2002) points out for China and David Barnhill (2005: 7) for Japan, East Asians did not contrast nature with humanity. They also did not contrast the natural with the supernatural. They contrasted living naturally with living unnaturally. Zhuang Zi (Graham 1981) held that humans in a confining society and horses in an overmanaged livery are alike failing to live their true natures; later thinkers agreed with this assessment.

Thus, as one would expect, there is no term equivalent to "wilderness" in Chinese. The nearest is an opposition of *ye*, "wild," to settled spaces—fields, towns, and cities. However, abandoned fields and settlements are ye. Even people can be ye. The *ye ren*, "wild man," is the Chinese Yeti, or Bigfoot, and the term can also be used for a real person who is uncontrolled and uncouth. The idea of wilderness can be, and is, expressed by descriptive phrases, but the lack of a simple word is revealing. Ye is normally unpleasant; wildlands as things of scenic beauty are called *shan shui*, "mountains and waters." When a Tang Dynasty poet equated them—"ye feelings are just for mountains and water" (i.e., "my feelings for mountains and water are feelings for the true wild")—he was doing it for effect. (The poem is in the Han Shan material but is stylistically rather different from pieces reliably by the original Han Shan; see Han-shan 2000: 191, with Bill Porter's freer translation.) Another word, *huang*, is even more tightly coupled with deserted places; an abandoned village is a *huang cun* (*cun* means "village"); an abandoned forest area is a *huang lin*, and neglected vegetation is *huang cao* (wild herbage). This implies that forests and herbage should be cared for. The great fifteenth-century guide to famine plants is called the *Jiu Huang Bencao*— (Herbal for use in huang, i.e., when famine has desolated the land).

The striking difference between China and the West in attitudes toward the nonhuman realm was already clear by the Zhou. The Western world defines "civilization" as urban; the word comes from the Latin for "city," just as politics, policy, and politeness go back to the Greek *polis*. This pro-urban bias goes back to ancient Sumer, as the *Epic of Gilgamesh* and many other texts show. The Arabs, too, in their medieval Golden Age, were intensely urban and—to use another revealing word—urbane.

In striking contrast, China defines civilized culture in terms of symbolic communication. The nearest Chinese equivalents to the English word "civilization" (as opposed to barbarism) are *wen* and *wenhua*. *Wen* in Shang times meant "marks"—any mark made with a pen, brush, piece of charcoal, or the like on an available surface. It soon developed the secondary meaning of "created symbols"—more than just writing (there is a different word, *zi*, for written characters specifically) but less than "marks in general." Over time, it came to mean "civilized knowledge and behavior." In modern Cantonese, for instance, a common description of a graceless boor is that he "lacks wen" (*mou man* in Cantonese). *Wenhua* means, literally, "marks transforming," capturing the ideas that the symbols themselves change and that they transform people—for the better, theoretically. *Zhongwen*, "Chinese marks," is Chinese literate culture—the marks the Chinese have left on the world.

The Western idea that the more urbanized a landscape, the better, and the more natural the worse, does not exist as such in China. There is no sharp contrast and no devaluing of the natural (i.e., the ziran, as opposed to the ye). China had many hermits living in the wild not out of self-mortification (as in the West) but because they preferred it. China also produced a large percentage of the world's nature poetry, and much of the very best thereof. (A rough but not uneducated guess, Chinese poets and China-emulating Japanese, Korean, and Vietnamese poets must have produced over 90 percent of the world's nature poetry.) Rural life was prestigious; farmers were honored, though, admittedly, more in rhetoric than in substance.

However, many or most Chinese did tend to prefer urban life, just as the West did. In fact, they may actually enjoy some aspects of it that Westerners often claim to hate. As noted above, the modern Chinese phrase for the excitement, interest, enthusiasm, variety, and general fun of the city is *renao*, which literally means "heat and noise." Urbane and civilized as Westerners may be, they do not usually think of the heat and noise of a city as its *good* features. There is a continuum in Chinese thought from cities to wasteland. Cities were idealized, but the mountains, waters, and remote fields were idealized and loved too. Best of all was to live among humans but to have a wonderful garden for escape. This ideal occurs over and over, from the poetry of Tao Yuanming (367–425) to *The Story of the Stone*, and, for that matter, to today.

Emotions were seen as part of human nature. Like groves and grasses, they should be properly socialized and controlled. They should be expressed in a duly managed way, which is one reason "Han Shan" used *ye* to shock readers. Geoffrey Lloyd (2007: 74–79) provides an excellent and incisive account of Chinese emotion terms and early philosophizing about emotionality and compares these with Western concepts. Lloyd tends to stress the differences with the West. I find more similarities, but there are indeed some key differences. Chinese culture focuses more on sociability yet also places greater stress on the joys of solitary contemplation in the mountains. The extreme sociability of Chinese culture makes the value of lonely meditation a quite reasonable and even predictable balancing response. Human minds, at least the more introverted human minds, need occasional rest or escape from what the Chinese call the "red dust" (*hongchen*, originally a Buddhist term).

Words for Knowing

Knowledge—religious, ethical, and scientific—is *xue*. This word implies an organized body of knowledge gained through study. It is now used to translate "-ology." Anthropology is *ren lei xue*, "knowledge of types of people." Significantly, *li xue*, which originally meant "knowledge of the basic principles of things," and thus included religious and meditative insight, has come to mean "physics." Agriculture could be just *nong*, but serious research on it is *nong xue*, "agriculture study" (a largely modern term). The term *xue* included literary studies, historical studies, and even religious studies, as well as the sciences.

The distinction between *jiao* and *xue* is interestingly made in the opposition of *dao jiao*, "Daoist religion," and *dao xue*, "study of the Way." The former is a specific religious tradition. The latter just meant any study of the right way to live, though it eventually was focused on neo-Confucian philosophy.

On the other hand, practical crafts were not usually called *xue*. Woodworking was just woodworking; one learned it by doing it, not by studying lore. Medical knowledge is *yi xue*, "illness knowledge," but traditional people were more apt to say they "knew some medicines" (*yao*). The modern term for "science" is *ke xue*, "study of categories," but it is a Chinese reading of a Japanese translation of the Western word. Neither it nor its referent, that is, Western-style science as a concept, had any traditional currency. On the other hand, it harks back to the classic idea of *ke wu*, "investigating things," established as an ideal by the rationalist Cheng brothers in the Song Dynasty (Graham 1958). *Ke wu* was close enough to the Western notion of "natural philosophy" that one wonders about contact across the Silk Road.

Skills were *shu*, and a good word for "science" in the practical sense was *yaoshu*, as in the great sixth-century encyclopedia *Qimin Yaoshu* (Ordinary People's Necessary Skills). *Yao*, "want or need" (a word unrelated to *yao*, "medicines"), is important in such contexts; the court nutrition manual of the Mongol Empire was the *Yinshan Zhengyao* (Drinking and Feasting Proper Needs), or, idiomatically, "necessary knowledge for drinking and feasting."

In short, the lack of a word for "science" did not stop anyone from talking about it. *Xue* with specifiers did fine, and there were other terms as well (such as *ke wu*). Still, it is significant that Chinese, like Native American languages, did not feel it necessary or useful to split "science" off from other ways of knowing.

Some disciplines that are close to their Western equivalents seem now to blur the magic-science-religion lines, but of course early Western science did that too. Modern writers may note a "curious combination of medical and magical thinking" (Wilms 2002: 33) in the writings of Sun Simiao in the seventh century, but Sun would not have found anything curious; he was merely writing up the medicine he knew. He did make skeptical remarks about many magical practices, however, so he seems to have some idea of the difference (Sun Simiao 2007). Western medical writings of the time were the same sort of "curious combination." Indeed, a state-of-the-art American medical textbook of 2013 will surely look like "a curious combination of medical and magical thinking" in a thousand years, if there is anyone around to read it.

Comparisons between Chinese and Greek science are apparently irresistible to historians and have been brought to a fine art by the collaboration of Geoffrey Lloyd and Nathan Sivin (Lloyd 1996, 2002, 2007; Lloyd and Sivin 2002) and by Paul Unschuld (2009). They find fewer differences between the traditions than do many others. However, Lloyd and Sivin point out that Greek science was more prone to define itself through controversy and thus to be more self-conscious about basic principles—not only the famous "axioms" but also ideas of cause, logic, and proof. The Chinese invested more effort in technical applications and in large-scale systematic and synthetic thinking.

Both Greek and Chinese scientific knowledge systems differed from modern science in similar ways: they relied heavily on induction and on received wisdom, they had little way of going beyond ordinary sensory experience, and they shared a deep belief in gods and spirits as active agents. Both failed to leave a legacy of free and spirited inquiry, in spite of their spectacular starts in that direction. Lloyd (1996), like almost everyone before him (including the

Greeks themselves), has emphasized the increasing dominance of imperial censorship over knowledge. Indeed, there was progressive stifling of free inquiry from the open days of Republican Athens and pre-empire China to the steadily more repressive Byzantine Empire in Greece and Ming and Qing in China.

Morality

"Good" and "evil" translate perfectly well: *hao* and *e* respectively. These were generally used as evaluative terms. They were as important in Warring States philosophy as in any other philosophies. "Good" (*hao*) in the ethical sense was understood to mean prosocial: good for society and good for interpersonal situations and interactions. Conversely, *e* referred to antisocial behavior: gratuitous harm or insult to other people. Mencius and Xunzi explained this particularly well. Interestingly, the Cantonese language parallels St. Augustine in describing evil as a privation of good; *m hou*, "not good," was usually used in Cantonese where Mandarin would use *e* or similar words for evil. (See E. Anderson 2007; Anderson et al. 2000. For the whole story of early Chinese thought, Mencius [e.g. 1970] is essential; the best survey in English of early Chinese philosophic logic and discourse is Harbsmeier 1998, but it has its problems; see Graham 1989 for a more readable and in many cases more accurate assessment.)

The proper "way" to act and the cosmic Dao were subjects for endless discussion. The equivalent of "ethics" in Aristotle's sense, that is, what is good for the *individual* as opposed to the collective, was not usually regarded very highly. When it was, the Dao was pressed into service, and people followed the True or Constant Dao rather than being "good."

So what we of the West tend to translate as "ethics" is really "politics" in Aristotle's sense, that is, what is proper for the social sphere. (Aristotle used "ethics" to mean what an *individual* should do. Thus a great deal of what modern philosophers call ethics would have been politics to Aristotle.) What we call Chinese philosophy is also more like Aristotelian politics than Aristotelian philosophy. This is only one example of the contrast of social-oriented East Asia with the individualist West—so often exaggerated, yet still so real.

Other words for "good" include *zheng*, "upright, straight, right, true," metaphorically extended as in English. Specific virtues like loyalty, courage, honesty, and probity had their own terms. Most interesting of all is *ren*, a derivative of the word for "person" (*ren*). As noted above, the moral *ren* is written with the character for "person" next to the character for "two." It is a verbal noun, meaning "the way two people should behave toward each other." The English extensions of "human" into "humane" and "humanistic" (in the moral sense) are exactly equivalent in both derivation and meaning. The old missionary translation of *ren* as "benevolent" is far out of line, and modern writers usually use "humaneness."

Most traditional Chinese believed that people were naturally good in the sense of eusocial. This position was convincingly argued by Mencius (fourth century BCE) in the Ox Mountain story and elsewhere. A major challenge by Xunzi (third century) held that human nature was thoroughly *e*. Both Mencius and Xunzi, however, agreed that education was necessary, either to keep people on the right moral path (Mencius) or to reform their innate badness (Xunzi). Mencius defined his entire morality as an extension of *ren*, and that term remained central. An old folktale tells of a family with five generations living happily under one roof—a Chinese ideal but rarely seen in reality. The local governor asked the aged head of the household how he managed it. The household head simply drew the character *ren* on the wall.

Over time, Mencius won out, mostly because his predictions were correct and Xunzi's were not. People were, and are, *generally* sociable and at least somewhat well-meaning, in Mencius' sense. When they were not, critics could point to poor education. This erased the distinction between "ought" and "is," so famously made by David Hume in the Western world. For Chinese, the natural (*ziran* or *xing*) "is" is the "ought." If people are naturally sociable and "good" and if society depends on their moral insights, the distinction is one without a difference. Hume answered similar charges in his own time by pointing to the un-British morals of ancient Rome, a culture highly admired in Hume's world but extremely different in morality. The Chinese had no such different yet respected society to contemplate. The "different" societies they knew were "barbarians," "lacking education," as shown by their economic and political marginality as well as by their cultural "otherness." This lack of a highly respected but very different comparison society cost China the chance to think more deeply about morality.

Dualism—the idea that good is heavenly, and earth, evil—has been common in Western thought throughout history. From original sin (Genesis 1 and 2) to Hobbes to Freud to Richard Dawkins, Westerners have generally concluded that humans are born evil and antisocial and must be whipped into shape—often quite literally. (In my childhood, people around me universally believed that children had to be savagely and frequently punished, and phrases like "spare the rod and spoil the child" and "beat the devil out of him" were invoked in a quite literal sense.) The belief has been that humans are driven by the devil, the "id," selfish greed (now called "rational individual maximizing"), or other dark inner forces.

This idea dates back to ancient Near Eastern dualistic thinking and survives in Christianity, thanks to Manichean and Neoplatonic influences. Thus proper Christians pray, "From all the deceits of the world, the flesh, and the devil, good Lord, deliver us" (this and similar lines occur in many prayer books, including the Great Litany in the Episcopalian Book of Common Prayer). Xunzi and his follower Han Feizi had similar beliefs but never took them as far. They never believed that evil was built in and ordained by the gods; they thought it was just natural selfishness, which was correctable by education. They also never dreamed that all human pleasures and enjoyments could be regarded as sinful simply because they were enjoyable. Xunzi and Mozi condemned luxury as wasteful, but they never condemned enjoyment per se.

In all these philosophic ways, from yang-yin cosmology and qi physiology to thinking of humans as prosocial yet needing education, the Chinese philosophy of the Warring States and early Han periods lasted until recent times. This does not mean that China was changeless or tradition bound. Belief in particular ideas and systems fluctuated greatly. New philosophies, notably Buddhist schools of many kinds, entered the culture and had great influence. Original ideas and original applications of old ideas abounded. The old core of Mencian, Daoist, and Legalist thinking persisted, just as ancient Greek and Near Eastern thinking did in the West—but, as there, it did not persist unchanged.

However, the modern world brought a genuine rupture. Modern European culture, especially Marxism, imported to China the Hobbesian view: the idea that humans are individual rational calculators, basically selfish, greedy, and mean and thus in need of strict governance. Also imported was the idea of "man" against "nature." These new ideas led to a catastrophic breakdown of Chinese moral, environmental, and political culture.

The Systematization of Environmental Management in Han

The above may seem too much philosophy for a book on the environment, but the present section will, hopefully, show otherwise. In Han, the above ideas developed into the Huang-Lao tradition of philosophy and statecraft (Chang Chun-shu 2007a: 119–20), which was loosely based on the mythical reign of the Yellow Emperor (Huang Di) and the teachings of Laozi. It was actually a syncretic tradition that integrated major and useful insights from the other schools but integrated them into a basic stock that was essentially the soft-path Legalism referred to above. The Yellow Emperor was recognized as a god in early centuries but was progressively euhemerized, becoming a "real" human ancestor by the mid-fourth millennium BCE (Chang Chun-shu 2007a: 122). In spite of the implications of some modern sources (such as Chang), the Huang-Lao was a very loose "school." Anyone who agreed that government should be moderate—not too light, not too strict—could be included, especially if he or she believed that cosmological principles encouraged such policies and operated in this world through subtle correspondences.

Later writings in the Han Dynasty considerably expanded this view, locking conservation policies into the imperial government (E. Anderson 1988). Xunzi's principles are found especially in the *Li Ji*, a record of court ceremonies and rules that dates from the Warring States period but was organized, arranged, and extended in the early Han Dynasty. In general, the *Li Ji* rules were designed to prevent overhunting, overcutting forests, and seasonally inappropriate behavior such as taking female animals in the spring. They also include specifications of how many people the lords were expected to feed, at least in the ancient days. By mid-Han, the seasonal rules had been forced into the straitjacket of Han cosmology, but they were not mere logical extensions of it; they are far too sensible to have started as anything but pragmatic environmental regulations.

Further research on conservation of resources in ancient Chinese thought has turned up a great deal (E. Anderson 2001). Han thought on the environment turns out to be strikingly complex, sophisticated, and accordant with twenty-first-century knowledge. We know that mainly from a series of huge compendia of Warring States lore, heavily reconstructed or actually created during Han times. Han authors loved to give distinction to their words by fathering them on a famous name or famous document. Indeed, they usually preferred to remain anonymous, submerging their work in the alleged writings of some earlier sage—a behavior rather surprising to a modern academic! The extremes of this tendency were reached in the Shen Nong herbal and the Yellow Emperor's classic of internal medicine. Shen Nong was a purely mythical ox-headed god of agriculture who supposedly lived in the twenty-eighth century BCE. (He is the source of those Western-secondary-literature claims that such-and-such a plant was known in China in "2737 BCE." This means it was mentioned in his herbal, which in present form dates from the sixth century CE.) The Yellow Emperor was similarly mythical, and even earlier in imagined time.

Similarly fabricated or reedited were Zhou court manuals (the *Zhou Li* and *Li Ji*) and various collections of lore. Authentic works like Zhuangzi's writings received gratuitous additions. Delightful fiction such as the Liezi material (Graham 1960) was passed off as real philosophical writing. I strongly doubt if educated people were fooled at the time. They no doubt took these attributions in the spirit that Berkeley hippies took the newspaper columns of "Dr. Hip Pocrates" (Dr. Eugene Schoenfeld) in the 1960s. But for modern scholars, who must try to sort out Han creativity from authentic Warring States thought, the whole business is either a nightmare or a fascinating detective story—depending on the scholars' sense of humor.

Conservation of resources had become scientific by Han times, if not by late Warring States. The early Daoist texts (Yates 1997: 163), the *Huainanzi* (Ames 1994, esp. 163, 201; Liu An 2010; see below), and other works specifically counsel the conservation and management of plants, game animals, agricultural land and resources, and other renewable resources.

The most thorough and insightful material by far is that compiled under the name of Guan Zhong, known as Guanzi—Philosopher Guan. W. Allyn Rickett (1965, 1985, 1998), in his monumental edition of the Guanzi material, does a particularly fine job of explaining the work in English. Guan Zhong (supposedly d. 645 BCE) was a leading political advisor to Duke Huan of Qi (r. 685–643 BCE). The book attributed to him is a vast and fascinating miscellany. It seems to have been the product of patronage in a grand intellectual establishment, the Jixia. This assemblage of government-supported intellectuals, planners, knights, and other statecrafters was a true think tank in the modern sense and had been created under the Tian kings of Qi (A. Meyer 2011). This was by no means the first intellectual academy in China; the state of Wei had had, a century or two earlier, a huge university-like establishment in which Mencius and other philosophers had taught.

The *Guanzi* and legalist works like *The Book of Lord Shang* counsel keeping statistics: detailed numbers on population, agriculture, and so on—a concept fairly new to the West in the eighteenth century. Useful backup advice includes "those who are skilled in shepherding their people are certain to know first of all the condition of their land" (Rickett 1998: 224).

The *Guanzi* contains much Qi material going back to the 300s and 200s

BCE. It was finally compiled under Han. The parts often contradict each other.. The writing styles are late Warring States or Han, and very often in the dialect of the old state of Chu, implying that this work—though starting life in Qi—may very well have been put together at the court of Liu An, along with the very similar *Huainanzi* (see below). (Thus, pace Meyer, who emphasizes its early Qi origins, I place it with the Han materials—they are much more comparable.) Most of it is Daoist or Huang-Lao (see below) in inspiration, but it wanders over the philosophic map, often combining Confucian, Legalist, Daoist and other ideas, as do other Han compilations. As Andrew Meyer (2011) and many others have pointed out, philosophers and politicians took ideas where they found them. Orthodoxy of the Western type was not a concept in ancient China.

The book is extremely detailed and sophisticated in regard to agriculture, geography, and economics. It is devastating to the old—and still commonly held—Western stereotype of the Chinese as dreamy sorts whose thinking was mystical and unworldly. For instance, a fascinating insight into the times, and an apparently accurate assessment, is "The most skillful peasant can support five people, those of medium ability can support four, while the least skillful can only support three. The most skillful women can provide clothing for five people, those of medium ability can provide clothing for four, while the least skillful can only provide clothing for three" (Rickett 1998: 441). Guan—or the Chu or Han scholar who used Guan's name—properly cautions against disrupting any peasant's work! "If a single peasant is not engaged in farming, someone will suffer hunger; if a single woman does not engage in weaving, someone will suffer cold" (459). With this level of production, there was very little scope for taxation, war, or mistaken policy. Every state operated at the edge of subsistence. As the Han emperor Wu Di was to discover, taxing the empire at a rate necessary for serious long-continued military action quickly brought ruin and could not be sustained.

Guan had much to say about how to use clever (sometimes downright Machiavellian) means to raise revenues. One of the more humorous ones involves tricking people with religion. Guan (or Guan's mouthpiece a few centuries later) advised the duke not to tax construction, animals, or trees, since it would lead to hindering the production thereof, but instead to tax ghosts and spirits—by getting everyone to sacrifice and taking a share of the revenues and production thus stimulated (453). The ruler can also take advantage of comets and other scary portents to hold expensive ceremonies and charge the rich: "Thus the wise make use of the spirits while the stupid only believe in them" (488). Cynicism was never more cheerfully deployed. One's heart goes out to the barefaced cheekiness of Guan's followers. (One may also be amused at the foolishness of certain later polities that exempt churches from taxation and thus lead to the creation of thousands of vast pseudo-churches that are nothing but economic and political scams.)

We have noted already the use of bulrush mats for sacrifices as a way of stimulating the bulrush industry in otherwise unproductive marshes (482). These passages perfectly anticipate John Maynard Keynes (see esp. 304ff.). Rickett thinks this was only for emergencies and not a general theory, but it is hard to read the translation that way—it seems to be a general theory, basically identical to Keynes's.

Advice also involves knowing the land—where to find metal ores, what lands can be used only for grazing, when to cull herds, and so on. Guan pointed out that landholders living in rocky, mountainous areas generally conquer those living in fertile lowlands because the mountaineers are forced to be more thrifty and prudent (470). (My Scottish ancestors would agree.) He sensibly advocated avoiding large reservoirs by having many small ones and cultivating more intensively, advice that is still state-of-the-art in international development. He mentions winter wheat specifically (473).

Guan took agriculture seriously: "Anyone who has claimed to be capable of being minister of agriculture, when found to be incapable, shall be killed and his blood smeared on his [i.e., presumably the government's] altar to Land" (Rickett 1998: 433). There is no evidence the advice was ever taken, but it deserves to be revived for economic advisors today, in China and elsewhere.

Some of the good management principles now associated with *fengshui* are attested in the *Guanzi*. It counseled the ruler to site his capital above the flood line but below the area that could go dry in a drought and to have an encircling canal and protecting mountains to provide water and storm protection (Rickett 1965: 74; 1998: 242ff.). All these are familiar tenets of modern fengshui. They were probably old by Han. There are excellent directions for flood control, including planting dikes with "thorns and brambles in order to secure their earth. Mix in [junipers] and willows to provide against flooding" (Rickett 1965: 79–80, correction taken from 1998 trans.). These and many other bits of excellent practical advice are mixed with cosmology and numerology in the *Guanzi*, just as in modern fengshui.

A long, brilliant, and highly sophisticated discourse on soils and crops (Rickett 1998: 259ff.) has been often described in Western literature (e.g., Needham 2004: 123ff.; his equations to modern soil types are shaky). Rickett's translation is more accurate about descriptions and trees than earlier versions, enabling us to see that Guan ranks loams formed under deciduous forest as the highest quality, and on down through alluvial clays, somewhat saline alluvial soils, and so on, to saline or alkaline soils as the worst. (Intruded into the account is an utterly irrelevant, and irreverent, humorous send-up of the Five Tones of the Chinese mystical scale; see Ricket 1998: 263.)

Guan recognized ninety soil types, but most are mere color variants; each major soil type has variants for each of the five colors. *Su* soils are best: "when wet, they are not sticky, when dry they are not totally lacking in moisture" (Rickett 1998: 268), and do not harden, erode away, or lose moisture; that is, they are loams with good water retention qualities. They are suitable for millets and (when unfarmed and undisturbed) grow tung trees, oaks, elms, willows, mulberries, poplars, and similar trees—that is, they are typical of second-growth valley forests. When they appear as deep loams on hillsides, they nourish second-growth trees like jujube, catalpa, and big-leaf oak. Marshes in areas with su soils are filled with fish, and in general the lands are fertile. Next come the *wu* soils, which are loose and porous, with earthworms. They are good for panic millet and support tung trees, oaks, catalpa, *Prunus* species, jujubes, pears—in general, similar trees as on the su soils. They are in fact forest loams, apparently somewhat more podzol-like than the rich su leaf molds. Then come the *wei* soils, which do not form hard clods or break into fine dust, and they too retain moisture and do not easily erode; they grow trees similar to the others, as well as medicinal herbs, ginger, smartweed, and other annuals characteristic of fertile woodland alluvium.

Then follow the *yin* soils, black and powdery. They grow rice and are good for animals but are 20 percent less fertile than the first three soil types. Trees are not listed, but from the description I take these soils to be alluvial and derived from forest podzols. Then come the *rang* and *fu* soils, described very briefly in similar terms. Following these are the distinctly inferior *ju* soils: wet, loess-like, and not very fertile; they are probably waterlogged alluvial soils derived from loess. *Lu, jian,* and *piao* soils follow, and then sandy (*sha*) soils, which have dust and sand and would appear to be low-grade wash from eroded hills. Then come the *ge* soils: "as rocky as a stone pile and unable to withstand flood or drought" (Rickett 1998: 280). Then comes *you,* which smells like manure, that is, soggy, waterlogged, poorly drained soil. Then *zhuang,* "the color of a rat's liver" (280; interesting in view of the fact that some Chinese of the time believed a rat had no liver—Guan's writers were, as usual, scientifically perceptive). Then come *zhi,* which "may become completely saturated and disintegrate, or [when dry], they may crack and lose their vitality," and they raise rice; that is, they are poor, clay rich, probably acidic alluvial soils. Then other poor types bring us to the worst: the *jie* soils, salty and bitter. But even they can raise some types of rice—a tribute to the tough, diverse, often salt-tolerant rices of old China.

Guan observes that people will fight for a country whose resources are adequate to maintain them (Rickett 1998: 141). Very many essays discuss ways (some devious) for assuring an adequate supply of grain for famine relief, war, and other hardships. A point very often emphasized is that the people must not be called away during the critical planting, weeding and harvesting seasons (177ff.), because loss of work at these times guarantees grain shortages. In general, a good ruler will help the people, adjust supply and demand to keep prices low, maintain a supply for famine relief, and so on, including quite modern-sounding (but impossibly idealistic) social welfare (227ff.).

Another focus of the *Guanzi* is on water management. One chapter is a sort of hymn to water, making it the basis of all things, from plant growth to national character. Chu has fine water, hence its virtuous people; rival states have turbulent, polluted water (more evidence for a Chu origin for the book). This chapter reminds one of Greek speculation on which "element" was the most basic. Other chapters are much more practical and discuss the actual ways of controlling rivers and floods. One source apparently thought the character for "water" could be analyzed as a symbol for a man and a woman with a stream of semen between (Rickett 1998: 103). This notion is quite consonant with Han sexual mysticism. More practical are references to various degrees of water need in land, up to "land that has been flooded in order to raise fish and turtles" (389); aquaculture was already well known at the time. It was supposedly invented by the semi-mythical millionaire Fan Li. In any case, it goes well back into Zhou days.

Major government rewards go to experts in raising animals, trees, melons and gourds, vegetables, fruits, silkworms, and so on, and to those skilled in medicine and in crop science (1998: 401). Directions for evaluating and managing land according to its potential include very specific and excellent ones (e.g., 419).

The geography, however, could be erratic. A famous passage about metals (see Golas 1999 for an extended discussion) states: "If, on a mountain, hematite lies near the surface, iron may be found below. . . . If lead lies near the surface, silver may be found below. . . . If cinnabar lies near the surface, gold ore may be found below. If magnetite is found near the surface, copper may be found below" (424). The first two are accurate enough guides to be useful, but not the second two; someone was overextending.

Possibly less useful, but extremely informative, are the elaborate calendars of what the ruler should do at any given time of year. The ruler had to plow a ceremonial furrow or two at the start of the plowing season, and the empress had to oversee rearing some silkworms, so that the forces of heaven would aid these activities for the whole country. Punishing criminals had to be done in the winter (the season of death; fall was possible also) but not in the spring or summer, the seasons of birth and growth. Some of these ceremonial calendars occur in the *Guanzi* and add a great deal of practical, homey advice ("Care for [the people] with kindness. Draw them to you with humaneness" and so on; Rickett 1965: 201).

A longer and more complete calendar in *Huainanzi* has a more elaborate cosmology but less advice (Liu An 2010). Many of the rules found in the *Guanzi* are taken and combined with Mencian and Daoist thinking in the *Huainanzi* (Liu An 2010), piled under the direction of King Liu An of Huainan in the 120s BCE in the Former Han Dynasty. This makes the *Huainanzi* a central conservation text in Chinese history, since it brings together the best and most nature-conscious of Confucian and Daoist traditions in one authoritative source. The same group of scholars apparently compiled the *Zhuangzi* in the form we know it today, and a great deal of the latter is repeated verbatim in the *Huainanzi*, showing that the environmentalist implications often seen in the *Zhuangzi* (see Girardot et al. 2001) are real, not modern romancing.

Along with the work of Dong Zhongshu, the *Huainanzi* was a main defining document in the cosmology of qi and the Five Phases. All things depend ultimately on heaven but operate through the endless circulation of qi through the world. It has hotter and colder aspects, and these become the yang and yin aspects of things.

Pragmatic conservation is worked into that cosmology. Thus, the obviously practicaland rational instruction that, in spring, "Nests must not be overturned nor the unborn young killed, likewise neither young creatures nor eggs" (*Huainanzi*, Liu An 2010: 183) is worked into a cosmological idea of spring as the season of birth and new life. Spring is also a time for nurturing orphans and the childless "in order that [these policies] may communicate . . . to the growing sprouts" (184). It is not a time for hunting, burning brush or weeds, or drainage or major public works (184–85). It is not a time for netting fish. For the same reason, it is the season for pardons, not for executions of criminals.

Summer is a time for guarding and tending crops. One cannot build up earthworks (it damages the fields) or cut down large trees (2010: 187). Burning off brush is still prohibited. One should not put out hunting nets till the dholes (wild dogs) have offered sacrifices in the fall (331). Apparently dholes finished raising their young by then and tended to leave some killed prey lying undevoured, as if sacrificing it. Fall is for hunting, burning, and executions. One can begin hawking, netting birds, and chopping wood, but not until fall is well along (331).

The alleged decline of China from an early golden age of peace and prosperity to later war, violence, and famine is due to people acting irresponsibly in search of profit. Among other things, they "ripped open pregnant animals and killed young ones, . . . overturned nests and broke eggs" (Liu An 2010: 68), set fires, piled up earthworks indiscriminately, dug and channeled and pounded and otherwise created great public works (269), and did violence to nature—reducing fertility and ruining farmland.

A later section repeats much of this rationale and adds that in the good old days:

> when hunting they did not wipe out herds;
> They did not catch fawns or baby animals,
> They did not drain marshes to get fish;
> They did not burn forests to capture [animals]. (331)

They did not chop small trees, kill pregnant animals, take fish under a foot long, or kill pigs less than a year old (331). In general, they were careful not to overhunt or deforest.

These practices of the old kings is very similar to the practices advocated in the *Li Ji*. It is also similar to recent practice of Tibeto-Burman groups in parts of China (Wang Jianhua 2013), and thus this passage may well indicate a realistic tradition, not a mere legend. To which one may add (472) that one early king did not want people to catch small fish, and they did indeed refrain out of respect for him.

A fascinating and environmentally significant bit of the *Huainanzi* bases government on yet another numerical association, the six regulating instruments. The metaphor was old by then—Confucians and Legalists had long made the point—but the *Huainanzi* took it to new cosmological heights. These were the simple tools used by ancient Chinese carpenters and craftspersons to measure and align their work:

Heaven is the marking cord.
Earth is the level.
Spring is the compass.
Summer is the balance beam.
Autumn is the square. [the carpenter's square, a simple right-angled
    metal piece]
Winter is the weight. (Liu N 2010: 204)

These six simple tools are not only symbols of good government; they *are* good government, through ganying. The government seasonally applies the basic ideas of which these tools are the simplest, most direct, and most straightforward application. The marking cord, for instance, is the simplest but most effective of imaginable instruments: a cord stretched between two points to mark a straight line. For carpentry, it was, and still is, inked and pressed onto the board to ensure a straight saw cut. I have seen this done countless times in China, as I have seen the other tools used too. They were and are "natural symbols" (Douglas 1970). The resonant, or metaphoric, application is that the government must be straight; in Chinese, as in English, "straight" (or "upright," *zheng*) has the metaphoric extension of "honest, true, open, consistent." Our "straightforward" and "correct" similarly have Chinese equivalents based on *zheng*. In fact, the word for "govern" or "government" in Chinese is the same word, *zheng*, written with a verbalizing marker (and pronounced in a different tone, because of an ancient verbalizing process). The *Huainanzi* provides similar discussions for the other tools.

This metaphoric use of tools lasted long and spread far. Korea's great poet and statesman Yun Sondo (1587–1671) used them in a song to start off a banquet. The song later became famous:

How is a house built?
It is the work of a master carpenter.
Why are the timbers straight?
They follow the line of ink and carpenter's square.
Knowledge
Of this home truth will bring you long life.
          (Yun Sondo in O'Rourke 2002: 91, slightly amended)

Little progress was made in conservation in later centuries or in later writings. There is not much evidence of people living by these rules of former kings. Widespread knowledge of these texts must mean that some people cared, but the ones who did were apt to be scholars who were not doing much hunting or woodcutting in any case.

The ordinary people certainly had their own ideas about conservation but were only indirectly influenced by these texts. Still, there must have been some carryover, since the literate tradition was widely known and directly influenced ordinary people via officials, landlords, and religious practitioners. One of the main things one learned from research in remote areas of China in the 1960s was that the literate tradition was quite well known even to illiterate peasants because it was constantly quoted in everything from religious services to plays, Chinese operas, and folksongs. It was not remote and cut off from ordinary society, as the Western "great tradition" was in America in my youth. I never heard anyone quote the Li Ji or the Huainanzi, but many people did know Mencius's Ox Mountain story—a staple of rural schoolrooms—and knew that taking small fish or pregnant animals was a fool's game.

Other calendars of this sort survive in varying degrees of completeness (Rickett 1965, 1998, e.g., 108–17). They indicate an exquisite sensitivity to the changes and moods of nature and a strong belief that these actually required that the ruler do different things at different times of year. Except for the matter of punishments and obvious farm-related matters like the ceremonial furrow, they do not always agree on what goes with what month. The Guanzi, for instance, allows one kind of nonfatal punishment in spring (Rickett 1965: 215).

A very similar conservation calendar to Guan's appears in the Lüshi Chunchiu (Lü Buwei 2000: 94–98). That work also makes some of the same conservation recommendations: not taking young animals (284), not taking small fish (471), not using fine-meshed nets (642). There is a particularly good story of an individual who advised his lord to triumph by deception; the lord replied that if you catch all the fish or burn all the forest, there will be no fish or trees, and if you deceive people you will similarly wind up in trouble. (He should have talked to the Guanzi writers.) Although the lord did use the tactic of deceiving enemies—once—he did not reward his advisor highly (317).

The first half of the Li Ji consists of elaborate ceremonial directions, including a great deal about timing and food. The latter half consists largely of teachings on ritual, ascribed to Confucius, followed by a long series of explanatory essays that provide sociological reasons and justifications for the rituals. These are fascinating in their anticipation of functionalist explanations of ritual in modern social science. They are apparently Han additions and certainly reflect Han social thought. (The latest and now most easily available edition of James Legge's classic translation of the *Li Ji*, originally published in 1885, now appears under the authorship of "K'ung-fu Tzu" [*sic*] on the mistaken belief that Confucius wrote it; I cite it here as Legge 2008.)

In the calendar sections and sometimes elsewhere, the *Li Ji* forbids taking pregnant game animals, setting fishnets in spawning season, burning forests for driving game, and even burning fields before (beneficial) insects have gone into hibernation (Ames 1994: 163, 201; see also Lewis 2006: 182 on rhapsodies that promoted conservation). The rules sound completely modern and—with some change of rhetorical style—would not seem out of place in a modern resource management textbook.

In the *Li Ji*, most of the rules are in the Yue Ling section (found in vol. 1, 155–84, of the 2008 edition). This calendar for the ruler explains dates, tells what happens at this season, tells what ceremonies to perform, and then tells the ruler what to do—including the conservation rules. In the first month, inspectors should check out the fields and repair boundaries. "Nests should not be thrown down; unformed insects should not be killed, nor creatures in the womb, nor very young creatures, nor birds just taking to the wing, nor fawns, nor should eggs be destroyed." In the second month, farmers should repair their houses and entries and temples. In the third, hunting with nets and disguises is ruled out. And so it goes, with many instructions to workers to keep everything repaired and up to the point and not to waste or misuse resources.

The *Li Ji* also has many notes on food customs among the elite: "The meat cooked on the bones is set on the left, and the sliced meat on the right; the [boiled grain] is placed on the left of the parties on the mat, and the soup on their right" and so on through minced and roasted meat, pickles and sauces, onions and steamed onions, drinks and syrups, with rules for serving, consuming, and finishing the repast (Legge 2008, 1: 61). "Do not roll the [grain] into a ball; do not bolt down the various dishes; do not swill down [drinks]. Do not make a noise in eating; do not crunch the bones with the teeth; do not put back fish you have been eating; do not throw the bones to the dogs . . ." and so on through other proper behaviors (62); "he who pares a melon for the son of Heaven should divide it into four parts and then into eight" and so on for less special preparations for lesser dignitaries (63). China's civilizing mission, in Norbert Elias's terms, came long before Europe's, but no one has yet compared the customs in the *Li Ji* with customs in the Western world at the same time period.

Presenting foods had its own rules: "When heavy rains have fallen, one should not present fish or tortoises. . . . He who is presenting cooked food, should carry with him the sauce and pickles for it" (64). Presumably the water animals are inappropriate for a wet time for reasons of resonance. Women presented lesser things, such as *Hovenia dulcis* stems, hazelnuts, jujubes, and chestnuts (82).

In sacrificial contexts, animals were referred to by indirect terms, evidently because the gods—and human dignitaries—wanted more high-class speech: "the ox is called 'the creature with the large foot'; the pig, 'the hard bristles'; a sucking-pig, 'the fatling'; a sheep, 'the soft hair'; a cock, 'the loud voice'" and so on through pheasant, fish, ale, various millets, rice, scallions, salt, etc. (81). Such references are strikingly reminiscent of the language of Zuyua in ancient Mayan texts, in which similar flowery and indirect terms are applied to foodstuffs in ceremonial contexts. Presumably a similar psychological process is involved. Meats of all the usual species and ale of many kinds are key, but water plants, grains, nuts, and other foods provide much variety.

Foods are listed at length and include not only the usual grains and domestic animals but also pickles of all kinds, quail, partridge, and wild game. Most dishes are not described in detail, but we have "snail-juice and a condiment of the broad-leaved water-squash [probably meaning water-spinach] . . . with pheasant soup; a condiment of wheat with soups of dried slices [of meat] and of fowl;" a suckling pig "wrapped in sonchus [sow thistle] leaves and stuffed with smart-weed . . . a fish, with the same stuffing and egg sauce; . . . brine of ants. . . . Pheasants and hares . . . with . . . duckweed" (262–63). Foods listed include sparrows, finches, curlews, cicadas, bees, chestnuts, water caltrops, jujubes, persimmons, plums, hawthorn fruit, and more. The five grains and the five animals were combined with appropriate seasonal resonances. Such rules included making minced meat in spring with green onions and in fall with Chinese mustard plant (263).

A great officer should not have both minced and dried slices of meat at the same meal or savory meat, evidently because it would be too luxurious. Several items were forbidden, and various rules for preparation, such as scaling fish and plumping up dried jujubes, were enforced. Anomalous-looking or strange-acting animals were considered bad food (264). Thus, an ox that lowed at night, a dog that was nervous and had red inner thighs, and a hoarse-voiced bird were to be avoided. Probably these were taken as marks of sickness, but in later millennia any unusual-looking domestic animal was apt to be shunned as uncanny (see, e.g., Buell et al. 2010).

An enormously long and complex set of passages on food occurs in the chapters on family rituals. The foods were mainly those offered to the elderly and to the spirits of the deceased. Today's failing elderly person was tomorrow's ancestor, deserving and receiving more or less similar foods in either state. (I saw this pattern in Chinese traditional households in the mid-twentieth century. A revered elder would be served her favorite foods, and when deceased, she would have them before her tablet on the family altar table.)

Such foods were the richest and finest of all. "For the Rich Fry, they put the pickled meat fried over rice that that been grown on a dry soil, and then enriched it with melted fat" (267). Dry-grown rice is generally more flavorful than wet-grown (paddy). "For the Bake, they took a sucking-pig or a (young) ram, and having cut it open and removed the entrails, filled the belly with dates [jujubes]. They then wrapped it round with straw and reeds, which they plastered with clay, and baked it. When the clay was all dry, they broke it off . . . they removed the crackling [skin] and macerated it along with rice-flour, so as to form a kind of gruel. . . . They then fried the whole in such a quantity of melted fat as to cover it," and then kept cooking it with herbs and served it with meat and vinegar (267). In short, the elderly had extremely fine food that was carefully cooked, high in protein, and easy to eat and digest. There are several other recipes given (see also Kwang-chih Chang 1977).

Drinks included both strained and unstrained ale, which were kept separate; the unstrained was presumably rather like the unstrained tapai of Southeast Asia, a rice beer with the rice mash left in so that one either eats it with a spoon or drinks it through a straw equipped with a strainer. Other drinks included millet water, rice water, and other thin grain preparations.

Many ceremonial and ordinary civil rules and prescriptions involved superior-inferior contacts, within the family and within the court (see, e.g., Legge 2008, 2: 4, 45ff.). This included elaborate rules for sitting at dinner and in ceremonies where food was provided.

One important lesson from all this is that fine food was so universal, and so integral to proper etiquette and civility, that there was simply no way for puritanism to get a foothold. Mozi had a hopeless task. He could not make either the elite or the ordinary persons go against all their training and sense of the right.

Final observations on Han synthetic philosophy are provided by the *Li Ji*, which is astonishingly modern in its use of functionalist explanations for ancient principles. Right from the beginning, it provides long and detailed explanations for the Rules of Propriety (as James Legge translated it in 1885; Legge 2008). These rules "furnish the means of determining . . . relatives, as near and remote; of settling points which may cause suspicion or doubt; of distinguishing where there should be agreement, wand where difference" and so on (53). The whole book reads like Durkheim or the early ethnonologists in its constant explanation of rituals and rules in terms of their pragmatic social functions. They keep society operating smoothly and predictably. This highly sophisticated and complex social theorizing might have put China two millennia ahead of the West in social thought, had it been extended in subsequent centuries.

The whole picture of Han conservation has been radically sharpened by an amazing find. Archaeologists working in the ruined city of Xuanquanzhi, near Dunhuang in Gansu, found a ruined wall painted with a long government proclamation. They patiently pieced it together, jigsaw-puzzle style, and found it to be an imperial edict on conservation and resource management. It had a date equivalent to 5 CE. Promulgated in the name of the Empress Dowager Yuan (Wang Zhengjun), it was apparently issued by her nephew Wang Mang when he was prime minister. Four years later he took over the empire in a coup. (Outside of remitting some taxes and freeing up exiles, he did not change policy much, having established a good deal of it before the coup. A countercoup displaced him in 23 CE and restored the Han.) Notable is the fact that this edict was found in a remote, isolated part of the Han Empire. We can safely assume that it was conspicuously painted on walls throughout China and had its due effect on behavior.

The edict has now been the subject of a detailed and meticulous study and translation by Charles Sanft (2009). Like many Sinologists, he is more interested in cosmology than in ecology and does not discuss the practical conservation advice. The latter, however, is worth quoting extensively, with ecological notes. (Notes in parentheses are mine; bracketed ones are Sanft's; diareses mark lacunae in the original.)

"The Grand Empress Dowager proclaims: Recently Yin and Yang have not been in harmony. Wind and rain have not come at the proper times, and the lazy farmers have been at ease, not striving at their work."

The order then starts from the fifth month and presumably is to start from the fifth month in subsequent years.

In the fifth month, "It is forbidden to cut down trees. This means that neither large nor small trees may be cut down, and it applies until the end of the eighth month. Only after the leaves have fallen from plants and trees may one cut down those trees that should be" (i.e., someone has marked certain trees for cutting—as in modern best forestry practice.)

"Do not gather birds' nests. This means that neither occupied nor unoccupied nests may be gathered. It applies for empty nests until the end of summer. [Gathering] occupied nests is constantly forbidden in all four seasons." (Someone has realized that unoccupied nests are very often reoccupied.)

"Do not kill young insects. This refers to immature insects that do not harm people. It applies until the end of the ninth month." (In spring, this could be mere cosmology, but the fact that it was ordered through the summer indicates that Han scientists recognized the value of insects in the ecosystem. As noted by Roger Ames for the *Huainanzi* calendar—see above—the insects would be hibernating by the ninth month in northern China.)

"Do not kill fetuses. This refers to wild and domestic animals that are pregnant and bearing fetuses. [Killing them is] constantly forbidden until the end of the twelfth month." (Thus it is legal from the first to the fifth month.)

"Do not take young birds. This refers to killing young birds so they do not get to grow up. It is constantly forbidden until the end of the twelfth month.

"Do not take fawns (here meaning any newborn mammal). This refers to four-legged . . . and domestic animals that are young and not yet steady, and it applies until the end of the ninth month.

"Do not gather eggs. This refers to the eggs of the type . . . birds and fowl, and it applies until the end of the ninth month. . . .

"Hide dried bones and bury flesh. 'Dried bones' refers to . . . birds and animals; those that still have meat are 'flesh.' This applies until the end of summer. . . .

"Do not encroach on waters or marshes, drain ponds. . . . Only then will people everywhere be able to catch fish. . . .

"Do not burn mountain forests. This refers to setting forests of fire for hunting, as it harms fowl, beast . . . snakes, insects, plants, and trees. . . . month until the end of . . ." (Alas, we have lost the dates, but probably burning would, like the other activities, start around the ninth month, when animals were grown and the forest was dry but not too dry.)

"Do not shoot birds with pellets, spread nets, or use other techniques to capture them. . . .

"Do not hold large hunts. This applies until the end of the eighth month" (Sanft 2009: 178–84).

There is a great deal more, but most of it is fragmentary. It calls on people to plant and sow, including wheat; to store dried vegetables; to repair and maintain roads, walls, and public works in general but not to overwork themselves with major projects (including new walls). It also establishes some bureaucratic reforms.

Overall, this is a stunning document. The measures quoted above are sensible and pragmatic. They are basically the same laws we have today in the most environmentally conscious polities, and they are well ahead of those in most current nations. The prohibitions on taking pregnant animals and on hunting during breeding season are, of course, more or less worldwide, since every cultural group that hunts has to have some such rules to keep in business (see, e.g., Berkes 2008; Pierotti 2011), but the concerns with trees, insects, birds, fish, and the whole environment are unusual—especially to find them posted on a wall in a remote corner of the empire.

Also notable is the indication that "hunting and gathering" were still very important in China at this time—as they were in many areas well into the late twentieth century. The Warring States documents show a world in which hunting still provided much of the food and forest, wetland, and river resources were critical. China still produced an incredible amount of game, fish, timber, and wild resources in general until the Maoist war on nature wiped out most of these "nature's services." Even today, China exports vast quantities of wild-gathered medicines and also tons of pine nuts, gathered from the wild (largely from *Pinus koraiensis* in the mountains of China's far northeast). What matters here is the extreme effort of the government to regulate it. In recent decades, exploiting the wild has ranged from weak control to a virtual lack of control in China, in spite of the public-show wildlife refuges (in which the wildlife is often being destroyed by overdevelopment for tourism), and as a result China has a vast number of endangered species, with recently highlighted extinctions (E. Anderson 2012). Obviously, Han had a far less difficult task than today's government, given Han China's much lower population and lower level of industrial development, but their efforts remain impressive.

Those efforts certainly provide yet more evidence for the pragmatic roots of Chinese cosmological resource management. The cosmological emphasis on maintaining life in spring and summer and taking it only in fall and winter is a reasonable extension of the wildlife management system. Bans on executing criminals till fall or winter make perfect sense in this framework.

In late Han, *The Comprehensive Discussions in the White Tiger Hall* (*Bai Hu Tong*, published as *Po Hu T'ung*, Tjan 1949) covered much of the above ground in a cursory manner, between long discussions of proper ritual and regalia. Seasonal prescriptions and proscriptions are repeated, the fivefold cosmology is briefly summarized (429ff.), and general remarks on nature appear. Little was added; the Han synthesis was well set in place. Millet appears as the staple food (384). The term is *ji*, which often means "panic millet," but it is evidently here used as a generic term. Sacrificial animals and sites of sacrifice are listed; they include ram, fowl, pig, and dog (378).

Philosophy moved in other environmentalist directions. Daoism taught retreat from the world, and in spite of its nature worship, it is strikingly silent on good management (E. Anderson 2001). It often incorporated earlier animal and nature cults, which declined in favor as time went on (Lewis 2007: 216–20). Confucianism became more focused on human society, although it maintained the conservationist rhetoric.

By Han, Buddhism was established in China, having surely come through Central Asia from such sources (Sen 2003). An early mention in 65 CE implies that there were even earlier communities (J. Hill 2009: 367). A few Buddhist objects and carvings survive, as around Pengcheng in Jiangsu, where stories place Buddhist encounters in the first century CE (Sen 2003: 5). The first dated Buddha sculpture in China comes from 338 (personal observation, San Francisco Asian Art Museum). Buddhism brought strict rules against taking life and provided strong advocacy for helping all beings. This had a major effect on China. Vegetarianism became widespread, and hunting gradually became less popular. Releasing captive animals became a regular practice, but, alas, sharp dealers quickly learned how to recapture the liberated captives—often training them to come right back to their cages! (I have observed this at Buddhist temples.) The degree to which Buddhism put a brake on overusing living resources needs to be assessed. Obviously it helped; obviously it did not stop the decline. Hopefully, some future environmental historian will calculate where, in the vast middle ground, Buddhism's effects lay.

CHAPTER 5

Dynastic Consolidation Under Han

A Summary of Han History

Qin collapsed in 207 BCE, but the imperial government of Han was not fully in place until 202. At this point Lu Jia told Liu Bei, the first emperor: "You won the empire on horseback, but can you rule it from horseback?" Liu saw he could not and set up a bureaucracy. The remark became famous and was re-cycled centuries later by Yelü Chucai, among others, instructing the steppe nomads who took over China in the Conquest Dynasties.

Early Han developed large cities of 200,000–300,000 people (Lewis 2006: 178), and later the capital reached perhaps a million. The huge towns that grew up around imperial tomb sites and housed workers and ritualists may have reached six-figure populations too.

A census in 2 CE revealed about 60,000,000 people, possibly an under-count. These were heavily concentrated in the North China Plain and Wei Valley, with smaller concentrations in the Sichuan basin and the lower Yangzi. There was another in the Red River Delta (now in Vietnam). Han conquered and held this area. The contrast with modern times is striking for the Pearl River area. It was then almost unpopulated, whereas it is now one of the most densely populated parts of the world. This census and one in 140 CE (Lewis 2006: 91) show that household size averaged around five persons, as it was throughout Chinese history.

Under Han, the centralization of China under one emperor in one capital became a reality. The founder (Liu Bang, Emperor Gao Zu) delegated power to his relatives, setting them up as kings. After his death, an empress, Lü, took over in a coup and declared a new empire (187–180 BCE). A countercoup restored the Han line in the person of Emperor Wen (r. 180–157). He relaxed the harsh Qin laws, supported learning, restored Confucianism, and tolerated other peaceful philosophies.

Wen cut land taxes substantially. His successor Emperor Jing lowered the tax on farmers from one-fifteenth of production to one-thirtieth in 155 BCE (E. Anderson 1988; Chang Chun-shu 2007a: 78ff.). This was the principal tax farmers paid (there was no separate income tax) and should be duly compared to modern world rates, typically around 40 percent of income in developed countries (unless one is rich and thus escapes). The figure of approximately 3 percent became enshrined in Chinese statecraft and was copied as late as the Qing Dynasty. Government services were, of course, comparably low. The government did not interfere very much in business or farming. The "good times of Wen and Jing" were remembered. They set a precedent, still alive and inspiring tax cuts in the Qing Dynasty.

However, Empress Lü's coup had taught the dynasty normal caution. While receiving popular approbation for their tax cuts and general kindness, Wen and Jing were quietly and thoroughly eliminating the restless and often rebellious local kings. This process involved eliminating entire families of immediate relatives. By Chinese—or any—standards, this was definitely hardline, but it was necessary for dynastic survival, and it worked. China remained centralized from then on when its government had any power at all.

Early emperors emulated the first emperor of Qin in having pottery armies to guard them in death; Emperor Jing's has recently been excavated (see Xu Pingfang 2002 for magnificent photographs of both Qin Shi Huang Di's and Jing's pottery armies).

Women were important, with a great deal of influence. This was not always viewed with enthusiasm, especially after yet another coup was brought about by Empress Yuan and her son Wang Mang, who established the Xin Dynasty. Most women were less rebellious. Many exemplary biographies of women—often written by other women—appeared. The women in them defer on the surface to fathers, husbands, and sons but managed to show a great deal of toughness, independence, and agency in the process—contrary to stereotypes (Raphals 1998). This tradition owes a great deal to Ban Zhao, a woman author who also continued the historical work of her father, Ban Bian, and elder brother, Ban Gu, finishing the *History of the Former Han Dynasty* (*Hou Han Shu*). She advocated proper deference to male authority but modeled what that meant by completing their work as a competent scholar fully equal to the men in the family. She was not a retiring person.

The great thinker and statesman Jia Yi, an early martyr to fearless speech (he reprimanded the emperor once too often), had much to do with redefining philosophy in a broadly Confucian mold. He followed a lead of Xunzi and anticipated Durkheim and other sociologists in providing startlingly modern functionalist explanations for ritual. He pointed out that rituals keep people together, teach individuals to do right, provide emotional grounding for morals, and represent the proper social relationships—for example, music uniting people and costumes showing the social differences through ritually prescribed dress (see, e.g., Lewis 2006: 200ff.). Jia Yi had a great influence on subsequent Chinese thinking, which ever afterward tended to give pragmatic, social-functional explanations for ritual and social norms. I heard many such explanations on the Hong Kong waterfront fifty years ago. These folk explanations may actually trace back to Jia Yi through convoluted historical paths.

The low-tax policy eroded as Emperor Wu's military campaigns forced raising of revenue. Emperor Wu (Wu Di, Martial Emperor, 156–87 BCE, r. 141–87) dramatically developed the economy with agricultural development research and implementation, including the world's first known case/control agricultural experiments and the first agricultural manuals (E. Anderson 1988; Bray 1984). However, it was his military drive that gave him his title and his fame. At his death, the Han Empire was the greatest on earth (Chang Chun-shu 2007a: 215). Han had conquered to the current western limits of China and beyond the current southern and northeastern limits. Wu Di's conquests amount to over 1.6 million square miles of real estate, conquered the Xiongnu Empire on the west (see below) and took over the Silk Road, just becoming a major artery.

In the southwest, the powerful Dian kingdom held sway until the Han conquest around 111 BCE. The area was to become independent again with the fall of Han. The Dian kingdom was a powerful, artistically brilliant, highly advanced polity centering on Lake Dian, on whose northern shore is the current city of Kunming (Yao and Jiang 2012). The Dian kingdom was based on advanced rice agriculture and had a diversified economy and superb metal work. It clearly had a highly multilingual and multiethnic citizenry, and the region is today one of the most ethnically and linguistically diverse in the world. The elite were probably speakers of one or even several Tibeto-Burman languages (Wang Jianhua 2013), and may have included Thai speakers also.

These conquests did not come without cost; the nearly contemporary *Han Shu* estimated that the empire's population was halved and the resources exhausted (Chang Chun-shu 2007a: 224). Wu Di also eliminated thousands of subjects and supporters who stood in his way or seemed to pose a threat. Wu Di was described by Chang Chun-shu as perhaps "the most brutal and neurotic ruler in Chinese history" (2007a: 94), which would be a true distinction in the land of Qin Shi Huang Di, Zhu Yuanzhang (of Ming), and other memorable tyrants. (I would, however, vote for Zhu over Wu Di any day.) Wu Di stands as one of those brilliant, merciless, isolated individuals—from Sargon of Akkad to Napoleon—who truly changed history through the sheer amounts of violence they used. Yet he also oversaw a dynamic program of expansion in agricultural development, research, and support, including into the newly conquered lands. Land there, and indeed throughout the country, was redistributed to yeoman farmers. Textile production greatly increased.

Then and later, Han also conquered southward into what is now Vietnam, where they encountered phenomenal resistance led by the Trung sisters, who were among the most militarily gifted women in history. Han prevailed but had nothing but trouble from its new subjects. (The Trung sisters became national icons and were much used in anti-American resistance during the 1960s and 1970s.) Thereafter, when China was strong, it dominated northern Vietnam, lost it otherwise, and faced indomitable resistance throughout—a history that caused many experts, including military ones, to warn American presidents to stay out of Vietnam in the 1960s. A similar overreach into hostile territory occurred in Korea, where Han troops were fought to a standstill. Vietnam was to have little effect on China, whereas Korea became a major trading partner over the millennia, supplying ginseng and other medicinal goods as well as more prosaic items, and China in turn sent fine cloth, ceramics, and other manufactured goods.On the whole, China reached a natural limit to its size, which has stood even until today. The only major extension since Han has been the Qing Dynasty incorporation of Tibet

The Chinese world-system was established: a huge, rich, powerful core depending on extremely advanced agriculture, surrounded by smaller but unconquerable states and peoples who slowly came to adopt much of Chinese culture but retained very different languages and rather distinctive arts, folkways, and foods. China had begun a long and fateful dominance over, and mixed response to, eastern Central Asia. Han cities in the Central Asian deserts still survive in ruins preserved with astonishing fidelity by the desert climate. Explorers in the nineteenth century could simply walk into buildings and pick up (some would say loot) the Han records and goods from exactly where they had been left 2,000 years before.

Han Foodways

As evidenced by archaeology and textual research, Chinese food suddenly came out of the shadows in the Han Dynasty. Apparently this was a time of major innovation and diversity, with everything from European grape varieties to the wok entering China (E. Anderson 1988). Fermentation technology seems to have spread, and developed technically. Even distillation seems to have occurred in Han, although it did not become common or well-known till Tang (H. Huang 2000).

Han saw the institutionalization of the "ever-normal granary" system (Li Linna 2007: 167), borrowed by the United States in the 1930s and developed there into the agricultural subsidy system. The major advances in agriculture in Han deserve further consideration (see Bray 1984).

Farming, of course, paid no better than it had when Lü Buwei warned against it. Chao Cuo in 154 BC talked in similar terms of the dismal life of farmers, though landlords had it easy. Farms averaged perhaps seven or eight acres (Lewis 2007: 110–11), but the average meant little, since farms obviously tended toward a few large ones and many small ones, as is true through so much of history.

Irrigation works, water and soil conservation, and seed-saving methods were developed. Moldboard plows with some iron bladework had been in China since perhaps 500 CE; before that, the ordinary ard plow had been known since time immemorial—or at least we have no real knowledge of when it arrived in China, presumably from the Near East. With advancing iron technology, plows with entirely cast-iron blades were developed in Han (Wang Zhongshu 1982). In fact, early Han saw, in the words of French world-historian Philippe Beaujard, "the invention of paper, the appearance of iron plows equipped with various types of moldboards, the invention of a multi-tube seed drill, of a rotary winnowing fan . . . , the use of various water wheels, and the invention of the driving belt, notably used in the winding machines of the textile industry" (2010: 31). All these were world-class inventions: they affected the world economy profoundly in the subsequent millennia.

An almost equally epochal invention was the agricultural extension manual. Fan Shengzi's book, the first known government-sponsored guide to agricultural methods (Shih 1974), has amazingly sophisticated directions for water conservation in dry lands, for selecting and protecting seeds, and in general for efficient farming that maximizes output for minimal input. This philosophy of farming remained the rule throughout Chinese history; F. H.

King's great work *Farmers of Forty Centuries* (1911) reflects exactly the same basic strategy. Chinese farmers learned to husband every drop of water, every bit of soil, and every shred of fertility, using these as efficiently as possible to maximize yields. Such agriculture was skill-intensive and labor-intensive; people used hard, knowledge-informed work to compensate for poor resource endowment. This did not, of course, protect the land entirely, but my personal sense is that the horrific erosion and other problems of the twentieth century probably have more to do with wars, civil unrest, and rampant exploitation of the people than with farmers' carelessness.

Spectacular tomb finds, especially at Mawangdui, have revolutionized the study of Han food. The Mawangdui tombs date from around 163 BCE. Careful embalming and subsequent burial in an anaerobic bog environment resulted in extremely good preservation not only of bodies and vessels (superb lacquerware is illustrated in H. Huang 2000: 101) but also of texts and individual food items. Many of the texts were medical (Harper 1998), and there is now a considerable scholarly literature on them (notably relevant to food is Lo 2001). Along with general principles, sexual hygiene, exercises ancestral to *tai ji* and *qi gong*, these medical texts provide much information about diet therapy and plant drugs. Many actual medicines are buried along with the texts—a dream come true for those of us who long agonized over what the old drug names "really meant" in botanical terms. Unsurprisingly, they usually meant what the same names mean now.

Almost as momentous was the discovery of two sets of distilling vessels dating from around 100 CE (give or take a few decades; see H. Huang 2000: 209–15). These predate by centuries the earliest previously known stills (which are also from China). Apparently the Chinese invented distillation. (An anonymous reader has pointed out that India also has a claim on inventing distillation and early use of distilled drinks; Paul Buell, who has been studying this issue, per email of March 28, 2013, responds that India may well have independently invented distillation at the same time as China, and there is even a fair chance that Mexico independently invented it shortly before European contact. It is not an incredibly difficult thing to invent.) Distilled liquor became common in Tang.

Another oft-claimed Han innovation is bean curd. Soy sauces had long been known, and liquid soy sauce as we know it may have been popularized in Han or just before (though there are no clear references till Ming!). However, bean curd (tofu) seems not to have been common until much later. A tomb from Han shows a quite clear representation of making bean curd or something very similar (H. Huang 2000: 305–33). Still, one wonders why references to bean curd remain totally nonexistent until the end of Tang. If bean curd was indeed a Han invention, it stayed amazingly obscure. One would think that such indefatigable chroniclers of foodways as Jia Sixie and Tao Hongjing could not possibly have missed it. H. Huang (2000: 333) is probably right in speculating that the process was "still undergoing development." The perfection of bean curd must have waited till Tang.

Yet another new product seems to have been tea. Tea is native to what is now far southwest China, but that area was not part of the Han Empire. Tea was an import. It is infrequently and doubtfully mentioned in Han but becomes better known in subsequent centuries and was common and well known by mid-Tang (see H. Huang 2000: 503ff. for the best history). The problem comes from the use of the word "tea" in ancient China, as in modern English, to refer to herbal drinks as well as to those from *Camellia sinensis*.

Han armies preserved meat—even rats—by drying, grain by parching or boiling and then grinding for meal (see Sinoda 1977: 486), and food in general by chilling. Fish could be preserved by fermenting with rice, which contains sugars that decompose into lactic acid that preserved the fish (487). This technique is still used in preserving food.

Literary sources provide diverse descriptions of food (Knechtges 1986), and some sources preserve less favorable impressions of minority foodways. Women married off to "barbarians," that is, steppe nomads, complained of "rancid mutton that to me was completely revolting" and "raw meat and koumiss" (attr. to Cai Yan, cited by Idema and Grant 2004: 122–23). Chances are that the mutton was neither raw nor particularly rancid, but obviously the fine court styles of Han were unknown on the frontier.

Folktales of nutrition leading to power—whether physical, magical, or spiritual—are as old as China. The Mawangdui texts have revealed a tremendous store of nutritional medicine, earlier and more elaborate than anyone thought (Harper 1998). Many (probably most) of the common medicinal foods were known and used then in about the same ways as they are now.

Another revealing burial was that of Emperor Wen of Nanyue (r. 137–123 BCE). The Nanyue kingdom was founded by a general of Qin. He had been sent to conquer Lingnan—modern Guangdong and Guangxi—and when Qin fell, he decided to set himself up as an independent king. Nominally a tributary to Han, he acted as a fully independent emperor. His son was less fortunate; Han Wu Di ended Nanyue in 111. The Nanyue kingdom thus became ruled by Han Chinese, but its people were Thai, with perhaps including some

Vietnamese and Austronesians. Nanyue Wen Di's tomb was hidden so well that although it was in the city of Guangzhou, it was never found until the hill in which it lay was sliced off for construction in the 1980s. The tomb is rather small, as ancient royal tombs go, but was crowded with vast amounts of gold, jade, precious stones, bronzes (including sets of bells), horse and chariot gear, and dishes (Li Linna 2007).

Of concern to us here is the food. Bronze vessels had held ale, stews, and soups. Two bronze grills—square, with a bronze floor for holding charcoal— were found; apparently meat was cooked over the coals on skewers, as with modern satay. More than two hundred skeletons of yellow-breasted buntings were found. These birds were extremely common in winter in the area until Mao Zedong's anti-sparrow campaign in the 1950s, when they became casualties because of their fondness for rice. (They also were fond of insect pests, however, and exterminating them caused terrible outbreaks of pests.) Medicines included the five colors: sulfur (yellow), realgar (red), purple crystal (black), ochre (yellow again—white is missing in this set), and turquoise (greenblue).

Perhaps the most interesting find was a considerable quantity of frankincense. The amount of this Arab-world import in the tomb of a small-scale backwater warlord is really astonishing. Trade with the Near East is confirmed by a large Persian silver bowl with cover, and some Persian (or at least Persianstyle) goldwork. Evidently, Guangzhou had already assumed the role of trading port with the Near East that would made it famous in Tang times. China's sea trade with the West was important earlier than we realized.

Han Food and Medicine

The classics of Chinese medicine that appeared during the Han Dynasty have been reanalyzed (notably by Paul Unschuld, e.g., 1986, 2003; see also Lo 2005 and several translations of traditional Chinese medical texts have been made (Sun Guangren et al. 1990; Zhang Wengao et al. 1990; Zhang Zhongqing 1987, 1993).

One thing that emerges is that these works (like medical textbooks everywhere) were revised regularly and do not necessarily resemble the original, any more than latest edition of *Gray's Anatomy* resembles the original work by Henry Gray in 1858. Thus the description and effective treatment of beriberi and the description of an effective oral rehydration therapy in Zhang

Zhungjing's *Shang Han Lun* (H. Hsu and Peacher 1981; Zhang Zhongqing 1993) may be Zhang's or may be later additions. Also, we are not sure that the alleged (but far from proven) derivation of the Yellow Emperor's term *huoluan* from the Greek word *cholera* is as early as Han; if so, it would constitute a uniquely early borrowing. Since these prescriptions or recommendations are extremely important historically—being by far the earliest descriptions of precise, effective food therapy in Asia—we need to know.

References to what seems to be beriberi occur early, with a strikingly good clinical description in 610 (H. Huang 2000: 580–81; this probably really is not later than 610, since it is preserved as a long quote in another early work, not as a part of an updated textbook.)

Common in classical times, and by no means extinct today, is the theory that eating grain feeds the corpse worms that are latent in all of us, shortening our lives and waiting to devour us when we die. This belief apparently stemmed from equating parasitic worms with maggots. It led to the conclusion that abstaining from grain would lengthen life. Reading old texts makes it fairly clear that people were observing the negative effects of a purely grain diet—deficiencies of iron, vitamin A, vitamin C, and other nutrients. They were quite aware that a diet rich in pine seeds and other high-nutrient foods corrected this. They thus tried to live entirely without grain—a logical overreaction. The locus classicus for this and other food myths came shortly after the fall of Han, in Ge Hong's *Bao Pu Zi* (Uncarved Block Master, fourth century CE; Ware 1966; Ge's other book, *Traditions of Divine Transcendents*, has recently been translated by Robert Campany, 2002). Ge advised people that pine seeds, wild herbs, and alchemically produced elixirs are necessary to long life.

Han Central Asia

At the start of Han, the north and west were dominated by large steppe empires—not by any means entirely "nomadic." Much of the region was conquered from Mongolia around 200 BCE by the Xiongnu, who had long been important in the area (Chang Chun-shu 2007b: 4).

It seems clear that the early Central Asian empires were multilingual, like Central Asian empires throughout history. No doubt Indo-European, Altaic, Sino-Tibetan, and other groups were involved in founding and peopling these empires. Groups like the Qiang, a fascinating and obscure Tibeto-Burman group, were powerful on the western frontiers, centered in modern Chinghai and Sichuan. (The current Qiang are only one part of the descendants of the ancient ones. Other Tibeto-Burman groups like the Lolo-Hani family trace their ancestry back to them; Wang Jianhua 2013.)

Central Asian empires, then and later, rose and fell at about the same time that neighboring settled ones did (Barfield 1989). The steppe empires fed off the settled ones through trade and raid. These two economic processes are often contrasted, but actually they form a continuum, and the relations of steppe and agrarian empires shows that fact well. Trade easily slid into "protection" (in the Mafia sense) whenever one empire was stronger than the other(s). Protection easily slid into raid, and raid was easily turned into trade, especially if the richer empire was weaker and could simply buy off the raiders with promises of ongoing economic activity. Border areas were always vulnerable, especially any cultivation there. Steppe empires always had settled agricultural zones, sometimes large and vital ones, and the agrarian empires could devastate these easily unless stopped by force. Even a weak agrarian empire could thus devastate a strong steppe empire.

Steppe empires could put pressure on two or three fronts alternately—raiding from Europe to Transoxania to China. Few except the much later Mongols could manage all three, and nobody managed to deal on any scale with all three plus India. (The Mongols tried with some success; Tamerlane later tried and failed.) However, knock-on effects from the China borderlands could lead ultimately to chaos on the Roman frontiers. If some fraction of the Xiongnu did indeed become part of the Hun war machine (see below), such effects began early. It then showed itself in the Rouran/Avar migration and in the countless excursions of Turks and Mongols. This had negative consequences on food production at the time but also led to foods and agricultural techniques being shared all across Asia by the end of Han.

Han conquered Central Asia, thus bringing this previously "West-oriented" region into the Chinese orbit. Settlement and administration followed (J. Mallory and Mair 2000). The Xiongnu Empire in early Han times occupied what are now Outer and Inner Mongolia, northeast and northwest China, and far southeast Russia. It threatened Han from the northwest, extending its control to the mountains north of the Wei Valley, and often striking down the river valleys that transect those mountains (Li Feng 2006). This allowed the Xiongnu to come very close to taking Chang'an on two occasions.

At this time, the Xiongnu held some 2 million square miles of territory with 3.5 million people; Han had only 1.5 million square miles (Chang Chun-shu 2007a: 158). Much of the Xiongnu realm was taiga inhabited by only a few wild hunting tribes. Still, the empire was rich and powerful. It included irrigated oases, fairly rich rain-fed farmlands, and highly productive upland forests. Farming was important and the southern parts of the realm had many large settlements. Recall that the Dadiwan area, just east of Lanzhou, was warm, wet, and lush, with warm-temperate forests, in the third and fourth millennia BCE; the Xiongnu lived in a somewhat less lush time, but still a time when the western loess plateaus were not the dismally dry and barren landscapes they are today. Xiongnu country had a great deal of fine farmland, and they did not neglect it. There was a lack of metal tools in some areas, but this does not mean there was no farming; it merely means the tools were usually of wood.

The traditional Chinese, and Sinological, view has always been that these steppe societies consisted of nomads, wandering at random with their flocks over vast steppes. In fact, nomads never do this. They have specific routes where they know they can find water and forage. They have camping areas for long stays in winter and summer. Moreover, the great Central Asian empires incorporated vast areas of farmland, ranging from marginal to rich, and grew many agricultural products. The recent view is that they were mixed economies in which the elite may have had nomadic origins but the population included nomads, transhumants, farmers, and urbanites (Barfield 1989; Di Cosmo et al. 2009).

Archaeology reveals that the Xiongnu did not deserve to be stereotyped by the Chinese as uncouth nomadic barbarians (Li Feng 2006; Rogers 2007). They were an urbane and civilized folk, having shared in East Asian civilization from long residence in what are now Shanxi, Shaanxi, Gansu, and neighboring core provinces of China. The nobility evidently traced descent from nomadic herding peoples.

The population of the Xiongnu lands was mixed. East met West biologically: three people buried together 2,000 years ago in high-status tombs included two whose skeletons and DNA are typical East Asian and one who was equally typical European (K. Kim et al. 2010)! The last was probably a Tocharian, but could, for all we know, have been a Germanic traveler or Iranian ambassador. In any case, we know the population of what is now Xinjiang and areas west of it was a zone of gradation, as Afghanistan and northwest Pakistan are today, with West and East Asian populations meeting and mixing.

Modern scholars, including Sanping Chen (2012: 90), speak of "mixed races." Central Asia has always been mixed. It is a meeting ground of West and

East and thus of broadly Caucasian and East Asian peoples. And the idea that the Chinese are *not* a mixed population is silly. They have been absorbing immigrants from the north, west, and south since eastern Asia was first settled. Meeting, mingling, and mixing European-type and East Asian-type physical stocks in Central Asia is a fact, established since the first human settlements there. One sees it in any Kabul market, and indeed in any west-central Asian city today, or among the Tatars of far west Xinjiang. Genetics shows that mixing goes back to the Neanderthals and Denisovans (at least Denisovan genes are common in modern populations to the far southeast).

The word "Xiongnu" is apparently the same as our "Hun," the Xiongnu being called *xwn* in a contemporary document, a Sogdian letter from Dunhuang around 313 CE (Hansen 2012: 117; Vaissière 2005: 43–45; see also Golden 2011: 33, 149). One letter seems a bit like the proverbial one swallow that does not make a summer, but this equation does seem reasonably definite. The Mongolian language refers to the Xiongnu as *hunnu* to this day. But the Xiongnu language, known from a few words transcribed by Chinese writers of the time, seems unrelated to any living language. Many languages have been claimed as relatives, but on far too little evidence. The Huns of Roman Empire fame used quite different languages: Turkic and Gothic ("Attila" is from the East Gothic word for "little father"). The Xiongnu fell before the Huns made an appearance, and of course there is a 5,000-mile gap to explain. Apparently the name, the general steppe cultural traits, and probably a few lineages of nomadic fighters were shared between the urbane, Sinicized Xiongnu and the wild, unruly, but militarily successful Huns (cf. Maenchen-Helfen 1973).

The Xiongnu are known primarily from references in early histories, especially that of Sima Qian (ca. 145–86 BCE), the Grand Historian, innovator of narrative history in China. A notably sympathetic observer of human affairs, even "barbarian" ones, he provided a much less biased account than did later writers. He noted that the Xiongnu practiced the levirate (to the astonishment and shock of Han Chinese), claimed descent of their royal family from the Xia Dynasty, and lived relatively wandering lives. In marked contrast to the Han Chinese, the Xiongnu gave the best food and clothing to young men rather than to the elderly. Sima, who preferred to seek out explanations rather than simply saying other ways were uncouth, reported that the Xiongnu told a Han envoy that the young needed it to fight to protect both young and old (Chin 2010)—a sentiment repeated in our own time in various martial societies.

Sima's attitude toward "barbarians" may have been typical of the time. He and others before Song and Yuan seem markedly less xenophobic and ethnicist than later Chinese—let alone Westerners. He did, however, have little respect for non-Chinese mores. He and almost all (if not all) early writers also clearly exaggerated the degree to which these empires depended on nomadic stock rearing (Di Cosmo 1994). As in Zhou times, the Chinese of Han had many words for ethnic non-Chinese: Rong, Hu, Yue, Man, and so forth. All these terms had specific referents—they are usually hard to pin down today but evidently were clear enough to writers of that time. Translating them all as "barbarian" is clearly inadequate. It also leads, inevitably, to back-projecting Western biases on early materials that do not have those biases.

Emperor Wu carried the fight to the enemy. In 129 BCE, he launched a major assault on the Xiongnu Empire. He learned he had to develop cavalry and thus supplies of horses and fodder. This he managed to do on a quite major scale (Chang Chun-shu 2007a: 176–80). In 104–101 BCE, his "army of over 70,000 soldiers, 100,000 oxen, and 30,000 horses marched over the Pamirs into Central Asia" (2). The army marched right through the Xiongnu Empire and reached Ferghana and Samarkand. China sent envoys to Rome, or at least in that direction. Over the years, the Martial Emperor hammered Central Asia with "over 1.2 million cavalrymen, 800,000 foot soldiers, and 0.5 million men in support and logistic roles" (2). China added to its territory the major part of what is now Xinjiang ("New Borders," or "New Territories").

The decline of the Xiongnu profited the Xianbei, who had established an enormous empire centering on Mongolia and expanded at the expense of the Xiongnu. (They may have spoken a Mongol language; Golden 2011: 31–33.) The Xianbei remain shadowy in spite of some coverage in Han annals. Their steppe empire or confederacy presumably included Turkic and Mongol groups as well as others more obscure.

In the 120s BCE, Wu Di sent one Zhang Qian west to try to form an alliance with the Yuezhi, a shadowy tribe of Central Asia. Zhang was captured by the Xiongnu but eventually reached the Yuezhi and cut a deal of some sort—but it bore little fruit. He seems to have introduced grapes and alfalfa to China on his return. Contrary to imaginative history, neither he nor any other known Han traveler reached the Roman Empire, nor did Rome have anything to do with the Han (Hansen 2012: 12ff.). Hansen points out that Roman coins abound in southern India, but there are none in China until mid-Byzantine times, and even then, very few. The Silk Road was an active concern by Zhang's time, but it did not allow much long-distance direct contact. It was not heavily traveled, and few if any travelers went all the way across Asia on it. The Yuezhi may have evolved into, or more likely joined with, the Kushans, a group that moved down from Central Asia into what is now Pakistan. The Kushans borrowed Hellenistic sculpture styles, adapted them to Buddhism, and thus created the Buddhist sculpture-in-the-round tradition, still dominant throughout eastern Asia.

A significant moment in history came when both Zhang and the Roman writers noted the fall of the Greco-Bactrian kingdom around 130 BCE, the first historical fact to be noted in both West and East (Christian 2000). Actually, a quite different polity, the kingdom called Shanshan in Chinese, and Kroraina in its own language (of obscure affiliation), occupied eastern Xinjiang, from Lop Nor to near Khotan. The name Kroraina was sinicized as Loulan, and used for the small capital city. Mummified remains show that the inhabitants (or at least many of them) were Caucasian in physical type, with sandy or red hair, pale skin, and a tall build. They raised some silk but depended largely on China for this commodity (Hansen 2012: 32–39). The kingdom was small and economically humble, but its place on the Silk Road made it important.

Han conquered Kroraina in 108 BCE and occupied the area, settling troops there. The resulting mixed-ethnic population ate almonds and walnuts, grew grains and fruit, including "grapes, pears, peaches, pomegranates and dates"; irrigation and plow agriculture were developed further, and metal tools introduced (Hansen 2012: 42). Historians claim the Han introduced irrigation, but this is clearly not the case; agriculture would have been impossible without it, and we know agriculture was important before the Han moved in.

Wu Di instituted colonization of the area by Han Chinese, thus extending to Central Asia a policy used by Qin and even earlier states. This policy is still being continued in Xinjiang by the Communist government. It may be assumed that in Han, as now, it was at the expense of the local people. Many farming garrisons were established. Chang Chun-shu (2007b: 16ff.) provides many details on promises made to the colonists; one wonders if they were kept. Han colonization increased farming in the riverine oases, but recent claims that these oases were little used before the Han conquest need confirmation. Such prime agricultural land could not have been neglected.

The conquest of Central Asia by Han led to the rise of the Silk Road as a great thoroughfare for commerce and contact. Here and later, Hansen's claim (2012) that the Silk Road was inconsequential in volume or value of trade simply cannot be sustained. She argues from lack of documents; however, as the proverb says, "absence of evidence is not evidence of absence," especially when we know that documents were destroyed wholesale. We have instead the evidence of many huge cities maintained solely on that trade. Cities were built, only to fall into ruin when Han declined. Saved by the dry climate, remnants of them still stand in Central Asia, where they were the wonder of early travelers such as Aurel Stein and Paul Pelliot.

An enormous number of documents survive, mostly as wooden slips on which missives and logs were written (Chang Chun-shu 2007b). These show, among other things, astonishingly high levels of literacy among a very broad base of the population in these remote and desolate outposts of empire. Chang (50) assembled some data on heights, and found the Han colonist adults were tall people. They averaged 169.59 cm (68 in.), statistically the same (given errors in assessing Han measurement) as the 168.5 cm recent average of the north Chinese. Then as now, China's population became shorter from northwest to southeast, with some of the world's tallest at the northwest end of the continuum and quite short and slight populations at the other end.

Colonies were limited to river and lake basins by the waterless deserts, and oases were heavily settled. In Han and today, they display a dense array of small neatly outlined fields, found largely along the upper and middle courses of desert rivers, where water is reliable and can be stored in reservoirs; the lower reaches are prone to flood, drought, and salinization. Less intensive upstream water use in Han meant that lower reaches could be more reliably productive than they are now (see Chang Chun-shu 2007b: 100–105).

These Central Asian oases—not only in China, but westward to Iran— were thus already very far from being natural habitats; they were totally managed, by irrigation technology and by farming. They were probably already leading the world in irrigation technology, as they had in the Tang Dynasty. Wildlife, such as the endemic red deer of the Aral Sea drainage and neighboring river basins, continued to flourish, showing that the habitat was not completely artificial.Even the surviving poplar forests were apparenlty used in the sustainable, resource-sparing manner seen today in parts of rural Mongolia, where substantial game populations and wild plant resources coexist with humans. (As elsewhere, the coming of modernity has led to the extermination of game and wild plant foods everywhere, *even without changes in population or technology.* We are looking at changes in ideology.)

Wheat and barley were the foods in Central Asia, with millet a very minor player, used for porridge and horse feed. It was commoner as one got nearer to China proper. The wheat and barley were ground for flour—relatively advanced milling came to China from the West during this period—and some fancy pastries were baked. A museum exhibition on the Silk Road organized by the University of Pennsylvania in 2010–2011 included a flour-and-water pastry that looks like a modern florist's chrysanthemum flower (E. Anderson 2010). However, the modern chrysanthemum had not been developed by Han times, so some other flower is evidently intended. A group of short spaghetti-like noodles, twisted together and deep-fried, was found in a Han site. I have eaten similar items in northwest China. These noodles are somewhat intermediate between the Neolithic ones noted in Chapter 1 and the well-documented noodles of later centuries. The West did not yet have any such commodity; in the Mediterranean world, noodles were invented or borrowed around 400–800 CE.

West of the Han Empire, Central Asia at this time was developing the fantastic irrigation technology that climaxed in the next few centuries (Harmatta et al. 1994; see esp. D. Hill 2000; Mukhamedjanov 1994). Complex webs of dams, diversions, and canals already covered the valleys. Important already were *qanats* (usually called *karez* in Central Asia, at least in later centuries): long tunnels, often high enough for walking, driven back into alluvial fans that fringe desert mountain ranges. Mountain streams create these alluvial fans by washing down rocks, sand, and earth. The streams sink into these fans and disappear; the water flows underground and is tapped by the qanats, which are dug at a very slight upward angle from the lower reaches of the alluvial fans. Qanat construction and repair is a highly skilled, specialized, and dangerous occupation. It has always been the specialty of a few families, who are secretive about it, leaving us less than totally knowledgeable about the technology. Qanats were invented in what are now the Iran-Iraq borderlands a few centuries BCE and spread rapidly east. Qanats (or karez) abound in the Tarim Basin but seem not to occur farther east. Outside the deserts, they would not work; rain, soft soil, and flooding make them nonviable.

They spread less rapidly west, but eventually they came to Moorish Spain and thence to central Mexico, where they thrived in the dry Tehuacan Valley. Mexican settlers brought them to San Bernardino, California, where "water tunnels" still supplied much of the city's water within living memory. Somewhat later, an Anglo-American water engineer who had worked in China introduced to the same city the concept of movable groins—huge "sausages" of rocks held together with netting, more recently with wire. These were used as movable levees or diversion dams. Thus East and Middle East met in modern southern California, as they had in the Han Dynasty in Central Asia.

CHAPTER 6

Foods from the West: Medieval China

Three Kingdoms and Northern and Southern Dynasties

In the unsettled period after the fall of Han, Chinese successor states fought each other to exhaustion, and "barbarians" conquered northern China. Starting in or before 311 CE, Central Asian states began serious conquests in China, sacking cities and later taking over all the north. The Xianbei, a group living under Xiongnu rule, emerged to acquire much of its territory when the Xiongnu state fell. Like other Central Asian empires, they ruled a clearly multicultural population. Many splinter groups went on to conquer various pieces of China and Central Asia. Victor Mair has sorted this out in a tour-de-force essay (Mair 2005), in which he notes that many of these conquerors were described as having big noses and full beards. The resulting statelets were more like nomadic chiefdoms than like Chinese dynastic states (Lewis 2009a: 72–73).

Northern China lost population, and some areas reverted to nomadic pastoralism. Although labor was in short supply for cultivation (Lewis 2009a: 78; Morris 2010: 298ff.), the north was a cultural dynamo. Buddhism and other foreign religions—notably Manichaeanism and Nestorian Christianity—flooded in. They brought a vast but now little-known freight of medicines, foods, clothing styles, and lifestyle habits with them. Again, Hansen's doubts about the levels of Silk Road trade are belied by the evidence; religions do not sweep across whole regions and profoundly influence their people and art styles without significant population fluxes and major political activity. (The "lone missionary" of heroic religious legend usually turns out to have had a powerful imperial state behind him.)

At this time, the Turkic peoples enter history. Apparently beginning as nomadic herders in the Upper Yenisei and neighboring areas, they were known as masters of metalworking. Presumably because of their skill with animals and metals, they became important components of the Xiongnu and Xianbei Empires. They then burst forth to become some of the most amazing conquerors and empire builders in the world.

The first Turkic move onto the world stage may have been the conquest of north China by the Tuoba (Tabghach), ruling as the Wei Dynasty. The Tabghach had some similarities to the Mongols too (Golden 2011: 36), but Chen Sanping has recently argued—on the basis of thin but credible evidence—that the core was Turkic, with some Mongol side groups (Chen 2012: 399–59). This would not be surprising; many or most Central Asian empires and confederations were multilingual. Wei lasted from 386 to 550 CE but held effective power only around 400–530. Like several minor earlier statelets in north China, Wei was founded by groups spinning off from the Xianbei Empire. The Tuoba clan broke out on their own as the Xianbei declined. Later, the Rouran, another mysterious people (very possibly Turkic like the Tuoba), were involved in the dynastic succession. They later moved west and were known in Europe as the Avars (Chen Sanping 2012; Golden 2011: 36).

Wei began as a typical nomad state but evolved rapidly into a true Chinese empire. Ian Morris sees them as having moved from a "low-end" state, that is, a patrimonial one based on personal ties, a nomadic, fluid organization, and a lack of developed bureaucracy and tax structure, to a "high-end" one—a centralized state with a rational bureaucracy and fiscal apparatus (Morris 2010: 336).

We have become more aware of the importance of Wei and other regimes for introducing Western and Central Asian ideas to China. Wei engaged in constant trade and diplomacy with Central Asian nomadic groups. In 520, they gave one nomad group "one thousand bushels of newly cooked rice, eighty bushels of fried [sic; evidently shao, here meaning "parched"] wheat, fifty bushels of fried [roasted] nuts, . . . two girl slaves . . . and two hundred thousand bushels of grain" (Jagchid and Simons 1989: 171, translating a Wei court document). In return, Wei received horses, livestock, furs, and the like. Contrary to Jagchid and Simons's wider point here, the nomads did not truly depend on Chinese foodstuffs. Trade was important and brought valuable commodities, but Central Asia had rich oases and some arable grasslands, and people could hold their own if they had to (Di Cosmo 1994).

Ongoing trade linked China and Central Asia throughout history but was never more important than in the 400s and 500s, when Central Asian dynasties ruled north China. The capital of Wei had a foreign quarter with up to forty to fifty thousand Central and West Asian residents, about a tenth of the population (Lewis 2009a: 115).

Immediately after the decline of Wei, the Gök (Sky or Heavenly) Turks (or Türük; Chinese *tujue*) took over the old Xiongnu-Xianbei lands and from 552 to 745 extended them, creating one of the most enormous empires in the world. Chinese sources reported that the Gök Turks descended from the Ashina tribe of the Xiongnu confederacy. Ashina seems to have been the name of the ruling dynasty, and probably comes from an Indo-European word for "blue" (probably the same root as "azure"). It seems that Ashina was translated as *gök*, "sky-blue," which itself was then borrowed into Mongol, probably as *kök*, now *khökh*. The names of Turkic groups in later times usually are after a powerful leader who organized a particular group along kinship lines or simply through personal attraction. Modern terms like "Ottoman" (from Osman) and "Uzbek" have this origin. We do not know if this was the case with the early groups. The Gök supposedly descended from the mating of a she-wolf with a human founder (Golden 2011: 37). Altaic and other Eurasian heroes often descend from wolves, and the Mongols were said to be descended from the mating of a gray wolf and a fallow doe (see below). These myths are metaphors that describe the savage fighting abilities of the peoples in question.

Climate deterioration resulted in the migration of peoples and agricultural shifts during this period. Crops changed according to rainfall, and farmed areas expanded or contracted. The size and depth of the Aral Sea have fluctuated greatly over the years. At some periods it even drains into the Caspian. It was at a low from 400 to 600 (Brite 2011; Brite and Khozhaniyazov 2010). Dewatering led to reduction or loss of wheat and barley cultivation. Farmers focused instead on foxtail and panic millet, cotton, and grapes. The Aral Sea region was abandoned by farmers around 400–600. Livestock were still raised, however, including pigs, which need a good deal of water.

Within China, kinship relations changed: lineages, tomb-temples, and graveyards grew more like those of later millennia. Individual small families were aggregated into huge oligarchic clans; however, more modern lineage systems (which more narrowly and exactly specify paternal relations) began their development at this time (Ebrey 1978; Johnson 1977; Lewis 2009a), which climaxed in Song. The great clans arose from leading landlord and court families of respectable age, but one has to assume that the clan organization of the Central Asians had some influence. The lineage system also had Chinese analogues. Its development over the centuries into a highly organized, bureaucratic, rule-guided institution seems to be an endogenous development, stimulated by the development of the bureaucratic empire. It imitated the latter's reliance on rules and local land ownership. It was also shaped by the imperial government's secular trend of suppressing aristocratic clans with hereditary privileges and great landed estates acquired as patrimonies and held in near-feudal conditions. The lineages held more modest, conventionally acquired lands—purchased or donated, and then passed on by ordinary inheritance.

Stirrups appeared in China at this time, the first known representation being in 322, with a real stirrup found in a burial in 415 (Lewis 2009a: 60). Stirrups greatly increased the effectiveness of horse-riding, especially cavalry.

Trade with and exploration of the south was also important. Ji Han's early herbal from 304 CE, *Nanfang Caomu Juang* (Southern plants and trees), gives startlingly accurate and modern accounts of many south Chinese and Southeast Asian products (Li Hui-Lin 1979). This work, too, had its revised editions, however, and not all the plants were necessarily well known as early as 304. The book includes the areca palm under its Bahasa Indonesia/Malaysia name, *pinang* (borrowed via ancestral Hokkien as *pinnang*; the modern Mandarin is *binlang*). This plant had already been attested in a late Han source (Beaujard 2009: 308). Ji Han also described many other southern plants, including sugar cane and the *Canarium album* tree, whose pickled fruit is known as Chinese olive and whose seed kernels resemble pine nuts and, even more, the closely related pilipili nuts of the Philippines. Ji Han repeats the old story that the sweet orange (*Citrus sinensis*) turns into the bitter, worthless trifoliate orange (*Poncirus trifoliatus*) when grown north of the Yangzi. What actually happens is that the trees are grafted. Hard freezes, which occur north of the Yangzi Valley, kill the sensitive sweet-orange scion wood, leaving the worthless, thorny trifoliate-orange rootstock to grow and proliferate. This was a common sight in California before global warming, and I have seen it happen in my own garden. My part of California got its citrus knowledge—grafting, trifoliate stock, and all—from Chinese immigrants.

In spite of violent and unsettled times, agriculture and gardening progressed, partly because of the influx of West Asian crops and techniques. Double-cropping of rice was known in the south (Lewis 2009a: 116), as was the single-ox plow, still common today, but then a new idea. It replaced a large plow requiring two oxen (121–23). Some of these plows had moldboards; all could probably turn sod. Harrowing and rolling were practiced.

The sixth century CE proved a major watershed, at least in regard to production of books. Tao Hongjing (456–536), a polymath rather like Leonardo da Vinci, dominated intellectual life in the advanced cities and temples of the southeast. His epochal work on botany, chemistry, alchemy, nutrition, Daoism, and medicine remains to be seriously monographed in Western languages.

An enormous and vitally important landmark of the period was Jia Sixie's encyclopedic *Qi Min Yao Shu*, a product of the declining days of Wei (Bray 1984; Dien 2007: 349–63; Shih 1974; major studies of this work by Françoise Sabban and other scholars are imminently expected and will revolutionize our knowledge of Chinese food history). Jia was writing for landlords and had farms of forty or fifty acres (16–20 ha) in mind (Bray 1984; Lewis 2009a: 120). Most farmers had smaller holdings, of course. Around three to five hectares was a small farmer's ideal; many, if not most, farms would have been even smaller. Jia talks much of clearing land. At this time most of north China and more and more of central China was deforested, though the far south was almost untouched. Jia was aware of needs for conservation and resource management and also that "ampler harvest can be achieved by less effort if the climatic rules are followed and the land suitability is taken into play" (Shi 2010: 159. Tian Shi's discussion emphasizes China's long tradition of sustainable agriculture.

In addition to the usual crops, Jia mentions pomegranates, evidently newly come from the Near East. He lists "thirty-one vegetables," including "cucumbers, pickling melons, musk melons, . . . wax gourd, calabashes, purple-flower garlic, . . . onions, scallions, Chinese chives, radishes, Chinese cabbage, white mustard, yellow seed mustard, . . . coriander, basil, water dropwort, eggplant, ginger, and Japanese peppers" as well as mallows, turnip-like roots, and other crops (Dien 2007: 360–61). Particularly noteworthy are his detailed instructions on fermentation: soy, vinegar, pickling, fish and meat pickles, and even fermented dairy products (H. Huang 2000).

Jia was aware of the importance of selecting the best seed and of presoaking it in various preparations of fertilizer and insecticide (Bray 1984: 245ff.), but these ideas were not new. Newer was a seeder, ancestral to modern ones. Rice was already being transplanted, transplantation having been first mentioned in late Han (Bray 1984; Lewis 2009a: 123–34). Jia was an expert on fertilizers. He gives us the first mention in China of green manures—beans plowed in before fruiting to get all the benefit of their nitrogen fixation—and discusses animal manures in detail. He also discusses crop rotation, describing several rotation systems. Grain was stored in pits;

Jia recommends parboiling millet to preserve it (it spoils easily). He details an enormous number of recipes for preserving food by salting, pickling, fermenting, and drying; early food preservationhas been the subject of major research (see, e.g., Huang 2000. Although living far in the northwest, he was aware of "lichees, loquats, bananas, and coconuts" as well as many varieties of more local fruits (Lewis 2009a:125).

Jia provides a recipe for duck that may be the first recipe involving stir-frying (So 1992: 23). The duck is cooked with spring onions, salt, and black bean sauce, and the directions make it clear that stir-frying is involved. Jia also gives a recipe for "golden pig"—roast pig with stuffing and a glaze that gives it a golden color when roasted (23–24). This dish is still necessary for any major fortunate-occasion ritual in southeast China.

Other recipes of the time, found in various works, range from water-lily soup and black bean sauce to congee with bean powder, minced fish, and meat dishes. One source claims that the nape of the neck of a steamed pig was reserved for the emperor (Dien 2007: 362). Presumably this was on the same logic that the native people of the Northwest Coast of North America used in reserving the corresponding part of a big fish for the chief: it is the highest part of the animal. Physical height seems to symbolize social "height" in every culture on earth; it is a natural metaphor.

At this time, milling became mechanized on a large scale. Buddhist monasteries, among other estate owners, milled grain and pressed oils (Lewis 2009a: 126; presumably from rapeseed, and possibly soybeans). Water mills were typical.

Elite gardens flourished and included many economic resources as well as strictly ornamental ones (Lewis 2009a: 86–90). Travel literature and garden poetry developed considerably. The two leading figures in the new literature could not have been more different. Xie Lingyun, the true father of Chinese travel writing, was an arrogant landlord who drove his armies of slaves to exhaustion working on his endless garden projects. Like Jia, he speaks of much clearing. Tao Yuanming, though of elite ancestry, was a retired farmer who lived in poverty and brewed his own beer, staying drunk when possible and writing rustic poems. He sometimes exaggerated his poverty and remoteness for effect, but he did not have an easy life. An early poem speaks of a couple of retainers; this mention has led some hasty readers to label him well-off, but his later poems do not mention the retainers, and instead describe major losses and serious want.

Tea entered China by this time; it is attested by 273 (Lewis 2009a: 126).

Chinese scholars have long maintained that it was known in Han, and this seems virtually certain.

Sui and Tang

China was finally unified, once again, with final Sui victory in 581, by one of the most striking figures in its long history (Wright 1978). Sui Yang Di was a powerful, brooding, intense, driven, remote warlord, a general in the constantly warring northern border country. Like many other northern aristocrats and military leaders, he had "barbarian" ancestry and rose from the ranks of the northwest frontier military. He was devoted to his lifelong principal wife, making her full coregent and slighting other women. I suspect this hastened the dynasty's downfall; the great lords all wished to ally themselves to him by marrying their daughters and sisters to him, in classic dynastic style. He rejected these offers, which, I suspect, turned the lords against him.

He and his wife were powerful enough to hold the dynasty together while they lived, but his son was weaker, and was soon displaced by yet another northwest-frontier general—the founder of Tang. The fall of Sui may be the greatest case in history of an empire destroyed by true love. The less romantic, however, hold that Sui Yang Di's remoteness and uncompromising nature were the problem. Either way, he alienated enough leading figures to provide the Tang rebels with a large, disaffected group of allies.

Sui Yang Di's greatest monument was the Grand Canal, China's lifeline in imperial centuries, now being rebuilt. He assembled it from earlier canals, channels, and plans. It runs for 1,500 miles, connecting the Yangzi with the north. In its glory days, it was possibly the world's greatest commercial artery, with entire cities and local governments depending on it in the way small towns in rural America now depend on freeways. Both the great cities at the termini and the small cities along it grew and thrived. It moved incredible amounts of grain, as well as luxuries of every sort, to say nothing of armies, scholars going for imperial examinations, traveling merchants, and other mobile citizenry. It is, today, going through yet another of its periodic refurbishments to clean out muck and pollution.

An analysis of the remains of one Yu Hong, buried in Taiyuan (northwest China) in 592, indicated European-type DNA (Morris 2010: 342). Was he a traveler from Europe, or simply a Tocharian from the near west? The Turks had taken over inner Asia by this time, replacing the Xianbei and Rouran and as-similating the Tocharians, but large Tocharian communities survived, speaking at least two, and probably three, closely related languages (see, e.g., Golden 2011: 55; J. Mallory and Mair 2000). From chairs to food to travelers, China was Westernizing fast—faster than it would do again until the twentieth century, when "the West" was a very different place indeed.

The Tang royalty, like the Sui before them, were at the very least thor-oughly Central Asianized by long service on the frontiers. They have long been thought to have had Wei blood, and now Chen Sanping (2012) has made a serious case for both the Sui and the Tang royal families to be straight de-scendants of the Wei elite—Turkic rulers of a united China. If so, they would certainly shift China's medieval history to one of Altaic conquests.

By the time of the Tang Dynasty (620–907 CE), Persians were selling breads on the street, and restaurants had waitresses with white skins and blue eyes (Schafer 1963; Sinoda 1977: 488). What is now Xinjiang was dominated by this time by Turkic peoples, notably the Uighurs, and Eastern Iranic groups, nota-bly the Sogdians, dominated Central Asia (Vaissière 2005). The Sogdians had an enormous mercantile network, going back to Han times, with merchants living in China for years. It seems to have been similar to early merchant net-works elsewhere, from ancient Assyrian (Beaujard 2009) to the amazing net-work of the Julfa Armenians in Abbasid Iran (Aslanian 2011). The Sogdians even had outposts in central Shanxi, where they were called the Jie Hu (Lewis 2009b: 82–83). (*Hu* generally meant Iranic peoples, but sometimes included Turks.) In Tang Xinjiang, Sogdian and the Tocharian languages were widely spoken. Central Asian influences at the time ranged from chairs (Fitzgerald 1965) to polo.

Bactrian camels carried a great deal of the load, and the Chinese loved to make beautiful and superbly executed pottery sculptures of them, often bur-ied as tomb furnishings—presumably to keep the deceased supplied with camel-borne luxuries. These camels have become favorites of modern art col-lectors worldwide. Elfriede Knauer (1998) describes their loads, which ranged from silk—of course—to glassware, silver dishes, garments, and even game and birds. Whole bands of musicians were often mounted on them. Knauer notes that today the camels more often carry yurts, salt, rocks, and other mun-dane loads, as they surely did in Tang also—but artists did not bother with such lowly matters. (I have seen camels hauling dirt carts in modern China and *ger*—yurts—in Mongolia.)

The Tang Dynasty was China's great period of contact with western Asia and also dealt with the remote south; mutual influences created a single cultural sphere, and China became much more a cultural center than it had been in Han (Lewis 2009b; Schafer 1963, 1967, 1977). More important was Buddhism (Sen 2003); many Buddhists arrived from India and Central Asia, and several Chinese made long pilgrimages to those lands. The most famous of the latter was Xuanzang, partly because he recorded the story of his travels in 629–645 (Xuanzang 1996), and his story led to the rise of increasingly wonderful and fantastic folklore that grew into Wu Cheng-En's great Qing Dynasty novel *The Journey to the West*. Envoys from the Muslim world came as early as 651 (Tan 2009: 81).

Major trade in medicines also took place, but they did not always provide beneficial results. In 648 the emperor Tang Taizong patronized a Buddhist longevity doctor, apparently from India, with unfortunate results: Taizong died at forty-nine in 649, and the doctor of longevity also passed on (Sen 2003: 47–48)—"Physician, heal thyself!" This incident did not help the cause of transnational translational medicine, but apparently did not hurt it deeply either, and ingestion of Indian medicines remained involved in the notorious deaths of late Tang emperors (49). Direct exchanges between China and India tailed off after early Song, but contacts continued. Extensive overland and maritime trade flourished, with Muslim traders and merchants becoming more numerous. Sugar and its related technology came from India, probably in Tang, and partly via Buddhist contacts (204–5). This point is interesting because it would have to have been via sea; the overland route was too cold and dry for sugarcane, and transferring the technology without the plant itself would not have been possible.

Arabs and Central Asian Muslims settled in far west China. The Central Asians—Persians, Sogdians, Uighurs, and others—were the most numerous, important, and influential foreigners. Central Asia became enough of an information highway to require useful phrasebooks translating, for instance, from Sanskrit to Khotanese; an example (Sen 2003: 86) shows that travelers' phrasebooks were as moronic then as they are today. ("Did you duly see the king or not? —I duly saw him. —Now where are you going?"). The Sogdian heyday lasted from around 500 CE, or earlier, to the mid-700s, when An Lushan's rebellion disrupted trade.

Ever seeking Central Asian influences, Chen Sanping makes a good case for the heroine Mulan and her ballad (famous enough to inspire a Disney movie) having been more Central Asian than Chinese in inspiration. It certainly does read like a Central Asian epic, and I find Chen convincing. He also has evidence that the Tang poet Bai Juyi had Central Asian ancestry. At the very least, China had a fusion culture in which Central Asia and the Yue- and Tai-influenced south seemed more important than anything we would recognize as "Chineseness."

Sea trade to the south, and onward to India, became important, but it was still uncommon and poorly enough routinized to be genuinely dangerous (see Hansen 2012: 164). We have records from Buddhist monks of long, storm-tossed journeys. Much of this trade was in non-Chinese hands. Arabs, Persians, and later Indian and Southeast Asian Muslims settled in and around Guangzhou. There were enough of them to cause a riot in 758; rumor said they should go home to their origin countries because they had been too close to pigs and pork-eaters in China (Tan 2009: 82). All these peoples, of course, brought major foreign influences. Sea trade also extended to Japan. Many items sent as gifts to the Japanese royal family survive in the Shōsō-in storehouse at Nara, which houses the treasures of the Emperor Shōmu (701–756) (Itoh 1973). These include some medicines with labels, which, like the Mawangdui tomb finds, provide useful truth control on translating early drug names into modern scientific equivalents.

Tang fell in 907, at a time of worldwide drought (P. Zhang et al. 2008), the same drought that brought down the Classic Maya and weakened the Khmer state centered on Angkor. (For a general history of Tang, see Twitchett 1979.)

Land ownership resided with the state, in proper nomad fashion. It was let out to farmers in exchange for taxation. This system did not always work well, but Dunhuang documents show it did work, and we have the land records (Morris 2010: 338).

Tang Environment and Farming

In Tang, environmental degradation began to attract attention. Mark Elvin quotes an extremely significant poem by the great writer Liu Zongyuan:

The official guardians' axes have spread through a thousand hills,
At the Works Department's order hacking rafter-beams and billets.
Of ten trunks cut in the woodlands' depths, only one gets hauled
          away.
Ox-teams strain at their traces—till the paired yoke-shafts break.
Great-girthed trees of towering height lie blocking the forest tracks,

A tumbled confusion of lumber, as flames on the hillside crackle.
Not even the last remaining shrubs are safeguarded from
        destruction;
Where once the mountain torrents leapt—nothing but rutted gullies.
Timber, not yet seasoned or used, left immature to rot;
Proud summits and deep-sunk gorges—now brief hummocks of
        naked rock.

                                              (Elvin 2004a: 18)

Mark Lewis also cites the poem and adds: "In what was clearly a political poem, the felling of trees symbolized the fate of talented men at the hands of a corrupt court. But the fact that the destruction of forests came readily to mind as a metaphor suggests just how common a sight the denuding of hills was during the Tang dynasty" (2009: 11). And the image shows that Liu has Mencius's famous Ox Mountain story very much in mind; that parable was evidently well known, and its full force appreciated. It is also significant that Liu was no marginal tree-hugger; he was, and remains, one of the most deservedly popular and highly regarded poets in Chinese history. Lewis quotes several further forest poems (see, e.g., 17) to show how conscious people were of trees and of the problems of deforestation.

Landholdings shrank as population multiplied. The classic well-field, or equal-field system, an ideal at best, became utterly unsustainable (see Lewis 2009b: 121ff.). Naturally, agricultural technology developed to keep pace.

The ox-drawn deep-moldboard plow, known since the second century, became common and spread south (Bray 1984; Lewis 2009b: 130). It allowed opening clay soils, dense grassland soils, and other refractory environments, and made rice cultivation much easier. The famous plow sole of rice fields developed: clay leached down to the depth of the plow furrow, accumulating there and sealing the field. Water was trapped, providing an ideal medium for rice instead of percolating away. The depth of plowing could be adjusted by the blade setting of the, allowing adaptation to different soils. With seed drills, sophisticated fertilizer, and a variety of crops, commercial cropping and local specialization became widespread; that in turn led to an explosion of shipping along canals, rivers, and seas (Lewis 2009b: 132–38).

Settlement of the south continued. "Between 742 and 1080 (two years for which comprehensive census records have survived), the population in the north increased by only 26 percent, while that in the south increased by 328 percent" (Lewis 2009b: 277). Forests began to disappear there too, but crops like Job's-tears and sago added to the Tang food reserves (Lewis 2009b: 125; Schafer 1967).

Tang Food

Early medical works and cookbooks multiplied from 600 on, but most are known only in fragments (see review in H. Huang 2000: 125–26). However, Sun Simiao's medical work *Prescriptions Worth a Thousand Gold* (2007; Chinese original 654) survives. It is one of the earliest books of prescriptions and one of the first to blend herbs and food into a comprehensive materia medica (see Engelhardt 2001).

With regard to food preferences, there was constant teasing between northern Chinese and southern. Mark Lewis focuses on these differences and finds plenty of material. He quotes a northerner who finds mutton and carp comparable but holds that tea is "'the true slave of yoghurt,'" while noting several southern counterclaims (Lewis 2009b: 127, from a Buddhist source). Conversely, one poor Yangzi Delta traveler to the north claims to have almost died from such a dreadful thing as yogurt. (Dairy products abounded in the north; Luo Feng 2008; Sabban 1986.) Of course he was exaggerating for effect, like Frenchmen today who claim to be nearly killed by British food. Northerners, in turn, said the southerners are so antisocial that "'they each boil their own rice . . . [and] cook their own fish'" (Lewis 2009b: 131), which was presumably an outrageous exaggeration then as it would be today. Shortly after the fall of Tang, when the Khitan people took over northern China, one Chinese called them "the hosts of the mutton-reeking tents" (Standen 2007: 30)!

The teasing between the stereotypically bluff, honest, sociable north and the sleek, polished, devious southeast is robustly alive today, and it is still often phrased in terms of a contrast between plain dull food (reeking of mutton) and exotic stuff made of weird water animals that no reasonable person would eat. The similarity between the constant mutual taunting of the English and the French is striking and amusing.

Probable Central Asian influence appears in the many forms of wheat cakes and dumplings described by Shu Xi (ca. 264–304) in his "Rhapsody on *bing*" (Knechtges 1986: 58–63). *Bing* then meant a wide range of prepared wheat foods. Many of these have relatives all over Asia and probably came from western parts; Shu Xi, in fact, remarks on how recent they are, tracing them back no farther than Han.

Filled dumplings—what would now be called *bao* and *jiao*—are included in the essay and described in mouthwatering detail. Large filled dumplings were called *mantou*, a word etymologized to "barbarian heads" and said to come from a conquest in which these dumplings were substituted for real heads in a sacrificial feast (Knechtges 1986: 60). This is a typical bit of Chinese fantastical folk-etymology. More significant than the story itself is its supposed date, the third century CE, just before Shu was writing. *Mantou* is in fact the Chinese reflex of a word known all over Asia (from Korean *mandu* to Greek *mantu* or *manti*). It is almost certainly Turkic, since the word is shared in various forms by almost all Turkic languages (Eren 1999: 286; Paul Buell, pers. comm.). The wheat-dough-wrapped filled dumpling came to China from Central Asia; it may have been invented there or in the Near East. (E. Anderson 1988; Buell et al. 2010). Indeed, meat-filled dumplings were all over Asia by this time. A mummified dough *jiaozi* was found in Xinjiang, along with a mummified spring roll that looks exactly like a modern one (pers. obs., Silk Road exhibition, Bowers Museum, Santa Ana, California, 2010; E. Anderson 2010). In the late sixteenth century, medical writer Gao Lian was still using the word *mantou* for filled dumplings.

Over time, *mantou* became a term for *un*filled loaves of steamed bread, *bing* became restricted to baked or steamed wheat cakes, and the filled dumplings became *bao* if thick-skinned, *jiao* if thin-skinned. Elsewhere, including in Xinjiang (see below), *mantu*, *mantou*, and cognate words still refer to filled dumplings, usually with meat fillings. *Mian*, previously a word for flour, became the word for noodles (Coe 2009: 90; he reports that egg noodles were not invented till around 1500, though this is hard to prove and I suspect they were earlier).

A Tang cookbook survives, but only as fragments in later quotations. It includes lamb (six recipes), beef, pork, many game animals, including the raccoon dog, and various fowl (So 1992: 25). Raccoon dog may sound unappetizing, but it is still eaten and said to be delicious. It has even been farmed for food. More interesting historically are 24 kinds of *huntun*—wonton (25), in the sense of small stuffed dumplings boiled in stock. This is the first known use of the word for this purpose. The word's root meaning is "the primeval chaos from which the universe formed," a poetic but apt name for a rich soup with small dumplings floating around in it.

Meanwhile, in the south, food was very different from the yogurt-eating north (see E. Anderson 1988; Schafer 1967). One area reported wildrice (*Zizania aquatica*—which is *not* wild rice; its English name is printed as one word to distinguish it), barnyard millet, crab eggs, nutmeg, betel nut, and water plants (Sinoda 1977: 488).

Tea spread rapidly from the southwest. In Tang and Song, monks and religious devotees took to consuming tea and medicinal soups on a regular basis as an aid to longevity, purification, self-cultivation, sophistication, and general religious virtue (S. Liu 2006). This was the beginning of the long East Asian cult of tea.

Tang Culture and Poetry

The famous civil service examination system, developed in Han, became more important as Tang wore on and education grew more advanced. The scholar-bureaucrats were highly trained. The old stereotype in the West has been that they were trained merely in "composing poetry and quoting classical literature" (Morris 2010: 338–39). Morris makes up for this nonsense by adding that when Britain copied the Chinese examination system in the nineteenth century, critics accused the English of "a sinister plot to 'Chinesify' Britain." In fact the exams demanded essays on genuine and serious policy issues. The candidates literally memorized all the early history books, knew the later ones almost as well, and knew every classic work on politics and political science. They were thus far better equipped than modern bureaucrats, whose training generally runs heavily to neoclassical economic theory, postmodern criticism of movies, and other matters that make composing Tang poetry seem burning with relevance by comparison. Knowing every detail of the history, philosophy, and ethical speculations of one's civilization certainly had its merits as an education for administrators.

Notable Tang scholars like Yuan Zhen, Han Yu, and Bai Juyi, all of whom made top scores in the exams, developed extended, trenchant, and brilliant critiques of government and statecraft. These commentaries kept them constantly in trouble (Palandri 1977), but their efforts may have saved the Tang state for a few extra decades. Moreover, not only did they become symbols of reform through their critiques, but their teachings on social justice, probity, and transparency influenced China from that day on; they are still widely quoted. All three continue to be regarded as among China's greatest writers, but in their time they were at least as well known for being statesmen.

One of Han Yu's scathing criticisms of incompetence and corruption got him banished to the Shantou area, then remote. There he was asked by the locals to read a government edict to a huge and annoying crocodile—surely the crocodile would fear the power of the state and leave the area. Han responded with an exquisitely crafted and hilariously funny prose piece, very obviously using the crocodile as a metaphor for his enemies at court (Giles 1923: 128 provides a translation into appropriate, humorously formal Victorian English). It reached the capital, where no one missed the symbolism. The crocodile went away, and Han Yu was recalled to the capital. I like to think that the court was too delighted with the story to maintain Han's exile.

Tang continued the traditions of four-line and eight-line verse but also developed new prosodic rules that both made the poems more beautiful and made them hard to write. These "poems" were actually songs. They were sung to well-known tunes or else chanted. Later paintings claiming to follow Tang models often show a sage out in the mountains, under a tree, playing a musical instrument and intoning songs. In Tang Chinese, these songs were masterpieces of rhyme, tone prosody, vowel harmony, and word music in general. This musical side is usually forgotten by modern Western, and even Chinese, readers. The Western readers usually see only prosy translations. The Chinese lose out, too, because the rhyme words often no longer rhyme, the tones are different, and thus the poem no longer sounds so good; also, younger Chinese today no longer learn to sing or chant them. The classical Chinese is often accompanied by translations into modern Chinese; the classical language is not as different from the latter as Beowulf is from modern English, but certainly not easy for a modern Chinese reader.

This poetry highlighted nature, and most poems idealized the mountains, waters, farmlands, and woods of China. They were thus an enormous force for environmental protection. Unlike Western classical poems, they were very widely known. Bai Juyi was proud to find farmers and villagers singing his works. Even illiterate country folk learned these poems, more or less as folk songs. Many were still able to sing them when I lived in Hong Kong in the 1960s. The effect of such widely known literature on popular ideology was enormous.

The greatest Tang poets remain among the greatest lyric poets in the world, but future imitators drifted farther and farther from their standard, as actual speech drifted even farther from Tang pronunciation. (Recall that classical Chinese was semi-artificial in the first place.) Tang poetry covers nature in exquisite detail, but, as Edward Schafer pointed out (in lectures and Schafer 1963), it tended to stick to a rather narrow range of images, such as orchids, pines, bamboo, mei flowers, the "bright moon," rivers, and seas. Images were recycled from ancient literature, being reused over and over and acquiring more and more layers of association. For example, a character in *Zhuang Zi*, praised for rustic poverty and independence, had a pigweed staff—a pigweed (a.k.a. goosefoot) stalk de-twigged to make an extremely humble walking stick. Du Fu seized on the image and made it his own: "testing the stream with my pigweed staff." Of course that opened the floodgates, and poets from Han Shan to the Japanese haiku genius Matsuo Basho all flaunted their pigweed staffs. I wonder if any of them actually had any. (I couldn't resist—I made one and have it by me as I write.)

Central Asia in Tang Times

At this time, the Silk Road was at its peak in importance. An enormous flow of information and commodities crossed Asia at the time: foods, foodways, ideas, technologies, medicines, and much more (Laufer 1919; Schafer 1963). It would not have taken a huge amount of traffic to introduce these, but it would have taken a good deal of serious intellectual exchange, which presupposes fairly steady and intensive contact. Even Valerie Hansen has to admit that in Tang considerable amounts of material flowed along the road (Hansen 2012: 99–104). The whole trade and transport economy was highly bureaucratized. It was also militarized, and Hansen is certainly right (at least for war-torn periods) in holding that governmental and military traffic outnumbered business traffic. On the other hand, even the surviving documents demonstrate impressive trade, with goods from far away such as camphor, pepper, and musk appearing in very early Sogdian letters (Vaissière 2005: 51). The Sogdians traded as far as India, as is shown by (among other things) their use of a word cognate with the English "pepper" for that commodity; both words come from Sanskrit (76). There also exist hundreds of Sogdian graffiti in northern Pakistan (79).

The Silk Road was a vital trade route for millennia. Classic works by Berthold Laufer (1919) and Edward Schafer (1963) document the enormous flow of plants, animals, and minerals from west to east. Major goods included, of course, silk. It was not just the staple trade item; it was usually the currency, especially in early centuries. Other fabrics and materials were not far behind, with cotton rising in importance and hemp probably falling. All manner of garments were traded. Coins were few, and silk bolts, or rolls, were the usual method of payment. Horses and sheep, medicines, incense, Buddhist texts, ammonium chloride for dyeing, and more ordinary food and clothing items were common. Precious stones, metals, hides, paper and books, art objects, and many other objects also traveled the routes (Vaissière 2005 gives long lists on 134, 138, and 294 from contemporary sources and from Schafer 1963). Many items traded were bulk utility goods, not luxuries. This was a serious trade that encompassed necessities and industrial items—not a mere luxury trade of the sort regarded as primitive or superficial by an earlier generation of historians (on such matters see Beaujard 2009, 2012).

A contemporary list of products traded along the Silk Road, by an Arab historian writing in 985, takes up a full page in David Christian's classic article about that route (2000: 8; the list is also found in Vaissière). Many kinds of cloth and foodstuffs were traded, along with furs, slaves, bows, metals, precious stones, horses, paper, leather, and all manner of luxury products (see also *The Silk Road* by Jonathan Tucker, 2003, 16–17). Medicines were also traded—not surprising, since, as Christian (2000: 23) points out, the Silk Road brought diseases and other undesirable items just as it brought necessities and luxuries. The bubonic plague was only the most famous of the diseases that moved west; we do not know what may have moved east. China sent ephedra, ginseng, snake bile, and seaweed westward and received the classic Mediterranean herbs, from lavender to bryony.

Inventions (Tucker 2003: 18–19) ranged from bridge types and irrigation technology to gunpowder, canal lock-gates, paper and printing. Of course, silk and all its techniques were the most obvious and one of the most enduring technologies to spread east to west by this route. The persistent story that silkworm eggs were smuggled across in hollow monks'-staff heads has not been substantiated.

Saddest was the thriving traffic in slaves of all sorts and origins. The effect of medieval slaving on world genetics has never been evaluated, but it was obviously massive.

More interesting from the viewpoint of the present book is the enormous variety of languages, religions, scripts, philosophies, technologies, and ideas in general, moving along the Silk Road and through the steppes, deserts and mountains of Central Asia. People speaking Chinese, Tocharian, Indian languages, and countless Iranian and Turkic dialects met and practiced Buddhism, Islam, Confucianism, Daoism, Manichaeanism, Church of the East (Nestorian) Christianity, Zoroastrianism, and various shamanistic religions without usually getting in each other's way. Islam eventually prevailed in most of the area, spreading rapidly in the time between the Battle of Talas River in

751 and a final complete conversion by 1500 (in most places by 1000). Buddhism survived, and survives today, in the Tibetan and Mongol areas. In Islamic realms, there was much less tolerance than in the older polities, but even Islam took notably tolerant forms, far from the current extremist forms of that faith.

In Central Asia, irrigation systems came to a spectacular climax, with dams rivaling the big dams of today (D. Hill 2000). Rulers competed to build the biggest and best irrigation systems. This was not mere show, or even beneficial economics; it was a matter of security. Whoever could feed the most soldiers had the advantage in the constant warfare that marked the region then as now. The Sogdians take the credit for much of this development (Vaissière 2005: 104).

Food in Central Asian China through the Tang Dynasty was still overwhelmingly bread, noodles, and other baked or boiled products made from wheat and barley. Bread similar to that of today seems to have dominated. Millet now constituted only about 15 percent of the grain used, and beer was its main use. It was also eaten as porridge. Both naked and hulled barley was grown, the former being classed with wheat, evidently because it was milled. Naked barley lacks tough inedible hulls. Hulled barley needs an extra step to get the hulls off the kernels. Wheat was soaked before milling, because the mills at the time were still inefficient. In Tang a vertical stone turning in the vertical plane was used to crush the grain on an anvil slab. Stone mills in the West used, and still use, two horizontal wheels, the upper one roughened with tangential grooves, to slash up the grain as well as grinding it. This process provides finer flour and better bran separation and is still the preferred way to mill wheat—far superior to the cheaper steel rollers of industrial grinding. White bread was made in large quantities for the elite and professional classes by bolting the flour (shaking it through a rather coarsely woven cloth, to separate flour from bits of bran). Hard manual workers had to depend on whole grain bread, bran and all. (This paragraph depends on the superb analysis in Trombert 2009.)

One assumes that Central Asia ate as the remote parts of Afghanistan and Pakistan did within living memory. Bread, usually much like Persian nan, was overwhelmingly the staple food, with dairy products, fruit, meat, and vegetables coming next in descending order, and the meat being often stretched by being chopped and incorporated into small boiled dumplings. Remains in cemeteries and Buddhist temples show a varied, cosmopolitan, high-quality diet for the well-to-do, and bran bread with some dairy and fruit for the rest. The basic diet had not changed since the days of the Beauty of Xiaohe, but the elite had a far greater range. Rice, now a staple of the region, seems to have still been lacking. It is commonly mentioned in the Mongol Empire, but the relevant sources come from Beijing, not the old Central Asian core. It had certainly reached Iran and the Near East by this time and must have been known in Central Asia, but mentions are few in the published and archaeological records.

From Central Asia and India, Buddhist missionaries and influences poured into China during this period, and some Chinese went to India to seek out more Buddhist knowledge. With this came vegetarianism, avoidance of alcohol and onions and garlic, and other Buddhist food rules (Sterckx 2005).

The Sogdian community continued to bring in Central Asian food. The tomb of the Sabao (caravan or community leader) Wirkak, near Chang'an, contained food sculptures apparently showing nan and dumplings similar to mantou (Dien 2008; cf. Dien 2007). After the Tang fell, Turkic peoples from the north and Persians from the west moved more actively into Central Asia. Sogdian and other East Iranic languages began to disappear, replaced by Turkic languages and later also by West Iranic ones such as Dari and Tadzhik. Today, a daughter language of Sogdian survives in one isolated valley in Tadjikistan. In his book *The One Hundred Thousand Fools of God* (1996), the ethnomusicologist Theodore Levin gives a wonderful and moving account of the Yagnab (or Yaghnob) Valley and its people and music, with songs transcribed and translated. Readers drawn irresistibly to the romance of Sogdia can find excellent poetry here. Levin notes that butter, mutton, black tea, boiled sugar, pepper, garlic, egg yolk, palav (pilau, pulao) and vinegar were "hot," while sour milk, veal, green tea, granular sugar, egg white, bread, noodles and greens in general were "cold" (213); this bit of Hippocratic-Galenic medicine surely goes back to early days, probably at least to the Tang Dynasty, as is shown by the similar codings at both ends of the Silk Road in that period (see below).

Tang was a period of learning and culture in Central Asia (Mirbabayev et al. 2000). Islam brought high levels of literacy and civilization. Learning in early Muslim Central Asia climaxed in the work of Avicenna and other medical and philosophical writers.

The Silk Road integrated the Western and Eastern spheres, or world-systems, but did not make them one. The Western world-system was dominated by Iranian and Semitic peoples. It was quickly conquered by Islam and by Tang were already almost 100% Muslim (though substantial Christian, Jewish, and Zoroastrian communities survived). The Eastern world-system was dominated by the Chinese, but Tibetans, Koreans, and farther afield the Japanese, Thai, and others had major roles. Islam never made headway there except in western Xinjiang, although in recent centuries more and more "Hui" (Chinese Muslims) have emerged in northwest China. The Hui had, and still have, their own distinctive cultural worlds.

The battle of Talas River, when the rapidly expanding Arab (or Arab-Iranian) armies clashed with Tang forces in 751; the rise of the Mongol hordes; and the slow decline of the Silk Road after 1400 failed to incorporate China into the expanding Western world-system. China remained its own core until the late 19th century, when it was incorporated into the newly emergent global system we know today. It has now reemerged as a core, but as one of several disparate ones in this modern system.

The Turkic groups and, ultimately and briefly, the Mongols bridged the gap, moving easily between world-systems. (The Mongols had previously been firmly incorporated in the Eastern system.) The Turkic peoples were classic borderland peoples, often spawning the semiperipheral marcher states that Peter Turchin (2003, 2006) found to be frequent sources of conquests in pre-modern state systems. In later centuries, they were identified as the Turan of the classic contrasts between Iran and Turan, roughly Persia and Central Asia respectively; however, in earlier centuries, both Iranians and Turanians spoke Iranic languages. The Turkic groups tended to move west, and now, of course, the vast majority of Turkic speakers are in the Western system; millions still inhabit China, however.

Shortly after the fall of Tang, the Sogdian world crumbled in the face of the rapid consolidation of the Arab and Persian conquests from the southwest and the Turkic ones from the north. Their languages, especially Turkic, replaced Sogdian. Trade began to be impacted by expanding sea trade and by the production of silk in the West. Trade would continue, but differently structured and under new masters. The "last contacts [of Sogdians] with China are attested around 930" (Vaissière 2005: 334).

Definitive Shaping of the Food System: Song Its Neighbors

Throwing on my raincoat, my rainhat askew, beyond a thousand
    peaks, I draw water and sprinkle vegetables in front of the
    Five Stars."
(The nun Miaodao, eleventh century; Idema and Grant 2004: 325)

The importance of the Song Dynasty, founded by General Zhao Guangyin, and its agricultural progress has been continually reemphasized by historians. (For Song history, see D. Kuhn 2009; Mote 1999.)

The general took power in a coup, the latest in a long series of coups that
had led to revolving-door changes of dynasty in the many small, dismal, nonviable states that filled the political void between the fall of Tang in 907 and
the final triumph of Song in 960. We have a fascinating near-contemporary
view of that bloody and anarchic period from Ouyang Xiu's great *Historical
Records of the Five Dynasties*, now translated (Ouyang 2004). Ouyang's meticulous history is complemented by his condign judgments of the morality of
the warlords of the time.

Above all else, Zhao Guangyin wished to stop the cycle of revolving-door
coups, and thus he definitively weakened the power of the military, putting it
under civilian control. He also began a tradition of greater respect for men of
peace, especially scholar-bureaucrats, and less respect for men of war. As Song
progressively lost to more martial peoples from the frontiers, the dynasty vac-
illated between defensive and compromising poses. Even individual emperors
changed their minds repeatedly, alternately facing the reality of savage enemies and the dream of a pacifist empire (Twitchett and Smith 2009). Lack of
military power is often blamed for the progressive loss of Song territory to
northern steppe and forest peoples, leading to a massively reduced empire—
Southern Song—by 1127. (The previous period of union is referred to as
Northern Song.)

Iron production skyrocketed as coal came into use as a major industrial
fuel; unfortunately, deforestation for charcoal continued (Hartwell 1962, 1982;
Wagner 2008). Deforestation was rampant by this time, because of the rise of
industry, notably iron but also printing, which caused a demand for wood for
blocks and pine to burn for ink. (Ink later came to be made by burning oil,
saving the pine forests.) Romantics have even suggested that the popularity of
poetry in old China led to deforestation and to paper shortages. This is exaggerated, but printing was a significant factor.

Rice yields doubled or tripled—ultimately, at least, but the process was
only beginning in Song or Yuan. Such yields were due not only to more intensive effort but also to the introduction of the Champa fast-ripening varieties
and other agricultural novelties. The Champa rice reached the lower Yangzi
from Fujian in the early eleventh century (the classic date is 1012). It had come
at some uncertain (but probably not much earlier) point from Champa, now
in southern Vietnam. It was rather poor quality and cooked up dry, thus hurt-

ing its appeal; its only advantages were quick ripening and some resistance to drought. It very quickly came to dominate the Yangzi delta (see, e.g., D. Kuhn 2009: 217) but did not take over all south China. It was slow to make its way, coming into its own in later dynasties when cooler and drier interior uplands were settled.

Li Bozhong (2003) argues that the full benefits of the Song introductions were not felt until Ming and that the new rices did not have as revolutionary an effect even then, as Elvin and others had argued. However, he has to admit that the Song crops and cropping systems had a powerful effect in the Yangzi Delta area, the economic powerhouse of the country—and one which, as he points out, did not suffer as much as other regions from the violence of the subsequent conquests. Thus, the issue is really one of what constitutes a "revolution"—the beginning and locking in of a basic change, or its final fruition. The latter was not completed, even in the Yangzi Delta, until Qing. In fact, the marginal parts of the south did not get their full "revolution" until the twentieth century. It seems possible to see Song as revolutionary, then, only if one remembers that the full benefits were not reaped (literally!) until later.

Sugar production soared in Song, because the government set a number of policies that favored it. Sucheta Mazumdar's study (1998) of sugar in Song found, among many other things, that the Chinese preserved smallholder dominance in sugar production with such ideas as mounting mills on barges and towing them among the sugar fields of the Canton Delta. (The delta of the Pearl River and several minor streams is referred to as the Canton Delta, from an old name for the city of Guangzhou, situated near the head of the delta.) Elsewhere, sugar is notorious for causing the worst excesses of plantation farming, because it takes tremendous capital to run a sugar estate (land, plants, and machinery to process the sugar are all expensive), yet the crop returns very little per unit weight. Thus the gap between extremely rich landlords and extremely poor plantation workers—typically slaves in the old days—is horrific, and slaves had a life expectancy of only a very few years on early sugar plantations; even today, sugar is notorious for causing rural inequality and poverty. (This fact has attracted notable scholars, producing three of the greatest classics in agrarian studies: George Beckford's *Persistent Poverty*, 1972; Gilberto Freyre's *The Masters and the Slaves*, 1964; and Sidney Mintz's *Sweetness and Power*, 1985.) China, throughout history, avoided the sugar plantation trap—an amazing achievement that deserves more recognition.

Certainly, the delta was doing well. Richard von Glahn (2003) translates one Fang Hui (1227–1307) as noting that families there had about 30 mu (a bit under 5 acres) of land. For a family of five, this meant a bit under an acre per person. The yields per mu were up to two *shi*, or *dan*, of rice. (The shi is a measure of weight, now 133 lb., but then a bit more, around 145 lb.; see Li Bozhong 2003: 170. Shi of rice are counted in dan, the way grain yields in the United States used to be counted in "bushels." Thus an amount of rice that weighs 100 shi is counted as 100 dan rice. In older European literature the shi was referred to by its Malay name, *pikul*.) Tenants sharecropped on a 50-50 basis, leaving them 30 dan. Fang Hui calculated a family of five would need 18 dan per year, leaving 12 for sale. Recall that this was often superior rice that would command a premium price. Assuming the family of five was two parents and three children, 18 dan would give about 4.5 dan per adult and 3 per child, or better than 600 lb. of rice per adult, certainly a liberal ration. Of course many a farm returned only half that yield per acre (Li Bozhong 2003, esp. 170), and outside the delta, the norm was probably lower still.

Official figures show yields from 20 to over 200 kg of rice per mu (D. Kuhn 2009: 214–15). The figure gives us about 2,800 kg/ha, an extremely high figure. European agriculture was getting 300–500 kg/ha maximum at the time, and United States maize farming in Iowa was getting only about 2,500 kg/ha in the early twentieth century. Yet Fang Hui's top figure is much higher, working out to a spectacular 4,000 kg/ha! This must represent double-cropping, which means Li Bozhong is being too conservative in doubting widespread high yields and double-cropping in Song.

The poor had trouble sharing in this bounty, as is true in most of human history. A good wage bought 200 liters of rice (D. Kuhn 2009: 242), enough to feed a family of five but not much more than that. Many people made half that much, so that a family of five would need two wage earners. Landowning households ranged from 3 mu—a mere fifth of a hectare—to an incredible 10,000 mu (214–15). The latter figure—around seven square km—shows that Song had its large estates. It is, however, extremely unusual. It may be compared to the feudal holdings in Europe at the time, which ran to many square miles, or even more in duchies and lordships. Soybeans were already important, as well as other pulses and a range of vegetables.

Northern Song coincided with strong monsoons, reliable rainfall, and good growing conditions all over China (P. Zhang et al. 2008). The dry north got wetter; the over-rainy south got drier (at least locally). By the end of Song, in 1279, the Medieval Warm Period was in full swing, causing better growing conditions in many areas but chronic drought in parts of the deep interior. It also caused more extreme climate events, since warming produces more evaporation, more wind, and more violent weather. Extreme rain events are much commoner when overall rainfall increases, for example. Thus at the height of the Medieval Warm Period, in the 1200s, Song was afflicted with major droughts in 1239, 1240, 1241, 1245, 1246, 1247, and 1252, and major floods in 1229, 1236, 1242, 1251, 1252, 1255, and 1259 (Davis 2009: 906).

In early Song, taxes were light. Paper money, called flying money, developed from merchants' bills of credit, and the government quickly adopted and adapted it, printing it by 1024. Soon there was more paper money than coin (D. Kuhn 2009; Morris 2010: 378). The Mongols continued to use it, to the amazement of Marco Polo. Trade also flourished; Kaifeng, the Northern Song capital, was full of all kinds of fish, although it is in a dry area and had to bring most of them from afar (S. West 1987). The flourishing state of printing (Chia 1996) allowed cookbooks, tea books, and very modern-seeming restaurant, food, and wine guidebooks to multiply inordinately. Of course it also allowed the government to print more paper money, and thus inflation occurred when the government was short on discipline.

Personal freedoms were strikingly evident. Song ran a nonmilitarist, open society. Criticism of government was incredibly free. The fiery interchanges between Wang Anshi and his critics in the late eleventh century rival those in the U.S. Congress today. Women reached what was apparently the highest status they held in imperial China's history. Trade flourished, and huge ships filled with the finest ceramics and other goods plied the oceans, some of them having been discovered where they sank along the sea lanes to Korea and Southeast Asia.

However, the "barbarian" invasions led to more and more taxes for paying "tribute" (in fact, protection money) to these increasingly powerful enemies. As Southern Song faced harder and harder times, a rather sour and reactionary ideology set in, as it generally does in worsening times. Personal freedoms, including women's status, declined. As in today's America, difficult economic times were followed by the rise of conservative theories about the family. The neo-Confucian Zhu Xi, dominant philosopher of the time, taught a doctrine that had some liberating and open-minded aspects, but his ideas on the family were sternly patriarchal. He has for centuries been blamed or credited for the long downward slide in women's rights and conditions since his time. Certainly he was no feminist. Even today, discriminatory and reactionary attitudes toward women and gays in places like Singapore are justified by appeal to Zhu Xi.

Song foodways were greatly elaborated, as we have long known (Freeman 1977). Dieter Kuhn (2009: 270) gives some detail, including a note that there were 54 kinds of "wine" brewed around Hangzhou. By this time, *jiu*, here translated as "wine," had expanded beyond its original meaning (basically, ale), to include distilled liquors, medicinal tinctures, and even actual wine. Tea had become a staple by late Song. Paul Smith (1991: 51–62) has more recently detailed the taxation of tea in Sichuan in the Song. A recent and very good popular summary of Chinese food history (Waley-Cohen, 2007) focuses overwhelmingly on the Song, Ming, and Qing Dynasties and specifically on the type of food and gastronomy that evolved in the Song Dynasty.

It is also thought that Yangzhou at this time invented Yangzhou fried rice, now perhaps the most common Chinese dish in the world. In the time of Emperor Huizong, people got tired of just making gruel out of leftover rice and started frying it with egg and other bits and pieces of leftovers; at least so thinks Antonia Finnane (2004: 290), with evidence from texts but no proof in the form of a Song recipe. (There are rumors that Yangzhou fried rice was invented in Hong Kong, or even in the United States, but these are dubious. The dish certainly existed before American Chinese food evolved.)

Central Asian foodways were still well enough established that Lu You, the famous patriot poet who had little use for Central Asian ways, could praise yogurt and mutton and refer to noodles with mutton (the criterial Central Asian dish) in his poems (see Cheng Wing fun and Collet 1998: 46, 48, 53).

An insight into the cuisine of Song is the cookbook by the great Yuan Dynasty artist Ni Zan (E. Anderson et al. 2005; So 1992: 29–34). Ni probably reflects Song tastes and provides highly refined recipes for a delicate, artfully simple cuisine. He also provides brewing directions (alas, garbled in transmission) that indicate that complex and highly flavored drinks were home-brewed at the time. A contemporary book, Zhu Gong's work on brewing, *Beishan Jiujing*, has more accurate recipes. Flour was stirred with water and a starter to cause lactic acid fermentation. Then glutinous rice was cooked and added. This mixture was fermented and strained (see H. Huang 2000; Sinoda 1977: 491).

Earlier was *Zhonggui Lu* (Records of home cooking) by one "Mrs. Wu, who may be called the first Chinese woman cookery writer" we know (So 1992: 26). She has, among other things, a recipe for a *zong* (glutinous rice dumpling wrapped in leaves) similar to modern ones.

Another scholar's cookbook was that of Lin Hong (thirteenth century), who developed a highly refined cuisine (Sabban 1997; So 1992: 27–28)). Based on vegetables, this cuisine could accommodate delicate meats and fish, but—

except for an odd stew of wildcat—few more robust meats, though mutton and venison did make it in. Delicacy can go no further than infusions, congee, and stuffings flavored with flowering-apricot blossoms; these have a marvelous but volatile and evanescent carnation or clove scent. (They were used to flavor tea in the Qing Dynasty.) Recipes included dishes of lotus, orange, wild mushrooms, hare, and various light-flavored greens. Like other scholars then and since, he warned against eating certain foods at the same meal, including crab and persimmon. This combination is still avoided, although no one has ever come up with a valid reason for it. Lin speaks of a "wind worm" (Sabban 1997: 42), a medical concept; the wind worm could be avoided by proper diet and regimen. Many, perhaps most, of Lin's recipes contain literary allusions. Although influenced by Daoism, he still could not give up grains or meats, but he minimized them and included various vegetarian "meat" recipes such as vegetarian duck. The book contains an early use of *huntun*—"wonton"—to mean a broth; it is, here, a medicinal one, using cedrela root (*Cedrela sinensis* = *Toona sinensis*) to treat diarrhea. Many of the recipes are medicinal, and probably all were considered to have medicinal value. He was devising a cuisine for scholars who had retired to the mountains—a cuisine simple and natural but still refined and tasteful (not to say expensive).

In Song, most Buddhist sects and regimens were strictly vegetarian, some sects of Daoism encouraged vegetarianism, and some Chinese scholars were simply too merciful to take animal lives—or so they claimed. Vegetarianism probably came with Buddhism before Tang. By Song it was more widespread and remains a part of the Chinese scene today. (On meat and the rise of substitutes for it, see H. Huang 2000; Sabban 1993.)

By contrast, many loved pork. The great poet Su Shi, known as Su Dongpo from his studio on the eastern slope (*dong po*) of a hill, was a famous gourmet and cook. He wrote poetry in praise of pork and so may have contributed significantly to its popularity (So 1992: 4; see his poem quoted there). To this day, in his homeland in the lower Yangzi valley, a deservedly popular dish is Dongpo pork, supposedly prepared according to his recipe. Just what that recipe was we do not know, for Dongpo pork is now made in so many forms that it defies reduction to one recipe.

Conversely, raw foods were still popular, as they had been in Tang. Not only fish, but pork, mutton, duck, goose, sparrows, and other foods were eaten raw (Sinoda 1977: 490). This habit declined steadily from Song onward, virtually disappearing in the twentieth century as the health hazards became widely known.

Many other cookbooks and food books are known from this period (Huang 2000: 126–28). There are also other observations on food, including many disparaging comments by exiles on the foods of remote regions. The south was infamous for its yams and taro, rats and bats, raw fish, and so on (Schafer 1967). Su Dongpo complained of these foods, strange to him;. His wife died after eating snake without knowing what it was; he attributed her death to the shock of finding out (Sabban 1999: 5).

An insight into the Chinese experimental approach to eating is provided by a Yuan Dynasty story about the Song Dynasty: "[In 1120 CE] . . . a creature somewhat like a dragon appeared in front of a teashop in Kaifeng County. It was about six or seven feet long [around four feet in modern measure] with blue black scales. It had a head like a donkey, but with fish-cheeks and a horn on top of its skull. It bellowed like an ox. As it happened, the shopkeeper was making up the beds that morning when he noticed something the size of a large dog beside him. When he looked closely, it was this dragon. He was so surprised he keeled over in fright. The teashop was situated very close to an arms manufactory, and when the workers in the mill found out about the dragon they killed and ate it" (Hennessey 1981: 41). Westerners would have fled in terror or collapsed praying. Nobody but the Chinese would have begun their acquaintance with such a creature by eating it.

Closely related to food was medicine. Considerable evolution in medical practice took place in Song, with food and nutrition taking an even more important place in medical practice than had been the case earlier. As we know from Paul Unschuld's work (1985, 1986, 2009), the Song Dynasty was a period of major medical transitions. We have little idea how this affected the courts of Liao, Jin, and Yuan. Did their medical personnel partake enthusiastically of the Song revolution, or did they hold off, avoiding contact with the enemy?

Liao and Jin

From the tenth century onward, North China fell into foreign hands: the Liao, Jin, and early Mongol invaders. (The most detailed history of these conquest dynasties is Franke and Twitchett 1994; for Song it is Twitchett and Smith 2009. These are basically narratives. For more interpretation, see Brook 2010; Mote 1999.) Little is known about food in north China during the earlier periods. The population declined; by early Ming, the North China Plain may have had as few as seven million inhabitants, comparable to Shang Dynasty levels.

The expectable Chinese prejudice against "barbarian" food came into play; one Chen Liang griped: "Is there none who thinks it is wrong to submit to the foe, whose stink of mutton spreads for miles and miles[?]" (D. Kuhn 2009: 167).

The Khitan from the northern steppes took over north China in 947 and founded the Liao Dynasty. Their word for "land of the Khitan," *Khitai*, gave us the old name of Cathay for China. Their origin myth is of interest (Sinor 1998). The Khitan were supposedly the offspring of a man riding a white horse and a woman riding a gray cow who met at the sacred mountain where the sacred rivers join. Possibly the original myth had only the horse and the cow begetting the Khitan. Among the early kings of the Khitan was one who was just a skull. He took human form only for the annual sacrifice, when in proper totemic style a white horse and a gray cow were sacrificed for the ancestral ones. Another king had the head of a boar. Another had twenty sheep—always exactly twenty. Every day he ate nineteen of them (a lovely thought), but next day there were twenty again.

Abaoji, the great founder of Khitan power, was born of a sunray. Like many Old World heroes, he allegedly had the body of a three-year-old at birth, could crawl on all fours as soon as he was born, could walk after three months, and at one year he could speak and foretell the future (Sinor 1998: 228). These were a horse-riding people, and horses can run within a few hours of being born. The temptation for humans to rival them, mythically if not in reality, was great.

Liao emperors were embalmed carefully; among other things, their bodies were stuffed with "fragrant herbs, salt and alum," and drained of body fluids, resulting in a dried mummy that an irreverent Chinese observer called "emperor jerky" (Steinhardt 1998: 226). Some corpses have lasted long enough to be excavated by modern archaeologists (such as Steinhardt). Copper wire suits and gold and silver face masks decorated the bodies, as the Liao court records had said. Food offerings were included but seem not to have survived. Liao, and Central Asian, food of the time consisted of the usual dairy and grain products, plus meat when available, wild vegetables, melons, grapes, and the other foods still familiar there (Kasai and Natsagdorj 1998).

The Jurchen Tungus conquered the Khitan, drove them from north China, and established the Jin Dynasty. The Khitan then set up an empire in east-central Asia that was notable for its religious tolerance. Like many central

Asian peoples, including the Jurchen and the Mongols (and, much earlier, Cyrus's Persians), the Khitan were quite prepared to welcome any and all religious communities (Biran 2005: 180–91). Their open-mindedness stood in extremely dramatic contrast to the increasingly rigid Muslims and Christians of the western approaches. One wonders what the world would be like if this attitude had prevailed. Unfortunately, it lost out during the succeeding centuries.

One thing is clear, however: their lack of religious bigotry did not prevent war. It did prevent anything comparable to the utterly gratuitous and horrific violence of the Crusades and the Wars of Religion, but it most certainly did not bring peace. The Mongol hordes needed no religious justification. Nor did Islam make Central Asia less peaceful (or more peaceful, either) when it triumphed. Central Asians fought quite openly for power and loot, whereas the Western world cloaked its struggles for power and loot under hypocritical guises of religion. In the West, and rarely in China too, religion often took on a hideous life of its own and led to mass bloodshed—supposedly pacific Christianity having as bloody a record as militant Islam. (It is all too typical, historically, that George W. Bush started a gratuitous and bloody war against Iraq because he wrongly suspected those Muslims were warlike—or simply because he wanted their oil—and that he called his war a crusade, thus alienating the entire Muslim world.) But in Central Asia, war was constant and terrible, as much under the tolerant Khitans and Mongols as among later and far less tolerant Muslims and Christians. The twentieth century managed to make things even worse: modern political ideologies—communism, fascism, and to a lesser but real extent corporate postcapitalism—mixed with resurgent Islam created violence that dwarfed even the Crusades and the Mongol conquests.

The subsequent Jin Dynasty is known, among other things, for introducing the word "shaman" to the world (Tao 1976: 12–13; see also Tillman and West 1995 and esp. Jin 1995: 217–20). The Jin were Tungus-speaking, and "shaman" is a word from that language. More to our point here are the surprisingly complex Central Asian recipes they prepared at court (Buell et al. 2000).

A trivial, but very revealing comment on Chinese food history concerns the fried dough strips known in ordinary Chinese as *youtiao* (which just means "fried dough strips"). They are colloquially known as "fried ghosts" (or "devils"), at least in the Cantonese world I know. They commemorate the betrayal of the great resistance general Yue Fei (1103–1142), who almost saved the northern part of Song from the Jin. He was betrayed and poisoned by a capitulation advocate, the minister Qin Gui (1090–1155), and his wife. Qin convinced the Song Emperor Gaozong to cashier Yue (see, e.g., D. Kuhn 2009: 77–78). The result was transient peace for Song and eternal hatred for Qin Gui. To this day, Chinese, when they fry the entwined dough strips, revel in thinking of him and his wife frying in hell. *Jian gui,* "fried ghost," sounds close enough to "Qin Gui" to make the point. Revisionist historians have recently tried to give Qin a fair shake (see D. Kuhn 2009 for full discussion), but my heart is with the traditional Chinese on this one. Yue Fei may have been excessively rash, but treachery and underhanded murder were hardly the best counter to that.

Populations crashed in each conquest episode. Apparently "a population of 108 million in 1210 fell to 75 million in 1292, rose to 87 million in 1351, and fell again to 67 million in 1381" (P. Smith 2003: 9, citing several authorities). Of course these figures are highly tentative.

CHAPTER 7

The Mongols and the Yuan Dynasty

Here is something about Furthest China, which I mention
as I find it and do not guarantee its authenticity. If it is true,
I will have achieved my aim; if it is not true you will know
what people assert.
—Yāqūt ibn'Abdulläh, Greek-Arab geographer, ca. 1229 CE
(quoted in Hopkins 1990: 320)

The Mongol Empire and Knowledge Flows Within It

For a very short while at the height of Mongol power, one huge global system
dominated all Eurasia. If Ferdinand von Richtofen had not blessed the Central
Asian trade route complex with the cognomen Silk Road in 1877 (Hill 2009:
xii), we could well have called it the Eurasian information superhighway. In
particular, in the late 1200s and through the 1300s, it was the Mongol information superhighway.

The Mongols, mythologically descended from a gray wolf and a fallow
deer, were a scattered set of forest and forest-steppe peoples speaking variants
of the Mongolian language. By 1100, they were taking notice of the rise of
steppe empires and conquest dynasties. Yet no one could have predicted the
rise of Genghis Khan (Chinggis Qaghan, Chingis Khaan in modern Mongol)
and his rapid conquests of most of inner Asia. He never conquered China, but
his grandson Qubilai did. At the same time, Hulegu was conquering the Near
East, sweeping away the last feeble 'Abbāsid caliph and establishing the rule
of the Ilkhans in Baghdad.

By 1279, most of the core of Eurasia was in Mongol hands. They never
bothered with western Europe after an early foray disclosed that there was

little loot to be had. They similarly avoided India after brief forays. They had been stopped at Ain Jalut, in Syria in 1260 by the Mamluks of Egypt. They briefly conquered Vietnam but failed to accomplish much there, and otherwise they did not control Southeast Asia. They also failed to take Japan, but otherwise, they ruled Eurasia. The story of the Mongol conquests has been told so many times that it would be tedious to recount it here (see Di Cosmo et al. 2009; Jackson 2005; May 2007, 2012; Ratchnevsky 1991; Weatherford 2004).

In world-systems terms, the Mongols started as an extremely peripheral society—a group of remote wandering tribes. Within a few years they had created a semiperipheral state, learned to administer it successfully, and skyrocketed not only to "core" status but to domination of most of the known world. They then shrank back to more local rule, but they still controlled the cores of the Eastern and Western world-systems (or subsystems) for decades. Never before or since has a group climbed so swiftly to power, and never before or since has a peripheral group taken over several cores and enjoyed such success for so long. Their exceptional abilities to learn from others and to draw on others for administrative and productive talent were the greatest single key to this; Genghis Khan's incredible generalship obviously was a sine qua non, but mere military prowess would not have sufficed. It is this ability to learn and borrow that lies behind the texts to be considered below.

Contrary to old ideas that the Mongols were forced out of Mongolia by drought (see May 2012), they rode out during the Medieval Warm Period, when conditions were the best they had ever been for nomadic steppe herding. Tree-ring studies in Mongolia confirm the good conditions of that time (Hvistendahl 2012). The warmth brought more rain, and above all freedom from the *dzud* (or *zhud*), the dreaded spring storm that ices up the grass such that the stock cannot paw through the ice to get their food. A dzud can eliminate a whole tribe of nomadic herders. Without such catastrophes, the Mongols rapidly increased in numbers, perhaps to a million or so (May 2012), and rode out in waves of well-fed young men who faced crowding at home as population increased.

Genghis Khan ruled from horseback, but his son Ögödei Khan established a capital at Karakorum in the early 1200s. After only forty years, however, Qubilai Qan shifted the capital to what is now Beijing. Karakorum (now Xar Xorim; *k* changes to *kh* in modern Khalkha Mongol) is now a small tourist and monastery town. It lies at the point where a small river exits the dry mountains and permits irrigated agriculture in a small mountain valley—a rare bit of fertile land in Mongolia. It was a cultural meeting ground for travelers from Europe as well as most of Asia. Mongol, Turkic, and Persian were spoken; Marco Polo seems to have spoken Persian when there. Apparently languages were easily learned and widely shared in old Central Asia, as they are in some places today.

The old stereotype of the Mongol hordes as brutal, bestial, and infamous for savagery is long dead (Weatherford 2004; "horde" comes from the Mongol word *ordo* and has nothing to do with "hoard").Although merciless and savage, Mongol warfare appears to have been no worse than other war of the time, except that the Mongols generally won and thus had more scope to kill and loot (see May 2007, 2012; Weatherford 2004). Warfare in medieval Asia was not a pretty sight. By all accounts the Crusaders were at least as vicious and brutal as the Mongols. The Mongols did kill vast numbers of people, but so has everyone else in war and conquest—certainly in the bloody thirteenth and fourteenth centuries (Mote 1999 for the Chinese world, Tuchman 1978 for the West).

The Mongols, moreover, exaggerated their bloodiness as a form of propaganda. They used the time-honored technique of circulating horrific stories about their atrocities, to scare cities into submitting without a fight. This approach frequently worked (Weatherford 2004). It goes back at least to the Assyrians (Van de Mieroop 2007: 231) and probably is much older. The Mongols included tales of killing a million people in a city with less than 100,000 inhabitants and other unlikely events. These stories, with a good deal added in transmission, became "facts" in the European literature of the time and have tended to remain in books. Less pleasantly, they sometimes appear to have served later conquerors as models.

Admittedly, there are various versions of a story attributing to Genghis a memorable description of the highest good: to "chase and defeat [my] enemy, seize his total possessions, leave his married women weeping and wailing, ride his gelding, use the bodies of his women as a nightshirt and support" (Ratchnevsky 1991: 153), but these stories are obviously embellished and may well be part of the propaganda machine. The stereotype of the savage Mongols is based not only on such stories and the fear they inspired but also—in both China and the West—on recycled war propaganda from earlier "barbarian" attacks.

Oddly, Weatherford (2004) repeats the old nonsense about the Mongols eating raw meat after warming it between their thighs and their horses' backs.

This story was started by Ammianus Marcellinus writing about the Huns and is a pretty typical bit of late Roman war propaganda:

> But although they have the form of men, however ugly, they are so hardy in their way of life that they have no need of fire nor of savory food, but eat the roots of wild plants and the half-raw flesh of any animal whatever, which they put between their thighs and the backs of their horses, and thus warm it a little." Ammianus goes on to say their clothes are "skins of field-mice sewed together," and once on they never take it off—it eventually wears out. (Ammianus Marcellinus 1939, Book 31, 382–83)

Not only is this ridiculous war propaganda rather than fact, it has nothing to do with the Mongols; the Huns were a completely separate people who lived 700 years earlier. Moreover, the Mongols believed boiling retained the spiritual essence of the food and therefore almost always boiled their meat. They had a religious horror of eating raw meat (they still shun it). In any case, no nomad—Hun, Mongol, or other—would butcher on the trail and carry bloody meat on his horse, if he could avoid it. Butchering wastes time, depletes livestock, and fouls horse and gear with blood. Mongol trail rations are known to have consisted of hard-dried dairy products, parboiled or parched grain products, and jerky if one was lucky. (The Mongols did sometimes eat the horses they led as spare mounts, but only in severe need.) Nor did the Mongols wear the skins of mice; imagine trying to keep warm in a mouse-skin shirt. Not that Mongols were necessarily clean feeders; they ate mice, rats, wild roots, and anything else they could get (Buell, Anderson, and Perry 2010). But they had common sense.

The Mongols were heavy drinkers, and many emperors apparently died of the effects of overeating and overdrinking. Genghis Khan had warned them in a rather self-deconstructing way: "If he is drunk only twice a month, that is better—if only once, that is more praiseworthy. . . . But where shall we find a man who never drinks?" (Ratchnevsky 1991: 192).

In fact, far from being constantly bloodthirsty, the Mongol Empire brought peace and order. This tranquility was extended with conquests to most of Eurasia, producing the Pax Mongolica, a period so stable that "it was said a virgin carrying a gold urn filled with jewels could walk from one end of the empire to another without being molested" (May 2012: 109). That would be from Russia to south China, or Korea to Baghdad. Of course that particular claim is as exaggerated as the stories of massacres, but the peace was real enough.

Compared to the oceans of ink spilled on recounting the Mongol conquests, surprisingly little has been expended in explaining their continued success. Basically, that success came from their ability to draw on kinship, ethnic, religious, and military ties to build enormous forces by working their networks to the hilt. Genghis Khan was the great master at this. The foundation of this ability is tolerance; they were not limited to fellow Mongols, fellow religious practitioners, or any other arbitrary grouping. Tolerance also showed itself in the Mongols' propensity to learn from others. They picked up military technology such as state-of-the-art knowledge of siegecraft. More important and difficult was acquiring the entire ideological and pragmatic baggage of running a bureaucratic state—not necessarily easy for a group of independent forest and steppe nomads! They managed to do so by taking over bureaucracies they conquered. Above all, they used advisors from groups that had made the same transition earlier, notably the Khitan and the Turks. The famous advisor Yelü Chucai, who played a critical role in the process of conquering China, was a descendent of the Liao Khitan royal family.

The Mongols were religiously and culturally tolerant to a degree inconceivable in the Western world. They followed a noble tradition of steppe empires, which never were dogmatic about faith. Most steppe peoples, including the Mongols, were shamanistic and thus accustomed to individual religious practitioners who followed their own counsel and conscience and were judged by results rather than dogma. If they could contact the spirits and bring luck, they were accepted. Attitudes toward religion were similar: holy men were judged by their ability to talk, act, bring good fortune, and otherwise do something, rather than by orthodoxy.

The Mongols brought ideas and people from all over Asia. Their religious tolerance now seems wonderful and inspiring, their warfare the opposite. But things were not always so. Europeans of that day understood warfare perfectly and lobbied the Mongols to unleash their hordes on the Muslim world so that the Europeans could succeed better in the Crusades. The lobbyists were not enamored of Mongol tolerance. Thus wrote Andrew of Perugia in 1326: "Each and all are allowed to live according to their own sect, for this is their opinion, or I should say their error, that every man is saved in his own sect." The great traveler William of Rubruck reported disapprovingly that the Great Qan Mongke said, "God has given mankind several paths" (both quotes from Jackson 2005: 273). The Iranian writer Juvaini (1958), a Muslim, noted the same latitude but was more tolerant of tolerance (see also Dawson 1955; Rossabi 1992).

The Mongols believed (and still believe) in Tenggri, or Tengger, heaven (cf. Chinese *tian*) and saw all faiths as simply other ways to reach it. Later, Buddhism replaced Tenggri shamanism as a religious mediator; Allsen maintains that Buddhist networks of information and commodity flows were superior (Allsen 2009: 145). The Tenggrists and Buddhists were certainly more tolerant than Islam, which dominated western Central Asia, and in the east the former were certainly more wide-flung and prevalent.

It is safe to say that historically most people have resisted borrowing such major matters as religion and ideology. The Chinese had their sense of cultural superiority, which inhibited—though it certainly did not stop—learning from "barbarians." The West was worse off, trapped in the exclusivist, often intolerant Abrahamic religious traditions. Only during periods in which its survival was dependent on learning from others did the West open itself to Eastern culture.

The Mongols created a crisis so desperate, and opportunities so irresistible, that Europe opened its doors to learning—thus, slowly but surely, acquiring from the Mongols the great Chinese cultural achievements. Most Westerners now realize that the inventions Francis Bacon called basic to the rise of science—the compass, printing, and gunpowder—were all brought from China by the Mongols (see, e.g., Weatherford 2004; on the spread of gunpowder, see May 2012: 145ff.).

Also important were the wheelbarrow and efficient production of paper (May 2012: 251). Use of the compass, often mentioned in the same breath, was obviously learned by seafarers and thus more likely came from Arabs in the Indian Ocean trade than from the Mongols. It seems possible, indeed likely, that this receptivity had further ramifications, leading to the dramatic open-mindedness of Italy, and then the rest of Europe, to ideas from the Muslim world.

Siege techniques traveled in both directions. Organizational skills did too, but seem largely to have gone from west to east. Medical innovations also followed that pattern (Buell 2007).

However, most revolutionary to the Western world was printing, which appears to have been introduced by the Mongols from China to the West (Allsen 2001; Carter 1955; Tsien 1985; Weatherford 2004; Allsen's rather thin doubts about the Mongol introduction and its revolutionary impact are not supported by the evidence, which seems unequivocally to point to the Mongols). Simple block printing was locally present in the West earlier, but set type and movable type and the entire idea of printing long books was quite new.

Blue-and-white painting, using Iranian cobalt blue technology, was applied to Chinese porcelain to make the great feast dishes the Mongols treasured (Carswell 2000); the finest today are in the old Ottoman treasury, the Topkapı Sarayı, in Istanbul. Supposedly this paint has a healthful effect on food served in it, a belief that probably stems from the sacredness of the deep sky-blue color in Turkic and Mongol belief. In Mongolia, invoking the color of heaven (especially by wrapping with a blue silk cloth) still conveys fortune, blessing, and safety on anything so decorated.

Mongol transfers to the East from the West included, among other things, art and painting techniques, foods, philosophy and religion, and medicines. They were perhaps a more dramatic force for "globalization" than late twentieth-century expansion. David Harvey's "time and space compression" was surely anticipated by the Mongol pony express, which shortened the time for a letter to go from Baghdad to Beijing from several months to a few days.

The Mongols were fascinated with the realms they had conquered, and some scholars at each end of the Mongol world became fascinated also. Mapping and geography flourished; impressive collections of maps were made, mapping lore traveled in both directions, and mapping advanced greatly as a result. The indefatigable Rashīd al-Dīn (1247–1318; see below) compiled an atlas, now lost. Several Chinese atlases, compiled under Yuan, fared better and display vast increases in China's knowledge of the Western world.

To the west, Mongol rule brought relief from the Assassins, a violent but powerful Ismaili community whom the Mongols conquered and exterminated (see Juvaini 1958). The term "assassin" comes from *hashishin*, hashish users, a pejorative term applied by their enemies. If they did not use it (I expect they did), other sects certainly did; one Haydar al-Zawah of Nishapur, founder of such a sect, was said to have discovered marijuana in 1211 by seeing a "small tree . . . that . . . was in a state of agitation, shaking its branches and leaves excitedly even though there was no trace of wind" (Lane 2003: 247).

Conquests took the Mongols and their followers into uncharted realms with dubious foods. Sufis traveled from Central Asia to the newly Islamized land of Turkey, where they hoped for a wonderful new home but found instead that "the whole garden was planted with celery" (Lane 2003: 233)—at that time a weedy, intensely bitter herb—as effective an image for a disappointing scene as any in literature. The newcomers complained that there were too many *qalandars* (holy men of suspect sanity) with serious marijuana habits and rings through their penises to prevent sexual intercourse (246). Not all was reformed in Mongol days.

Under Mongol rule, there flowed textiles of all sorts, books, new inventions, paintings and art objects, ceramics, and indeed everything portable (Komaroff 2006). The Mongols did much to encourage trade, including long-distance trade. Western painting styles incorporated Chinese landscape art (reaching Renaissance Italy around 1400), as well as Chinese dragons, phoenixes, and other unlikely fauna, which were adopted early as far afield as Armenia (Kouymjian 2006). Pottery styles were homogenized across the Islamic world (O. Watson 2006), with, again, much Chinese influence on decoration. There is even a border in Phagspa script, a scientific writing system devised under Qubilai Qan, shown on a robe in an Italian painting from 1306 (Morgan 2006: 432).

A vast range of artistic methods and motifs spread across Asia (recently reviewed in a very valuable survey, *Islamic Chinoiserie* by Yuka Kadoi, 2009). Kadoi traces countless themes in painting, book design, ceramics, metalwork, cloth, and other arts. It remains only to be mentioned that Chinese landscape art, as filtered through Persia and Arabia, transformed European art after 1400. Most interesting for our purposes are the animal illustrations from the *Manafi-i Hayavan* by Ibn Bakhtishu' (ca. 1300; Kadoi 2009: 128–39). This is a work on animals, including their medical uses. A copy in the Pierpont Morgan Library, New York, is magnificently illustrated with paintings strongly influenced by Chinese art.

Allsen speculates on why and how some kinds of knowledge spread and were adopted, others spread and were lost, and others never spread. Clearly, the Mongols and their Turkic and Iranian courtiers knew good things when they saw them. They stockpiled skilled craftsmen, sponsored fairs, saved and often enslaved skilled workers and scholars when they conquered cities, and compiled encyclopedias and assembled libraries. They mapped, recorded, described, and sampled. They kept what was most useful and did not bother with the rest—unless it was luxurious for the court! The question of what survived and what did not remains to be addressed.

The Mongols brought back ideas and people from all over Asia. They deliberately captured and took home, or resettled as needed, the learned men, scholars, skilled craftspeople, and other valued workers (Weatherford 2004). This was another practice the Assyrians had perfected (Van de Mieroop 2007: 233), so the Mongols had only to copy a tradition already millennia old. Often the artisans were treated as loot and sent into de facto slavery, but if they were distinguished experts or particularly valuable workers, they were given the highest respect and treated very well (see Allsen 1997: 31–32).

The Mongol Empire had to have a rather astounding clerical staff to handle the languages; "each senior minister needed a host of scribes fluent in the principal languages of the empire, that is, Chinese, Tibetan, Uighur, Tangut [an ancient Tibeto-Burman language], Persian, and Mongolian" (Allsen 1994: 397), and obviously military leaders, large-scale traders, and other such would need similar staffs. Enormous diversity of language, religion, and culture existed and was tolerated. Uighurs and other Central Asian Turkic individuals were particularly important, partly because of their linguistic competence.

The Mongols moved thousands of Chinese and other East Asians to the Western world; Chinese were farming and cooking in Azerbaijan and Iran, and West and Central Asians in China (Allsen 2009). The Mongols sent Chinese doctors to Iran, where Rashīd met some and translated Chinese medical texts into Persian.

Trade and commerce flourished, of course (Allsen 1997; Haw 2006, 2008; Jackson 2005), as the Polos' journey famously attests. Marco Polo did make his trip and served the Mongols from 1274 to 1291, though his amanuensis Rusticello exaggerated his status in calling him a "governor." Polo describes many things that only an eyewitness could have known accurately, such as the different species of cranes in Central Asia and the huge pears in Hangzhou. The case against his trip rests on such arguments as his failure to mention the Great Wall—not surprising, since it was built 150 years after his time. The Polos were trading in luxury goods, what they called spicery and the Dutch later called rich trades. Much of the spicery was actually porcelain, fine fabrics, and the like. On the other hand, much of the Mongol trade was bulk staples.

Over the years, an amazing range of people traveled around the Mongol world (Allsen 2001: 6; Lane 2003, 2006). In addition to the Italians, Europe sent French, Flemings, Greeks, Germans, Scandinavians, Russians, and Hungarians. They were craftsmen, miners, and businessmen when they were not simply ambassadors or envoys. The Near Eastern people were represented, notably Armenians and Georgians, who were often at high levels as envoys, clerics, scholars, and rich merchants. (Georgia's brief but glorious Golden Age in the twelfth and early thirteenth centuries was still a living memory.) Even a few Alans turned up. Turkic peoples of Central Asia were pivotal—they tended to be mediators between the Mongols and the more sophisticated, urban peoples. Khitans, heirs of China's Liao Dynasty, provided much of the elite in the East.

Tibetans and Tanguts were well represented. Of course it was Arabs, Persians, and Chinese who staffed most of the middle and minor posts, and some rose to elite positions. They ranged from leopard keepers to cooks, from singers to stonemasons. Persian astronomers came to Beijing to build observatories and design state-of-the-art astronomical instruments. "Muslim" astronomy retained a place in the Chinese court astronomical bureau for centuries, until the Jesuits brought a better version (Elman 2005: 67–68). A Nestorian named Mar Sarghis made sherbets for Qubilai's court, possibly using sugar made by a combination of Western and Chinese technologies and Near Eastern types of lemons or limes grown in southeast China (Allsen 2001: 155–56).

Of course, there was a huge flow in the other direction. The Nestorians Rabban Sauma and Markos traveled from Yuan China to the Holy Land, where they found themselves elevated to high office; Rabban Sauma became an ambassador from the Mongols to Europe and left interesting descriptions of Italy and France (Budge 1928; Rossabi 1992).

Much of the flow of people consisted of slaves. Chinese conquest dynasties had a tradition of slavery; many, possibly most, citizens of the Wei and Jin Empires were in some form of servile status (Martinez 2009). This seems less true of Yuan, but in the West, the Golden Horde traded countless thousands of slaves to Byzantium and beyond; Genoese dominated the trade, basing it in Caffa (modern Fedosiya, near Odessa). The slave trade, already enormous, reached flood proportions; the West was deluged with Inner Asian slaves (Jackson 2005: 308), as it would be later by Tamerlane and other conquerors. The slave trade must have had a huge effect on demography then and since (think how many Italians have surnames like Slavo and Rosso), but no one has stepped forward to examine this issue. An almost equal lack of curiosity has bedeviled the question what cultural knowledge the slaves spread abroad. Many of them were specifically taken as skilled craftspersons. One assumes they had an enormous effect on the spread of technology and the arts.

Slavery was, of course, no new industry; the ancient Greeks and Romans had already developed that trade. Millions of people flowed outward from southeast Europe, southwest Central Asia, and points beyond. This movement is part of the reason for the rather uniform black-haired, brown-eyed, pale-skinned physical type of the Mediterranean. It is also part of the reason for the chronic failure of that part of the world to develop a great civilization. Foreigners (from Jews to Germans to Turks) flowed into the region, over time, to fill the demographic void. This item of information would seem to take us far from China, but the Western slave trade was an intimate part of Mongol power and enormously affected political development all over Eurasia. Imagine a counterfactual case in which the Black Sea had been a center of a more moral trade: given its central position, fertile soil, accessible seas and land routes, and rich resources, it would surely have become a great center of civilization and industry, like China, India, and western Europe. One remembers the point, made by countless writers from Adam Smith on, that slavery corrupts and debases the owners almost as much as it oppresses the slaves. The Chinese wisely moved away from it during history. In spite of having various forms of servility, China was usually a land of free, small-scale farmers—not peasants, serfs, or slaves.

The Mongols organized communications and trade into a comprehensive system. The *morin* (horse) mail was ancestral to America's Pony Express, but there was also a *narin* (careful) pathway for direct communication with the central government and a *tergen* (wagon) network for hauling bulk goods to the dispersed nomadizing hordes and migrating governments. In Thomas Allsen's felicitous wording, these comprised a part of the "interlocking networks that account for the extensive circulation of commodities, ideologies, technologies and pathologies that so characterizes the history of the Old World from ancient times" (Allsen 2009: 145). These were so incredibly successful that gyrfalcons, delicate birds from the arctic and subarctic that invariably die in hot climates unless superbly handled, traveled the sea lanes as far as Iran (146), Japan, and probably China.

It was at this time (ca. 1250) that Frederick II of Hohenstaufen wrote the world's greatest treatise on falconry, *still* a standard text in actual use by falconers and still in print (Hohenstaufen 1943). It is a thoroughly scientific work. In line with the relative tolerance of the times, he dedicated it to the neighboring sultan, a fellow falconer. It is dramatic proof that extremely rigorous, self-conscious, fully developed science did not have to wait for Galileo and Descartes. There were, obviously, equally skilled falconers in Japan, China, and Mongolia, as paintings and poetic references show (pers. obs., esp. of Chinese and Japanese paintings; the Chinese, ever fond of exotic "barbarians," loved to show Mongols with their eagles and falcons). They did not go into the meticulous and comprehensive historical and medical realms that Frederick covered, but they, too, were scientists in their way. It was during the brief period of unity, when it became as easy to go from Samarkand to Beijing as to Baghdad, that the *Huihui Yaofang* was born.

The integration of the Western and Eastern realms might have had world-making effects, but, ironically, it was the Mongols' own introductions that helped end the opportunity. The Mongols brought improved compasses, navigation instruments, printing, and related technologies to the West, enabling Europe to develop the sea trade that in the fifteenth century ended once and for all the dominance of the Silk Route.

An astonishing example of Mongol irrigation technology, recently described, is a dam built in Iran in the early fourteenth century (Hill 2000: 266). It still survives. Built across a river in a deep V-shaped gorge, it is 26 m high and 55 m along the top. The dam was built into limestone, which dissolves slowly over time. A similar dam in soluble rock in southern California failed in 1926 when the rock softened, leading to many deaths and to river system damage that is still not healed. Already by the fourteenth century the Mongols were beyond such foolishness; they dug grooves back into the solid rock and extended the dam several meters into them. Moreover, the dam is the first known arch dam: rather than stopping the river by sheer mass, it forms a curve, distributing the weight of water as an arch distributes the overlying weight of masonry. Somebody, somewhere, had had the brilliant realization that an arch rotated 90 degrees—to face upstream rather than upward—could stop water just as a regular arch bears the load of a building. Dams like Hoover Dam today still use the technique.

Humans have a maddening tendency not to record useful inventions of this sort. People would rather list battles or write about abstruse theological points. Thus we have no written record of this dam or of any like it until modern times. Probably the Mongols did not invent it; the Persians, great water engineers, may have been building such dams for years. In any case, the Mongol Empire had the good sense to build this one.

The Mongols also maintained and presumably expanded the networks of qanats, those greatest of all works of water engineering, invented in Persia or Mesopotamia a millennium or more earlier (see Chapter 5). Also popular were norias—sophisticated water-lifting wheels—which were known in both Rome and China by the first to second century CE, implying an origin possibly in Central Asia (Hill 2000: 269).

In addition to the trade and contacts across Central Asia, focal to this narrative, there was a huge amount of contact via the Indian Ocean, with India as the intermediary; Indian merchant groups such as Gujeratis joined Arabs (often Hadramautis), Jews (Wink 2002), and even Indonesians and Africans in a vast international enterprise.

Thomas Allsen, in *Culture and Conquest in Mongol Eurasia* (2001), documented a great deal of the knowledge transfer under the Mongols. He summarizes a great deal of information, mostly in Western sources but also in Chinese ones, on relations between the Ilkhans in the Near East, the Mongols in the steppes, and the Yuan Dynasty in China. Long after these were separate realms, they stayed in touch and exchanged information and goods. The relationship ended around 1335, when the Ilkhanid Abū Sa'īd died and the Yuan court ran into desperate straits.

Lists of gift exchanges from 1324 to 1332 show that the West sent a range of goods, especially Western products (Allsen 2001: 44). Notable were animals—lions, tigers, dromedaries, and the like. Precious stones, medicines, and minor manufactured items traveled. The Chinese sent silk and money, and once some medicines. Apparently this was more a question of the Chinese court buying exotica than of real exchange or tribute.

To some extent, this economic activity was in the family; the Golden Horde still held south Russia and the neighboring steppes. Ibn Battuta stayed with the Golden Horde's royalty in 1332 and accompanied Khan Üzbak's third wife, a Greek princess from Constantinople, on a visit to her home (Ibn Battuta 1959: 498–517). It was quite a trip, with all the requisite courtiers, jurists (he being one of them), servants, beasts of burden, presents, and luxury items. A single such progression conveyed a vast amount of material wealth across vast spaces.

In an earlier work, *Commodity and Exchange in the Mongol Empire* (1997), Allsen studied the flow of cloth and cloth technology through the Mongol world. The Mongols reveled in silk brocaded with gold, the most luxurious thing they could imagine. They not only dressed in it; they lined their tents with it. (They still love silks and fine clothing.) Textile art has always been a major fine art in Asia, not a "mere craft" as in Europe, and cloth technology (including dye chemistry) became a major part of global knowledge transfer in the Middle Ages.

Marco Polo and other European travelers played important roles in documenting the life and culture of the time (Haw 2006). The most important, however, was the great polymath Rashīd al-Dīn, a Persian dietitian and physician who served under the Ilkhans. Rashīd was said to have been Jewish, but converted to Islam. In addition to his atlas, he compiled a history of the world and several science books (many now lost) in conjunction with teams of experts and writers. Rashīd knew the elites of the time and worked especially with a Mongol named Bolad Aqa (Allsen 2001). Both had been leading nutritionists and dietitians in their respective courts. Bolad apparently occupied the position of court nutritionist (130), later occupied by Hu Sihui, of whom more below.

Rashīd al-Dīn, "a Sunni administrator, wrote, with his research team that included Buddhists, a history of Buddhism for a Shi'a Mongol khan" (May 2012: 188). Rashīd introduced Chinese medicine to Iran and had something to do with growing Chinese seeds in Tabriz and spreading Chinese rice agricultural techniques to the Caspian lowlands (Allsen 2001).

One interesting observation (from among many) was Rashīd's description of a rice variety popular with Indian elites (Allsen 2001: 137). From the description, it was a basmati. The Persians tried to grow it, but it would not flourish under Persian conditions. Allsen further speculates that this was the time when rice began to spread rapidly in the Near East. Of course it had been known before, but rice cookery may have become more advanced. One strong possibility is that pilaf was invented at this time. The pilaf or pilau technique— frying the rice in fat before boiling it and then adding spices and other items— appears to be a Persian invention. (Chinese fried rice is fried *after* boiling and drying.) Nothing like pilaf is attested in any medieval cookbook. Yet, the technique was widespread as far as Spain in the early modern period—early enough for it to be part of the package of Moorish-Andalusian cuisine transmitted to the New World in Spanish colonial times. Clearly, it was invented sometime before then and spread swiftly.

Agricultural manuals were one of the types of scholarship that flowed in both directions. The knowledge industry Rashīd al-Dīn developed was involved, and a manual compiled by him actually survives (Allsen 2001: 117–18): *The Book of Monuments and Living Things*. It contains much Chinese lore, studied with the help of his Mongol collaborator Bolad. It was part of a larger work that ranged from calendrics to dam building to mining. The agricultural part covers seeds, trees, grafting, fertilizer, melons and other crops, domestic animals, bees, "crop failures and their prevention," and product storage (118). Much of the information is direct from China, and Allsen suspects "that Rashīd al-Dīn had access, albeit indirect, to the vast Chinese literature on agronomy" (118). I wonder if it really was indirect. Rashīd certainly could have acquired Chinese manuals had he wanted. If he could not read them himself (and he may well have been able to), he certainly had staff members who could. In any case, he includes data on classically Chinese products like oranges, rice, jujubes, and mulberries; he knew the Chinese had different kinds of mulberries for raising silkworms and for making paper. He was aware that the Chinese had varieties of millet unknown or barely known in the West. One millet variety had been introduced to Iran.

He gives quite recognizable Persian spellings of the Chinese words for coconut, cinnamon, black pepper (which the Chinese called Iranian pepper), betel nut, sandalwood, litchi nut, and, of course, tea—which is still known in Persian by the Chinese name *cha*. The word has evolved into *chai* in Persia and its old sphere of influence by adding a Persian nominative suffix. One can tell today that Eastern Europe, India, and even—surprisingly—Mongolia got tea initially from Persia, by their use of this form. The Persians already had already been acquainted with tea before Mongol times, but not very well; the Mongols were the ones who brought it to stay. A fusion cuisine developed. Even chopsticks were known, acquiring a Turkish name borrowed into Arabic (Allsen 2001: 136).

Chinese medicine was already somewhat known in the West; there are Chinese medicines in al-Kindī's work in the ninth century (Savage-Smith et al. 2011:217). Our irrepressible friend Rashīd al-Dīn noted and summarized various Chinese books on medicine, "translated into Persian and then into Arabic" (Allsen 2001: 144). He and one Safī' al-Dīn compiled a book called *Tanksūq-nāmah īl-khānī* (Treasure book of the Il-qans); Allsen 2001: 144; see also Adnan 1940; the work is referred to as the *Ilkhan Compendium Concerning the Sciences and Arts of the Chinese* in Nasr 1976: 182). This book remained unique in Near Eastern literature, but from it, knowledge of Chinese medicine spread rather widely in the Western world. Amazingly, a first volume survives, covering pulse, anatomy of the head, pregnancy, and fatness. The illustrations look very Chinese. It was preserved in Istanbul and is now being studied by Vivienne Lo and other scholars. A pair of anatomical drawings showing the internal organs from front and back was copied faithfully from a text by the Song Emperor Huizong's physician Yang Jie (twelfth century); the original and a copy in a Persian manuscript of the fourteenth century are shown by Shih-shan Susan Huang in her great work on Daoist art, *Picturing the True Form* (73–74).

Much medical lore in Rashīd's book seems to have been taken down directly from Chinese teaching—evidently everyone, or at least many key people, knew both Chinese and Persian, to say nothing of Mongol, Turkic, and Arabic. The work shows familiarity with the *Nanjing*, the Yellow Emperor's Classic, the "Hua Tuo" material, and other classic Chinese medical texts. Hua To—a surgeon of the third century CE who had legendary powers and became a mythic figure—inspired a much later work called the *Hua Tuo Nei*

Zhaotu (Hua Tuo's illuminating illustrations of internal medicine; Allsen 2001: 145), and this was drawn on heavily in Rashīd al-Dīn's text. The Persians were particularly impressed by pulse diagnosis. They translated the *Mai Jue* (Secrets of the pulse), a composite book dating from the Sung or Yuan eras and mistakenly ascribed to Wang Shuhuo of a much earlier era (Allsen 2001: 145–46; see also Savage-Smith et al. 2011: 217).

A great deal of herbal lore spread with this. Chinese rhubarb (*Rheum palmatum* and *R. officinale*) became popular to relieve constipation. Use of Cubeb pepper, cassia, and many other drugs also expanded. Cinnamon was known as *darsīnī*, "Chinese cinnamon," in Arabic and Persian, so when cassia—the Chinese equivalent—became known, it got a double dose of "Chineseness": *darsīnī-sīnī*. Allsen does not note, but we should here, that cinnamon, *Cinnamomun zeylanicum*, comes not from China but from Sri Lanka. Spice cassia, *C. cassia* and related species, is from China and is so similar to true cinnamon that few people can tell the difference. Among medicinal foods, *Coptis teeta*, *Smilax china*, Chinese rhubarb *Rheum emodi* (Akira 1989), camphor *Camphora officinalis*, and cassia *Cinnamomum cassia*, and some less important items, were adopted by Near Eastern medicine in early days (Said 1997). Opium entered with the *Huihui Yaofang*, becoming regular Chinese practice in the Ming Dynasty (Allsen 2001: 159).

Among things that spread the other way were mastic, theriac (much discussed in the *Huihui Yaofang*), and medical uses of sharbat (see Allsen 2001: 154–56). Allsen believes Galenic medicine was hard to accept—though made easier by the diversity of medical traditions in China. Actually, Galenic medicine had been filtering into China for centuries. The Chinese fused it with yin-yang cosmology without much difficulty.

Allsen devotes much notice to the *līmū*, a citrus that seems to have started its career in Persia, or perhaps India, and spread to the Near East and China shortly before the Mongol period (Allsen 2001: 122–24). The word is, of course, ancestral to our "lime" and "lemon." This one was probably a variety of lime since it grew commonly in Baghdad, which is too hot for lemons. The Yuan established a botanical garden at Litchee Bay near Canton, and grew, among other things, 800 of these citrus, to produce a thirst-quencher (*keshui*) "explicitly equated" with *shelibie*, the Chinese spelling of *sharbat*. (*Sharbat*, from the Arabic root for "drink," gives us the English words "sherbet," "sorbet," and "shrub"—the rum drink, not the bush.)

Meanwhile and later, Near Eastern knowledge was merging with Indian knowledge and influencing Tibet (Buell et al. 2010, whence it fed into the

Mongol and Chinese data pools of herbal references, medical texts, local knowledge). Central Asia was placed at the meeting ground of Near Eastern, Indian, and Chinese lore and boasted an enormous wealth of local herbs and herbalism to draw on. The Mongols took full advantage of this. (For chronicles of the many Mongol and subsequent encyclopedias intended to propagate medicine there, see Richter-Bernburg and Said 2000: 312–15.) The Mongols set up medical schools and raised the status of the medical profession significantly, probably inspired by Near Eastern norms. The Mongols seem to have seen Western medicine as more advanced than Chinese and did all they could to bring it to China. Four medical schools were founded over time in the Mongol capital, and all had heavy Persian (and thus Arabic) influence (Rall 1970; Rossabi 1994).

Moreover, the Mongols also transferred veterinary medicine around their empire, and thus a major Central Asian tradition of veterinary medicine (Richter-Bernburg and Said 2000: 315–17) reached China in Yuan (Buell, in progress). Moreover, knowledge flowed both ways. Ibn al-Baytar (1197–1248) introduced many Chinese drugs to the Near Eastern world, including varieties of aconite and rhubarb.

The great plague of 1346–48 (Dols 1977) may have been started by Mongol armies or Mongol slaving or trade with the Mongols; it supposedly spread from Kaffa, on the Crimean peninsula, via Genoese merchant ships. It did not affect China significantly. Li Bozhong (2003: 138) correctly dismisses the claims of bubonic plague episodes contemporary with or earlier than Europe's great epidemic. There is absolutely no evidence for a Chinese equivalent to this one. For many reasons (some addressed memorably in C. Benedict 1996 and more recently in Buell 2012), bubonic plague is endemic, not epidemic, in China. It seems never to have been a major killer, judging from the lack of descriptions of this unmistakable disease in the records we have (Brook 2010: 65–66; Buell 2012). It is somewhat depressing to read Western histories that assume China "must have" had the same plagues as Europe. Diseases are not like that. They do what they do, not what a historian thinks they "must have" done.

By contrast, this epidemic devastated the Western world. It hurt the Near East more than it hurt Europe. In Europe many of the elite lived in castles in the country and were thus relatively safe from rats. Thus after the plague, the workforce was depleted, the elite less so. Further cycles of plague continued the process. Wages rose, innovation flourished to make up for shortages of labor, and the economy eventually prospered greatly. In the Near East, elites lived in crowded cities, where the plague was worst. The country folk were less affected. Thus the plague created a shortage of employers and a surplus of labor, leading to economic problems. More to the point, scholars, scientists, and craftsmen were almost exterminated. The Near East lost its lead in the world and never recovered it.

Mongol Rule in China

The perfect epitaph on Song, and comment on the rise of Yuan, was made by Marco Polo:

> Yet the province of Manzi [Song, specifically the Song heartland in the Yangzi Valley] is very strong by nature, and all the cities are encompassed by sheets of water of great depth, and more than a crossbow-shot in width; so that the country never would have been lost, had the people but been soldiers. But that is just what they were not; so lost it was. (Polo 1927: 207)

The Mongols conquered the north in 1234 and all China in 1279, establishing the Yuan Dynasty. By this time Chinese and Altaic peoples had come to work together in north Chinese administrative bureaucracies, and the Mongols could simply fit in. They were advised by an heir of the Liao Dynasty, the noted statesman and thinker Yelü Chucai. At least one Mongol chief proposed, probably not seriously, to clear out the Chinese to create pasture land. However, China supposedly has selenium-deficient soils, which are not good for horse grazing (May 2012: 225), and there are other feed issues as well as climate and disease problems (P. Smith 1991), although horses are raised in many areas today.

The Mongols knew where their real wealth lay and were, at first, good administrators. On the other hand, the conquest of China took an incredible toll of lives, especially in the north. China's population fell from 100–120 million in the early 1200s to 60 million or a bit more (according to a Yuan census of 1290; May 2012: 223; May thinks this is a serious undercount, however). Most of the most losses were in the north. The fall of Yuan eliminated any gains under that dynasty, and Ming began with the same lowly figure, not regaining pre-Mongol population levels till the late sixteenth century (Mote 1994: 618–22). The Song Dynasty had experimented with a pacifist policy; it was founded by a general who took power in a coup and did everything possible to prevent a strong military from doing as much to him and his heirs (Twitchett and Smith 2009; see Chapter 6). Unfortunately, pacifism did not work at that time, so the Mongols did not take that path.

The Mongols had learned about autocratic rule in Central Asia, and Liao and Jin had pioneered pathways to centralization. So the Yuan introduced to China a more autocratic form of government than that of Song. However, the problems of rule—including weak emperors and war-torn successions—prevented Yuan from being very effective. Taxes remained low, around 3.4 percent of grain produced (Brook 2010: 107). This meant, among other things, that the government establishment could not be very large and could not even remotely approximate the penetrance and authority of modern governments. This mix of autocracy at the top and weakness on the ground was not a formula for success in governing, and Yuan was one of the shortest-lived Chinese dynasties. The following Ming Dynasty was to succeed better at rule.

It was at this time that the ethnically Chinese Muslim community began to take shape on a significant scale (Tan 2009: 87ff.). The merchants who had begun to flock to China in the 600s now came in droves, settled down, and married into the Chinese population. Widespread Muslim communities resulted; however, the immigrants were of higher status than the Chinese, so attempts to maintain Islamic culture were the rule. These were the people who later became the Hui, but in Mongol times that term would have been understood as referring to the people of the Uighur kingdom, which had only recently been eclipsed by Mongol and other powers.

The Mongols inherited a China already westward-looking (Haw 2008; Jackson 2005; Ratchnevsky 1991; Rossabi 1988), thanks to earlier dynasties, all of which started in the northwest—generally in the Wei Valley area of Shaanxi—and conquered eastward. Sui and Tang were downright frontier societies in origin (Twitchett 1979); the Tang royal family was said to be part "barbarian," probably Turkic. The Liao and Jin Dynasties were in full contact with the West; Michal Biran (2005) has recently documented Liao's westward stance and Islamic contacts.

Chinese skill was taken for granted in this world, and very widely circulated was a Chinese claim that only the Chinese see with two eyes; those of Byzantium (or other skilled areas of the West) are one-eyed; the rest are blind (Allsen 2009: 152–53). This is possibly not the first or last time the Chinese were a bit less than modest about their skills, but it seems clear that the Western world did not disagree strongly with the assessment.

The Chinese had a type of low-rated cotton before Yuan, but the Mongol regime introduced better cotton and propagated it widely. It finally became a major fabric, at the expense of hemp and other bast fibers. China's enormous and fantastically productive cotton industry was beginning, but its full development had to await the introduction of New World cottons, a few centuries later on.

The Mongols succeeded in taming the Yellow River, taking only half a year (Endicott-West 1994: 576). This feat was never repeated in the entire history of imperial China; the Yellow River was not controlled again until the Communist era. The striking findings are that the Mongol Empire was very far from being a brief irruption of nomads who settled down to become just another Chinese dynasty. In addition to the Yellow River control mission, other water control projects flourished (Li Bozhong 2003).

Meanwhile, in China, the Yuan court issued *Essentials of Agriculture and Sericulture* (*Nongsang Jiyao*; Allsen 2009: 138). Food was easily spread. Gastronomy was well established at both ends of the Mongol world, and the Mongols soon picked it up. (If one's cuisine is limited to boiled meat, noodles, and fermented mare's milk, one's resistance to borrowing Chinese and Persian gastronomy is probably low.) In addition to the work by Paul Buell, Charles Perry, and myself (Buell et al. 2000; Perry 2005; Rodinson et al. 2001), Allsen notes that sugar technology spread to China and elsewhere in Asia, and saffron became a food spice in China. Laufer (1919) and later Franke, Buell, and others discovered many food-related Persian loanwords in Chinese (see Franke and Twitchett 1994; Buell et al. 2010). Buell dissected these and showed that many had been borrowed via Turkic languages, for the Chinese words represent transliterations of various Turkic dialectic pronunciations of the Persian words (Buell et al. 2000). However, away from the Mongol court and the "barbarian"-influenced north, Chinese food remained totally conservative. The great cookbooks of the period do not show any Mongol influence at all (E. Anderson et al. 2005; Sabban 1997, 1999).

In medicine, the level of exchange is shown by the presence of a Lombard doctor at the Yuan court (Allsen 2001: 142) and of Greek medicine in Tibet. Medical schools proliferated under Yuan and were heavily influenced by Western knowledge (Shinno 2007). A new medicine arose from the fusion of the dramatic advances made in the Song Dynasty (Unschuld 1985, 1986) and the new Western knowledge.

Food Under the Mongols

The Mongol Empire and its foods and agriculture are now well known (Allsen 2001; E. Anderson 2005b; Barfield 1989; Brook 2010; Buell, Anderson, and Perry 2010; De Rachewiltz 2004; Ratchnevsky 1991; Rossabi 1988). Allsen (1997) notes interesting food-related color symbolism. White was spiritual and special; white mares were used for *kumys* (59–60). White was associated with dairy foods, red with blood and meat, black with black tea and soup, yellow with butter, and green with vegetables and herbs (58). This color-coding of foods still exists in Mongolia (see below).

Scholars once believed that pasta came from China to Europe. The reality is much more complex. We have observed noodles in China in the Neolithic (Chapter 2. They were apparently extruded—the dough forced through a colander or sieve to make the noodles. This is the classic Chinese way to make noodles. Apparently quite independent was the invention of dumplings wrapped in dough skins, probably a Near Eastern idea. It reached China via the Turks by Tang. Yet another invention was Mediterranean pasta. This started with thin flat dough sheets that the Greeks fried or baked and called *laganon*. These were layered with cheese and honey. Eventually somebody got the bright idea of boiling them, and in Sicily the Arabs created the dish of layered boiled laganon and cheese that soon evolved into lasagna. Meanwhile, the Greeks had begun to cut flat sheets of dough into thin strips called *itria*—noodles. Cut noodles may have spread to China with the steppe nomads in the period just before Tang. The Chinese, however, added new tricks that eventually spread back to Europe. (See the classic history of pasta by Serventi and Sabban 2002). Nobody knows who started or from whence came the idea of mixing the dough with egg. Noodles of various sorts remain basic to Central Asian cuisines, even more than to the Chinese.

The *Huihui Yaofang*

The *Huihui Yaofang* (*HHYF*; "Western medical formulas") was a typical Mongol project: a vast exercise in learning from other cultures. The *HHYF* was probably compiled by "the Guang Hui Si, the ministry of Islamic drugs" (Kong et al. 1996: 3). Its signal failure to affect Chinese medicine is fairly typical of medieval Chinese attitudes toward foreign realms and their knowledge. The

Chinese were relatively open as traditional societies went, but they were not like the Mongols in this regard.

The *HHYF* was the most spectacular product of the Ilkhan-Yuan knowledge exchange. *Huihui* originally meant "Uighurs," but by this time had become a general term for people of the Near Eastern and Muslim world. The term included not only Muslims but also, at least by implication, the Christian (especially Nestorian) and Jewish doctors who abounded in the Near East and Central Asia and whose imprint is clear in the *HHYF.* Galen, Rufus of Ephesus, and many Christian doctors appear in it as hui.

The *HHYF* was unique in transferring Near Eastern medical knowledge to China directly but has to be seen in context. The Mongols also oversaw massive transfers of medical knowledge around their domains in Central Asia and the Near East. This was not innovative, as is obvious from what has been discussed before, but the point to be made is that the single (though huge) case of eastward expansion is not a strange and unprecedented occurrence but simply an extension of what was routine in the Western world. In Timothy May's assessment, "the Mongols preferred Islamic medical care to other forms and that the publication of this work is evidence of the Mongol court's attempt to promote it" (May 2012: 17).

A western specialist, 'Isa the Interpreter, founded an Office of Western Medicine (*Xiyu Iyao Si*) in China around 1263; it survived throughout Yuan. There was a Western medical classic, possibly Ibn Sīnā's canon, in the Yuan library (Allsen 2009: 139). Allsen argues that the Mongol belief that "the seat of human life force, the soul, was located in the blood and circulatory system" made the Mongols sympathetic to Chinese medicine, with its focus on circulating qi and blood and its use of pulse diagnosis to assess these; this may be why Rashīd al-Dīn made a point of translating a Chinese pulse classic into Persian (Allsen 2009: 148). The Mongols found the Chinese doctors and astronomers shaman-like. The Chinese scholars did not go into trances and voyage to the other world, but they did divine illness and keep watch on the stars, like shamans.

The *HHYF* was heavily derivative of standard Near Eastern medical works by Avicenna and the post-Avicenna writers. One suspects that Central Asian writers are especially represented—in particular, the leading Persian medical encyclopedia, compiled for the kings of Khwārazm by Sayyid Zayn al-Dīn Ismā'īl al-Husaynī al-Jurjānī. This is the book that really introduced Avicenna and the great pharmacologists to thirteenth- and fourteenth-century Central Asia, and is probably the direct source of the *HHYF.*

Allsen thinks Western medicine had little effect on China (Allsen 2001: 156), but this was not the case. Even Allsen reports (briefly) not only on the *HHYF* but also on the *Hui-hui I-shu* (Book of Muslim medicine) in the Ming encyclopedia, which apparently is not surviving (Allsen 2001: 159). There had already been considerable incorporation of Galenic ideas into Chinese medicine, dating back to the Wei and Tang Dynasties.

Arguably, most important about the *HHYF* from a modern point of view is what it says about globalization and international knowledge flows in the medieval period. This encyclopedia appears to be genuinely unique in world history. Few books even in modern times so comprehensively summarize one tradition's science for the benefit of a different and separate civilization.

The *HHYF* survives in fragments. The Yuan original from the early 1300s was lost, but the Ming had the sense to republish it, and some of that edition survives. It was edited and published, with wonderfully valuable botanical identifications, by Y. C. Kong (1996). About 400 pages' worth of material exists from what once must have been a 3,500- to 4,000-page work. Surviving is the twelfth *juan* (section, originally a separate volume in Chinese) on treating stroke and psychological conditions; juan 30, on complex prescriptions; juan 34, a long and exceedingly complex treatise on wound treatment; and the table of contents for the second half of the work. The original was written in Chinese, with Arab and/or Persian glosses carefully written next to many Chinese transliterations or translations.

The botanical identifications were done via two approaches: noted economic botanist Hu Shiu-ying and her students (including Kong himself) worked on the Chinese, while Kong and associates studied the Arabic. They came to good agreement. (Much more work with documentation is needed; medieval Arabic medicine remains poorly known, in spite of Levey 1966, Levey and Al-Khaledy 1967, and others.) Kong et al. (1996; Kong and Chen 1996) cite 128 Chinese drugs and about 517 Near Eastern ones (the latter number being uncertain because of identification questions). This somewhat overstates the diversity; discounting unidentified entries, duplications, and entries in which several virtually identical species serve the same function, there are only 416 clearly distinct drug categories in the surviving parts of the book, and several of these are known only from being listed in the index. Many of the latter cannot be identified. About 398 of the 416 are identifiable. They include 258 identifiable plant species, 27 minerals, and over 70 animals and animal products. (These total 354; the other items are either unidentified or represent multiple products from some species.)

The book has also been reissued in a modern Chinese edition by Song Xian (2000). This edition includes a version in modern Chinese with the Arabic transliterated in Roman script and a long, thorough listing of the medicinals and diseases. The identifications appear to be based on Kong et al. (1996) (The last would be more helpful if the authors had more consistently used scientific terms rather than often falling back on the idiosyncratic and annoying pseudo-Latin affected by practitioners of traditional Chinese medicine.)

Most plants mentioned in the *HHYF* are Western ones. The foundation of the entire herbal construction is Dioscorides (Gunther 1934; see also Riddle 1985). This great second-century Greek writer had wandered across the Mediterranean world and knew his plants. Much of his herbal lore is still used today, and not only in folk medicine. Later Greek writers added to it, and then Syriac, Arab, and Persian traditions fused with the Greek. By the time of the *HHYF*, there were hundreds, probably thousands, of plants in Near Eastern medical practice. These are known from a large range of herbals produced by Christian, Jewish, and Muslim authors.

However, many of the plants in the *HHYF* are native Chinese ones. Mongol drugs are presumably among these but are hard to separate from Chinese herbal drugs and require further research. Also unsurprising is the presence of several Indian plants from Ayurvedic medical tradition. (Fortunately, Nadkarni 1976 provides a superb encyclopedic reference on Indian medical botany.) There are also Tibetan influences on medical practice, though not on the plants. Tibetan medicine and ethnopharmacology are finally becoming known in the West, thanks to the recent work of Denise Glover (2005), Frances Garrett (2007), and others. The Mongol Empire was truly a world empire and incorporated every bit of knowledge it could find; doctors from the West, Tibet, and China were present at court, and probably Indian medical experts too.

The biggest problem in dealing with the *HHYF* is that most of the illness terms are incomprehensible so far. Near Eastern terms were translated into China's medical language. Unfortunately, the Yuan was a time of medical transition (Unschuld 1985, 1986), and we do not know what most of those terms really meant, especially when used to translate Arabic and Persian terms that also have uncertain referents. We have to work with translations from Greek to Arabic to Chinese and then to English.

Sometimes this is easy. The Greek term *alopecia*, "fox condition," for hair loss (shedding hair the way a fox sheds its winter coat) managed to survive all the way from Greek to Arabic to Persian to the Chinese words for "like the molting of a fox" (see below).

Melancholia becomes Arabic *malinkhuliya*, which is given in the *HHYF* text in clear Arabic. It is glossed in Chinese as "lack of peace in the heart and wild talk due to wind." Wind as causal is a purely Chinese touch. Melancholia in Greek medicine originally referred to black bile, the blackish mixture of dead blood cells and other disease products that choke the bile duct and drain into the intestine in severe cases of hepatitis or malaria. Since anyone with this condition would be utterly miserable, the term took on the psychological implications it still has today. However, there is no evidence that black bile was a concept in China or in the *HHYF*. In fact, the four humors of Galenic medicine (blood, bile, phlegm, and black bile) remained poorly known. Blood, of course, was obviously important, but Chinese and Greek beliefs about it differed radically. Phlegm was important in Chinese medicine from very early— possibly as a borrowing, but choler and melancholia in the Galenic sense were not concepts that took hold in China.

Other terms are much more mysterious. *Qulnaj* is defined as "abdominal wind internal knotting," and both its Greek original and its Arabic meanings are obscure. Usually we do not have even this much to go on in the *HHYF*; the Chinese terms are often given without the Arabic or Persian originals and are substantially incomprehensible.

Chinese medicine is based on qi. Much illness is caused by *feng*, literally "wind," but the word actually refers to a number of external and internal vapors, influences, and humors that are obscure to us. Conditions are blamed on stagnant qi, evil feng, inadequacy or weakness of the organ fields, and other causes whose fourteenth-century meanings are now quite unclear.

In modern Chinese medicine, which uses the classic sources and probably preserves the broad outlines of medieval medicine, these entities were diagnosed on the basis of suites of symptoms that do not define modern biomedical nosological entities. For instance, in the excellent descriptions of illnesses in *Chinese Herbal Medicine: Formulas and Strategies* (Scheid et al. 2009), Chinese categories do not correspond to Western ones. Sometimes the Chinese illness is completely refractory to understanding in biomedical terms, but far more often the symptoms define some type of respiratory, digestive, or systemic condition that does not map perfectly onto modern biomedical categories. Respiratory illnesses, especially, can be caused by any number of problems with qi in Chinese medical thinking, or by any number of viruses, bacteria, or environmental irritants in biomedical thinking. Although all are respiratory illnesses, the classification according to wind and qi is not the same as the classification according to viral or bacterial causation. And Chinese "excess heat" may manifest as rashes, pustules, sore throat, chapped lips and mouth, mouth sores, flushing, dry skin, stomach cramps, or constipation.

These symptoms define a perfectly clear and well-defined nosological entity to traditional and modern Chinese but are a meaningless congeries of unrelated symptoms to a biomedical doctor; they can be caused by scurvy, or by various infections, or by allergies. These different causal explanations lead to dividing the vast set of "illnesses" into countless subsets, and the divisions are different in China from those in biomedicine. If the purpose of taxonomy is to "carve nature at the joints" (as a biologists' saying tells us), China and biomedicine both see "nature"—the respiratory symptomatology—but they have totally different perceptions of where the joints are and how to find them. One could go farther and say that biomedicine wants to "carve nature at the joints" whereas Chinese medicine wants to trace nature's qi flows instead of carving it up.

Even the relatively straightforward terminology of the body used in the section on wounds, breaks, and dislocations is often incomprehensible. Historians of Chinese medicine have not yet analyzed Yuan anatomical terms. Words that must have been perfectly clear to a Yuan practitioner are not so now.

Contrary to Allsen's assessment (2001: 156), the Chinese acquired a good deal of Near Eastern theory, including Galenic material. The revolutionary changes in Chinese medicine in Song and Yuan are only now beginning to be appreciated. Much more is to be learned. Suffice it to say that the Chinese did not ignore Near Eastern lessons, although that may be truer for animals than for people; Buell and coworkers have shown that Chinese veterinary medicine is largely a Yuan import. Near Eastern and Central Asian veterinary learning was so far ahead of Chinese that the Chinese simply engaged in mass replacement (Buell et al. 2006).

Previous studies of the *HHYF* have emphasized its relationship with the great *Qānūn fi al-tibbi* of Avicenna (Ibn Sīnā), a standard medical encyclopedia in the Islamic world. The relationship is distant at best. The *HHYF* was clearly compiled from a variety of sources. Al-Bīrūnī is one source, at one or two removes (see Al-Bīrūnī 1973). Al-Samarqandī's work seems surprisingly unrelated (see Levey and Al-Khaledy 1967). All the drugs that he recommends are in the *HHYF*, but his simple, eminently practical formulas are extremely different from the long-complicated, often part-magical formulas in the

HHYF. Al-Samarqandī's book is so rational and sensible that it could still be used perfectly well as a guide to herbal remedies today; its formulas have stood the test of time, and my personal observations show that they are often essentially the same as home remedies used successfully in the Near East, Mediterranean, and (thanks to Moorish Spain) Latin America.

I suspect that especially important was Sayyid Isma'il Juzjānī's *Zakhīra-i-Khwārazmshāhī* (Thesaurus of the Khwārzamshāhs), a monumental twelfth-century Persian work known to have been very important in Central Asia (Elgood 1951, 1970), where it was apparently written. Unfortunately, no translation of this work exists; copies are hard to find and little scholarship has been expended on it. Proof that one of these Central Asian Persian epitomes of Near Eastern medicine was a source is found in juan 30, 357: "I saw a person in Balkh" who used a particular medicine, and "was cured, I believe." In Balkh at that time, Arabs were unlikely and Chinese doctors nonexistent. The individual who saw this cure must have been an Iranian doctor.

Distilling, a critically important medical technology, was first invented in China, probably in the Han Dynasty (H. Huang 2000, analyzing Han illustrations and actual Han stills archaeologically discovered; I have separately examined the pictures and agree with Huang; early distilling also existed in India, possibly an independent invention). Allsen (2009: 150) notes that distilling was also invented in Sicily in the 1200s, though I wonder if there is an indirect Chinese origin there. Allsen also notes that distilling fermented mare's milk (Turkic *kumys*, Mongol *airag*) was clearly an idea of Muslim-world inventors—rather ironic in view of the Muslim prohibition on alcohol—because the Mongol word for it was *araki* (now *arkhi*), from the Arabic word for distilled liquor (Arabic *'araq*, "sweat," a good descriptive term for simple distillation). Distillation was well known to both Mongols and Chinese at this time, and some small stills survive. The Mongols distilled black kumys, a strong, prized drink. Mongol and Yuan Chinese distillation and its history have recently been monographed in detail by Luo Feng (2012). These stills seem ancestral to the rather distinctive "Mongolian" type of still as classically distinguished from the Chinese type by Rudolf Hommel (1937: 141–47).

Kong et al. (1996; Kong and Chen 1996) cite 128 Chinese drugs and around 517 Near Eastern ones (the latter number being uncertain because of identification questions). This somewhat overstates the diversity; discounting unidentified entries, duplications, and entries in which several virtually identical species serve the same function, there are only 360 clearly distinct drug categories in the surviving parts of the book.

At least 148 foods are cited in the *Huihui Yaofang*, some of which occur in the formulas. Many (including odd items such as weasel, bat, lizard, and crocodile) are noted in the table of contents, but we have lost the section on foods, in which they were described.

Many of the *HHYF* drugs are effective by modern biochemical standards. Some are narcotics: opium, henbane, marijuana, and the like. Others are stimulants: cinnamon, saffron, black pepper, and many others. There are also many soothing drugs: lavender, myrrh, lemon balm, and other herbals. Vermifuges, such as wormwood, were known. Some drugs are antiseptic and antifungal, like rose oil, saffron, and the metal salts. Diuretics, purgatives, and emetics were also known. In many formulas, however, these effective drugs figure as only a few ingredients among many. Unless the patient took vast quantities of the formula, the effective ingredients would be diluted to the point where they offered small value.

The *Huihui Yaofang* mentions some 67 strictly Western food items. It mentions 17 Chinese foods and many more Chinese herbs, including many Chinese items clearly used only as a substitute for something Near Eastern. Eleven foods are from India; these have clear medicinal activity by modern biomedical standards. Southeast Asia supplied seven foods, all medicinal in modern terms. Seventeen of the foods are widespread. About half of these are medicinal in modern terms: for example, pine seeds, bottle gourd, rose, and radish. Licorice and wolfthorn species were different and the uses slightly different too. Honey, the item most often mentioned in what survives of the *HHYF*, was universal. It was already used as a common vehicle for drugs, soother of patients, and nourishing and safe food everywhere in the world that bees could flourish. Its importance in the *HHYF* mirrors its importance in Western medicine of the time.

One typical, effective group of drugs comprises the genus *Artemisia*. Wormwoods were known throughout Eurasia to be vermifugal. The Chinese were well aware of abortifacients, presumably including wormwood, but did not often employ them (Sommer 2011). By contrast, Dioscorides' herbal (Gunther 1934), the basis of all Western herbal medicine, lists countless abortifacients (not all were effective). Wormwoods also treat digestion; one of them, *A. annua*, *qinghao* (the drug being *qinghaosu*), cures malaria, a fact known very early in China; all wormwoods are somewhat antiseptic. They kill insects, a fact that led to their use as early as the Han Dynasty to line the interiors of granaries. The leaves were also powdered and mixed with the stored grain—to be carefully sieved and washed out later (Shih Sheng-Han 1974).

Many remedies in the *HHYF* involve enormously long lists of drugs. This may be related to the tendency of Near Eastern physicians to use almost anything for almost any condition in the hopes that if they tried enough drugs something would work. This is shown by the Cairo Genizah material (Lev and Amar 2008), in which this pattern is clear.

The *HHYF* also uses theriac. Endless recipes for theriac existed in Europe; one attributed to Nicholas of Salerno had 58 ingredients (Wallis 2010:177). The *HHYF* includes three closely related recipes with even more: 77, 83, and an incredible 97 ingredients. A large percentage of these were effective stimulants or stomachics, so these recipes might actually work as general tonics. A few other formulas, however, reach 40 drugs. This sort of everything-and-the-kitchen-sink approach would be familiar to the Chinese, although they never (to my knowledge) elsewhere used so many drugs in one formula. Chinese formulas usually contain fewer than 20 drugs (Scheid et al. 2009). One is reminded of the Chinese tendency to supplicate enormously long lists of gods (Johnson 2009; see esp. 39–51) in the hopes that one might actually help, or at least that the supplicator would not offend any god by leaving him or her out.

The *HHYF* was apparently prepared in the hope of improving Chinese medical practice, at least for the court, as well as serving as a basis for medical education. This was not a work of pure theory or speculation but a working manual. As such, it should be studied to understand how it appeared to its Yuan compilers. One assumes they thought it was full of important knowledge—that Near Eastern medicine worked well for what ailed the dynastic elite. Rarely before modern times has a culture attempted to graft another culture's medical science onto its own stock in this comprehensive, systematic way. Significantly, one of the few other cases was Europe's adoption of Near Eastern medicine in the same time period. Moreover, the Yuan writers were apparently quite selective about what they copied and how they systematized it.

In *juan* 12, dealing with stroke and wind illnesses, the section on stroke is particularly revealing, since we have a condition that was very well recognized and described in both the Near East and China, with surviving texts from both. The *Huihui Yaofang* explains stroke thus: "If a person indulges frequently in sex, or overexerts himself, or suffers a fright, or climbs to a high place, or is overwhelmed by joy, the heart main artery . . . strongly starts and the body struggles. . . . heavy inebriation, overconsumption of chill liquids, and food that is not dissipated, will . . . give rise to turbid [corrupt] illnesses. If the root is obstructed, the strength of the *qi* does not go through and cannot reach the body" (Buell's translation, Buell n.d.: 10). If corrupt moisture "is full within, the main arteries expand or contract" and moisture goes down from the brain to the body" (29). Wind conditions occur. "Much of this is a consequence of urgent heat" (29–30). There will be dryness, and/or "moisture is roasting and cooking the brain cavity and the nostril cavity" (30) and arteries become obstructed. So it appears that the Near Easterners and Chinese, at least the ones reading this literature, were aware that obstruction of the arteries is the cause of stroke. They also anticipated the modern opinion that excessive emotion or effort or drunkenness can precipitate this condition. All of these precipitating factors were well known in the Arabic medical literature.

That description may be compared with the very different traditional view, as seen in the major early Chinese *Mai Jing* (Pulse classic): "The disease of wind ought to develop [i.e, normally leads to] hemiplegia. . . . Headache with a slippery pulse is wind stroke. The pulse of wind is vacuous and weak. . . . When vacuity and cold are contending with one another, the evil is in the skin (and flesh). . . . Since the vessel networks are empty and vacuous, the murderous evil is impossible to drain away. Therefore, it lodges either in the left or right side. The evil qi slackens (the affected part), while the righteous [normal, proper] qi makes (the opposite part) tense. The righteous qi tries to draw the evil. Thus there arises deviation (of the eyes and mouth) and hemiplegia. When the evil lies in the vessel networks, there is insensitivity of the muscles and skin. When the evil is in the channels, there is unsurmountable heaviness (of the limbs). If the evil enters the bowels, (the sick person) will be unable to recognize people. If the evil enters the viscera, (the sick person) will suffer from difficult tongue in speaking and drooling at the mouth" (Wang 1997: 274–75; parentheses Wang's, brackets mine). In other words, wind has caused coldness, and if there is vacuity or emptiness of the vessels, stroke results.

Chinese formulas for dealing with hemiplegia generally assume that it is wind stroke (*zhong feng*, lit. "centering wind"). Originally this was taken to be a literal strike by a wind, but over time more and more ideas of internal involvement of such interior problems as "fire, phlegm, yin deficiency, and ascendant yang" (Scheid et al. 2009: 620). Various forms and degrees are now recognized. Volker Scheid and his associates give several classic formulas for treating it. They use drugs that are, in biomedical terms, stimulant or soothing. Apparently the stimulant drugs are the more important ones; they are generally more apt to be the "master" drugs as opposed to adjuvants. The idea is to stimulate qi flow, regulate blood flow, and augment qi—preventing stagnation. With the exception of one formula that includes myrrh (631), none of the formulas in Scheid's book involves Western drugs or bears any resemblance to formulas in the *HHYF*. On the other hand, the basic idea is the same: stimulation and warming. Some of the drugs—ones known everywhere—are the same, notably cinnamon, ginger, licorice, and one Western drug: myrrh. Long established in Chinese practice, it was common in Chinese formulas before the *HHYF*'s time.

One HHYF recipe is specifically—but not believably!—credited to Galen himself. It treats excess phlegm and thus the polluted body, stroke hemiplegia, and wind disease (Buell n.d., 47). Several following recipes also stress an excess of phlegm, as do recipes for other types of wind illness, later in the book.

Showing that all these recipes were very close to Near Eastern practice are the prescriptions for stroke in a manuscript from Cairo, dating to 1260 (Chipman 2010). The author was a Jewish Cairene druggist, of which there were many in that relatively tolerant era. The book shows that the medicine of the *HHYF* was flourishing abundantly at the other end of the Islamic world. At the very time of its composition, the Mongols were ravaging other parts of the Near East, but they were soon to be stopped suddenly by the Mamluk sultans, giving our pharmacist a break and Egypt another few centuries of freedom.

The Cairene book includes some recipes for stroke and paralysis that are comparable with those in the *HHYF*. One includes "various myrobalans, pepper, long pepper, ginger, opoponax [*sic*], dorema, Persian fennel, turpeth, fresh rue, fresh caltrops, cabbage, castor oil" (Chipman 2010: 249). All these except the dorema are (or probably are—given some ambiguities) in the *HHYF* remedies. Another is made of "wild oregano, mandrake, lesser centaury, marjoram, blue iris-root, wild thyme juice, milk"; another of "aloe, nigella, horehound, opoponax [*sic*], white and black hellebore, saltpeter, mandrake, castoreum, saffron, marjoram water"; yet another of "hiera picra, sweet-flag, mountain grapes, harmala, pellitory-of-Spain, ginger, nigella, oregano, blue iris-root, celery root bark, oxymel" (this one also treats epilepsy); and another of "verbena, resin, white wax, olive oil" (Chipman 2010: 267–69). Of these, marjoram, iris, saffron, opopanax, hellebore, thyme, oregano, olive oil, castoreum, celery root skin, and oxymel are in the *HHYF* remedies for these conditions. The minerals, resins, verbena, and grapes are somewhat hard to identify, but I suspect they are the same as those intended by the terms in the *HHYF*. Other sections of the *HHYF* contain most of the other drugs. Only hiera picra (probably a specific compound; see below) and pellitory-of-Spain seem absent from the *HHYF*.

There are also close European parallels from the same time period. The French Jewish physician Isaac Todros wrote a short essay on the subject around 1370 (Bos 2010). Todros was trained in the finest Galenic tradition, a

state-of-the-art practitioner of the very tradition the *Huihui Yaofang* was trying to transmit to China. He describes facial paresis as "crooked mouth,"
much as the *HHYF* refers to "wry obliqueness." His explanation was that it was
"obstruction of the pneuma in its course" (192), which is so close to the *HHYF*
as to sound downright eerie. (There are philosophic differences between the
concepts of pneuma and qi, but one suspects the fine points would be lost on
Isaac Todros and the authors of the *Huihui Yaofang*.) He thought this was in
turn due to "phlegm . . . in most cases" (193) and could be treated with lavender, oxymel infused with squill, sage, sweetflag, hyssop, and fennel to concoct
the humors, and then if this was successful, to go deeper (i.e., to deal with the
physiological roots of the problem) with ash of fig, myrobalans, turpeth, ginger, lavender, dodder-of-thyme, salt, and gum Arabic, with fennel juice and
wormwood syrup.

The following days the patient was supposed to take mithridates (a complex electuary; theriac can be used) with wine, acorus, and sage. Then the
patient's neck was rubbed with a mix of oil of iris and lily, spurge, castoreum,
vinegar, *Anacyclus pyrethrum*, and wax. Boiled meat of hare could be applied
too, also mouse-ear plant (*Myosotis*? *Anagallis*?) in the ear, or ginger taken
with sweet reed and honey. Another possibility was Hermes' hiera (a mysterious compound). If there was diarrhea, the patient could take nutmeg, myrrh,
frankincense, nard, and clove along with the acorus. (These would indeed
have an anti-diarrheic effect.) A small sack on the head, holding mace, cloves,
roses, marjoram and other scents, was useful. These are all fairly mild warming and stimulant drugs, that is, targeted against phlegmatic humor. Of these,
only sage and fig ash are missing from the *Huihui Yaofang* lists. One of the
Huihui Yaofang recipes even lists using game meats as a poultice (30), though
hare is not among them.

Todros advised that taking lavender with rosemary honey warmed the
nerves. Pine seeds, pistachios, and almonds were good foods. Honey water,
wine, and a hydromel with more aromatics were then used (Bos 2010). All
these are paralleled in more general *HHYF* practice. A further treatment, fortunately absent from the *HHYF*, is bleeding; the Chinese never accepted that.

A great deal of herbal and food lore about treating strokes is found in "A
Case of Paralysis," written by a student observing Guillaume Boucher and
Pierre d'Ausson in early fifteenth-century Paris (Wallis 2010: 396–99). The lists
of herbs and food somewhat overlap those in the *HHYF*. The main difference
is that in Paris the herbs were those found in Europe or regularly imported;
the Indian and Chinese herbs were, unsurprisingly, not available, and only a

few common ones from the Near East were used. Castoreum, mustard, iris, wormwood, mint, lavender, rose, euphorbia, and many other herbal drugs are included. Recommendations for a light diet are also shared.

More than a century ago, E. Wallis Budge discovered an anonymous Syriac Christian medical manuscript in Mosul and translated it (Budge 1913). It remains the only medieval Near Eastern encyclopedic medical work to be fully translated into English. (It includes an astrological text and an odd collection of thoroughly non-Galenic folk cures and magic, as well as the solidly Galenic major text.) It also has recommendations for treating stroke (hemiplegia), including many of the familiar herbs: castoreum, mint, all the peppers, amber, euphorbia, fennel, hellebore, and others. Less rational or beneficial are jackal fat, camel urine, and bitumen (Budge 1913, 2: 58). The Syriac writer had a startlingly good knowledge of nerves (see esp. vol. 2, 120ff.), paralyses of various kinds, and anatomy in general.

In short, as far as stroke goes, we really are dealing with a single medical tradition here. The description is essentially the same, the cause is the same, and the treatment is the same: recipes involving a variety of stimulant and warming drugs. In modern biomedical terms, these would not be a good idea, since all they would do is make the blood flow faster and harder, potentially making things worse. It would be better to use a blood thinner, but such were apparently unknown at the time.

As to insanity, the *Huihui Yaofang* again blames it on phlegm and strong emotionality and drinking, which is presumably why it was put next to stroke in the book. Budge's Syriac author blamed it on black bile; phlegm was associated, yellow and yellow-red bile caused milder mental problems, but serious chronic madness was a melancholic condition (Budge 1913, 2: 14ff.). Some recipes in the *HHYF* mention hellebore, a strong heart stimulant. As noted, the anonymous Syriac author used it, as did medieval Islam (Dols 1984: 53).

Similar attribution of insanity to excessive worry and anxiety and to overindulgence in alcohol, food, and sex is common in Chinese medical literature, from its most ancient surviving records to today. Chinese texts and formularies tended to use either cure-all drugs—the things they list for every condition, mostly mild diuretics and things of that nature—or magical remedies. None mention psychedelic drugs, although these were well known. Most mention soothing and mild stimulant drugs, some use a variety of minerals (see, e.g., Scheid et al. 2009: 639), and one classic formula depends simply on wheat grains assisted by licorice and jujube (471). Insanity and stroke were closely linked in Chinese medicine, both being caused by attacks of wind affecting a body weakened by substance abuse, worry, or qi and blood problems.

Madness was treated by Galenic means in the formal medical tradition (Dols 1992), but the Greeks had not said much about it, so local traditions and innovations were important. Mental hospitals existed but were not well supported by the state; they tended to depend on local charity. Thus the lot of the mentally ill was often chains and beatings and sleeping on straw. Treatment of the more fortunate, however, was designed to deal with the melancholic humors. Some of these were burnt choleric humors—the yellow bile somehow burned internally, becoming black. This explained agitated and frantic madness. Passionate love was considered a form of melancholic madness and could be treated by laxatives and moisturizers and other Galenic remedies as well as the more common-sense remedies such as distracting a male lover's mind with slave girls, or simply marrying a pair of starstruck lovers to each other (Ibn Sīnā, quoted in Dols 1992: 485).

A sovereign remedy for madness (and almost everything else) in both the Islamic world and the *Huihui Yaofang* was dodder-of-thyme (*Cuscuta epithymum*; see Dols 1984: 53–54), a plant singularly lacking in any demonstrable value. Medieval Arab sources also noted wormwood, frankincense, polypody, myrobalans, agaric, lavender, colocynth, yellowish thyme, turpeth, oxymel, hyacinth bean, euphorbia, mustard, safflower, beets, and Armenian stone and salt (54). Most of these plants have demonstrable and obvious medical effects, but none on mental illness. (Lavender does have a slight effect; its oil is tranquilizing, even as a scent.) Of these, polypody, myrobalans, agaric, lavender, turpeth, wormwood, Armenian stone, salt, and colocynth are included in the *HHYF* recipes. Most of the other plants mentioned in the *HHYF* are mere soothing items. All the other items in Dols's list occur in the *HHFY* as drugs, though not for this condition specifically.

In later Islam, aromatherapy was used for madness (Dols 1984: 173), but we have no indication of that application in Chinese sources. In fact, medieval Near Eastern medicine featured all kinds of soothing, cheering, and diverting treatments for madness: music, horse riding, outings, good food, rest, calm, fresh air, flowers, and even lovely girls for cases of love-stricken noblemen (173 and throughout). None of these are found in the *HHYF* or any Chinese sources, to my knowledge. In so far as the mentally ill were treated at all in old China, it was generally by religious or magical means; certainly in my experience in rural Hong Kong and Malaysia half a century ago, serious mental illness was considered hopeless by medical practitioners and left to the Daoist priests and spirit mediums. Some minor mental problems, from blanking on exams to excessive fear, were ascribed to loss of a component of the soul. The medium would go through a ceremony to call it back. Other, more serious conditions were due to haunting, and the medium or—more often—Daoist would drive the gui from the patient. Yet another cause was a curse by a witch or magic worker, in which case, the curse had to be neutralized. In all cases, mediums and priests often provided charms to be ashed and then drunk in herbal tea, but this was their only physical intervention.

Juan 30 is a collection of cure-all recipes, beginning with one supposedly invented by Rufus of Ephesus; it has been added to since. It is recommended for practically everything, including the above-mentioned alopecia (Buell n.d. 282; many other recipes treat fox condition too). Alas, a recipe that cures everything is informative about nothing.

Interesting is the lack of Chinese ingredients. An exception that proves the rule is found on page 369 (Buell n.d. : directions for "sending down" a medicine, i.e., taking it such that it will be effective) include a number of Chinese medicinal soups calling for standard Chinese remedies like ginseng, mandarin orange peel, and apricot kernels—items conspicuously absent in most of the rest of the *HHYF*. Here they appear to be mere adjuvants.

A revealing comment (Buell n.d. 376–77) lists "urgent" medicines as including ephedra, euphorbia, scammony, colocynth, and agaric. With the exception of agaric—which may be a misidentification—these are all medicines with clear and dramatic effects. Ephedra clears up some allergies, euphorbia is a violent spasmodic, and scammony and colocynth are quite dramatic purges. The passage goes on to contrast "middle category medicines," including opopanax, castoreum, gum ammoniac, and asafoetida. These indeed have mild soothing and other qualities but are not obvious strong medicines. The writer—whoever is translated here—knew the effects of these products. This system of classification is clearly quite separate from and independent of the classical Chinese classification of "master, minister, and servant" drugs.

Juan 34 deals with treatments of wounds, obviously a major concern in the Mongol Empire. These are mostly arrow wounds and other matters expected in battle but also include bites, including human bites as well as rabid-dog bites. Ulcerated wounds, wounds with bits of weapon material within, broken bones, and other damage are all dealt with. Surgical procedures are treated in great detail and are generally sophisticated and thorough. They make harrowing reading when one considers that anesthetics were few. Opium was well known, and is called for in many *HHYF* recipes, so one hopes and trusts that at least some sufferers benefited from it. Many must have been treated on the battlefield, where opium might be unavailable.

The herbal cures are often extremely long recipes involving everything medicinal that could be imagined. Most, naturally, are poultices and ointments involving protective material (gums and resins), desiccants (powdered shell, minerals), and emollients (oils and salves). They would seal the wounds and have a soothing effect.

Several antibiotics and antiseptics were used, including frankincense, myrrh, saffron, and rose oil. So were astringents such as oak galls, willow leaves, and pomegranate skin paste or tea. However, they were often in quantities too small to do anything. This is more than strange, since both the Chinese and the Near Easterners knew that substances like rose oil and thyme would treat skin infections. Actual pragmatic experience does matter in things of this sort, and it is surprising to see the minimal use of it in the *HHYF*. Al-Samarqandī's work of the early thirteenth century gives recipes for a number of balms for use on wounds, sores, and aches, and these balms are made of soothing, softening, and antiseptic drugs in quantities that would actually work (Levey and Al-Khaledy 1967: 132–35. Even one for epilepsy would at least have felt soothing.) One wonders why more use was not made of such materials. Quite probably, on the battlefield the arcane and excessively complex recipes of the *HHYF* would have been impractical, and simple treatment with oil and a few antiseptic drugs would have been all that was available.

Chipman's Cairene manuscript from 1260 is very similar and has some of the same remedies. A group of them for wounds includes, among other things, "pig fat, olive oil, litharge, green vitriol, green palm leaves; violet oil, white wax, ceruse . . . camphor; hawthorn, . . . pearl, saffron, . . . rose oil, wine vinegar, pine-nut mastic [probably pine cone resin], Iraqi verdigris . . . petroleum" (Chipman 2010: 243); most of these are the same as or close to items called for in juan 34 of the *HHYF*. A few other items are ambiguous or quite different from anything in the *HHYF* (e.g., "green palm leaves"). Most would be sterilizing (drastically; green vitriol, camphor) or soothing (from fat to wax). Rose oil, which is both soothing to humans and deadly to bacteria, would be the ideal treatment. Violet oil should work similarly; however, like the other effective drugs, it is called for in small quantities.

In the *HHYF*, a subsequent section on burns is more hopeful; it is based on poultices of egg white, with litharge, copper salts, and rose oil or mint or other antiseptic herbs. These mixes would work, although it is conceivable that the copper could further damage the skin and that the lead from the litharge might be absorbed and poison the victim. We also have a particularly clear example of Galenic heating and cooling concepts: "Also, the medicines that are used at first to prevent burn lesions from forming are uniformly ones with cold natures and are not heating and drying; for example, such as egg white combined with rose oil brushed onto the burn with a chicken plume" (Buell n.d. 76. of *juan* 34). There are many other references to this Hippocratic-Galenic heating-and-cooling system scattered throughout the book. Of course the system had been known since at least the days of Tao Hongjing and Sun Simiao (Engelhardt 2001), but the *Huihui Yaofang* used it more systematically and in a less Sinicized way.

Trauma was treated quite differently in Chinese medicine, with, for example, the use of an erythrina wash (a very effective anti-inflammatory and anti-rash medication; Scheid et al. 2009: 902).

Medicinals: Numbers and Classification

A total of around 398 entries appear in my tables of medicinals (not counting synonyms and several completely unidentifiable items, which would bring the total to approximately 416). This does not translate to 398 species, because there are entries for generic things (dung, soil) and some entries that cover several species of plants that seem similar and were apparently used similarly. In some cases we are not sure which species was actually used in the *HHYF* and thus include data for two or three similar ones. Actual numbers of species involved are impossible to state because we have not identified or confirmed all the identifications. (Hu's team came up with some identifications that do not seem to check out with the reference books and need further research. Given that Hu and her team are leading scholars in this specific area, while the reference books are old and often very general and not well checked, it is probable that in all or almost all cases the books are wrong and Hu is right.)

We have about 302 entries for plants, 69 for animals, and 27 for minerals, with an unknown number of species involved. The animal and mineral substances are not much used. In fact, animal drugs barely appear at all, and when they do, it is often in recipes that are more magical than practical. It is quite clear from context, to say nothing of other Chinese texts throughout history, that the Chinese knew the difference. They would not have had the same concept of magic versus scienceas a modern biomedical doctor, but countless comments in the medical literature show that the realm of spirit mediums, street pitchmen, and folk magic workers was a different one from that of serious doctors and druggists. I observed this in rural Hong Kong in the 1960s and 1970s.

The terms in the *HHFY* often refer to genera that comprise several medicinally used species, so 302 plant entries means more species than that to consider. It is often impossible to determine which species of a widely distributed, widely used genus—*Astragalus* or *Ferula*, for example—would have been available to the Mongol court. Moreover, the Chinese often used a Chinese plant name to translate an Arabic one; usually they got the genus right—they found a plant of the same genus, with, one hopes, the right drug properties— but sometimes they were very wrong. As an extreme example, they managed to confuse saffron with gardenia, because the Chinese names were similar. Moreover, sometimes the Persian or Arabic names are ambiguous; *shitarāj* normally refers to *Lepidium latifolium*, and surely does herein, but the same word is used in India for *Plumbago rosea*, utterly different in appearance and properties.

Spices and herbs abound in the *HHYF*, and indeed most of the prescription formulas include some. This is to be expected, since, as medicine specialists knew even before Theophrastus and Dioscorides, herbs and spices do have medical activity, often a great deal (Billing and Sherman 1998; Moerman 1998). Some, such as mint (menthol and other volatiles), aloe vera, and artemisia, continue to be used in contemporary biomedical practice.

Plant families that are abundantly represented include the Apiaceae (the celery and fennel family), Brassicaceae (cabbages and mustards), Fabaceae (beans), and Lamiaceae (mints). This is true of medicinal herb lists all around the Northern Hemisphere, for instance in indigenous and pioneer-settler North America (see Moerman 1998, here and for what follows) and in Mongolian folk medicine (Bold 2009 and my own field research). The Piperaceae (black pepper and relatives) and Zingiberaceae (ginger, turmeric, galangal) also show up frequently. Conversely, again as in North American data, Asteraceae (asters and sunflowers) appear less frequently relative to their incredible abundance in the regions involved. The Poaceae (grasses), the most common of all in numbers of individuals on the steppes, are hardly represented at all (there are a very few). The Cucurbitaceae (gourds), Rosaceae (rose relatives), and many minor families are in between, with a few major drugs from each.

The biomedical fact is that the chemicals that apiaceous, brassicaceous, and lamiaceous plants use to fight off pests and predators are also effective against things that bother humans. We seem to have evolved with them and developed an ability to thrive on their toxins instead of summarily dying. By contrast, the many and rich chemical defenses of the Asteraceae are strangely less valuable to us, although a goodly number of the Asteraceae still make it into the *HHYF* and into Chinese and Mongol medicine. Wormwoods, a large asteraceous genus, are a major exception; mentioned abundantly in all medieval herbals, they are very important medically today. Grasses generally figure as the least useful large family, because their defenses are mechanical—quick growth and silica granules in the leaves—rather than chemical. Yet a fourth possibility is represented by members of the buttercup, nightshade, and some other families. These have chemicals often intensely toxic to humans but of considerable medical effect. These families are well represented in the *HHYF*.

It is striking to note how many of the plants in the *HHYF* are still used today and proven by biomedical research to have actual value. (My database of *HHYF* remedies, with summaries of major herbal sources from the west and China, is available on request.)

Places of Origin of Major Medicinals

The places of origin of the major medicinals—the 258 taxa that get extensive coverage in medieval herbals and were widely used in Eurasia—make an interesting study. In the first place, many of the *HHYF* taxa, such as rose, poplar, rhubarb, dock, and willow, include several species that are distributed all over Eurasia but with different local species being used medicinally in China and western Eurasia. Rhubarb, for instance, was *Rheum rhabarbarum* in the West (having astringent and irritating action), the purgative *Rheum emodi* in China, and the abundant and widely used *Rheum nanum* in Mongolia and neighboring cold dry areas. Honey comes from the domesticated bee *Apis mellifera* in the West, but it was also introduced as a domesticate to China very early; however, the exceedingly similar East Asian *A. cerana* was also known and used. Honey is regarded here as in the "widespread" category geographically, being found everywhere in Eurasia.

Second, some individual species, such as apricot, sweetflag, and hemp, occurred throughout the Eurasian heartlands from very early times and were used medicinally throughout their ranges. Third, some species, such as citron, barely reached Yuan China and were probably not known medicinally there. (Citron's home includes what is now southwest China, but the domestic citron was developed in India or the Near East, and the Chinese would not have known or recognized the wild ancestor in Yuan times; only through Mongol conquests had they acquired control of the relevant territory.) These last seem to be treated as "Western" plants in the *HHYF*; their names given are Near Eastern ones, and the indicated uses tend to follow the Dioscorides-Galen traditions. We are thus dealing with Western *uses* of the plants, however Chinese or universal the plants may be.

On the other hand, the *HHYF* does separate some groups, for example, *Artemisia* and mints, into roughly species-level categories, and different species of the plants in these groups were used in the East and West, sometimes for different purposes. These can be scored more precisely.

Many medicinals were widespread in India, the Near East, and Europe long before the time of the *HHYF*. These have all been coded as Western, since this is a book of Near Eastern medicine (written for Chinese in China, but strictly Near Eastern in content), although some are known to have come from India originally. "India" thus becomes something of a residual category for plants that clearly came from India and were not known, or at least not widely used, in the Western world much before the *HHYF*'s time. Sugarcane, for instance, had rather recently come from India to the Western world, but it had been known since around Han times in China, which it reached via Southeast Asia. It probably originated in New Guinea. In Yuan, to all intents and purposes, it was a fairly new introduction from India to western Eurasia.

Similarly, some medicinals made it to China slightly before the *HHYF*'s time, but they have all been scored as Western here because they were recent arrivals as of the fourteenth century and had not been well assimilated into Chinese culture. This, also, is obviously maddeningly ambiguous. Grape is scored here as Western, for instance, although it was known in China since the second century BCE; it remained as of the fourteenth century an overwhelmingly Western crop, even though widely grown in western China (often or usually by Hui peoples). Walnut, which is probably native to China as well as to west Asia, scores as Western because it is called Iranian peach in Chinese and the common large edible form is evidently an import (Laufer 1919).

The eleven plants that have a Southeast Asian origin are, similarly, plants that would have been seen at that time as rather exotic Southeast Asian items, though long known in India and China. They are mostly spices and incenses. Cloves are the extreme case here; they were still strictly an import, but the importation had started by 400–300 BC. Black pepper had also been long known and was a major import, though it may possibly have been locally grown (it is today, but largely as a new crop). It is actually one of the most often mentioned item in the *HHYF* with 91 mentions—second only to honey, with 114. The *Yinshan Zhengyao* (*YSZY*; see below) also features it. Marco Polo noted the heavy use of pepper in China; some have cast doubt on his claims (Haw 2006: 140–41), but the *HHYF* and *YSZY* provide clear proof that he was right.

> Plants:
> Found in all regions, 31
> Western, 152
> India, 26
> China, 38
> Southeast Asia, 11
> Total, 258 taxa
> Number of these mentioned in Dioscorides: 136
> Mentioned in Li Shizhen's *Bencao Gangmu* (2003): 148 (as well as
>   most of the animals and animal products)

Note the importance of India even after it has "lost" many of its drugs to scoring as generically Western.

The lists of *HHYF* plants mentioned in Dioscorides and in Li overlap considerably, and many of the plants that occur in only one list are quite obscure. The rest of the exceptions are several plants in Dioscorides that cannot be grown away from the Mediterranean and several native to East and South Asia that were not known to Dioscorides. In very many cases, however, the genera are the same but the species used by Li was (or were) slightly different from the one(s) used by Dioscorides. *Rheum* is one example.

Since Dioscorides has priority by about fourteen centuries, and since most of the overlap involves Western-origin or Indian-origin plants, we can safely infer that the botanicals in question spread from West to east. However, in very many cases—from *Artemisia* and *Asparagus* to *Ricinus* and *Vicia*—the genus, if not the species, is widely distributed and independent discovery is possible. When the plant has such obvious medical value that no one could miss it, as with *Artemisia* and *Ricinus*, independent discovery becomes probable.

Among foods specifically, there is less overlap. The only clear and unmistakable Western borrowings shared by the *HHYF* and Li are common foods and a few other products of early (often very ancient) presence in China (see Laufer 1919; Schafer 1963): ball onion (*A. cepa*), dill, celery, beet, frankincense, cabbage (*B. oleracea*, specifically said by Li to be Western), safflower, myrrh, coriander, saffron, carrot, asafoetida, fig, fennel, barley, flax, basil, poppy, pistachio, almond, apricot, pomegranate, possibly sumac (but there are native sumacs in China), rosemary (Li says it came from the West in the Wei Dynasty), madder, sesame, styrax, fenugreek, wheat, and European grape (but there are also native Chinese grapes). This totals thirty species. Some, such as wheat and barley, go back to very ancient times in China. Others, such as grape and coriander, reached China in very early imperial times.

The only clear borrowings from India or Southeast Asia are galingale, *Aquilaria*, *Areca* (its Chinese name is a loanword from Malay), turmeric, zedoary, *Daemonorhops*, *Dryobalanops*, nutmeg, *Phyllanthus*, the *Piper* species, sugarcane, clove, and *Terminalia chebula*. Several other largely Southeast Asian species probably ranged into China in ancient times. Possibly even turmeric and zedoary did.

The Moral: Chinese and Western Medicines United

One thing is clear and deeply important: nobody thought that it was impossible to incorporate Western nutrition and medicine into Chinese practice. No one claimed that the traditions were different enough to be "incommensurable" (T. Kuhn 1962) or even very different. It is, however, possible that they were different enough to block widespread adoption by the Chinese of the Western techniques and medicines.

Nathan Sivin has recently edited key documents of Joseph Needham's work with Lu Gwei-djen on Chinese medicine (Needham 2000; Sivin 2000). Needham died in 1991, leaving Sivin the task of completing the "Medicine" volume for the monumental project *Science and Civilisation in China* that had become Needham's life work. Sivin is a leading authority on Chinese medicine, and his introduction to this book provides a superb guide to the state of the art—brief yet extremely clear, informed, and authoritative. However, he and Needham differ on a key point. Needham saw Chinese medicine as part of a world medical science, although developing in some isolation from other emerging medical traditions. Sivin points out that almost all contemporary scholars of Chinese medicine see it strictly on its own terms: as a unique tradition that cannot be discussed in connection with others except to show how different it was. (Paul Unschuld 2009 takes a middle course.)

To Sivin, Chinese medicine is utterly different from biomedicine. He fixes his gaze on the underlying principles, the philosophy of the system. To Needham, the difference is real but can be overcome. Needham fixed his attention on practices and remedies rather than on underlying principles, so to him the difference is merely a minor roadblock rather than a total barrier. Also, Sivin cares that the Chinese *did not* mathematize the system; Needham cared that they *could have*.

Another way to look at this is to view Sivin as basically interested in cosmological principles, especially the most exotic ones, like the fivefold correspondence theory. Needham was much more interested in practical matters, which is where Chinese medicine is much closer to Western—if only because one cannot ignore the reality of sprains, broken bones, rashes, dietary regimens, and so on. Whether you believe in fivefold correspondence or biochemistry, willow-bark tea works for fevers, and oral rehydration therapy effectively treats diarrhea. Since practice is more apt than theory to be based on actual working experience, it is more apt to be commensurable across cultures.

Sivin correctly emphasizes throughout his introduction that Chinese medicine is itself incredibly diverse; by his own logic, we should not really be talking about Chinese medicine, but instead about Chinese medical traditions, some of which might be incommensurable with biomedicine. Certainly the magical material, with its dragons and demons, is not commensurable. So, I think, is the fivefold theoretic that is basic to Han medical writing. But the practical lore that actually mattered in daily medical behavior is more directly translatable. So is the yin-yang theory, which is so close to Galenic humorism in its basics.

There are two ways to salvage Needham's view. First, we can point out that the Chinese of the great dynasties were under no illusions of "incommensurability" between East and West—as the *HHYF* clearly shows.

Second, and this point is made by Needham, practice really has some privilege over abstract theory here. Medical science is not an example of philosophers spinning beautiful dreams in isolation. It is about maintaining health. It is tested against results. To be sure, most Chinese physicians, like Western ones, rarely question their systems when they fail in curing—they usually blame the unique situation at hand. But, in the end, the system has to deliver. All medical systems are kept on course (and occasionally even forced to change) by being tested against results. Chinese medicine has always featured "knowing practice" (Farquhar 1993) first. It is a hands-on, practice-based trade (E. Hsu 1999).

Biomedicine has found a somewhat better way to test (though be it noted that the Chinese invented case-control experimentation—for agriculture, around 150 BCE; E. Anderson 1988). So much the better for biomedicine; we can now test traditional Chinese remedies and prove that many of them work. Ginseng, artemisinin, chaulmoogra oil, ephedrine, and many others have entered world medicine, proving that the systems are commensurable. Survival rates are the common measure, and a very fine measure they are, too.

Of course, the fourteenth century was a time when medicine was probably more similar between West and East than at any other time in history. The Golden Age of the Silk Road had climaxed and was soon to end with the fall of the Mongol Empire, the rise of sea trade, and the coming of the Little Ice Age, which made parts of the Silk Road almost impassable. The Chinese could reinterpret Near Eastern medicine in their terms without doing great violence to it.

At least some of the people involved in this transmission were thinking about practice, not theory. In the *YSZY* Hu Sihui had relatively little theory, and most of that was snippets of old stuff. The book is almost all recipes, practical tips, useful advice, and summaries of working knowledge. Obviously, a cook would not worry much about the incommensurability of Five Phases theory with Platonic or Aristotelian dogma. But Hu was clearly something of a scholar, not just a cook, so he was breaking the scholar-bureaucrat mold. In fact, his focus on real-world practice is exactly what the classic European stereotype of Chinese scholarship says the Chinese never had. Possibly Hu was enough of a *semu*—a Central Asian in Mongol employ—to be outside the Confucian value system, but the existence of perfectly good working recipe books by people like Ni Zan and the Ming doctor Gao Lian makes that hard to accept. The fact is that Chinese scholars sometimes interfaced with the real world and knew perfectly well how to deal with it.

The *HHYF*, too, is largely practical, even though the more theoretical sections can be very dense reading for anyone not highly expert in medieval Chinese medical terminology. The doctors, however, were interested in treating patients, not in philosophy. They were trying to find practices that they could actually use. The Mongol information superhighway brought them a vast bounty of good ideas.

The *HHYF* shows that medical systems spread rapidly, mix, merge, and go on. Nothing could be a more extreme contrast to the current reigning wisdom of medical history, which holds that every culture or region has its own medicine, completely and hermetically sealed and closed off from every other.

Sivin tells us to interpret the medicine of China only in the light of Chinese tradition, and often only in the light of literate texts from that tradition.

The reasons are clear enough: the historians fear, above all things, dismissing the past as nothing but an inferior run-up to the present—at worst steeped in error, at best merely a place to mine for innovations that later paid off and ideas that later proved correct—in either case, present knowledge is what mattered, and the past was evaluated only on presentist bases. Early histories of medicine very often did this, and histories of Chinese and Near Eastern medicine were particularly notable for it. The current fashion, however, is a sad overreaction. It mercilessly essentializes cultural traditions. It sees these traditions as wholly separate and distinct, despite overwhelming evidence of massive borrowing. It segregates them from each other behind Chinese walls.

The authors of the *HHYF* believed otherwise. They knew that China had been learning from the West for hundreds of years. They knew that Hippocratic-Galenic medicine and the Theophrastus-Dioscorides herbal tradition had spread over most of the known world, being readily accepted, adapted, and adjusted to local conditions wherever it went. They knew, above all, that patients were in need of all the help they could get. They knew from experience that many Near Eastern, Chinese, and Indian herbs worked, and they were not in the least interested in limiting their herbal medicine to one tradition or region.

Yet, they were not mere atheoretical pragmatists like some of Galen's rivals. The authors of the *HHYF* were schooled in highly sophisticated medical theories, which were fully scientific by the standards of the day. They must have had many a learned discussion of the relative merits of Galenic humoral theory and Chinese correspondence theory. They did not see these as closed, sealed jars of specimens to put on a museum shelf; they saw them as living bodies of theory to be used as tools and adapted as needed.

The historian and anthropologist need, first, to try to see what the doctors saw and try (hopelessly—but there is benefit in the attempt) to think as they thought. They were not playing word games or spinning out theory in a vacuum. They were treating patients. They tried to find what worked and to explain or understand it in light of what theories they knew. We most certainly cannot project our knowledge or views on them. We have to understand them on their terms.

We cannot view the Galenic and Dioscoridean traditions as different from or alien to China. It certainly was not alien to our own modern bioscientific world; in fact, it was ancestral to it. True, modern biomedicine is based on a classic Foucauldian "rupture" or Kuhnian "revolution": the germ theory and the consequent explanation of contagion, infection, and epidemic disease. But, on the other hand, Galenic medicine never died. Regimen—diet, rest and activity, lifestyle—was never forgotten. The *Tacuinum sanitatis*, a Latin version of an Arab text based on Galen, was so influential that in my youth I heard various folk versions of John Harington's (1966) translated verse from it:

> Keep three physicians: Doctor Diet,
> Doctor Merryman, and Doctor Quiet.

I had no idea that "Doctor Diet, Doctor Merryman, and Doctor Quiet" came from a literate scientific source going back 2,000 years.

Looking back on it all, we can see an interesting pattern, with the *YSZY* and *HHYF* squarely positioned on a key node. The ancient Babylonians and Egyptians seem to have gotten the idea of a specialized, self-conscious search for pragmatic and empirical knowledge and a further hope of systematizing it, deducing it, and possibly even explaining it. This was the dawn of self-conscious science (as we usually understand that term today). The Greeks and Chinese both developed it into an actual specialized realm of human enterprise, variously called *episteme* and other names by the Greeks, *dao shi* and other names by the Chinese; the Latin label "science" was much later. Persia and India had their own equivalents.

This activity included self-conscious medical traditions from the start. From early civilized periods, the Chinese had doctors (*yi*) and medicine (*yao*). Medical science developed to a high level with the Greeks, spread from them throughout the Mediterranean world with the Greek and later Roman empires, and thus became international. It contracted sharply in the West with the Dark Ages. Even in the East, it stagnated; there was virtually no medical progress from 400 to 800. At least the tradition survived. Finally, in the 700s, a huge boost to its international spread was provided by Islam, which adopted Greek medicine wholesale and spread it wherever the Muslims went. Thus while science almost died in the whole of Europe, it exploded in the Near East. It was then reintroduced slowly and fairly steadily to Europe until a spectacular rush in the 1200s not only brought southern Europe into parity with the Near East, but also started it on a path of growth that put it far ahead of the Near East within a couple of centuries. The geography of science had shifted rather spectacularly.

Meanwhile, Chinese medicine, which developed in the early states, spread slowly through East Asia, following the progress of civilization. A dark age (the Three Kingdoms Period), which was somewhat earlier than the Western one, set China back, but it recovered fast.

The two spheres touched by the 700s. With the continuing triumphal spread of Galenic medicine through the Western world, a climax of internationalism appeared in the 1200s and 1300s. During that period—it must have been an exciting one to be a doctor—there was a single vast medical enterprise from Spain to the Yangzi delta and from central Africa to Siberia. Serious, intensive scientific research, development, and education were found in colleges from Cordova to Beijing and from Timbuktu to Samarkand. There has never been anything quite like it before or since.

After the plague of 1346–48, science contracted again. Scientific activity, including medicine, declined in the Near East. North and central Africa went sharply downhill, especially after the slave trade began to devastate entire civilizations there. Central Asia also regressed. India and the Near East progressed slowly and haltingly, especially after 1500. China built on its traditions and developed rapidly but did not break through to biomedicine. Only Europe went from strength to strength.

Today, once again, medicine and other sciences are moving forward everywhere in the world, and a great medical tradition links humanity. The hopes embodied in the *HHYF* had been diminished by plague, war, climate, and human frailty but are now renewed. Yet, once again, our human enterprise is threatened by these horsemen of apocalypse. It remains to be seen whether the twenty-first century will recapitulate the fourteenth, with overpopulation, militarism, and intolerance all spiraling out of control, leading to a deadly downward cycle in Europe (Tuchman 1978) as well as in China. We have the chance and the opportunity to prevent them and to control our destiny. The wonderful dream embodied in the *HHYF* may provide inspiration.

Today, lifestyle-conscious doctors like Andrew Weil and Mehmet Oz teach versions of the Arabic regimen advice immortalized in the *Tacuinum*. (It is almost too perfect that one is Jewish and the other Turkish; verily even the nationalities have not changed.) We are all, once again, cognizant of the need for healthy eating and drinking, healthy exercise and adequate rest, healthy sex and social relations.

"The past is a different country," and historians do well to treat it as one, but we are all human, and we are all heirs of accumulated human wisdom. We are, in addition, the heirs of the medical traditions in the *HHYF*. Both the Western and the Chinese medical ideas in it have gone worldwide now. We cannot treat the *HHYF* as something alien to humanity or to our own culture. It is part of all our lives.

The *Yinshan Zhengyao*

The Mongol court's official book of food, nutrition, and dietetics, the *Yinshan Zhengyao* (Essential knowledge for drinking and feasting"), was assembled by Hu Sihui (Buell, Anderson, and Perry 2010) and presented to Emperor Tugh Temür in 1330. It is a stunning work of synthesis and includes a great deal of Near Eastern culinary and medical lore. Both Hippocratic and Chinese medical traditions privileged diet as the most important form of medical care. Hu Sihui was charged with making the imperial food healthy as well as sumptuous and exotic. Thus the book is a major primary source on the medical beliefs (notably eclectic) of the Mongol court, particularly its nutritional and herbalist experts (Buell, Anderson, and Perry 2010; see also Anderson 1994; Sabban 1983, 1986; the Mongolian traditional medical authority Sharav Bold has independently discovered and commented on this work, Bold 2009, esp. 83–99). In general, Chinese and Turkic foodways were mixing (cf. Golden 1994).

Hu Sihui, the court nutritionist of the Yuan Dynasty, was Turkic in origin, and Paul Buell believes, from the linguistic usages in the book, that Hu came from the eastern reaches of Chinese Turkestan—from somewhere east of Xinjiang. The *Zhou Li*, the Han Dynasty reinvention of the rituals of the Zhou Dynasty, listed the nutritionist as the highest in status of medical practitioners, since the Chinese always recognized that nutrition is the most important aspect of medicine. Several other works on medicine and medical nutrition survive from Yuan, some written by Chinese, some by Mongol authorities (Bold 2009: 199–203).

As Francoise Sabban has pointed out (in conversation with this author, November 20, 2011), the *YSZY* is the only book known to have been written by a court nutritionist. It provides a large number of recipes with their nutritional values as perceived by Chinese medicine of that time. The recipes come from as far afield as Baghdad, Kashmir, and eastern Europe. Most are Central Asian: Turkic, Mongol, or Iranic. Many are Chinese, but these are definitely in the minority, although the book was compiled in Peking. Many recipes are examples of fusion cuisine: Chinese ingredients in Central Asian recipes or outright blends of the two traditions.

The process of distillation in China apparently goes back to the Han Dynasty, as noted above, but here it reentered China from the West. (A possible independent origin of distilling in India at an uncertain date, and certainly the great development of it in the Near East in the medieval period, seems responsible for the need to bring in Western technology.) Hu gives directions on making arak—using the Arab word (*a-la-ji* in transcription, from the Arabic 'araq, "sweating," referring to the distillation process).

The Mongols and others at their court wished to demonstrate their sophistication by serving foods from all over the world. They loved to impress visitors by providing them with the foods of their homelands. They were famous for assembling skilled people and knowledge as part of their insatiable thirst for anything that would help them conquer and hold the world. But, beyond this, the Mongols were deliberately and openly showing off their power. The message of their feasts was: we can command foods and recipes from the entire known world; we not only conquered these lands, we really own them, and we can take their people, their cultural ways, their skills, their expertise.

The cuisine of eastern Central Asia became increasingly Chinese-influenced. In fact, knowledge spread farther: Peter Golden found in a dictionary compiled in Yemen in the fourteenth century words for chopsticks and for "Chinese duck" (1994, 2011: 88).

By contrast, ordinary Chinese seemed rather unaffected; Sinoda (1977: 491) has noted that the contemporary novel *Shui Hu Quan* mentions only standard Chinese foods. Chinese medicine was more eclectic, with Western, Tibetan, and Korean influences prominent, but the *YSZY*'s influence seems to have been rather limited. Among major foods, only the carrot appeared to be introduced as late as Yuan. The cultivated carrot is often said to have been developed in Afghanistan in the late Middle Ages, but there are perfectly unmistakable pictures of domestic orange carrots in Dioscorides's manuscripts from Europe, going back to the Juliana Anicia codex of 512 (see Collins 2000 and the Carrot Museum website, www.carrotmuseum.co.uk). The case for medicines is less well known (except for those Laufer 1919 mentions), but few indeed of the Western medicines in the *Bencao Gangmu* were introduced in Yuan times.

More Chinese manuals survive largely to the extent that they were copied in later manuals. They cover the same general topics, including a vast range of crops. Expectably, the Chinese paid far more attention to silk production and bamboo, as well as to domesticated fish, than the Persians did. Fish, especially carp species, had long been domesticated in China—supposedly, and believably, since the Warring States period. The Mongols introduced domestic fish and fish-farming to the West, or at least to eastern Europe, where it underwent a dramatic development in subsequent centuries. It soon spread west, and carp ponds became common on feudal estates and monastery grounds.

The Chinese appear to have gotten the carrot from the Iranians at this time (Allsen 2001: 124; Laufer 1919). It is still called Iranian radish (*hu luobo*) in Chinese. (*Hu* covered, focally, Central Asian Iranics, not Persians, who were *posi*. We can be pretty sure the carrot came from the Central Asian peoples— Sogdians or Tadzhiks—as opposed to Persia, because spinach, which was borrowed directly from Persia just a few centuries earlier, was and still is forthrightly called *pocai*, "Persian greens.")

Conspicuous in the *YSZY*, but much less so in the *Huihui Yaofang*, is the cosmology of qi and the Five Phases. In the *YSZY*, qi is clearly taking on the role of the great unifying flow of energy or subtle fluid or substance-behind-the-material that makes everything what it is and brings everything into one unified field. Concepts of harmony (*he, heping*) and resonance (*ganying*) are implicit. Foods, medicines, and diseases are consistently described in terms of qi flow or stagnation and the Five Phases, including the Five Major Organ Systems, Five Tastes, Five Scents, and so forth. In addition to the Five Tastes (pungent, sweet, sour, bitter, salt), there are five levels of heating: Hot (*re*), warm (*wen*), neutral (*ping* "level" or "balanced"), cooling (*liang*), and cold (*han*). These Galenic concepts were assimilated to yang and yin fairly early. Hu also drew on folk beliefs that have no obvious roots in formal medical theory, such as the tabooed combinations, the lore on fox spirits and other spiritual issues, and Mongol ideas of taboo and purity. Near Eastern medical influence is shown in the Hippocratic-Galenic values ascribed to Near Eastern medicinal foods (such as the cheering influence of saffron), the heavy use of sweet drinks and syrups, and a few other odd cases.

The *Yinshan Zhengyao* is explicitly a guide to court feasting (*shan*) and thus evidently reflects, especially in its exotic recipes, the great *qurim* feasts at which the Mongols entertained guests, dazzling and impressing them with dishes from every part of the empire. One recipe is actually called *qurim* bonnets (it is a very elaborate and unique recipe for dumplings that resemble the tall bonnets of the Mongol royal women). These feasts also were the true home of the huge, exquisite blue-and-white dishes such as those surviving in the Topkapı in Istanbul (Buell, Anderson, and Perry 2010; Carswell 2000).

Its three juan cover an amazing range of foods. The first juan is made up of some general nutritional advice, followed by ninety-five "strange delicacies of combined flavors": recipes for principally Near Eastern and Central Asian dishes. The second is devoted to medicinal recipes, including fifty-seven drinks and liquids, sixty-one brief medicinal recipes for different sorts of animals and the like, another six recipes for Daoist preparations for immortality, and miscellaneous nutritional advice. This advice includes foods to avoid, food combinations to avoid, excesses to avoid, and other caretaking advice. The third juan provides accounts and pictures of the major foodstuffs mentioned in the other juan, as well as some further food animals and plants, for a total of 221 headings. These briefly provide medicinal values: heating or cooling, poisonous or not, and so on. (In Chinese medicine, *you du*, "having poison," does not necessarily mean a food is poisonous; it may merely potentiate poisons in the eater's system.)

The *Yinshan Zhengyao* mentions at least 242 species of animals and plants. Surprisingly few plants, only 28, are from the West. Also, the standard domestic animals (cattle, horse, sheep, goat, donkey, dog, domestic honeybee) are from the West. Six plants are from India and Southeast Asia. Everything else mentioned is native to China. However, many of the animals are game animals common in Mongolia but rare in China: cranes, swans, wolves, bears, marmots, and the like. These reflect the Mongol aspect of the work.

As court nutritionist, Hu Sihui was in charge of cuisine. He had to make it both tasty and healthy. He had the unenviable job of trying to get the Mongols to eat and drink sensibly. Starting with Qubilai Qan himself, they used their position to feast. Many appear to have died from obesity, stroke, probable diabetes, and alcohol abuse. Therefore, Hu Sihui's book is full of good advice about moderation in eating and drinking, the health benefits of fruits and vegetables, the benefits of clean fresh water and healthful ingredients, the virtues of simplicity, and so on.

However, the recipes reflect what the Mongols and other Central Asians were actually eating. The major recipe section, "Strange Delicacies of Combined Flavors," includes seventy-two recipes for lamb and mutton out of ninety-five recipes total. Most involve cooking the lamb with considerable starch, usually wheat: noodles or dumpling skins (in twenty-three recipes—plus four more in juan 2), whole grains of wheat or rice, and so on. About sixteen recipes involve bread, which when recognizably described is Persian *nan*. Often, other heavy items are added. Sometimes millet enters the picture. This dominance of wheat and the rarity of millet accords with Central Asian, not Chinese, foodways of the time.

Most recipes call for light spicing, often the classic cinnamon-cumin-black

pepper mix of the Near East, often also involving China's own large cardamoms and brown pepper. Large cardamoms in particular occur in 24 percent
of the recipes in this and the following sections. This is the most pervasive of
the Chinese contributions to the flavors of the book. Several Chinese-style
recipes call for soy sauce.

Some recipes use chickpeas, which was not a normal Chinese food; these
are among the most clearly Near Eastern-derived recipes in the work. Some
of these, and some other recipes, produce soups that boil down into a solid
mass, that is, the *sopa seca*, "dry soup," of Mediterranean cuisines. Significantly, there are no stir-fried dishes and very few dishes that involve a topping
put over a starch staple (in the manner of Chinese *cai* and *fan*). Most dishes
are boiled; the Mongols preferred boiled food, believing that boiling concen-
trates the essence of the food. On the whole, the dishes run heavily to meat
and flour, with some beans and a fair, but not heavy, amount of spicing. Vegetables are rare, but fruits abound in the recipes of the second juan. Nothing
appears in these recipes about appropriate times, occasions, or sequences of
eating, although these were often feast dishes.

The first recipe in the book is a revealing one, and can stand for the whole:

Mastajhi [Mastic] Soup. It supplements and increases, warms the center, and accords *qi*. Mutton (leg; bone and cut up), tsaoko cardamoms
(five), cinnamon (2 oz.), chickpeas (half pint, boiled, skins removed).
Boil ingredients together to make a soup. Strain broth. [Cut up meat
and put aside.] Add 2 more oz. of cooked chickpeas, a pint of rice, an
ounce of mastic. Adjust flavors with salt. Add the meat and garnish
with cilantro." (Buell, Anderson, and Perry 2010: 270, modified)

This would stand as a type of *shülen*, Mongol meat soup (modern Mongol
shöl, "soup"), but it is clearly a variant of the classic Near Eastern recipe *harisa*,
which is found in almost every Near Eastern cookbook from the Middle Ages
on down (although in North Africa the name has been transferred to a hot
sauce, presumably on that was originally used on this dish). The dish involves
lamb boiled with chickpeas, flour, cinnamon, cumin, and black pepper (in the
most basic recipe; it varies from place to place). A very similar recipe was
recorded from the other end of the Arab-influenced world: Hispanic New
Mexico, where Cleofas Jaramillo learned it from her grandmother in the 1940s
(Jaramillo 1981). The Jaramillo family is known to have had *converso* Moorish
roots (Gary Nabhan, pers. comm., May 16, 2013). New Mexico was settled to

a large extent by converted Spanish Moors and Jews whose conversion was suspect after 1492; they were exiled to the farthest reaches of the Spanish empire. From 1600 until recently, Hispanic New Mexico was a veritable museum of Hispano-Moorish and Hispano-Jewish culture.

The third recipe is a recipe from "Balpo" (Nepal, Kashmir, and area) for lamb with radish and is quite like a modern Kashmiri dish. And so it goes, down to poppy seed rolls (Buell et al. 305) indistinguishable from those found in any delicatessen today.

Some fifty-three of these recipes provide medical indications; the others lack them. When there are medical indications, they are in strictly Chinese terms: what is supplemented or tonified (*bu*), which qi is strengthened, what illnesses are alleviated, and so on. Usually it is the "center" that is tonified, but various organs are sometimes those helped. In traditional Chinese terms, most of the recipes are warming and supplementing; the latter term refers to certain tonic herbs but also especially to foods like lamb and game meats. These were seen to supplement the body's strength, vigor, color, and healing abilities. In modern biomedical terms, they are high in easily digestible protein and easily assimilated mineral nutrients, including iron.

Recipes range in complexity from "willow-steamed lamb," which is lamb pit-cooked in an earth barbecue (302), a truly simple and straightforward Mongol dish, to the elaborate *Qurim* bonnets (304–5). The latter recipe involves a range of ingredients from eggs, safflower, and vinegar to sheeps' stomach, lungs, and tripe! Interesting is its usage of "pine pollen" for pine nuts. The recipe calls for these, apricot kernel paste, pistachio nuts, and walnuts; these nuts, and the whole obsession with tree nuts that it reveals, unmistakably ties this recipe to a Persian or Afghan background.

The cuisine is heavily Near East-derived, but recent recounting shows more local or Central Asian influence than at first seemed the case. Some twenty-one recipes from the ninety-five in the "Strange Delicacies" section in the first juan are fairly straightforward Near Eastern ones. Another twenty-one are simple Central Asian recipes for bear, wolf, and other game, as well as various parts of the sheep. Some eleven recipes are straightforward Chinese ones. One is Indian (a dish still made in Kashmir), with Arab and Persian ancestry. The other forty-two combine Near Eastern, Central Asian, and Chinese foods and influences in various ways, ranging from simple to exceedingly complex and innovative (E. Anderson 2011; Buell, Anderson, and Perry 2010). Some similar recipes exist in other cookbooks of the time, and some survive in western China, Afghanistan, and neighboring areas today (from author's personal observations in Afghanistan and Shaanxi and in Xinjiang-style restaurants around the world). Interesting in some of these exotic recipes is nut paste, a very rare ingredient in world cuisine except in Spain and parts of Italy. The expected paste in Near Eastern cooking would be sesame, but it is not that in the YSZY. Instead, we find almond paste, though some recipes specify peach kernels, the standard Chinese substitute for almonds. Several recipes also mention pine nuts, a food unusual except in the eastern and central Mediterranean (from *Pinus pinea*), although it is also found locally in Afghanistan and Pakistan (from chilgoza pine, *P. gerardiana*), in Korea and neighboring parts of China (from *P. koraiensis* and close relatives), and, important here, in Mongolia (from *P. sibirica*).

Dairy products are strikingly absent. There are a few mentions of cheese, possibly a cheddar type like that of Afghanistan's Baghlan province or a fresh white cheese such as the Mongols enjoy.

About sixteen recipes mention bread, usually as nan used to eat the food. Another twenty-three mention noodles. Chicken, fish, and game meats are found in some recipes. Much of the spicing is Near Eastern, with cinnamon, black pepper, cumin, sesame, occasionally saffron. But, to balance this out, ginger, green onions, soy and mung beans, Chinese large brown cardamoms, and other classically Chinese flavorings are very widely found.

Rarely does Hu Sihui the person appear in the book, but in some places a gentle, low-key humor breaks through. This is clearest in the recipe for roast wolf soup (286). He writes: "Ancient *bencao* do not include entries on wolf meat. At present we state that its nature is heating. It treats asthenia. I have never heard that it is poisonous for those eating it. In the case of the present recipe we use spices to help its flavor." (The recipe is in fact a recipe for lamb that has been retooled for wolf.) This description conjures up a vivid image of an uncouth Siberian tribesman throwing down a wolf and saying "Cook that!" This concept is particularly disturbing since Mongols (then and now) do not eat wolves, because the ancestor of the Mongol people was a gray wolf who married a fallow doe, and of course the many Muslims at court avoided all canids as *haram*. (There is no detectable link with the ancient uses of wolf and similar animals as medicine in the Near East.)

The second section includes more strictly medicinal foods, and many of these are Near Eastern preparations of fruit and sugar in which fruit juice is boiled down with sugar. If it is boiled down to a drinkable liquid, we have a syrup, from the Arabic *sharab* or *sharbat*, something drunk. If boiled down to a thicker liquid, we have a rob, Arabic *rubb*. If it is a paste, it can be cut into lozenges, Arabic *lauzanj*. However done, it is mostly sugar, and its health benefits rather small.

Comparison of a few food accounts with Galen's and with Sun Simiao's *Recipes Worth a Thousand Gold* proves that Hu stayed close to Sun and did not follow Galen. Of course, Sun was not without Near Eastern influences himself (Engelhardt 2001), so there is some common ground.

I have elsewhere quoted several descriptions from Sun Simiao's *Recipes Worth a Thousand Gold* and compared them with the *YSZY*'s and with Galen's. The *YSZY* is usually close to Sun and not to Galen (Anderson 2011: 16–19). It appears that there is *no* clear Western input to the *Yinshan Zhengyao*'s medical assessment of foods that was not already developed in Sun Simiao's time. Ute Engelhardt (2001) and I have both pointed out elsewhere that Sun was an amazing individual in his ability to adopt Western ideas and blend them with Chinese ones (see my introduction to Sun Simiao 2007). He was ahead of his time in many ways, although he was certainly equaled in his comprehensive, rational, and innovative thought by Jia Sixie and Tao Hongjing in the previous century. But Hu Sihui, much later, was derivative.

Hu's medical texts are also extracted from earlier material. A long story of a woman who became a Long-lived Person by eating Solomon's seal is close to the one in Ge Hong's *Baopuzi* (fourth century; see Campany 2002: 22–23). A number of other blocks of text in the *YSZY* are obviously copied from older material.

Fox meat "cures infantile convulsion epilepsy, spiritual confusion, indistinct speech, and inappropriate singing and laughing" (Buell et al. 2010, 409). This is basically fox-madness, as seen in Chinese folklore.

Interesting are the very long lists of recommendations. These are almost all avoidances. Many are common sense: do not consume spoiled food, food of uncertain origin, polluted drinks, and so on. But most are mysterious. They are part of a very ancient tradition of avoidances, which was transmitted both in literature and orally from earliest times. Many involve combinations that were regarded as dangerous; this is a particularly distinctive Chinese tradition, again known in both literary and oral transmission for many centuries and continuing today.

Approximately 168 foods are discussed by Sun Simiao (2007; fourteen are of Western origin, four are Southeast Asian.) In most cases, Sun categorizes them in terms of hot/warm, balanced, or cool/cold. (Hot and warm, and cool and cold, are somewhat poorly and inconsistently distinguished in Chinese medicine and will be consolidated into two categories here.) Of the 210 foods discussed in much detail in the *YSZY*, most are similarly coded; 33 have the same classifications as Sun gives them, while 19 are different.

In almost all cases in which Sun and the *YSZY* differ, the codes in the latter are the same as the modern ones I collected in studying folk medicine in rural Hong Kong in the 1960s and 1970s. In a few cases, the *YSZY* differs from Sun, but the moderns side with Sun. Only one item—sesame—is different in the three: balanced for Sun, cooling in the *YSZY*, warming in modern Hong Kong. Galen discussed sixteen foods well enough to give a good sense of his perception of their heating and cooling qualities; six are coded as in the *YSZY*, three are different, and seven are not found in it. Galen also says that "Everything pungent has been shown to be warming," astringent foods are cooling, and sweet things are more balanced (Galen 2003: 84; see also 85–86). This is basically true of Chinese food coding today and of modern Mediterranean and Latin American folk belief as well. My own research in Mexico and China shows that the codings are usually identical; the logic is almost identical; and even the words used are the same, allowing for translation problems (E. Anderson 1996).

The relationship of Near Eastern and Chinese food codings is far too close to be coincidence. We are dealing here with one system that has been transmitted worldwide. I once thought it was Greek but am now convinced that the flow went both ways, because the influence of Chinese medicine on Near Eastern thought can no longer be denied and because Galen seems far less thorough and clear on the codings than were later authorities who wrote after the Chinese connection had been established.

During and After . . .

Ordinary Chinese seem to have been rather unaffected by all this Near Eastern and Central Asian borrowing. Ordinary non-Imperial Yuan cookbooks, including the one by the great artist Ni Zan (Anderson, Wang, and Mair 2005), are singularly lacking in Central Asian recipes. A classic work on food and health was the *Yinshi Xuzhi*, literally "Drinking and eating needed knowledge" (1969, orig. ca. 1400). This was a long list of recommendations from a countryman, Jia Ming, who was supposedly 105 years old when interviewed. His wisdom was written down in early Ming for all to emulate, but he spent most of his life under Yuan. Note that the title means exactly the same as the *YSZY*'s, except that it uses more ordinary synonyms for the words; it seems quite impossible for this to be mere coincidence. Few Western foods occur, and most of them had been in China for centuries (wheat, barley, sesame, fennel, . . .); however, carrots and watermelon had now entered the picture. Ming's advice is broadly similar to Hu's in that it is strongly based on moderation and avoidances, and these are—again—a mix of common sense and incomprehensible prohibitions against eating certain foods in combination.

Some of these forbidden combinations are shared between the two texts. This may indicate a Yuan focus, but it has been a common Chinese folkloric trait from that day to this. In the twentieth century, Libin Cheng risked his life trying them out and found them all to be harmless (L. Cheng 1936). I recorded many in my own field work in Hong Kong in the 1960s and 1970s (E. Anderson 1988). Jia Ming also recommends many waters from various sources, various kinds of tea and salt, and other useful local items. In this he anticipates the much longer and more detailed work of Gao Lian in later Ming (see below).

The effects that the *Yinshan Zhengyao*, the *HHYF*, and comparable works (if any) had on Chinese culture remain to be assessed. One thing, however, is clear: there were few. Of course, it was very difficult, perhaps impossible, to obtain the rarer, more obscure, and more expensive medicinals mentioned in the *Huihui Yaofang*. And if Chinese medicines were routinely substituted, we would have a hard time teasing out the Western influences in later books.

This being said, it is clear that their influence was not great. The encyclopedic compilation *Chinese Herbal Medicine Formulas and Strategies*, by Volker Scheid et al. (2009), shows absolutely no change in the use of foreign plants between pre-Yuan and post-Yuan formulas. Actually, neither period shows much use of foreign items. Wheat and barley are often used, but no one in old China would have thought of them as foreign. Apricot kernels are very common in the formulas, but if the apricot was not native to China, it certainly got there early. Of the actual drugs used in the formulas in Scheid and his colleagues' great compilation, only areca nut, benzoin, catechu, fennel, fenugreek, garlic, myrrh, natron, and safflower stand out as foreign. All of these were familiar very early on (and of course areca was from Southeast Asia). Saiga antelope horn, which was often used, would had to have been brought from Central Asian territories that China rarely held. A single mention of *Sinapis* (western mustard) is probably a mistaken identification (I am sure the original formula referred to Chinese mustard, *Brassica* sp.).

On the other hand, there are generic similarities. The treatment of stroke by warming and stimulating drugs, typical of the *HHYF*, is also typical of Chinese medicine (Scheid et al. 2009: 631ff.), and some of the drugs are the same: cinnamon, ginger, licorice (a soothing and harmonizing adjuvant), and, significantly, myrrh—one of the very few Western drugs that stayed popular in China. Insanity, closely related to stroke in the *HHYF*, is related to it in Chinese practice also, and in both cases attacks by wind and internal problems from anxiety, worry, and overuse of alcohol, food, and sex are considered causal. Some influence seems likely here and, of course, is certain in the case of myrrh. All these similarities held long before the *HHYF*, but the latter may have helped establish them in Chinese medicine.

A huge book on medicinal eating by Gao Lian was printed in 1591 and includes several Western recipes, but it mentions only seven Western foods, mostly those known since the Tang Dynasty. Novels like the *Jin Ping Mei* and the Qing Dynasty's *Hong Lou Meng* have very little on Western food; the only significant Westernization of life reflected in the latter book was the coming of accurate timepieces—Western clocks. In spite of the enormous amount of medicine in the *Hong Lou Meng*, I can find no Western influences except the general, long-established concern with heating and cooling—long assimilated to traditional Chinese ideas of yang and yin.

A book by Gao Lian, a litterateur and amateur physician with nutritional interests, is more hopeful (Su 2004). In a vast assemblage of lore on foods, drinks, and medicinals, dating to 1591, he mentions anise, coriander, dill, fennel, garlic, poppy seeds, and sesame seeds—all Western , though long established in China by that time. (Historian Sumei Yi has prepared a translation of Gao's work on food, available from me.) He provides recipes for sweets that are clearly West Asian (83ff.in Yi's translation ms). One is a pine nut shortbread essentially identical to those found in New Mexico today. Another is much like a *kourabiyeh* (an Arabian, stuffed small cake). There are recipes for halwa. One sweet is actually called by that name, transliterated as *hailuo* (sea radish). Among several others is a milk dessert similar to Persian and Indian *barfi* (Farsi for "snowy").

A recipe for a fried jiaozi is called *shilaier*—literally "eat-come-let," but obviously a transliteration of a Central Asian term (89). An Azerbaijani cookbook has a very similar food under the name *shor* (Akhmedov 1986: 155). Probably *shor* and *shilaier* are cognate words and recipes. (A Central Asian sweet called *chekchek* and a Manchu *saqima*, Perry 1995, could be related.) Gao sees the shilaier as a type of mantou; evidently the word had not yet taken its modern meaning of an unfilled small loaf of wheat dough. (Gao also describes very modern wonton soup under that name—*hundun*). Yet Gao's medicine appears unaffected by Western knowledge.

The End of the Mongol Information Superhighway

The Mongol Empire fell apart slowly but surely. The Golden Horde converted to Islam for complex reasons; the process was not simple or merely political (Deweese 1994). Settling in Russia, they gradually mixed with Russians and Turkic peoples. The last of them became "Tatars," whatever that word may mean, and were largely exterminated by Stalin (the Crimean Tatars were especially affected by outright genocide; see E. Anderson and B. Anderson 2012; Rummel 1998).

Near Eastern medicine transformed Europe and had much to do with the making of modern science. The knowledge transfer seen in the HHYF is dwarfed by the sheer volume of the transfer from the Near East to Europe in the medieval period. On the other hand, the latter transfer took place slowly and in small packets from the 700s to the 1600s. There was a burst of activity in the 1200s, when the total mass of translations of Arabic works into Latin reached enormous proportions. Gerald of Cremona, the most diligent scholar, translated (or at least oversaw the translation of) dozens of works. Medieval Europe began the process that reached fruition in the "scientific revolution" (Gaukroger 2006); many now think there was no revolution, only a slow process.

Europe was rising fast, and its expansion after 1400 diminished and eventually replaced the dominance of Asia in world politics. European powers rapidly seized control of the sea lanes at just the point when marine transportation was becoming more efficient and cheaper than caravans. The Silk Road was doomed. With European dominance of the seas, and the resulting vast wealth flows to the relevant powers, Europe took the lead from Asian medicine in the sixteenth century.

Even before that, medicine was past its acme in the Near East. A recent concise summary attributes this to "military invasions [including the Ilkhans], massacres and infrastructure destruction; a long period of drought beginning around 1250 AD [the Medieval Warm Period]; and a series of plague epidemics between 1347 and 1515" (Silverstein 2007). Nevertheless, medicine continued to exist, and some real advances were made. The idea of unrelieved decline is simply not the case (cf. Dallal 2010; Stearns 2011), but the problems were overwhelming. The Near Eastern doctors had long known of contagion and did what they could to fight bubonic plague and other epidemics in spite of much controversy, but they had nothing that could stop them.

The Yuan Dynasty fell and the Mongols were expelled in 1368, following the amazing popular rebellion led by Zhu Yuanzhang—the only case in all of Chinese history when a popular movement led by a plebeian actually brought down a dynasty and established a new one (see, e.g., Mote 1999). The Mongols fled back to the steppes, where they kept harassing Ming. They even once succeeded in sacking Beijing. They preserved their state for centuries—solid disproof of the old nonsense about China absorbing her conquerors.

The Ilkhan dynasty in the Near East, checked by the Mamluks, rapidly unraveled and fell into the usual fratricidal conflicts of the declining Mongol empires. Then Tamerlane appeared from Central Asia (Marozzi 2004). His conquests devastated all of the Near and Middle East, but he created little that lasted. The region was so devastated that it could only fall into increasingly destructive wars. The cycle of savagery goes on today, preventing Central Asia from rising again.

In fact, the Song Dynasty, conquered and destroyed by the Mongols, was in many ways a golden age of innovative thinking that China was never to repeat. The Ming lost Yuan's fascination with the West (P. Smith and von Glahn 2003) and turned its attention eastward. Allsen (2001) notes that the Ming compilation of the history of Yuan devotes more attention to the Ryukyu Islands than to the Mongols in Russia! Surely the Yuan would not have had such a priority. This indicates a shift in trade from land-based across Central Asia to sea-based toward Japan and Southeast Asia.

The Ming Dynasty, which arose as an anti-Mongol movement, was relatively xenophobic. Chinese traditions triumphed, but Ming copied the Mongols in one major way: they maintained and greatly strengthened the Mongol centralized autocratic government. China became authoritarian in a way that it had not been before. I follow the widespread (but still controversial) view that this is what eventually slowed Chinese science and enterprise (see Mote 1999 and Pomeranz 2000). China fell behind the West from the middle Ming onward, though it remained somewhere in the competition until the comparably repressive Qing Dynasty (1644–1911).

Most scholars still seem unaware of the extent to which East and West fused under the Mongols (Buell, Anderson, and Perry 2010; May 2007). Perhaps more to the point, they still have, somewhere in mind, racist stereotypes of Chinese science. As recently as 1944, even so widely tolerant a scholar as A. L. Kroeber—the antithesis of a racist—could write that Chinese "Observation, except for practical utility, inclined to be casual and summary. . . . The bent of Chinese civilization . . . was toward an interest in human behavior and relations, rather than toward the physical world. . . . Nature was something to be taken for granted, dealt with, or enjoyed aesthetically, but hardly to be curious about" (Kroeber 1944: 183). Joseph Needham changed all this. We often forget, now, just how revolutionary Needham's findings were. Quotations like the one from Kroeber remind us that even the least intolerant Westerners still believed stereotypes. Even after Needham, scholars often dismissed Chinese science as nothing but mystical nonsense (e.g., Wolpert 1993).

This attitude has led to the assumption that Ming simply kept the tradition going. In fact, Ming slowed an interaction that should, by all rights, have kept China fully participant in the modernization of science after 1500. If the impetus of the previous 2,000 years had been maintained, China would have been as much a part of the developing European world as Germany, or at least Sweden or Hungary. Instead, China turned inward or eastward. It did not stand still—science continued to flourish, observation went on—but by the end of Ming, China had begun to fall behind the Europeans.

CHAPTER 8

Shifting Grounds in Ming

Ming and Impossible Rule

The most amazing thing about Ming is that the dynasty lasted almost 300 years—in spite of a definitely eccentric royal family, a corrupt government, and an incompetent and thinly stretched bureaucracy. Ming's royal family had a touch of paranoia (literally; not a loose use of the word), which led to mass murders of intellectuals and innovators. The founder, Zhu Yuanzhang, killed an estimated 100,000 elite individuals, not counting people in the lower classes (Marmé 2005: 76; cf. P. Smith and von Glahn 2003, passim), and his successors were often as bloody. Over time, they imposed an increasingly strict control on writing, advocacy, and political activity. They were not as despotic as they sometimes appeared to desire to be, and not as despotic as many a modern state, but they succeeded in limiting intellectual probing. They targeted specifically anyone interested in change or in loosening up the imposed intellectual crust on the country.

The Ming Dynasty coincided with the first part of the Little Ice Age, and that meant horrible weather—freezes, snowfalls, droughts, floods (Brook 2010, esp. 50–78)—with consequent famines and epidemics. Yet, not only did the dynasty survive murderous rule and bad climate, but after the Yongle emperor's takeover by coup in 1402, there was never even a significant challenge to the government until its last days.

In Ming, the West and Central Asian immigrant communities faced forced acculturation, or at least the attempt of it. Zhu Yuanzhang decreed in the very year of his ascension that foreign surnames, dress, and hair styles should be Sinicized. The foreign surnames rule was unenforceable, but names usually changed anyway, as in the routine change of Muhammad to Ma. In 1372, after only four years of rule, he made an amazingly audacious decree that "the Mongols and *Semu* people are free to intermarry with Han Chinese . . . (but) they are not allowed to marry their own race" (Tan 2009: 99; his translation; I assume "Han Chinese" was indeed *Han ren*, "people of Han"). *Semu* was the Mongol term for their Central Asian allies, the largely Turkic and Iranic people they brought in as administrators and skilled workers. The result of these decrees was, of course, massive Sinicization, with the Hui community really coming into its own as a formidable power within Han Chinese society (see Tan's lengthy account). One unanticipated result was an astonishing fusion of Islam and Confucianism—the Muslims agreed with some later Jesuits that Confucianism was a philosophy, not a religion, and found its teachings very similar to those of Islam! (See Tan 2009: 117–23.)

Ming Fails in the West but Thrives in the Southeast

Zheng He's voyages continue to amaze (Tan 2009), not only because of their scope and range but also because they did not usher in a whole age of exploration. These seven voyages meant almost continuous seafaring for the intrepid Zheng, who died far from home, in Calicut, in 1433. But after that the Ming Dynasty dropped such huge expeditions, citing their expense and the lack of a commensurate return. Unlike the later European voyages to the East, Zheng He could not bring back a cargo that would guarantee severalfold profit. Zheng He opened up connections with Africa, but China had no need for giraffes, as one emperor pointed out. China lost the chance to drive science and capitalism by long-distance seafaring and trade.

The voyages of Zheng He were merely the most spectacular of a long-term expansion of China into the Indian Ocean, at that time an incredibly busy place (Chaudhuri 1985; Sen 2003). Philippe Beaujard's enormous recent history shows that every nearby realm, from Borneo to Italy and Egypt, was sending ships all over this vast sea. Beaujard, a Madagascar expert, traces the formation of the Malagasy people from Indonesians and others, including some Africans (Beaujard 2009, 2012; from my own research there, I believe he understates the African contribution). China already had a spice trade and major maritime links with India and Southeast Asia (Deng 1997; Sen 2003). These links had flourished from Han onward. In spite of their steppe background, the Mongols had not been remiss in following up that trading tradition, as we know from Marco Polo's experience voyaging homeward. They had not conquered much of the region, but they opened it for settlement and trade.

Trade in fabrics flourished, with competition from India. The Malay world came to depend on imported fine fabrics, a fact delightfully reflected in a wry Malay saying on poverty: "Even though ten ships come, the dogs have no loincloths but their tails."

Notable from the beginning were the communities from southern Fujian and northeast Guangdong who speak dialects of the Southern Min language, known in Southeast Asia as Hokkien (from its pronunciation of "Fujian"). Southeast Asian languages are riddled with Hokkien loanwords. One has gone worldwide: "ketchup." Hokkien *ke tsiap* refers to fruit or sea food sauces. In what is now Indonesia, the term came to be used for soy sauce, *kecap* in modern Bahasa. It then was borrowed into English for a product that diverged farther and farther from soy.

Conversely, Chinese has many loans from Southeast Asian languages via Hokkien. We have already encountered the earliest: Malaysian *pinang* for the areca palm. This carried straight across into Hokkien as *pinnang*, but became *bin lang* in Mandarin. The borrowing is already attested in Ji Han's book of 304, but is probably a later interpolation, since it is doubtful modern Hokkien had developed by 304. Many other such borrowings have accumulated since. Fusion foodways developed in Southeast Asia (Cheung and Tan 2007; some of the authors in that collection speak of "hybridity," but the foodways of China and Southeast Asia had never been separate in the first place and were merely continuing a long history of mutual influence, not "hybridizing"). Today's Nonya cooking and the special cuisines of urban Bangkok, Saigon, and Hanoi reflect centuries of Chinese-Southeast Asian fusion, and certainly the result has been some of the finest food on earth.

Ties of language and foodshows how close and extensive the economic ties were between China and Southeast Asia from very early on; they became far more extensive under Ming. The Mongols tried to conquer Southeast Asia by force of arms, with dubious success; Ming won it commercially (Lieberman 2003, 2009; Wade and Sun 2010).

By contrast, the Silk Road was virtually closed. In the aftermath of the Mongols, violence escalated out of control, climaxing in the apparently psychopathic killings of Tamerlane. The Little Ice Age brought both cold and drought—ironically saving China from Tamerlane, who died on his way to

China in one of the first of the particularly savage winters the Little Ice Age brought. The Little Ice Age made Inner Asia's high passes almost unbearable and its deserts almost impossible for caravans. Meanwhile, the sea trade routes expanded, undercutting the caravans and taking all the business.

Perhaps in consequence to the economic failure of Zheng and the climatic failure of the Silk Road, Ming stopped not only long-distance voyaging but also most attempts to keep up on, learn from, or borrow from the West. The Mongol books remained in print, and Central Asia continued to be a zone of influence and interaction, but no new projects comparable to the *Huihui Yao-fang* emerged. This has been taken as the Chinese norm for so long (in spite of recent revisionist views) that one must emphasize, over and over, the dynamic, open, eager-to-learn nature of Chinese civilization in previous centuries. The profound influence of West, South, and Central Asia on China climaxed in the Mongol period.

One reason was that however much the Ming Chinese wished to forget Central Asia, they were not allowed to. The Mongols, far from being "assimilated" or "absorbed" (as earlier generations of Western historians taught), continued to be formidable enemies. Expelled from China, they continued to hold most of the rest of Eurasia for another century (and locally even longer). In 1449, they captured the Emperor Zhengtong (who had waged an ill-advised campaign against them) and held him hostage (Brook 2010: 95–96). They exerted continual pressure on China. Ming never came close to restoring the boundaries of Tang, let alone approaching the size of later Qing. Yet, with the Silk Road ruined, Ming could not profit from its Central Asian forays. There was no hope of turning the Mongols into peaceful, prosperous traders. Ming could not focus on lands across the sea.

What if the steady expansion seen in Tang, Song, and Yuan had continued? China would have immediately leaped on Portuguese and Dutch seafaring and mercantile knowledge, seeing the imperative need to compete if it was to keep a hand in Southeast Asia. It would have introduced many plants and animals, learned new bookkeeping techniques, borrowed metals technology. It would have participated in the modernizing enterprise (whatever that may be or might have been), as Japan did after 1868. World history would have been very different. Conjectural history is always fun. But, then, to quote a remark beloved of my historian father, "Cleopatra's nose: Had it been shorter, the whole face of the earth would have been changed" (Pascal 2005: 6). ("Snub" noses were not liked in Pascal's day, and his idea—a satire on conjectural history—was that a snub-nosed Cleopatra would not have captivated

Caesar or Mark Antony, in which case the Roman republic might have been saved and the fall of Rome averted.)

The great exception was the arrival of New World food crops. They reached China in late Ming and steadily gained ground (Ho Pingti's study, 1955, has never been superseded, but see Mazumdar 1999). Maize was widespread but rare in the 16th century. Maize may have come first through southwest China and Tibet. Sweet potatoes were introduced by a Chinese merchant from the Philippines in 1590 and possibly also by earlier but unrecorded merchants. White potatoes came via the Dutch in Taiwan in the seventeenth century and were separately introduced, later, by European missionaries in the western mountains. These new crops did not, however, take China by storm (Li 2003). They were introduced by local merchants and farmers, not by an enterprising government. Through Ming and perhaps even early Qing, they stayed local and were sporadically cultivated.

Yet, the extent of New World penetration of China is evidently far greater than has been realized. Roderich Ptak (2011) has recently analyzed the natural history of introductions by the Portuguese to Macau (from the early 1500s) and by the Jesuits to Beijing and other cities, and it turns out that there was a great deal coming into China. Many kinds of New World (largely Brazilian) parrots were well known around Macau, and Ptak reproduces a very accurate Chinese painting of a macaw (plate 2). If even macaws were well known in at least one Chinese port, it is clear that far more useful things like food crops would be spreading rampantly. Diligent searching of the relevant works is needed.

Maize was not important until Qing (Li Bozhong 2003), and in most of China only in late Qing (Myers and Wwang 2002: 581). It then spread rapidly in the twentieth century. Sorghum and millets had long prevailed in areas where maize is now central; they yield less well but are much better food. Maize, sweet potatoes, peanuts, chiles, and other New World crops made a huge and dramatic difference in the Qing Dynasty but were slow to arrive and spread. Sweet potatoes were widespread by the 1730s. Maize remained commoner in central and upland south China, sweet potatoes in the southeast (Vermeer 1998: 266).

The New World crops allowed more agriculture in the mountains of the center and south, where they grow well but rice does not. This in turn led to further deforestation (Vermeer 1998: 267). The principal contribution of the New World crops was expansion of agriculture; they would grow on steep mountains, sandy fields, dry areas, and other unlikely habitats that had previously been low in productivity. Almost as important, though, was a rarely appreciated fact: they permitted the poor to be reasonably well nourished. Peanuts provided protein and oil. Maize, tomatoes, and chiles provided vitamin A. Chiles, in fact, provide all the vitamins and many important minerals—unlike most other easy-to-grow, highly productive plants. The Chinese already had cabbage and mustard greens. They had Chinese wolfthorn, which is closely related to tomatoes and chiles and has even greater nutritional value. But they needed still more. Significantly, the chile caught on in precisely those parts of China where other vitamin-rich crops were relatively hard to grow, especially the mountain west. It also became popular in Korea, where people were even more food-stressed and chronically short of vitamins and where many of China's best vitamin sources can be hard to grow because of cold and mountainous conditions.

One dubious legacy of this expansion allowed by New World crops was the steady and rapid encroachment of Han Chinese on the formerly free and isolated realm that James Scott (2009) calls Zomia. This formerly vast realm comprised upland southern China and the northern interior parts of India, Myanmar, Thailand, Laos, and Vietnam. It was occupied by a vast number of societies speaking extremely diverse languages, though practicing broadly similar forms of agriculture. They were fiercely independent and resisted incorporation into or dominance by the down-country states. Zomia is now substantially incorporated into those states, and the independence of its people is a thing of the past. Scott sees it as having been something of an anarchist utopia, and friends and students of mine who come from there are prone to feel sympathetic, though uniformly admitting that Scott rather overstates the case. In any event, New World crops allowed these hill peoples to expand their population and economy considerably but also allowed the lowland majority peoples to move rapidly into the mountains and take over political power.

During Ming and Qing, vast numbers of Chinese migrated to the Nanyang—the Southern Ocean, that is, Southeast Asia, including the Philippines and Indonesia—to make a living. More Hokkien words entered Indonesian: *tauge* for bean sprouts, *tauhu* (the Hokkien pronunciation of "tofu") for bean curd, and so on.

In the Rijksmuseum in Amsterdam, there hangs a Dutch painting done around 1660 of a market stall in Java, which the Dutch had recently taken. The stall-holder is Chinese, and he is selling not only Southeast Asian fruits such as coconuts, bananas, rambutans, langsats, durians, rose apples, and mangos, but also New World foods: pineapples and cashews.

Ming Learning and Development

Otherwise, agriculture continued to develop, slowly but surely, in Ming. (For standard histories, see Brook 2010; Li Bozhong 1998; Mote 1999; Mote and Twitchett 1988; Twitchett 2001.) Suzhou in Ming focused on high-quality rice, trading it widely. The people who grew it had to sell it to buy cheaper rice, as did farmers in Hong Kong in the last century, when low-yield, salt-tolerant, excellent-flavored rice grew in the outer New Territories. The Suzhou gazetteer (a local guidebook with a local-products list) in Ming reported "seventeen varieties of nonglutinous and twelve varieties of glutinous rice, six strains of wheat and six types of beans . . . nine kinds of fruit in addition to eleven different tangerines and twelve varieties of plums . . . thirteen types of vegetables and six of melon" (Marmé 2005: 23), as well as many fish, water plants, medicinal herbs, and so on. The fishermen were boat-dwellers, as in early modern south China generally.

According to a Ming account, it was in Suzhou that the merchants began avoiding the old word for chopsticks, *zhu*, because it sounded too much like "to block"—as in blocking one's shipments. So they started to call them *kuai*, "fast," to counteract the bad luck (Brook 2010: 112). Chopsticks are *kuaizi*, "little quick ones," to this day. "Chop" was "pidgin" English for "fast," hence the English word.

Both the end of Yuan and the end of Ming (like the end of Tang) coincided very closely with dramatic decreases in the strength of the monsoon, associated with the Little Ice Age. It appears almost certain that famine and unrest associated with these events helped bring down the dynasties (P. Zhang et al. 2008). All these climatic problems coincided with dry or cold periods elsewhere in the world.

Scholars in China have been accused in Western stereotypy of being otherworldly, concerned only with ancient philosophy. Chinese scholars often had their practical side and connected with the "real world." A notable event—notable to people then, not just to modern researchers—was the publication in 1406 of the *Jiuhuang Bencao* (Basic herbal for famines; Read 1946). This was a book intended for local distribution and use; the victims of famines could not read it, but it was well illustrated, and local scholars and officials were expected to explain it. It was published under the patronage and official editorship of imperial prince Zhu Xiao (1380–1425). The actual lead author was Zhou Dingwang (1382–1425). A later, enlarged edition appeared in 1559. It described 414 plants, all edible but not usual foods; most were wild greens of a coarse nature and bitter or tasteless. Several wild fruits and grains were mentioned.

Bernard Read (1946) compiled modern identifications for the plants. He also looked into their nutritional value and found it substantial; the Chinese scholars knew what they were doing. Nothing could be farther from the stereotype of the "Chinese mandarin" than an imperial prince compiling a genuinely excellent and well-targeted work for use by the poor in hard times. Nothing comparable existed in Europe at that point. The book was widely distributed, though apparently not as widely as intended; its effects were less than had been hoped, but similar works of utilitarian knowledge appeared in large numbers in Ming.

China's greatest single intellectual achievement in the practical side of literary endeavor may be the *Bencao Gangmu* of Li Shizhen (2003 [1596]; Métailié 1989; Nappi 2009). It is finally available in English, running to six huge volumes. It was the climax of China's long herbal tradition. It describes almost 1,900 medicinal items, including many from Europe, the Near East, India, Southeast Asia, and elsewhere. Li summarized and evaluated everything that had gone before and added his own observations—many of them shrewd and perceptive and based on his own experience. It must be admitted that many other data were credulous and speculative and based on hearsay, though he did sharply dismiss a great deal of truly ridiculous lore that had accumulated over the centuries (see Nappi 2009 for detailed discussion). He managed to hear and include the story of the vegetable lamb, in almost exactly the same terms as Europeans of the time (2009: 111). Since this story of live lambs growing on plants derived from an early report of cotton, and since the Chinese had had cotton a long time, the story must have reached China from the west via Central Asia. He also has many tales of wild folk, cannibalism, dragons, and other wonders. The vast majority of his entries, however, are solid, reasonable, pragmatic medical lore. Much of it is wrong or dubious by modern biomedical standards, but so much of it is correct and empirically successful that the book continues as the major reference for modern Chinese herbalists.

He includes at least 67 Western medicinals. This figure is a minimum, since I do not count the varieties and subvarieties of plants or any of the minerals—minerals being universal, though the uses Li describes were often Western derived. Li includes at least 31 plants and animals from India and Southeast Asia, but only four from the New World, including maize and squash. Li was quite conservative and tended not to list Western or New

World items unless they were well established in the old herbals. He did not deal with several of the plants in the *Huihui Yaofang*. He missed tobacco and chile, both probably well established in China in his time. Li mentions some 203 of the medicinals in the *HHYF*, including about 46 of the Western ones and 15 from India and Southeast Asia. He generally ignored minor Western and south Asian items; the overlap is extensive in regard to widespread medicinals. His book does describe local equivalents or congenerics for many west Eurasian herbs, but the uses tend to be different.

This can be compared with the final count on introduced food plants in China, as found in Shiu-ying Hu's comprehensive *Food Plants of China* (2005). This book lists 79 introductions from western Eurasia, as well as 40 from south and Southeast Asia, 10 from Africa, and 60 or more from the New World. (These are not complete lists. I am aware of at least one further, very recent, introduction that is not in Hu.) These are only food plants, not animals and medicines.

When *Bencao Gangmu* was published in 1596, shortly after Li's death, it was probably the greatest herbal in the world, but already Western European botanists such as Leonard Fuchs and Rembert Dodoens were closely approaching Li's accomplishment. Within a few years, European herbals such as those of Gerard (1975 [1633]) and Parkinson (1976 [1629]) challenged Li's herbal in scope and considerably surpassed it in scientific accuracy and value. Even more to the point, John Ray (1627–1705) developed the scientific taxonomy that was to climax in Linnaeus's system. Li standardized Chinese terminology in a quite similar way, typically using binomes comparable to Ray's genus-species terminology. Li also had a sense of natural order, comparable to Ray's idea of divine order. But Li did not parallel Ray's awareness of plant anatomy and the importance of reproductive anatomy, and no Chinese Linnaeus stepped forward to create a full, formal, scientifically based taxonomy with reproductive systems as key (an extremely important foreshadowing of Darwinian evolutionary theory). In Chinese medicine today, Li's great herbal remains the standard. Chinese chemists have now found the active ingredients and begun testing the biomedical effectiveness of the remedies, but this literature is not widely circulating in current Chinese medical practice. Much of the testing is based on small samples and lacks full double-blind case/control structure.

Another fascinating work, slightly later in time, was Song Yingxing's *Heavenly Work, Creating Things* (*Tiangong Kaiwu*, Sung 1966, original ca. 1630; *kai* means "to open," and thus to originate, create, put forth). Song (1587–

1666?) was a failed exam-taker who became a local teacher. Seeing the tragic decline of the dynasty, he sought ways to bring heaven's will back into popular life. He became obsessed with crafts—with how people mined metals and coal, made sugar, spun and wove silk, and anything and everything else. He had an elaborate, highly rationalized version of qi theory, studied in detail by Dagmar Schäfer (2010). Song saw qi as basic to everything, and yang and yin qi in particular as the creative forces; hence fire and water were vital in industrial processes. (Recall the cook Yi Yin saying something similar thousands of years before; early Chinese medicine also held that yang and yin qi were all-important.)

He started by explaining how grains are grown, especially rice, by that time the most important grain in the empire. His detailed and vivid accounts give one a good enough understanding that a reader, with some prior knowledge of farming, could go out and start gardening forthwith. The same cannot be said for most Chinese literary accounts.

Song believed the old Chinese idea that metals and coal would grow back in the earth if not exhausted by overexploitation (Schäfer 2010: 170). This was a reasonable view, in spite of its error, since the Chinese observed that crystals and speleothems often grew (slowly but surely) in caves and that alluvial deposits often replenished themselves as water carried more minerals downstream. He noted that silver prospectors looked for "heaps of surface stones that are 'slightly brown in color and scattered in such a way as to present the appearance of forked paths'" (Sung 1966: 238; see also Schäfer 2010: 171), that is, dikes, probably pegmatite, colored by oxidized iron—exactly what prospectors still seek.

He also knew the effects of lack of salt: "A man would not be unwell if he abstained for an entire year from either the acrid, sour, sweet or bitter; but deprive him of table salt . . . for a ten-day week and he will be too weak to tie up a chicken and feel utterly enervated" (Schäfer 2010: 90; Sung, 1966: 109; Vogel 2009 205, cite the same passage, Vogel delightfully adding "or overcome a duck"). Indeed; and no one has ever said it better.

Song tells us a great deal about flour milling (Sung 1966: 94ff.) and vegetable oil making (214ff.). Oil was made of sesame, Chinese cabbage, soy, and Chinese radish seeds; a lesser but still good oil came from perilla and Chinese rapeseed; a rather inferior one from tea oil (from *Thea sasanqua*, closely related to tea for drinking). Other plants provided oil for lamps and the like; many of these oils were toxic and thus inedible. Song details the production processes, which were highly sophisticated. Perhaps the most interesting section to a food historian is that on yeasts and fermentation (289–94). Long and detailed recipes are provided for ordinary, medicinal, and red yeast preparations.

Similar books were becoming common Europe at the time. Song's life is amazingly parallel to that of Sir Hugh Plat (1552–1608), another less-than-brilliantly-successful individual who was fascinated, indeed obsessed, with everything technical (Thick 2010). But Plat was writing at the beginning of the scientific revolution and was followed by ever more accurate and detailed accounts, whereas Song wrote at the end of Ming and had no successors. There were countless Chinese books on crafts and industries, but they focused on just one topic, for example, cooking, printing, weaving, pottery, agriculture, or the like. Only Song seems to have been obsessed with understanding absolutely everything.

For the rich, food became ever more sophisticated. (See H. Huang 2000: 129 for a list of major culinary works; see Waley-Cohen 2007 for brief but very good history of gastronomy .) Novels of the period reflect an extremely sophisticated, diverse cuisine and provide the best picture available. Sarah Schneewind (2006) tells a hilarious story of an attempt to fool a Ming emperor into thinking an auspicious omen had appeared in the form of two melons growing on one stalk. In Imperial times, bearers of such good omens were liberally rewarded by emperors—if the emperors believed the omens to be genuine. This particular emperor was not fooled.

Connoisseurship flourished in horticulture:

When someone in antiquity who was gripped by an obsession for flowers heard speak of a rare blossom, even if it were in a deep valley or in steep mountains, he would not be afraid of stumbling and would go to it. Even in the freezing cold and the blazing heat, even if his skin were cracked and peeling or caked with mud and sweat, he would be oblivious. When a flower was about to bloom, he would move his pillow and mat and sleep alongside it to observe how the flower would go from budding to blooming to fading. Only after it lay withered on the ground would he take his leave. . . . This is what is called a genuine love of flowers. (Yuan Hongdao 1568–1610; in Zeitlin 1991: 3)

Garden art reveals the extreme wealth and sophistication of the agricultural sector in imperial China (Clunas 1996, and, for a more personal view, see the great novel *The Story of the Stone* by Cao Xueqin, 1973–86 [Chinese original, eighteenth century]). China's gardens reached heights of lavishness and beauty. Chinese had a major love of the environment, shown not only in travels and nature writing (Elvin 2004 and Strassberg 1994 give examples) but also in art—notably the miniature gardens that captured the beauty and spiritual power of the wild for city-bound people (Stein 1990). Of course, loving natural beauty does not often stop exploitation. However, behind the aesthetic appreciation lay a genuinely religious bond with the landscape, and this did serve to save forests, wetlands, brush, and mountain environments.

CHAPTER 9

Overview: Imperial China
Managing Landscapes

Don't fear going slow, just fear stopping.
(*bu pa man, jiou pa zhan*)

—Chinese proverb

Patterns and Pasts

China—that is, something like the current geographical expanse we call China—has been united under seven dynasties. First was Qin, which, though short-lived, united the country and gave it its name. These dynasties lasted an average of around 250 years, but the range was vast: from 14 years for Qin to more than 400 for Han. The modal value was around 300. Also, Han (twice) and Tang (once) were interrupted by coups that transiently brought empresses or their protégés to power, followed by countercoups that restored the dynasty. Han's coups, successful countercoups, and 400-year reign are all very anomalous in world history and deserve more study than they have received.

Coups by one branch of the imperial family against another were occasional, with the victory of the Yongle Emperor of Ming in 1402 being the major one in terms of effecting major change. One rebellion—An Lushan's—briefly toppled a dynasty but was quickly suppressed; the violent rebellion of the Three Feudatories almost brought down Qing, and later the Taipings and many other rebels came even closer in the 1800s, leading to a genuine reinvention of Qing in the Tongzhi Restoration of 1862. Averaging these deadly crises indicates that coups occurred about every 75 years, but this number ignores many lesser crises that were serious but not regime-threatening.

Again, the range is dramatic: from Qin's 14 years to a full 242 years for Ming after Yongle's coup.

Dynasties failed when they lost the Mandate of Heaven: that is, when they misgoverned so badly that ordinary environmental fluctuations turned into disasters, ordinary bandit activity grew into mass rebellions, inevitable but manageable corruption turned into free-for-all, and ineptness of a particular emperor or minister swelled into a court of incompetents.

Western textbooks are fond of treating the Mandate of Heaven as typical Oriental superstition and mysticism, but no Chinese histories seem to have labored under such illusions. Western studies of Chinese history have been seriously handicapped by the irrepressible tendency of Westerners to see the Chinese as lost in obscurantism. Not often do Westerners realize that the Mandate of Heaven might be a perfectly hard-headed concept, if extended a bit too far into religious realms.

Political theorists now often hold that governments depend on perceived legitimacy, which in turn depends on the government doing something remotely like its job. It also depends on the government manipulating symbols of legitimacy: the flag, the military parades, and such. Religion, be it worshiping at the altars of earth and heaven or swearing on the Bible, is always bent to the service of legitimizing rule—a very difficult rhetorical trick when the religion is Daoism or Christianity!

The Chinese tried to shore up their legitimacy by saying the emperor was divine; Western states used to speak similarly of the divine right of kings but have since come to speak of democracy and the people's choice instead. At least in the contemporary United States, where corporate money has taken over politics, democracy has become as real as the divinity of Chinese emperors. Claiming divinity or free democracy serves the same function: shoring up legitimacy through dishonesty.

One might think of national politics as a pressure cooker. There is always steam building up in the form of power-hungry rebels waiting in the wings. They fail to achieve their goals as long as the government can keep the lid tight. The lid is "legitimacy" and some enforcement capacity. With those, even if the government is singularly inept, people stay loyal.

The seventy-five-year cycle of coups, however loosely approximated, reminds us of the ideas of the great fourteenth-century Tunisian social scientist Ibn Khaldun (1958). He postulated hundred-year cycles. A government would start with a band of brave, united individuals, typically "barbarians," or, as we would call them in modern jargon, semiperipheral marcher polities (E. Anderson and Chase-Dunn 2005). They were united by *'asabiyah*: solidarity, loyalty, and mutual aid, created in battle and in tribal life and reinforced by successful looting and sharing of the loot. These persons would conquer the empire and run it well as long as they were united by 'asabiyah. The next generation would reach heights of power and glory but would begin to lose the 'asabiyah as power blocs began to emerge and compete, paying more attention to their own benefit than to that of the nation. The third generation would succumb to luxury and selfishness. In the meantime, population would grow and land would become scarce accordingly, causing more and more pressure on the regime. By the end of the third or fourth generation, people would be rebellious because of limited land and opportunities; selfish power blocs would dominate the government; and the rulers would be lost in luxury and selfishness, having lost most of their old tradition of solidarity.

This pattern fits perfectly with Chinese experience and traditional Chinese historical theory. Zhou, Qin, Yuan, and Qing were established by states that could be described (perhaps with some doubt in the early cases) as semiperipheral marcher states. The major dynasties that held only north China but not the south—Wei, Liang, and Jin—were all semiperipheral marcher states when they conquered the north. The first emperors of Sui and Tang were generals from the northwest frontier and were both probably part Turkic, which puts them in a somewhat semiperipheral situation.

On the other hand, almost all the other regime changes were the result of coups by imperial or military leaders. Han, Sui, Tang, and Song were all started by leading generals. So were most of the short-lived dynasties and kingdoms of the periods of disunion. Two coups were staged by empresses, and two others were led by empress dowagers (Wang Mang's and the Tongzhi Restoration). The only genuine popular rebellion that toppled a dynasty was Zhu Yuangzhang's (Ming), and the only other one that came even close was the Taiping. So China suffered slow rotation at the top—it was nothing like the revolving-door coups of old-time Latin America, but still a form of change that produced little change.

Conspicuously absent from Chinese history are cases of government change that resulted from group rivalry. The West was constantly torn by religious wars, which ruined many a state, especially in Europe in the sixteenth and seventeenth centuries. Such things were almost unheard of in China, though some major rebellions—from the Yellow Turbans to the Taipings—were millenarian. Meltdowns due to ethnic hate, as in Hitler's Germany and 1990s USSR and Yugoslavia, were also alien to Chinese tradition, though, again, not totally unknown; ethnic bias was certainly a factor in the fall of

Yuan and the fall of Qing. Ethnic rivalry, repression, displacement, and killing were routine in imperial times but never led to the sort of breakup that faced the USSR and Yugoslavia—if only because China's ethnic minorities were too few to be successful against the state. Instead, when China did collapse during interregnal periods, the cleavage was along regional lines. Warlords took over economic macroregions, as famously argued by G. William Skinner many years ago (1977, 2001).

It appears, but is far from certain, that the first rulers of Qin and Sui were so autocratic and yet so poor at consolidating a regime that their descendants lost control long before an Ibn Khaldun cycle could finish. Yuan lasted one Ibn Khaldun cycle. Tang had regular crises at Ibn Khaldun intervals: the Empress Wu "catastrophe," An Lushan's rebellion, and Huang Chao's rebellion. Song faced something similar in duration if not in causation: the progressive losses to Liang, Jin, and finally the Mongols. Qing, similarly, was shaken by the rebellion of the Three Feudatories, the crazy last decades of the Qianlong emperor (from the "literary inquisition" to He Shen's power grab), and the rebellions that climaxed in the Taiping devastation. Ming has been noted above.

This leaves only Han as truly anomalous and requiring explanation. At present I have none. Emperor Wen's countercoup and consolidation in the second century BCE seems to have been so brilliantly done that the empire lasted without too much damage. Wen managed the trick described by old-time Western historians as "the iron hand in the velvet glove"—or possibly the velvet hand in the iron glove. He and his successors consolidated autocratic rule based on Legalist principles but did so much for agriculture and the ordinary people, and propagated so many peaceful and beneficial ideas and ideologies, that they won respect such as few dynasties have enjoyed. Emperor Wu undid much of this, but the empire survived until Wang Mang's coup (9 CE). The restoration after that coup seems to have sobered everyone—disruption and violence were too obviously the result of trouble. Yet a succession of weak emperors in the second century CE should have brought down the dynasty, but as in late Ming, they did not. More research is needed to understand why.

Environmental History

The Chinese have always known they had developed socially from a simple hunting-gathering society: "We no longer dwell in nests or pry open mussels for food!" (Ban Zhao, first century CE, cited Idema and Grant 2004: 24). Their nowledge of simpler ways was based on experience with remote ethnic groups, especially in the south, though the belief in a nest-dwelling phase seems to have been a purely logical deduction. China's many origin myths tell of legendary emperors who tamed the land: Shen Nong invented agriculture, the Yellow Emperor learned medicine, and so on. Great Yu drained the swamps and was so busy he did not enter his own door for three years, in spite of passing it time and again. Even traditional Chinese found this antagonism to nature a bit excessive, and many poems condemn him for so neglecting his natural desires for home in favor of an unnatural desire for artificial landscapes. But the bottom-lands did get drained, and it did take hard work to do it. The imaginary Yu was a metonymy for the millions of anonymous humans who did that work.

China's environmental history has received much recent study, and now with Robert Marks's *China: Environment and History* (2012), there is a fine, authoritative, comprehensive environmental history of China available. Several other important works have also stressed the extremely successful, sustainable, intensive nature of Chinese agriculture, which fed hundreds of millions of people over the millennia (see below, esp. H. Huang 1990; Ruddle and Zhong 1988; Wen and Pimentel 1986a, b; Wong 1997).

However, there were long-term consequences of environmental degradation, especially the steady rise of the south and relative decline of the north. In Shang and Zhou times, the north was a rich, lush, mostly forested landscape, well watered, with game, wild foods, and incredibly fertile soil. Increasingly serious overuse devastated it all by the Song Dynasty.

The biggest difference within China in agroecology was the contrast between the dry north and wet south. The north, with extensive farming of wheat and small grains, was cursed by nature with problems. The soil could easily be eroded by wind and water. The rivers were extremely vulnerable to differences in rainfall and were constantly either flooding or drying up. The higher lands were drier and poorer all the time; the low-lying ones often succumbed to buildups of salt (salination). Already by the second century BCE, however, farmers had learned to deal with this; the stunning sophistication of Fan Shengzhi's book from that date is remarkable. The government protected and encouraged yeoman farmers, aware that they made the best use of land and resources. Their husbandry was offset by the tendency of the elite to form large estates that were worked by servile labor and inevitably poorly managed. The grand estates peaked in Han and the following period of unrest but declined through later history.

In the south, yeoman farmers and an intensively managed rice ecosystem prospered and protected the land, as we have seen. Large estates were almost impossible to manage, because of the need for intensive on-the-ground oversight of rice irrigation. Also, the government routinely opposed large estates, fearing a buildup of local power. Measures of intensification made the system ever more successful.

The south, formerly riddled with malaria and other diseases and difficult to farm because of dense forests and swamps, was tamed over millennia. With better conditions for plant growth, it soon took the lead in both forestry and agriculture. This changed the dynamics of empire, particularly between 300 and 1400. The Ming Dynasty sensibly moved their capital to the south (Nanjing—which means "Southern Capital") but foolishly moved it back to Beijing ("Northern Capital"), where it remains.

The same gradual transfer of power took place between the Near East and Europe, partly for the same reason: as the Near East was progressively trashed environmentally, Europe was progressively opened up. A "tilt" point came in the 1200s and 1300s, when the core Near East was substantially devastated ecologically at the same time that Europe was tamed and converted into its present cultivated landscape—roughly the same time that the south (the lower Yangzi and points south of it) became dominant in China. Europe at this time borrowed much Near Eastern agricultural lore—from crops and harness methods to irrigation technology and rural organization. These all became part of the infrastructure that lay behind the later rise of Europe. China at the same time borrowed heavily from west and south Asia.

The result in both regions was often a well-managed landscape, but short-term calculation, not to say desperation, led to mismanagement on a wide scale. Community over both individual and top-down remote management is the key, as in other situations worldwide.

Major books by Marks (1998) and by Mark Elvin (2004a), document a great deal of Chinese concern with the environment—both love and appreciation of it and serious fears about the extent of deforestation, erosion, flooding, and other major problems. However, their main conclusion is that the Chinese took enormous care of their farms but little care of their forests and other natural resources. Elvin is too harsh; among other things, he barely mentions the millions of acres saved as temple groves and sacred forests or the millions more saved by the Qing Dynasty as reserved land in Manchuria (Menzies 1994). The Chinese also carefully avoided building on the most productive farmland when there was an alternative.

What is surprising is not that the tigers and elephants retreated, but that a few are still left after a million years of human presence. (Europe had exterminated its lions and North Africa's elephants by late Roman times.) However, Elvin and Marks are certainly correct in noting the steady and exponential increase of deforestation and consequent erosion, siltation, biodiversity loss, desertification, and general decline in China's environment. Marks stresses the sustainability of agriculture, which kept adapting and intensifying as the trees went down, but concludes that China wound up as of 1900 with a terribly abused environment—and things have gotten much worse since.

Part of the problem was constant "improvement" that was often shortsighted or misguided. People expanded cultivation into lakes and floodplains and then suffered from floods (see, e.g., Schoppa 2002). They cut forests and then suffered from erosion. They pushed cultivation too far into drylands and suffered desertification. (Many stories are told in the various papers in Elvin and Liu 1998.) However, restraint in premodern times was generally noteworthy. The worst such stories have occurred since 1900, especially since 1950.

However, in spite of chronic famines, epidemics, floods, earthquakes, deforestation, erosion, and other human-caused disasters, China never collapsed ecologically. Some cultures, from the lowland Maya to the Easter Islanders and the ancient cultures of southwestern North America, may have ecologically ruined themselves (Diamond 2005a; his book is controversial). Instead, China displayed a cyclic pattern of collapse. Dynastic failures took place "when the government lost the Mandate of Heaven," as the Chinese said: that is, whenever the government became weak, overly far from its grassroots, overly corrupt, and overly torn by palace factions. The loss of the Mandate of Heaven was often announced by the types of disasters that we of the West call "natural" or "acts of God" but which the Chinese knew were caused by governmental incompetence and irresponsibility: floods, famines, landslides on deforested slopes, and the like. They overinterpreted the general principle and blamed even droughts on the emperor, thus going to the other extreme from that of the Western world, but on the whole they were more insightful than Westerners. Most Western "acts of God" are acts of men playing God and doing a bad job of it. This point was repeatedly made after Hurricane Katrina almost completely destroyed New Orleans in the early 2000s, thanks to a century of incredibly inept projects by the Army Corps of Engineers and other meddlers (Fischetti 2006).

Environmental stresses were not the only reason the people became desperate. High taxes, uncontrolled bandits, buildup of population, widening gaps between rich and poor, general corruption, and above all the loss of collective morality and the rise of selfishness, all bulked large in their minds (see Mote 1999). Usually, the Chinese seem to have managed their environment better than they managed their government, so it was the latter that gave way first. The land stayed productive, and loss of land to erosion was balanced by opening new lands in the south or reclaiming new lands from deltas that were building seaward because of erosion upstream.

In the end, China took care of its environment enough to maintain a growing agricultural system that fed its people without totally destroying the environment. Doing so depended on conserving every possible nutrient. As my friend Hugh Baker said, the success of nutrient recycling in China "must make nitrogen atoms unfortunate enough to be in other parts of the world feel unloved" (Baker 1989: 661–62, in a review of *The Food of China*).

J. R. McNeill holds that "China was, from about 650 A.D. to 1800, almost always the most ecologically resilient and resourceful state on earth" (1998:34–35; as quoted in Li 2007: 14). Chinese management had its costs, and McNeill later admits that "According to Elvin, China has pursued ecologically unsustainable patterns for three thousand years" (McNeill 1998: 41). China prospered because much of its agriculture was sustainable, especially the rice system. But its forest management and dryland management were problematic and often unsustainable. Actually, Southeast Asia and Japan were the regions that deserve McNeill's grand prize.

In spite of China's major role in inspiring permaculture and other modern systems, there is little research on the values of the traditional system. A notable recent exception is a study of raising fish in rice paddies, carried out at Zhejiang University in the famous old city of Hangzhou (Xie et al. 2011). Xie Jian and coworkers found that raising fish in rice paddies reduced the need for fertilizer by 24 percent because the fish fertilize the paddy (but the fish have to be fed some), and pesticide use is reduced 68 percent (or more) because the fish not only eat the pests but also dislodge them from the rice stems. And of course the fish themselves are a much more valuable food than the rice.

We have noted (see introduction) the findings of Hayami and Ruttan (1985) on China's "biological" agriculture. Hayami and Ruttan were wrong in suggesting that China's biological system developed as a result of the population pressure on the land; China was thoroughly committed to that course long before the population was dense. The real reasons were lack of a highly developed mechanical sector (in early times) and, more important, the needs of marketing. Chinese cities and armies grew to enormous size early, and they had to feed themselves from nearby fields, given the primitive levels of transportation in ancient China. To make money, farmers had to be as near the city or road as possible. That situation led to tremendous pressure to maximize yields per acre, even before overall population became crowded (E. Anderson 1988). By Han, yields were already high (Bray 1984; Shih 1973, 1974).

Biological technology naturally leads to a more conservationist approach to resources, since it is based so heavily on composting, cropping systems, and the like. It was, in China, also forced to be sustainable, by the interaction of tight family and community structure accompanied by the constant danger of mass famines and disasters. Everyone knew that floods, droughts, and the like would come, and everyone had dependents and descendants to worry about. The result was memorably described by F. H. King in his classic *Farmers of Forty Centuries* (1911). He emphasized the superior use of organic materials and farming in China and Japan and the consequent higher yields (compared to those in the West at his time) and more sustainable agricultural systems.

Biological technology also naturally favors the small owner-operated farm, because it requires constant application of skilled labor. Vast latifundia—giant estates worked by slave labor—defined Roman agriculture and flourished through the history of Europe (though, in later centuries, only in overseas European colonies). They never flourished in China though they did exist, and in early times were fairly widespread. But their numbers declined over time, because they simply could not compete. In a market economy where cities and courts had to be supplied, small-scale, diversified, skill-intensive, efficient farms were superior. Also, the rulers realized very early—even before the beginning of the Chinese empire, in fact—that a large class of stout yeoman farmers was best for stability, whereas a large class of powerful, idle landlords was worse.

The comparison with imperial Rome is striking: Rome had constant coups, almost no emperors died in bed, and a dynasty of three generations was a rarity. This was, in large part, because of the dominance of the great landlord families, who dominated the senate. China's dynasties were usually stable for centuries, lasting for long cycles of 3–4 seventy-five-year cycles (on the general case of such cycles, see Turchin 2003, 2006; he provides documentation and explanations, on a worldwide scale). A great part of the reason was their prevention of an independent power base in the form of a large latifundia class. China had its rich landlords, but they were increasingly brought to heel over time. At the end of the imperial period, they were lords of a few hundred acres at most, and often only a couple of acres. In earlier dynasties, many nobles—as well as lineages and religious orders—did become independent lords of thousands of acres, but the imperial state always tried to crush such estate development, and emperors often found pretexts for convicting such people of crimes and expropriating their property. In Han and Tang, in particular, there were major moves against the great families or clans.

Mark Elvin (Elvin and Su 1998), Robert Marks (1998, 2009), and I (E. Anderson 1988; E. Anderson and M. Anderson 1973) have emphasized the degree to which China's rice landscapes are human creations. The old Dutch saying "God made the world but the Dutch made Holland" could easily be transferred to the Yangzi, Pearl, and other river valleys and deltas. Burning fields for agricultural and other reasons in the mountains led to silt washing downstream, eventually leading to buildup of alluvial deposits, which restored fertility of existing fields and allowed reclamation of new ones. In lake and sea deltas, these became polders, known in southeast China as sand fields (*sha tian*) or sand flats (Marks 2009: 21–22). This process was still under way and observable when I lived in Hong Kong in the 1960s and 1970s.

The result was the most incredibly productive ecosystem in the premodern world, yielding 2,500 pounds of rice per crop, 2–3 crops per year, and side benefits including fish, silk (mulberries were raised on the dykes), vegetables, and so on (E. Anderson and M. Anderson 1973; Ruddle and Zhong 1988; Wen and Pimentel 1986a, b). Biological control was the rule. Insects that ate insects were well known, but better still were control agents that could themselves be eaten. Ducks controlled rice insects, frogs controlled other pests, fish ate aquatic insect pests, and weeds were fed to pigs (E. Anderson and M. Anderson 1973; Needham 1986: 519–53). Sparrows controlled flies and larvae, and the killing of sparrows (as grain eaters) under Mao Zedong led to huge outbreaks of pests.

Biological technology continues with the continual breeding of new and better rice varieties. A breakthrough was discovery of male-sterile lines and breeding of domestic and wild rices in the 1960s and 1970s; the most important developer of this new technology was Yuan Longping, who continues to develop improved rices. Varieties developed by Yuan now produce over half the rice grown in China, making him a major national hero. However, the groundwork for this was laid by Japanese, Taiwanese, and American efforts in breeding short-stalked, high-yield rices from ancient Taiwanese strains in the 1950s and 1960s. (This involved selection and some crossing but not the systematic hybridization of very different lines using male-sterile plants that

Yuan developed. See Virmani 1994.) And that effort dates back even farther, to the development and subsequent crossbreeding of japonica and indica rices 7,000 years ago (see above, Chapter 2). Contrary to claims in the literature, different strains, and even different species, of rice do hybridize without laboratory treatments; Asian rice naturally hybridizes with African rice (*O. glaberrima*) quite frequently in West Africa (Nuijten et al. 2009). Today, hybrid rice yields run around 10 tons per hectare and even an incredible 15 tons (Yuan Longping 2002), but both conventionally bred rice and selected seedlings from hybrid strains (but still breeding true) can do as well. Recall that the traditional yields of rice in China were around 2.5 tons per hectare.

Unfortunately, there have been complaints about such rice (see, e.g., GRAIN 2005). The rice seeds are very expensive, are complex to produce, and do not always yield well or produce quality grain. There have even been lawsuits in the United States over underperforming seed (see Fox16.com, News, "Arkansas Farmers Sue Company over Hybrid Rice," July 16, 2012). Although China and Vietnam are heavily committed to hybrids, other countries are not, and other approaches are being pursued. Plant breeding is an old science, and one ever more important and sophisticated. The future depends on it and on other biological technologies.

The above-cited accounts stress the successes of the system, but deforestation, water pollution, waterborne diseases, and sheer numbers of people pressing on a fragile environment were also a reality.

Since 1950 the Communist regime has done more damage to both upland and downstream areas than all previous mismanagement. Similarly, in Taiwan, Qing Dynasty deforestation was extensive and hard to control, but deforestation after 1949 was far worse. In both China and Taiwan, damage eventually was slowed by the coming of modern conservation ideas in the 1990s (Ch'en 1998), but things seem to be getting worse again, at least on the mainland (Abe and Nickum 2009).

Historian Robert Marks was led to a somewhat negative assessment by his belief that "Slash-and-burn [was] the earliest and most rudimentary form of agriculture" (Marks 2009: 11). This is not the case. Slash-and-burn was certainly not the earliest form of agriculture, and it is usually a very sophisticated, carefully managed system. In China it is not usually the rough, unsophisticated shifting cultivation Marks is describing. Such rough cultivation did and does exist in China, however, usually when lowlanders are driven into the mountains by war or famine. It is less common than highly sophisticated, environmentally fine-tuned swiddening, involving forest management, orchard planting, protection of forests (often as sacred groves), special management of crops, and a wealth of other techniques. Especially in minority areas, shifting cultivation in China was well managed and integrated with landscape care (this from twentieth-century evidence, but presumably true throughout history; see detailed studies of similar agriculture in China and nearby countries, e.g., Conklin 1957; Klee 1980; Spencer 1966; Wang Jianhua 2013).

China's minority peoples were, in fact, usually better resource managers than the Chinese themselves. The south Chinese minorities shared a Southeast Asian style of management that involved sacred trees and groves, sacred mountains whose resources were protected, and exceedingly tight restrictions on use of most resources, especially vulnerable ones like forests and bamboo groves (Xu Jianchu et al. 2005). The best studies are of the Akha, but many are unpublished (Sturgeon 2005; Tooker 2012; Wang Jianhua 2007, 2008, 2013).

Minority peoples have, on the whole, stronger ideologies about conservation than the Han Chinese. One finds stories surprisingly similar to North American cautionary tales about respecting nature. The Tujia of central China live partly on fern rhizome starch, which must be laboriously dug up and processed. They tell that once the starch could be just shaken off the leaves, but then someone treated the plants with disrespect—either using the starch to cover a baby's excrement or using the leaves as a sitting pad—and the Jade Emperor ordered the starch to grow underground, where the people would have to dig for it (Xu Wu 2011: 95–96). A version of this story is now told about maize, a new crop.

The Mongols are another example; they invoked and maintained a range of grassland conservation methods that succeeded extremely well, even recently at high population densities and under substantial pressure. Collective ownership and management, often by kinship groups, has provided the background. The success of these practices is shown by the very rapid degradation that has followed from recent forced changes in ownership and management regimes under Communism in China and "free market reforms" in Mongolia (Buell and Le 2006; W. Li and Huntsinger 2011; Sternberg 2012; Williams 1996a, b, 2000, 2002; an anonymous reviewer of the present book has argued that preservation of the grasslands was primarily an inadvertent result of die-offs of livestock, but the articles referenced here, as well as my own research, clearly refute that case). Tibet similarly conserved wildlife and grassland until recently, with dramatic recent changes (in a negative direction) showing how effective the traditional systems were (D. Anderson et al. 2005; Glover 2005; Jan Salick, pers. comm. over years; Salick et al. 2005; Zelda Liang, Ed Schmitt, pers. comm. January 2013). The Tungusic peoples also had conservation traditions (Arseniev 1996), maintained to some degree by the Jin and Qing rulers (for instance, Spence 1974 provides details on the Kangxi Emperor's hunting management).

Some astonishing innovations were made in water control. Not only were many aspects of irrigation and canal technology developed in China, the Chinese invented the cantilevered bridge, and minority peoples in what is now the China-India border area invented the suspension bridge (Needham et al. 1971). Gabions—long sausages of rocks tied up in bamboo canes—were used to make instant levees and dykes; they could be many feet long but could be lifted by a gang of workers and carried into place in minutes. Fascines, similar rolls of vegetable materials, were also used and may have been more effective. These may have been invented in the Song Dynasty. (On these matters, see Lamouroux 1998, esp. 530.)

As Lillian Li (2007: 15) points out, "human efforts to control nature may have prevented disasters in the short run, but they increased the likelihood, or severity, of human disasters in the long run." This is particularly famous in regard to building levees higher and higher, causing the river bottoms to aggrade as silt settles, and thus leading eventually to rivers perched above their floodplains—making disaster inevitable (W. Mallory 1926). As usual, the Chinese were quite aware of this chain of events from early times and did what they could about it. In Sichuan, the great Li family of engineers designed the Min River irrigation system that waters the lands around Chengdu. They split the Min into three channels and ordered that these be dug out every few years. During low water, the river is diverted into only two channels, and the third has its bottom lowered; this is done in rotation, so every channel is dug out periodically (E. Anderson 1988). They left a slogan of four words carved in huge characters on the rock at the head of the system: DYKES LOW, CHANNELS DEEP. The system is still in use and still maintained after 2,000 years.

The problem was that this system was impossible to implement in much of China, especially the Yellow River plain, which is bedeviled with every sort of catastrophe from drought to flood. However, where low dykes and deep channels could be managed, they often were. (No one seems to have surveyed this on a nationwide basis until modernity had irrevocably changed old practices, though several of the local case studies in Elvin and Liu 1998 make the point. One problem is that the best documentation of premodern systems is for the Yellow and lower Yangzi Rivers, where low dykes and deep channels are virtually impossible to maintain because of the flat landscape and the flood-drought cycles that lead to great fluctuations in discharge.)

China's environment was influenced by the truly enormous level of industrial production from the Warring States period onward. Ceramics (Kerr and Wood 2004), metallurgy (Golas 1999; Wagner 2008), and other industries were well developed by 300 BCE. Robert Hartwell's classic work on production of iron and steel (Hartwell 1962, 1982) notes the deforestation of entire mountain ranges. Hartwell thinks the iron industry may have been critical in deforesting north China, especially in the Song Dynasty.

The back-and-forth balancing of destructive practices versus constructive ones is well reflected in Chinese literature. Already in the early Han Dynasty, the extreme care with which cultivation was practiced (E. Anderson 1988; Shih 1973, 1974) shows that even then the population was pressing against the resource base, although the problem was one of raising production near the huge cities, not of raising production overall (E. Anderson 1988). Walter Mallory (1926) and more recently Lillian Li (2007) point out that China had chronic general famines, about one every other year in Mallory's calculation. Li (2007: 6) notes that Europe did not have anything approaching that rate, though it had plenty of famines and a few widespread and devastating ones (as in 1312 and in the great potato famine of 1846–48). Famine was well known before China unified into one empire under Qin (221–207 BCE). The following Han Dynasty (206 BCE–CE 220) coped well and started China on a path to success, partly through astonishingly enlightened methods ranging from advanced water-saving technology to the first case-control experiments in the world (E. Anderson 1988). However, then and later, bad reigns and devastating interdynastic crises could reverse years of good planning. They also reduced the demographic pressure on the land—admittedly by horrific means—and thus allow it to rebound when stabilization came.

More and more actively over time, from the Zhou Dynasty onward, the government diked the rivers, reclaimed land, and eventually developed a huge and fairly successful famine-relief capability (Lillian Li 2007; Will 1990; Will and Wong 1991). During periods of breakdown, the economy went into decline and the wild areas crept back, but no one was able to enforce measures to preserve or protect anything, so the damage to forests and game could still increase. Probably most of the damage by wildfires, military actions, and the like was done not during stable times but rather during the horrific interdynastic crises that regularly shook China. Population declined as much as 25 percent, and more than 50 percent locally, during some of these. Some of the worst times were in the nineteenth century, with the Taiping Rebellion the greatest crisis of all. The result was a country sadly depleted and impoverished by the early twentieth century.

Explaining Foodways

The reasons for early intensification of agriculture are fairly well laid out in early texts, from Confucius and Mozi to Sima Qian and the Discourses on Salt and Iron. The need to feed cities and armies has been noted above. There was also the court, with its thousands of people, and also local government bureaus. Second, China had a highly advanced and developed marketing system. Third, China had a government dedicated to the idea of "agriculture as the basis of the state." The Warring States competed with each other to see who could most develop agriculture, and the Han rulers were perceptive enough to realize that dynastic survival depended on using all the best ideas from that long competition. They drew on Confucian, Legalist, Daoist, and any other good ideas they could find. Fourth, China had already learned that maximum productivity lay with independent yeoman farmers and had begun (but only begun) to eliminate slave estates and other enterprises involving servile labor. Han's great contemporary, the Roman Empire, was handicapped by its slave economy. Fifth, China did not rely heavily on grazing animals. It did not have to have vast areas in pasture because it could concentrate on maximizing production in small areas that were conveniently close to markets and cities. Effective demand did the rest.

Once China was started on the path of biological development, path dependence and lock-ins kept the system intensifying rather than radically changing. Once one is committed to an agricultural system based on free small-scale farmers trying to wring the most they possibly can out of tiny plots, it is almost impossible to change. The difficulties of change were shown quite dramatically in the Great Leap Forward, when Mao Zedong tried to turn China from a nation of small farmers to a European-style world of vast fields worked by landless teams. Such change was not only impossible in practice, but it would have been a disaster even if it had worked. Machines, agrochemicals, and landless laborers are already proving a disastrous combination in the United States; they have had worse effects in China. It is interesting to remember that a very large percentage of the advances that have made Western agriculture so productive—more productive than old China's—were actually made after 1950, and almost all after 1800. In spite of the rise of agricultural science in Europe from about 1400, European and American agricultural productivity in the early twentieth century still lagged well behind China's.

It remains to ask who did the work—who developed China's agriculture. Almost all the credit belongs to the billions of nameless farmers. From domesticating rice to discovering that silkworms fed on mulberries to the spread of tomatoes and papayas in very recent decades, all was due to the men and women on the ground. We do not know when or where most innovations were made, let alone the names of the developers. A few gentry were comparable to England's "improving squires," and we do know their names and creations, but they are a drop in the ocean.

The government, however, gets full credit for their policies of furthering agriculture, publishing encyclopedias of farming and medicine, experimenting, and developing crops and techniques. The government published famine manuals and carried out famine relief on a mass scale. Governments built dikes and canals, maintained irrigation works in general, relieved droughts, and protected farmers, albeit somewhat erratically, from abuses. The wonder is not that China's national and local governments often failed; so did all early governments, and so will all our governments today, in the long run. The wonder is that China's governments functioned as well as they did given the problems of running a premodern society.

Last (and perhaps least), the scholar-bureaucrats defended the small farmers and agricultural interests. They retreated from science, they were often corrupt, they maintained to the last that moral reform would solve problems that only better agroecological systems could really solve—but at least, as a class, they cared. They constantly advocated for tax relief, famine relief, public works to protect farms, justice for peasants, and consideration of the farming sector as at least as deserving—if not more so—than the military or merchant sectors of society. They are, however, singularly absent from the ranks of agricultural experimenters and developers.

From China's 3,500 years of recorded history we have the names of countless generals, outlaws, corrupt officials, and scoundrels of every stamp. We do not have the names of the persons who really *made* China.

Forests

Thus agroecological economics made the biggest difference, but the fate of the forests shows that ideology mattered also. Forests were preserved in proportion to how much protection they got from religion, spiritual and magical beliefs, aesthetics, and—last but not necessarily least—awareness by landowners and bureaucrats that trees were valuable for ecosystem services as well as for timber (Elvin and Liu 1998; Menzies 1994). When I worked in Hong Kong in the 1960s and 1970s, the only groves surviving were those protected as fengshui groves. Some had been taken over and expanded in size under protection by the government. Natural vegetation was also protected in graveyards and tomb areas, gardens, and village religious sites. No natural vegetation was left alone unless it was protected for one or another of these reasons, but the combined total of protected acreage was nevertheless very large, and some of the woodlands were wild old growth—not bad for an area where four million people were jammed into a tiny space. Neither Elvin nor Marks mention the sustainable logging of China fir (*Cunninghamia lanceolata*) practiced for centuries in south China in connection with agriculture (Chandler 1994).

We need a more balanced assessment. A beginning is Nicholas Menzies' history of Chinese forestry (1994). He shows that temple groves, village groves, commercial plantations, and orchards saved trees, whereas the imperial parks and refuges did not. He traces the history of the latter from the enormous imperial hunting parks of the Warring States and Han to the small but still significant preserves of Qing. Pressure from well-meaning but shortsighted ministers to release land for cultivation led to steady decline, but more serious were the cyclic collapses of dynasties, which opened any and all areas for devastation.

He quotes a Buddhist account of an abbot in the Song Dynasty who "ordered his disciples to plant *Cunninghamia* around the monastery and over an area covering a circle of one hundred *li*. The master said, 'There are remote places on this peak where none of the *Cunninghamia* are in good condition. This means that we cannot be sure of the flow of the water and the supply of firewood to our retreat" (Menzies 1994: 69). Note that the master is aware of the extremely important point that a healthy forest helps provide a reliable water supply. In spite of such accounts, Menzies somewhat downplays the conservation value of temple groves, though he calculated that perhaps several million acres of sacred groves and forests existed in early twentieth-century China. From my experience, I think he significantly underestimated the extent and importance of the temple and village groves. (Menzies is rather a cautious scholar given to British understatement. He has recently become more aware of the value of groves; pers. comm. over recent years.) Certainly there were many thousands of acres of these groves in the New Territories alone in the 1960s, and they preserved countless plant and animal species otherwise gone.

Deforestation was especially serious, with Song almost finishing off the forests of the north. One main cause was the iron industry, which used thousands of tons of wood for fuel until coal eventually came into use (see Hartwell 1962; Wagner 2008). A more romantic reason was that mass printing of books became common at that time, and poetry and other literature (as well as more mundane publications) took up trees for paper and for ink (Marks 2012). At the time, Chinese ink was made by burning resinous woods. Thus bookmaking and printing (Chia 2002) also required forests for making paper and ink. In the Song Dynasty, noted scientific writer Shen Gua complained that whole forests were being burned for pine soot to make ink. Folklore held that the level of poetry writing alone was a serious drain on forests. Vaclav Smil speaks of the irony of writing "glorious accounts of civilization underwritten by the destruction of its natural foundations" (Smil 2004: 142; of course, the folklore is much exaggerated). Fortunately, the forests were saved by developing (around Song times) a better process for making ink by burning vegetable oil. Paper could be made from anything vegetal, but it too was produced in enormous quantities. Again, there is folklore: a single poet caused paper to become more expensive in the capital city of Luoyang since everyone wanted copies of his poems. "Paper is dear in Luoyang!" later became a staple bit of flattery for poets.

Really destructive deforestation, overcultivation of permanently cropped land, and excessively careless shifting cultivation were problems at all times (see, e.g., Elvin 2004; Menzies 1994). A writer complained that in urban areas "even the gorgeous flowers, the beautiful bamboo and the pines and the catalpa trees that grow upon the burial mounds have all become bare earth" (Menzies 1994:24). In the eighteenth century, for instance, the mountains of southern Shaanxi were invaded by "drifters . . . [who] tilled fields for a few years using slash-and-burn techniques, then moved on when the soil was depleted. As a consequence, a huge pool of late eighteenth-century mountaineers led rootless, impoverished,and desperate lives" (McMahon 2009: 94). In the late Ming, as in many other periods, large areas of old-growth forest were logged.

Writing in 1618, Xie Zhaozhe encountered some tall tales from the woodcutters: "I have seen men who have been to cut Imperial timber. They say that there, in the depths of the mountains and in the empty valleys, where none have been before, there are trees from the [ancient] days of wilderness and chaos. But it is wild and extremely dangerous. Venomous snakes and blood-thirsty animals roam in and out of the mountains. There are spiders the size of cartwheels whose webs hang down to the ground like nets to trap tigers and leopards which they eat" (quoted and translated by Menzies 1994: 112). Some of the largest orb-web spiders in the world live in south China—I have seen some with leg spans of several inches—but catching tigers is a bit beyond them. Menzies's author had been listening to tall tales (similar stories are not wholly unknown in rural China today). Menzies traces fear of these vast southern forests to early times (1994: 28).

With frequent fires and military actions periodically devastating cities, urbanization also had its costs. Even so, China in the mid-twentieth century was an incredible mine of resources. Millions of acres of prime forest survived. The grasslands of Inner Mongolia, Xinjiang, and Tibet were unsurpassed. Vast wetlands supported millions of birds and produced thousands of tons of fish and other protein foods. Some of the world's most fertile soils were enriched by thousands of years of composting and careful planting (Bray 1984; Buck 1937). Compared to southern Europe or the Middle East, China was in good environmental shape. The loess plateaus of north-central China were desolate and eroded, but the rice-farming deltas of the southeast became more and more extensive and fertile with time. Mountains of the center and east were often deforested, but those in the north and southwest retained vast rich forests. China was less well off than north Europe or Southeast Asia, but it had a far larger and denser population to support. However, it may have been relatively more damaged in per capita terms than India—where Hinduism protected forests and wildlife—or Japan, reforested under the Tokugawa (Totman 1989, 1995).

Modern Folk Views Continued Much of the Old Ideology

Folk worldview held that within the mountains were giant spirit dragons and tigers, whose pulses were also energy-flow channels in the earth. Cutting the dragon's pulse caused disaster. The earth also had its qi, which, in the earth or in humans, was regarded as purely natural. No one thought of it as shen or fate or as needing incense or sacrifices. It was regulated through means assumed to be purely natural—in humans, use of herbal drugs.

I have often described my moment of truth in understanding traditional science. Construction for a new hospital had cut deeply into a hill by the bay where I stayed. Local peasants warned that this would cut the dragon's pulse and disaster would follow. I made no sense of this, but in the next big rain the undercut slope failed, and several houses were destroyed by the landslip. The peasants said: "See, this is what happens when you cut the dragon's pulse." At that time, Western science had no better explanation for slope failure; geologists invoked the angle of repose, an entity as obscure as the dragon. Since then, our understanding of materials and their failure points has advanced, but the point remains: traditional people, and many modern ones too, can perfectly well link cause and effect. Where they go wrong is in the inferred linkage: what is inside the black box where the cause actually operates to produce the effect.

The Chinese think of storms as caused by dragons in the air and also as judgments. One can offend the dragons. Many a storm is punishment for foolishness. The short-tailed dragon is especially irascible—some say because his tail was cut off—and his fury causes typhoons; so I was told on the Hong Kong waterfront. My sailor friends had sometimes seen him, or thought they had seen him, in the writhing, wind-torn clouds. Indeed, in the dark and violent storm, one's fear can easily make one see huge reptilian forms half-hidden in mist. Many a Chinese painting shows this dramatically. Weather in general was natural, but was under control of these dragons and of the Sky God, who could be implored for help. Sailors burned incense to him at dawn and evening when they were going to sea.

In old China, ordinary people were much more prone to see the earth as having dynamic channels and fields of energy, as well as supernatural animals and spirits, within it. Mountain gods, locality gods, rock spirits, tree spirits, and other local shen were universal and intimately involved in people's lives. Every specific, localized, conceptualized feature had its spirit. The spirit of the house was worshiped at a tiny shrine to the right of the front door as one entered. The kitchen god was worshiped at the large brick stove, or, in households lacking that, at a small shrine in the kitchen. Family ancestors were worshiped at a household shrine, lineage ancestors at a lineage hall or local temple. Ghosts haunted particular spots. In addition to millions of localized shen, there were countless general ones. (For general descriptions of Chinese religion, see E. Anderson 2007 and sources cited there; Mair 2005, with selections from relevant texts of all sorts.)

People had no idea why weather, illness, and luck happened as they did. The gods were assumed to have some disposal over these, but one of the commonest proverbs was "Even the gods are subject to luck." (A variant made them subject to fate rather than to luck; the concepts were very close. *Ming* "fate," *ling* "disembodied supernatural force," and *jie* or *yun* "luck" are at issue here.) Luck and fate were disembodied natural forces, and luck could be made better by many behaviors. Tangerines were called lucky fruit because it was fortunate to have them at New Year. Other citrus, as well as peach flowers, lotus nuts, and many other flowers and foods, were lucky or had special powers over gods and fate.

Such "black box" situations are always the test of science. There is a strong human tendency to assume agency until proved otherwise (Atran 2002). Countless surveys show that most Westerners still believe that God or saints or other active, conscious beings are in the box: classic dei ex machina. Today's Chinese are much less prone to do so, after six decades of "atheistic" Communism, but the old beliefs are far from dead.

Connecting these folk beliefs with the higher and more abstract religious thought of classical China has rather rarely been done, but the gap is not large. Chinese elite and folk cultures were not separate; they constantly intermixed and blended. Elite ideas trickled down through the temples and temple fairs, and folk concepts rose upward through these and through household, village, and town connections. Readers of novels like *The Story of the Stone* (eighteenth century; Cao 1973–1986; Y. Zhou 2013) will know that even the highest elite were constantly dealing with servants, estate overseers, and impoverished relatives. My work in Hong Kong showed that elite poems, philosophical taglines, and stories were widely known; illiterate farmers and sailors could quote many, especially from the hallowed works of Confucius and Mencius (E. Anderson 2007).

Chinese science seems, today, to blur the lines between magic, science, and religion. Of course, early Western science did that too. Modern writers may note a "curious combination of medical and magical thinking" (Wilms 2002: 33) in the writings of Sun Simiao in the seventh century, but Sun would not have found anything curious; he was merely writing about the medicine he knew. However, he did make skeptical remarks about many magical practices, so he seems to have had some idea of the difference (Sun Simiao 2007). Western medical writings of the time were the same sort of "curious combination."

A wonderfully concise insight into this viewpoint is found in a tract on iron mining by Qu Dajun of the early Qing Dynasty. After giving a perfectly factual description of iron mining in Guangdong, he says:

> Splitting a body of iron ore layer by layer, one finds that each [layer] has a tree-leaf pattern. . . . If the mountain has a certain type of tree, then that tree's leaf pattern will be found in the iron ore. . . . When it is extremely cold in south China . . . the leaves do not [normally] fall

from the trees; it is only on mountains which produce iron that the leaves fall, and these are absorbed by the essence of the iron. . . . This is an example of the Way of "metal conquering wood." The iron ore has a spirit, and to this the furnace-master must sacrifice devoutly before he dares to operate a furnace. . . . According to tradition, the wife of a certain Mr. Lin, when her husband was in arrears in his official iron quota, threw herself into the furnace in order to make it produce more iron. Today those who operate the furnaces always sacrifice to her. (Wagner 2008: 49–50)

Here we have what to Qu was a simple, straightforward description, but it seems to the modern Western reader to be a wonderful mix of fact, religion, and folklore. Note that, as in very many Chinese sacrificial-rite stories, the woman was supposedly a real person, revered only after her death. More interesting is the accurate observation interpreted according to cosmology. As Wagner points out (52): "The leaf pattern is fairly common for water-deposited minerals," but it would not take the form of the local trees' leaves! The shedding leaves are real too. Iron ore bodies tend to be high, rocky, and infertile, and sometimes the mineralogy makes the soil stunting, dry, or even downright toxic to plants. I have myself observed leaves being shed prematurely in iron-rich hills in south China. But Qu has interpreted it according to Five Phase theory.

Management ideology and religion played out on the ground via fengshui (for more extensive accounts see E. Anderson 1988, 1996 and references therein; E. Anderson and M. Anderson 1973). *Fengshui* literally means "wind and water" and is the art of siting dwellings and graves such that wind and water will benefit them rather than damaging them. It thus taught that houses should be leeward of hills, thus protected by side ridges from storms and other damage. They should be sited where water pools up, not where it rushes by to be lost.

Fengshui taught that groves should be preserved around villages, houses, and temples, not only because trees have good spirits, but also for the wholly practical values of their shade, timber, firewood, fruit, and so on. Common experience taught that without the spiritual aspect, groves were always quickly depleted. Spiritual values as promoters of good fortune were key to motivating communities to work together to preserve the groves. I saw this happening in the New Territories in Hong Kong; the government was continually trying to lay out roads, power lines, and other public works through the fengshui groves but was always stopped by public protest. Sometimes these protests were all too negotiable for money, leading to a good deal of cynicism about fengshui. But in the end most groves were protected, and many are there yet. No groves not considered keys to sacred security were saved from such threats. In China proper, fengshui and Buddhist temple practices preserved groves for thousands of years, until the Communist government ended such "feudal superstition" and did incalculable and irreparable harm by eliminating the groves (E. Anderson 2012). All or almost all the minority peoples had comparable sacred or protected groves.

Fengshui also taught that houses should not sprawl onto cultivated land or be built on floodplains. Disregard of these rules has had the inevitable consequences. I first realized the importance of this during the great June floods of 1966 in Hong Kong; all the traditionally sited villages were above water, but all the new construction on the plains was flooded.

The supernatural element entered through the belief in immaterial influences of good and evil. Evil travels in straight lines, so doors, gates, winding roads, shrines, and trees were set to block it. These also discouraged more tangible evils, like bandits and rogue soldiers. Good influences are attracted not only by trees but also by pagodas, sacred rocks (often shrines to local spirits), and the like, so these were positioned appropriately.

Among the crystallizations of yang and yin energy are the dragons and tigers that live in the hills. A high, rough mountain ridge looks like a dragon and has the dragon's yang qi in it; less educated traditional people believe (or believed in the 1960s and 1970s, anyway) that there was an actual dragon within any such ridge. Lower, smoother, rounder ridges and hills are tigers—that is, they have tigers' yin qi or have actual giant spirit tigers within. A house should be located where the dragon dominates the tiger, as yang should dominate yin—a bit of old-fashioned sexism playing out on the landscape.

Over time, magic took became predominant, and today's fengshui is usually used to plan offices, house layouts, and other environments far from the storms and droughts of old China. Such attitudes have led to confusing it with mere chicanery or to diluting it to the level of an amusing game. But the original fengshui was deadly serious and thoroughly pragmatic.

The traditional landscape was shaped by a pervasive spiritual component. Large and strange-shaped rocks, large old trees, striking hills, and waterfalls were the residences of spirits, whose power was proportional to the size and dramatic appearance of the feature. Gnarled and twisted trees, knobbed and cliffed crags, and dramatic outcrops of earth and rock showed by their appearance that they were centers of the flow of powerful qi. Such places were worshiped, usually by burning three sticks of incense morning and night—the standard practice at household shrines and other religious spots. From the small crags around Hong Kong to the fantastic slopes of Mt. Emei in Sichuan, the size and dramatic quality of outcrops was proportional to their sacred power. We will examine below the effect of these beliefs on art; those magnificent trees and cliffs in Chinese paintings are not mere wood and stone.

All these beliefs had the function of saving large old trees, but also made the entire landscape a sacred and powerful place, or at least a world peopled with sacred and powerful places. "Peopled" is the proper term, because the spirits were in fact persons, though often very far from humanlike. Anything could have a conscious spirit. Spirits varied greatly in degrees of cognition and will—from mute and frail spirits of pieces of paper or wood to the powerful, world-changing gods of the great mountains. Actual communication via spirit mediums came usually from ancestors or other deceased humans, or from real gods, most of whom had been humans at one time. These gods carried the messages from the spirits of fish or hills or trees, if the latter needed to send word.

Animals were safeguarded largely because of Buddhism, which tried to protect all life and was relatively successful in regard to cattle, turtles, and songbirds. Temples in some areas still stock turtles, fish, and birds to release for karmic merit. The birds are often trained to fly back and be recaptured; some are veterans of years of doing so. Certain trees were sacred in Buddhism and Daoism because of powerful qi or associated mythology; banyan trees are associated with the Buddha and also are often huge, gnarled, and venerable, showing great qi. Ginkgo trees were revered, which is why they still exist; they are apparently extinct in the wild, having survived only in temple groves and other protected woods.

Many other species are protected locally. My fisher friends regarded sawfish, porpoises, sea turtles, sturgeons, and giant groupers as sacred and full of qi and thus would not catch them if possible. If they did catch them—especially the sawfish and sturgeons—they offered them as sacrifices in temples. (I have provided a much fuller discussion of this in E. Anderson 2007.) These and other taboos and "power animal" beliefs are often explicable because the animals are anomalous or are "natural symbols" (Douglas 1966, 1970). They look and act strange, thus showing both supernatural power and impressive qi. Dragons are, of course, the ultimate in impressive creatures.

In general, Buddhism teaches that all animal life is sacred and must be protected, though taking animal life to sustain one's own life and one's family's is not condemned as strongly as is wasteful killing. Daoism teaches something similar, especially in regard to animals somehow sacred or rich in qi. Confucianism teaches conservation, restraint, and sustainability. None of these religions ever came close to eliminating hunting, let alone fishing, but they at least slowed the pace and prevented much needless or useless killing.

As in so many other cases, one need only look at the results of Westernization—including the attitude of "struggle against nature"—in the last sixty years. Prior to that time, China was still quite rich in game and fish. Today, China has eliminated almost all of its wild food resources by uncontrolled hunting, overfishing, and habitat destruction. Clearly, economic rationality, economic need, ecological facts, and "progress" all greatly underdetermine environmental management. Obviously they affect it, and indeed are basic to our use of environments and resources, but the way use, management, and economic agency actually play out on the ground is due to choices and acts that are directly and heavily impacted by particular complexes of knowledge, ideology and, belief. Economics, like religion, involves belief systems cast as ultimate truth (Foucault 2008). Unfortunately, absent the infinite wisdom of the more remote subjects of religious speculation, we mortals must do with imperfect information. We thus act from partial knowledge filled in by inference, hope, self-delusion, blind faith in the past, and other shortcuts (Kahneman 2011).

A Summary of the Old Ways

There is a rather clear pattern of good management and bad management. Good management existed in orchards, temple and fengshui groves, wet-rice agriculture, remote areas of the country everywhere, and gardens—both commercial vegetable gardens and ornamental gardens. Bad management dominated most forestry (especially late), much dry-grown grain farming, much commercial agriculture in general, and at the pioneer fringes. It was particularly bad where the Chinese were displacing minority groups or warring with each other. Industry led to much ruined land. Overall, the north did worse than the south.

The clearest determinants here are industrial or exploited forests versus religiously protected ones, and dry-grown crops versus wet rice. However, at a deeper level, it appears that the rapacious and usually corrupt government and the merciless market were the ultimate causes of the problems (see Elvin 2004a). They demanded everything straightaway and thus forced short-term accounting on the farmers, who had to maximize their immediate income to pay taxes and bribes and still have enough money to buy clothing and metal tools. There was always some surplus, but it was unpredictable and had to be saved or invested in more secure ventures, rather than used to maintain and improve sustainability and efficiency of farming. Some old established farm families could and did invest in the latter, but largely where they could feel secure in tenure of fields and orchards.

The only way to avoid government rapacity and market squeeze was to have powerful community and religious forces that were even stronger and more persuasive on the local level. Thus, either religious ideology (temple groves, sacred groves) or elite taste (gardens, estates) or economic rationality (rice paddy systems, tree-planting) or a combination of all these (fengshui groves, elite involvement in landscape protection) could save environments and promote wise use of resources against wreckage of the environment and the resource base. Lack of any or all of them led to waste.

One had to think of the lineage descendants, even the poor relations, as far into the future as one could see. Thus, the extreme cut-and-run attitudes of modern industrial agriculture did not exist, except on frontiers and during troubled times. On the other hand, the needs of the living necessarily took precedence, and many a short-range decision was made with full knowledge of—and sorrow about—its long-term costs.

Worldviews and ideology mattered in many ways. The basic background ideology of working with nature—of harmony with earth and waters—was never lost in dynastic times. The basic ideology of sustainability was certainly present in rice farming, tree cropping, and related branches of agriculture, thanks to a constant feedback between economic realities and ideological preferences.

The result of economic rationality combined with a balance-of-nature worldview was a lock-in of sustainable agricultural practices, at least in rice agriculture. Innovation and intensification involved using more labor, rather than innovative machinery and pesticides, to rationalize rice paddies, canals, dikes, and soil preparation (Hayami and Ruttan 1985).

Grazing, brushlands, gardens, vegetable farming, and other types of land use all had rules and models, and sustainable management was found where culture, religion, or aesthetics demanded; otherwise, overuse was common. In ancient times, game was reserved by the imperial court and other elites for hunting purposes, but there seems to have been little sense of the value of wild animals, and conservation was rather limited. Animals that caused actual danger, like tigers and wolves, were hunted for elimination when possible. A broad respect, and even love, for wild animals was present and general but seems not to have been strong enough to be a major protective force.

One resource that was usually extremely vulnerable to exploitation was fish. I never heard of general fisheries management or conservation among the fishermen I lived with for two years in Hong Kong and have found no references to such in the literature. They did, however, save the sacred fish; as in the case of forests, religion protected when common economics did not.

The modern Chinese state has destroyed its fisheries thoughtlessly, leading to extinction of the white-flag dolphin and the imminent extinction of the Yangzi porpoise (Stone 2010), and extirpation or commercial extinction of countless species.

On the other hand, the Chinese fishermen I lived with in Malaysia (E. Anderson and M. Anderson 1978) were often strong conservationists, managing their stocks and protecting local fisheries by methods up to and including outright killing of trespassers. Presumably these Malaysian Chinese had had some sort of equivalent systems back in China, and one wishes for reports.

China's elite nature-loving ideology clearly affected practice via educated estate owners and even small farmers and via the massive influence of elite culture on folk culture (far greater than in most of the Western world). Ideas matter, but the important ones are the working ideas of how to farm, not so much the abstract religious models. The working models not only more directly influence the environment, they are also far more widely shared, and usually at a deep, even subconscious, level. Abstract philosophical and aesthetic models are less deeply held.

China's ability to feed itself over 2,000 years is due to several factors.

First, China has always been willing to adopt and accept new and valuable crops.

Second, China early developed a balanced crop roster that supplies maximum nutrition for minimum space and inputs.

Third, China developed a "biological" technology that emphasized fertilizing, soil improvement, superior varieties of crops, careful cultivation techniques, and other ways of winning more with less. There was enormous investment in what geographers call "landesque capital": reshaping the land by such things as terraces, dykes, leveling, building drainage ditches and canals, and improving the soil.

Fourth, China's imperial government often tried to keep agricultural taxes low, develop agricultural science that really worked, and invoke policies that benefited agriculture in many ways. The government was, however, also frequently arbitrary, tyrannical, brutal, and overtaxing. But it was rarely as damagingly bad as were many other governments of the time.

Fifth, China developed a general ideology, or cosmology, or environmental science, that was accommodating to conservation and wise management. It incorporated wise management ideas in its philosophical systems.

Sixth, Chinese religion also incorporated some conservationist and resource-sparing ideas.

Seventh, the entire concept of civil and personal responsibility in China was based on following the broader ideals of religion and cosmology, including some ideas about conservation. Much more important was a more specific idea of responsibility about food, feeding the hungry, maintaining the agricultural system, regarding farmers as valued citizens, and regarding agriculture as the most important of all activities. These latter may be contrasted with Europe's traditional social scale, on which warmongers ranked highest and peasants lowest.

Eighth, China had an aesthetic based on a true love of the rural scene and a love of plants, trees, forests, waters, and other natural resources—one that contrasts very sharply with the traditional Middle Eastern aesthetic. China's aestheticis closer to the romantic strain in European arts but is considerably more positive about rural experiences.

Ninth, in the end, we have to credit the indomitable Chinese people. They survived disasters, wars, evil emperors, oppressive landlords, and all the other problems that broke and crushed almost every other ancient civilization and many modern ones. They survive today, unbowed and unbroken.

The future ahead is cloudy. China has abandoned the traditional cosmological and aesthetic views that encouraged sustainability. Recent developments have not always been sparing of agronomic resources or encouraging of farmers and farming. Above all, conserving soil, water, forests, and biodiversity will be a great challenge for the future.

Conservation Among China's Neighbors

China is surrounded by the most explicitly conservationist societies in the world (E. Anderson 2009a). The "myth of the ecologically noble savage" (Redford 1990) is long dead, and we know that many traditional societies lack even the concept of saving natural resources or managing wild plants and game (Alvard 1995; Beckerman et al. 2002; Hames 2007; Kay and Simmons 2002). On the other hand, many traditional societies do manage resources extremely well, and none do it with more explicit attention to sustainable use and conservative management than those of south and inner Asia. The conserving societies stretch in a vast arc from India to the Bering Strait.

Many of China's minorities were much better in their treatment of the environment, especially forests (Marks 2012). The Qing perpetuated Manchu traditions in saving their own original habitat, the forests of Manchuria. Minorities often cultivate by slash-and-burn agriculture, which is often condemned but which results in healthy forest regeneration if managed correctly. Some groups plant trees to reclaim swiddens for managed forests; they may use nitrogen-fixing trees like alders or commercial trees like cinnamon, a practice attested as early as 1639 (Menzies 1988) and surely much older. Toni Huber's book *The Cult of the Pure Crystal Mountain* (1999) documents religious forest-saving in Tibet; on the sacred mountain, all life is strictly protected.

The ideology of all these societies has one common theme: people are in nature, not outside it and opposed to it. A further belief, almost universal in the region, holds that spirits inhabit the natural world, especially its mountains, waters, and forests (in about that order of importance), and they must be kept on one's side. Doing so requires a genuine "harmony with nature," one of a religious sort. This is a broadly "animistic" tradition (J. Campbell 1983; Harvey 2006; Tylor 1871). It is, however, also quite practical. Being part of the cosmos means that humans have to take care of other lives at least well enough to keep human societies functioning. Since all these societies depended, until recently, on their own immediate production, they could not neglect nature (in the sense of nonhuman beings) for long. Most lived by a mix of agriculture and stock raising, supplemented with some hunting and gathering of wild resources. Many were largely pastoral, and several were strictly hunter-gatherers. Agriculture and herding *force* people to sustain at least their crop strains and their livestock herds (Alvard and Kuznar 2001), but even hunters have to manage their game well enough to keep it available.

The attitude of caring for nonhuman lives is very ancient: Jainism and Buddhism crystalized from humans-in-nature mind-sets around 500 BCE, and their complexity and sophistication bespeaks a long prior history. Buddhism certainly influenced Asia as far north as the Mongol world, but beyond that it had little traction, and when the Yukaghir or Ainu demonstrate concern for game animals, we can be sure there has been relatively little outside influence. Even within India itself, the sacred groves of the Toda (Walker 1986) and the Munda tribals (Archer 1974, and even those of the major ethnic groups, seem to go back well before the rise of world religions. The concept of *ahimsa* (nonviolence—nonslaughter and protection), first applied to cattle then progressively to other animals, is certainly old, having developed in Vedic times.

Tibet has been a major pupil of India, but again the sacred mountains that are totally protected (Huber 1999; Snellgrove 1967), the careful management of medicinal herbs (D. Anderson et al. 2005; Glover 2005; Salick et al. 2005), and the sensitive management of herds in systems that maximize wildlife too, all seem to have indigenous roots rather than being merely borrowings that came with Buddhism. Conservationist views have certainly been reinforced and informed by Buddhism (and Bön too), but they have enough indigenous content to make one suspect a long prior history. The vast herds of game on Tibetan plateaus and mountains excited amazement and wonder until the Chinese invasion and takeover from 1959 onward; the Communists, with their motto of "struggle against nature," soon exterminated them. The Ersu Tibetans in China once had a successful forest conservation system, religion based and enforced, but the Communist Chinese ended this, with the inevitable results of flooding, drought, timber shortage, fuel shortage, soil depletion, and so on (Schmitt 2012).

Highland Southeast Asian societies range greatly in their concern for the environment, but many are exemplary, maintaining independence from governments (Scott 2009) and thus from many pressures to destroy one's life support system. Widespread is an idea that the forests belong to the spirits and must therefore be protected, lest the spirits attack humans. Some societies have an entire sacred order, from absolutely protected trees to ancestral and burial groves to generally protected forests to working forests that are used intensively but allowed to regrow (Wang Jianhua 2007, 2008). Particularly careful environmental management is reported for the Akha in earlier times (Sturgeon 2005; Wang Jianhua 2007, 2008, 2013) and the Karen (Pinkaew 2001). Less careful—prone to work their way through forests, exhaust them totally, and move on—are some Hmong groups. W. R. Geddes (1976) portrays the Blue Miao as rather destructive, but a much more conservationist picture of the same people emerges from an account by Chindarsi (1975); Geddes is describing observed practice, whereas Chindarsi is more focused on ideals.

Thailand and its neighboring countries were 90 percent forested in the early twentieth century, and the rest of the landscape was carefully managed for intensive yet sustainable agriculture; tens of millions of people were supported with no major ecological damage, a unique accomplishment worldwide. Elephants, rhinos, and such unique and fragile species as the Vietnamese saora antelope flourished. Most of Southeast Asia is highly degraded today, and much is total wasteland. This has happened without any great benefit to the actual incomes of the mass of inhabitants. The difference is due to changes in land use strategy, not "economic development." Buddhists continue to work hard to save trees (Darlington 1998 and my personal research). Most Southeast Asian societies have complex and beautiful rituals connected with rice, and these often serve to inculcate values of sustainability and good management (Hamilton 2003; Klee 1980)

Mongolia, like Tibet, has been influenced by Buddhism, but the country entered history before Buddhism had much purchase, and even then the Mongols were conservers and protectors. Their totemic story of descent from a gray wolf and a fallow doe linked them with nonhuman lives from the beginning. They share with other Altaic peoples a long list of sacred fauna and flora (Roux 1966, 1984), sacred trees, sacred sites, and sacred landscapes. As among the Akha and other Southeast Asians, large areas were protected for the spirits and for burials. Genghis Khan's grave is unknown; following custom, he had himself buried in a wilderness, which was then totally closed to entry—a vast tract of untouched, untouchable wild for his tomb and memorial. (For this and much else about medieval Mongol reverence for nature, see De Rachewiltz 2004.) Ögödei became ill in 1231 while fighting in China, and

"Mongolian shamans attributed this to 'the lords and rulers of the land and rivers'" of that land (Allsen 2001: 208). Genghis's heirs established their capital, Qaraqorum, near the old Gök Turk capital, "because they believed that there inhered in that particular locale a special good fortune" (Allsen 2001: 208). Throughout recorded history, the Mongols paid enormous attention to sacred mountains and rivers, to forests and pastures, and to landscapes in general.

Today, Mongols still fight ferociously—with politics, not with the old swords and arrows—to protect the purity of their water (Metzo 2005). The key concept is *shutekh*, "respect"—the word means respect for parents and elders and is extended to the whole natural world and its plants and animals (information from field work, especially from Mongolian ecologist Purevsuren Tsolmonjav, interviews of May 26–June 9, 2013). All these have spirits (on Mongol animism, see Humphrey 1996), which must be treated with respect for safety's sake, but ordinary everyday respect for the real-world animals, plants, waters, mountains, and landscapes is evident and goes far beyond mere fear of spirits. Polluting waters is avoided, and some springs cannot be touched at all; no one washes in them, stock are watered downstream, and even taking clean drinking water is done a few feet down from the spring head (I have personally observed this). Trees are protected; many trees of good size are tied with blue silk scarves, the mark of sacred space. *Ovoo* (sacred cairns) mark important spots, often delineating large taboo areas, such as Yolin Am in southern Mongolia, where hunting, firewood cutting, and other destructive activities are forbidden. In practice, of course, all these practices do not prevent serious overgrazing, overcutting of firewood, and other ills, but it certainly makes them incomparably less frequent than they are in neighboring China, where Communism removed such "superstitions" and left the land unprotected.

From the Tuvans, neighbors to the north of China, come the songs and teachings of the shaman Mongush Kenin-Lopsan (1997), recorded by Hungarian ethnographer Mihály Hoppál. Kenin-Lopsan's teachings are some of the most explicitly and uncompromisingly conservationist of anything recorded from non-Western peoples. There is some possibility of Russian influence, but given other documents we have and the general lack of Russian interest in conserving, I see no reason to doubt the fully traditional nature of Kenin's views (cf., for example, Vainstein 1980, which reports similar beliefs and practices for the same area). Other shamanic records from Altaic cultures (e.g., Nowak and Durrant 1977; Arseniev 1996, but the latter is a somewhat romanticized source) are less explicit but confirm the general emphasis on nature.

The Ainu, who speak a totally different language, have a quite different belief system, but it nevertheless involves some of the same ideas of sustainable management as part of a spiritual, or "animistic," view of nature (Batchelor 1901; Fitzhugh and Dubreuil 1999). Ainu songs include a great deal about nature spirits and the natural world (Philippi 1982). The Japanese have a shamanistic substrate to their culture (Blacker 1986), as do the Koreans (Kendall 1985), and this is clearly part of the "story behind the story" of both countries' stunningly successful reforestation campaigns (Totman 1989). The Japanese have in the past succeeded in other conservation activities, including the careful regulation of fisheries that Japan once had (Ruddle and Akimichi 1984) and has now so signally abandoned.

Similar ideas stretch far westward into Europe. On the borders of Asia, the Uralic Udmurt still maintain vestiges of their ancient tree worship, which once involved worship of a birch tree that could not be ringed round by three sets of arms (Shutova 2006). Similar reverence for birches, oaks, and trees in general characterized ancient European religions, while concern for wildlife is attested in such things as Georgian folk songs (Tuite 1994). The conservation region also stretches onward through northern Asia and down the American west coast, but that is another story.

It seems obvious that there is a vast common ground throughout the northern parts of the Northern Hemisphere, based on the needs of nomadic herding and hunting people to maintain their food source and characterized by broadly "animist" and often conservationist views. Many societies are not as concerned with management as are the Tuvans and Udmurt; the Yukaghir, carefully and thoroughly described by Rane Willerslev (2007), are less devoted, and so apparently were the Chukchi and some Native American groups in former times. But the general ideological underpinning is the same. One clear predictor—simple population density—explains much of the variance in which societies will be self-conscious about saving. Other factors, including direct or indirect Buddhist influence, are involved as well, but population density coupled with the fragility or resilience of the resource base explains a great deal (cf. Beckerman et al. 2002 on South America).

China is thus ringed by societies are very much more conservationist than China itself has been. Civilization spared the Chinese elites the need to worry about rapid and terrible feedback if the environment was mismanaged. Peasants could and did die, but the decision-makers could always eat. By contrast, hunting and fishing people who overhunted their game and overfished their waters died quickly and unpleasantly, and there was no escape unless neighboring lands were extensive and very poorly defended.

However, there seems to have been an ideological difference from the start. Mencius and Zhuangzi notwithstanding, early Chinese texts have nothing like the Buddhist, Jain, or shamanistic ideas of the neighboring cultures. Buddhism took deep root in China but had somewhat less than total penetrance—in fact, very little obvious influence—in regard to things like hunting and forest protection. *Ahimsa* was not part of China's way, though it did greatly temper Chinese wastefulness. China's early culture clearly shared deep animistic and shamanistic roots (see, e.g., Waley 1955) with surrounding societies, but the Chinese seem not to have developed this into the pervasive view that one simply had to preserve a great deal of the natural world. On the other hand, the entire thrust of the present book is to point out that China did share a good deal of the basic ideology and values system—enough to keep it a mix of conservation and waste, throughout history, in contrast to the vicious and total onslaught on nature that has characterized the last seventy years.

An Introduction to Central Asian Food

Central Asia today is a vast but surprisingly homogeneous food region. From Xi'an to Turkmenistan, there are broad similarities. The most obvious of these is the basic importance of wheat. It is the subsistence grain everywhere, except insofar as local poverty or famine force people to rely on barley (and, in the past, millets). It most commonly appears in three forms:

Bread: The typical Central Asian bread is the Persian *nan*, a yeast-raised bread that often involves shortening. Its Chinese form is the familiar *shaobing*, a miniaturized nan probably derived from those introduced by Persians in the Tang Dynasty (Schafer 1963). However, other breadstuffs exist, from chapatis near the edges of the Indian subcontinent to bagels (see below). Rolls, cakes, and cookie-like sweets exist in great variety. Bread is sacred to most of these groups and cannot be thrown away or treated without respect; this is the eastern limit of a custom universal until recently in Europe and the northern Middle East. In those areas I have repeatedly encountered the idea that crumbs of bread must be carefully swept up from the floor, lest someone step on them, a cardinal sin. A Finnish consultant was told as a child that the crumb would carry you down to hell. Bread is usually Persian style: large, oval, flat loaves baked by sticking them to the sides of a huge tandoor oven. Large breads remain more popular in Central Asia and Ningxia.

Noodles: Wheat noodles are universal and abundant, especially in Chinese Central Asia and Uzbekistan. They are usually found in soups and are not very different from those mentioned in the *Yinshan Zhengyao*.

Wrapped filled dumplings: These are a quintessentially Turkic food, and their most widespread name in the region—*manty* or some variant of it—is clearly Turkic. But they go by many other names, from Afghan *ashak* (from Farsi *ash*, stew) to Russian pelmeny, Polish pierogi, and Ukrainian *vareniki*— all three of which words appear to be Turkic in origin. The Yiddish word *kreplach* is harder to explain. Italian ravioli are probably a fairly recent derivative, possibly from Greek *manti*. Thousands of variants are found, with many local names; *shor* is one Azeri form. In spite of their Turkic identification now, these dumplings are almost certainly of Near Eastern origin, being related at some remove to Arab *samusa* and the like. I suspect they were invented in ancient Mesopotamia and spread via Iran to the rest of the world. Archaeologically recovered manti have emerged from western China (Anderson 2010). There seem to be no records of them from ancient Greece or Rome.

Barley bread and soup were known, and millet was usually used for porridge (as elsewhere). Millets are very ancient in Central Asia; panic millet was quite possibly domesticated there (see above, Chapter 2). Maize has come in recent centuries, and cornbread now exists locally, especially in China.

The other very important grain in Central Asia today is rice. This is usually a special food—for feasts, celebrations, and special dinners—at least in western Central Asia. Especially in the western half or two-thirds of the region, it is normally found in the form of pilaf (pulao, pilau, polo, pilu, etc.). This dish consists of rice cooked in stock, usually meat stock; in many areas the rice is fried first, while raw. (Chinese fried rice is fried *after* being boiled and then dried—it was originally a way to deal with leftover rice.) Pilaf is an Arab or Iranian invention and evidently fairly new, because recipes for it do not appear until the last few centuries (Charles Perry, pers. comm. and in Buell, Anderson, and Perry 2010). It is now a staple—locally *the* staple—at feasts and festivities. Among local variants, that of Kabul is particularly famous: it involves fried onions, carrots, and raisins, as well as bits of lamb (or goat) and some spices. In Kabul, it tends to be made with sheep fat and is consequently stodgy, heavy, and greasy. Lighter variants have appeared elsewhere.

Throughout all recorded history, the usual diet in much of Central Asia has been wheat for everyday; dairy products as the usual accompaniment; and meat, lots of it, for special occasions. Dairy products come in a dizzying variety. Fresh milk is rarely consumed in any quantity, because of lactase deficiency. Dairy is thus usually prepared by lactic acid fermentation (and sometimes other fermenting processes). Lactic acid fermentation by *Lactobacillus* spp. produces yogurt, kefir, and sour milk. Add yeast to a sugary milk, and one can obtain *kumys* (kumiss, koumiss), which is usually made from mare's milk because it has enough sugar to feed the yeasts. It is mildly alcoholic and is the standard drink of nomadic herders if they can afford it. Settled people, unless they come of nomad stock, rarely like it; it tastes like a mix of buttermilk and flat beer. Ibn Battuta sampled it with Queen Taitughlī, head wife of Khan Ūzbak of the Golden Horde, and found it "disagreeable" (Ibn Battuta 1959: 487), as have many since. Distilling it produces a powerful vodka-like drink, generally known as *arak* or some similar derivative of Arabic *'araq*, "distilled liquor" (from *'araq*, "sweating").

Cheese is also produced, ranging from fresh white cheese (pot cheese, *queso fresco*) to the cheddar-like hard cheese made in Baghlan Province (Afghanistan) and other places. Rock-hard whey cheeses and dried curd are produced as a storable ration; they can be carried anywhere under any circumstances and grated when needed for food. Dried milk products are another travel ration.

Game used to be common and important and was somewhat conserved by the need to kill it according to either shamanist conservation principles or *halal* rules—an observant Muslim cannot just shoot a deer and then eat its carcass; he has to capture it alive and slit its throat. Today, the game is thoroughly shot out, except in the most extremely remote and isolated regions, and Central Asia's large mammals are on the endangered species list. However, the classic Central Asian feast, involving a whole sheep, or several of them, slowly roasted to fork-tender delicacy, is only for special occasions and often only for the elite. The ordinary individual must be content with small bits, if that.

Traveling in remote parts of Afghanistan forty years ago, I found that food normally meant bread and, with luck, a bit of cheese or a kabab made of tiny scraps of very tough and rank meat alternating on the stick with equally tiny bits of tail fat. The fat-tailed sheep has a huge fat storage system in its rump and tail, held in place with connective tissue, so that cooking it produces a chewy, fatty morsel rather than mere melted lard.

The "poor man's meat," legumes, are for the settled poor rather than the nomadic ones—the poor nomads live on dairy foods and wild foods in addition to what grain they can get. But for the settled people, chickpeas are generally available, as are various local pulse crops. New World beans have entered the picture recently. Legumes get much commoner as one gets nearer to India, the great home of vegetarian and legume cookery.

What saves Central Asian food from monotony and lack of distinctiveness is the pervasive use of fruits and vegetables—especially fruits. The common domestic apple comes from the mountains of eastern Kazakhstan, where the principal city preserves the name Alma-Ata, "father of apples." Other apple species were domesticated in north China and Korea. The apricot is Central

Asian. The jujube comes from northwest China, not far from the eastern ends of the Silk Route. The common domestic grape comes from the Caucasus and Black Sea area, but it found a haven in Central Asia. (The Greeks under Alexander probably popularized it.) Superb table grapes are raised, and wine is made where Islam is less strict than usual.

The fruiting mulberry, Near Eastern as opposed to the silk-raising Chinese mulberry, abounded in historic times but is rarer now; its fruit was a staple food until recently, but scorched-earth wars that destroyed the orchards eliminated it as a staple (at least in the areas of Afghanistan known to me). Almonds and pistachios, both from the Near East, are universally common. Pine nuts are traded from forested regions north and south, and occur surprisingly often in dishes in the *Yinshan Zhengyao*. Raisins, almonds, and pine nuts are regularly used in pilafs and similar elaborate rice and wheat preparations. Unlike the European tendency to confine fruit to desserts and sweets, the Iranian and Central Asian world routinely uses fruit—especially raisins—in meat dishes.

Most distinctive of all, however, are the melons. The sweet melon is a Mesopotamian or Persian creation and reached its full splendor in Central Asia. Melons need hot dry days and cool dry nights to reach perfection, and they have them there. Anyone who has tried a real Hami melon (or one from Green River, Utah, where the same conditions obtain) will understand that melons differ as much as wines do. Melon gastronomy flourished in old Central Asia just as wine snobbery does in France or California. Watermelons came much later, from Africa, but have caught on. When in 1978 some of us asked a north Chinese farmer what he would do first if he had a bit of money, there was no hesitation: "Buy a watermelon!"

Whence came this diet? Where identifiable, it was largely from the Near East. Wheat, barley, sheep, goats, cattle, and most of the other plants and animals came from there. So, almost certainly, did the idea of stuffed dumplings. Rice, of course, was Chinese originally, but the cooking styles of the Near East once one is west of the Eighteen Provinces are clearly from India and Iran; dish names like *pulau* leave no doubt.

The sophisticated cuisines of urban areas have been influenced by more rich and powerful neighbors. Southern Afghanistan, especially the Kabul area, was strongly influenced from India (see, e.g., Saferi 1986, which reflects a rather Kabul-oriented background). Western Afghanistan is thoroughly Iranian; the northern regions are more classicly Central Asian, with Tadzhik and Turkic foods. Xinjiang has been influenced by China and is becoming more so literally by the day. The north and west of Central Asia, formerly Soviet, have been Russian-influenced since before the USSR took shape. The recipe names in an Uzbek cookbook (Visson 1999, for one example) are not hard to read for one who knows no Uzbek: the food words are almost all from Russian, Farsi, or Arabic (via Farsi). *Plov* is obviously from "pilaf." *Lovia*, for beans, is from Arabic *lubiya*; *tovuk* for chicken from Arabic *tawuk*. *Laghman* for noodle soup is straight Farsi. And so it goes. An Azerbaijan cookbook (Akhmedov 1986) is much more Turkic in its vocabulary.

As Elisabeth Rozin (1983) pointed out, a cuisine is best defined by its signature spicing. Central Asia relies on the classic Near Eastern mix: black pepper, cumin, coriander (the ground seeds and the fresh leaf), and cinnamon. This is exactly what we find in the *Yinshan Zhengyao*, and what we find today, with the frequent addition of New World chile pepper. Mint and poppy seeds appeared in the *Yinshan Zhengyao* and are found today. Black cumin (nigella) is occasional.

Toward the west, more strictly Near Eastern spices like sumac, saffron, and dill appear; toward India, turmeric becomes rapidly more common. Within China, but not even in western Xinjiang until recently, one finds among Central Asian foods some or all of the classic Chinese signature mix of ginger, large cardamoms, soy sauce, and green onions. All are common in the more Chinese-sounding recipes of the *Yinshan Zhengyao*, and the large cardamoms are even in the Near Eastern dishes. (They were probably used widely in the Near East at the time of the *Yinshan Zhengyao*, in the fourteenth century; they rarely are today.) Soy products were not normally used at any time in Central Asia except in Chinese territories.

Turkic speakers of Central Asia—China's Xinjiang province and neighboring former Soviet republics—include the Uzbeks, Kazakhs, Kirghiz, Uighurs, and others. They live on bread and meat, with a very large consumption of noodles and wrapped dumplings (known almost everywhere by some variant of the word *mantu* or *manti*). Boiled noodles in soup with mutton is widely popular. Meat can include goat, horse, and camel but is usually sheep. Fermented mare's milk is popular among the Kirghiz, as among some other groups farther north and east. Vegetables are not popular, except for carrots, but fruit is popular and common. Melons are favored. Grapes are common and wine is produced. Apricots do especially well and abound where conditions have been stable enough to allow trees to mature. A 2005 book by Martha Weeks details Kirghiz cooking thoroughly. This cuisine preserves many dishes similar to those of the Yuan Dynasty.

My own observations, and especially information provided by Gulbahar Mammut (a Xinjiang Turkic student), adds the following details of Xinjiang Turkic cuisine. Rice pilaf becomes *polo* (Uighur and related dialects, and also some dialects of Farsi; Uzbek *plov*). *Manta* (yeast-raised, or sometimes unleavened; Uzbek and others, *manti*) are stuffed with meat and onions, more proof that the modern North Chinese *mantou* is a recent degeneration from a filled pastry. *Manta* or *mamanta* is a common local variant of the widespread word (Fuchsia Dunlop, email to author, June 4, 2012). Smaller, thinskinned versions are *chüchür* (Uzbek *chuchuar*, but, from the description, *chuchuar* is more like the Xinjiangese *hoshiang*: fried, then steamed, dumplings). *Toqash* is a small bread; many other breads exist, such as *pitr nan* (pita) and *qatlama nan* (layered with onions, cheese, and such), and the similar *güsh* (meat) *nan* (layered with minced meat). A strudel-thin bread filled with yogurt is *holuq nan*. Filled pastries are *samsa* or *sambusa*, from the Arabic *samusa* or *sambusak*. *Qoldama* is a dumpliing. The tandoor oven is *tunur* or *tanur* in Xinjiang. Red pepper is *laza*, from Chinese *la jiao*.

Noodles are, of course, vitally important in the Turkic areas, and include the very long *lang men*. This name appears to be a sort of fusion of Chinese *mian*, "noodles," and Persian *laghman* (cf. Uzbek *lagman*). *Ash* is "soup," as in Persian. Ordinary cooked rice is *gang pen*, from Chinese *kan fen*, "rice cooked dry." Fish is rare and locally taboo. Qıtaq (with a Turkish short i) is yogurt, a basic food; dried, it is *qurut*. Sheep, of course, is the really choice food, and as in the Mongol days, almost all of it is eaten, including lungs, stomach, and brain. Kababs are popular—I assume they are like those in Afghanistan, small and much like the *sate* of Southeast Asia, and alternating bits of meat with bits of tail/rump fat. The skin and feet, however, are not eaten (the *Yinshan Zhengyao*, however, has gourmet recipes for them), and Islam forbids eating the blood, formerly consumed. For the lungs, dough is mixed with water or spices and poured in, with much care to fill all the alveoli. Then the whole is boiled for an hour and then eaten with a spicy dip. The intestines are stuffed with finely cut vegetables, rice, and water and boiled whole. The meat-and-chickpea stews of Mesopotamia, featured in the *Yinshan Zhengyao*, have disappeared. Noodles in soup dominate instead (as in Ningxia).

In addition to the ubiquitous peaches, apricots, and melons, sweets include *halva* (Arabic *halwa*), here made of lamb oil, sugar, and flour and often served as an appetizer! Cookies, some at least of Russian origin, occur (Russian types include *pichina*). The Uighurs eat a fair amount of dairy products—yogurt, cheese, and now condensed milk—but, in general, Xinjiang's Turkic groups are much less dairy-dependent than groups to the north and west of them.

In short, modern Turkic speakers' food in China food is quite similar to that in the *Yinshan Zhengyao*: rather bland noodle soups with lamb; chicken red-cooked with star anise; nan (Persian bread); and others. Polo is new since Mongol times. As in Afghanistan, carrots are important and occur in polo, among other dishes. Potatoes have become a major stew ingredient in the last couple of centuries. Thus the standard stew can be very much like an Irish stew: lamb, potatoes, and carrots, without much spice beyond salt and pepper. The familiar manta dumplings are supplemented by samsa. Soup goes by the good old Arabic word *shorba*. Lamb kebabs and whole roast lamb remain featured. Most of the dishes are very similar to those of Afghanistan, Uzbekistan, and other points west, but many Chinese dishes are found, especially west Chinese dishes. (See also Alford and Duguid 2008.)

A fascinating and unique research project concerns the bagel. Cyril Robinson (1998) devoted years to a search for Central Asian origins after discovering ringbreads, very similar to bagels, in Xinjiang. The links are lost, but there seems no question that there is some kind of continuity from these to the doughnut-shaped boiled-dough breads so familiar in America. The bagel we know today was picked up by the Jews from northeast European usage, in or around Bielarus, centuries ago, and became a characteristic Jewish food though not of Jewish or Palestinian origin. It may date back to ancient Indo-European breads.

The Dungan or Dong'an, a Muslim group in northwest China, eat food typical of that region. They speak Chinese, but their food is a cross between Turkic (pilaf, apricots, mutton in all forms, etc.) and Chinese (noodle dishes including bean threads, chicken with ginseng, Chinese vegetables of all sorts, cold dishes, and the like; see Weeks 2004).

Mongol subsistence today is quite distinctive from Turkic forms, and is clearly continuous with descriptions in Genghis Khan's time (see Buell et al. 2010). It is still dominated by dairy products, meat, and grain, the dairy products being primarily available in summer. Milk, *süü*, is normally processed into *airag* (kumys), *aaruul* (dried curd), and *aarts* (dried yogurt); these are similar to the Arabic *kishk* and Central Asian Turkic *qurut*. *Byasag* is a fresh cheese; *tarag*, yogurt. Dumplings range from *bansh* to *buudz*; larger fried dumplings, like large heavy samusas, are *khuushuur*, very popular; sidewalk stands sell them. Noodles are *goimon* in general, but several kinds exist, and noodle soups are generally known by the name of whatever is the most interesting ingredient in them; the commonest is thus "soup with mutton." The worldwide, stodgy fried dough is *gambir* (a more elegant filled form is *boov*). Many other terms for flour foods and flour-and-meat combinations exist. Fruit and vegetables are popular when available, but herders have little access to them; orchards and kitchen gardens are hardly compatible with thousands of hungry livestock milling around. Livestock, incidentally, is known as the Five Snouts (or Five Muzzles, *tavan ichoshuu*). The less tractable ones, camels and goats, are "cold-snouted stock"; the more tractable horses, cattle (including yaks) and sheep, are "warm-snouted stock." Interestingly, all the above food words are quite different from those in Turkic, except the most basic of all; the word for milk is an obvious cognate of Turkic *süt*. Once again it is maddeningly difficult to tell whether there is an "Altaic phylum" or not (information from field research, supplemented from Sanders and Bat-Ireedüi's very valuable textbook, 1999).

Everywhere in the modern Mongolian world, meat is the prestigious protein food, and the *Yinshan Zhengyao* is not alone in talking constantly about it while avoiding mention of lowly dairy products. The meat is usually sheep, often goat, very rarely anything else. Cattle are restricted to warmer parts of the region and usually to settlements. Pigs are now taboo, of course, in most of Central Asia, because of conversion to Islam. Horses and camels now share that taboo but were once common fare; they were favored by the Mongols and also were emergency rations, since a Mongol soldier could, in a pinch, eat the spare horses he always led. The Mongols, Buddhists who are not very serious about the vegetarian teachings of their religion, still eat horses and Bactrian camels with relish, as well as what pork is available (Mongolia is not good hog country). Reindeer reach their southern limit in the Altai and northernmost Mongolia, just north of our areas of concern.

The Mongols eat every part of the animal, partly because it shows respect (Mongol *shutekh*) for the animal. Widely in northern Eurasia and North America, it is believed that animal spirits must be shown respect, which involves no unnecessary killing—game is killed only when needed for food—and no waste (for Siberia, see, e.g., Kenin-Lopsan 1997; Willerslev 2007; the best discussion of "respect" in this context is in Atleo 2004, describing the beliefs of the Nuu-chah-nulth people of Canada; their beliefs are startlingly similar to Mongol ideas). Not eating parts of the animal is highly disrespectful. This belief system is now confined to marginalized traditional people but was once widespread, though even in early days market hunting and royal hunts (Allsen 2006), learned from Persia and China, led to sad compromises of the traditional belief system. Respect, however, does not stop people from having preferences. The Mongol equivalent of "a bird in the hand is worth two in the bush" is "better today's lungs than tomorrow's fat" (Sanders and Bat-Ireedüi 1999: 78)—that is, better the worst part of the animal today than a promise of the best-liked part "some time." Fat is still conspicuously preferred in Mongolia. Even so, the *Yinshan Zhengyao*, explicitly a book of feast food for the court, includes recipes not only for lungs but also for skin and feet. Respect had to be shown.

Mongol food continues to be simple, based on the familiar boiled mutton, wheat and millet products, and above all, fermented dairy products. As in medieval texts, boiling continues to be respected as the way to capture the essence of meat. Wild plants are still used. Liu Pei-Gui (1999), among others, has studied Mongol uses of mushrooms. Mongols use large numbers of both individuals and species from many genera of mushrooms (Buell et al. 2010), including the common *Agaricus*, *Boletus*, and *Tricholoma*, as well as less-known genera. Such bizarre plants as the bitter and acrid but edible *Cynomorium soongaricum*, a parasite on the roots of desert shrubs, are eaten. So are many berries, including rose hips (Tungalug and Jamsran 2012); wild roses are, for some reason, known as "dog muzzle bushes" (cf. English "dog rose"). Medicinal herbs abound and are widely used. Shamanism lives on and affects foodways, and even though it is dying out, it supplied us with a particularly fine account of shamanic practice: Caroline Humphrey's work with the Mongol shaman Urgunge Onon (1996).

Medical foodways are still very important in Mongolia. Foods are color coded in Mongol culture, and what is eaten sometimes follows on that coding because relatively more of certain colors of food are consumed at certain seasons: black and yellow (i.e., hard liquors—long considered "black" in Mongolia—and butter, cream, and barley flour) in spring; white (dairy foods other than butter) in summer, green (vegetables, herbs and fruits) in fall; red (meat; marmot is recommended) in winter (Bold 2009: 121–25).

BIBLIOGRAPHY

Achilli, Alessandro et al. 2012. "Mitochondrial Genomes from Modern Horses Reveal the Major Haplogroups That Underwent Domestication." *Proceedings of the National Academy of Sciences* 109: 1449–54.

Agamben, Giorgio. 1998. *Homo Sacer: Sovereign Power and "Bare Life."* Trans. Daniel Heller-Roazen. Stanford, Calif.: Stanford University Press.

Akhmedov, Akhmed-Djabir. 1986. *Azerbaijan Cookery.* Baku: Ishyg.

Akira, Haneda. 1989. "On Chinese Rhubarb." In *The Islamic World from Classical to Modern Times: Essays in Honor of Bernard Lewis.* Princeton, N.J.: Darwin Press. 27–30.

Akkermans, Peter M. M. G., and Glenn M. Schwartz. 2003. *The Archaeology of Syria: From Complex Hunter-Gatherers to Early Urban Societies (c. 16,000–300 BC).* Cambridge: Cambridge University Press.

Alberuni (Al-Bīrūnī). 1973. *Alberuni's India.* Trans. Edward Sachau, ed. and abridged Ainslee Embree. New York: Norton.

Al-Bīrūnī. 1973. *Al-Bīrūnī's Book on Pharmacy and Materia Medica.* Ed. and trans. Hakim Mohammed Said. Karachi: Hamdard National Foundation.

Alford, Jeffrey, and Naomi Duguid. 2008. *Beyond the Great Wall: Recipes and Travels in the Other China.* New York: Artisan.

Allan, Sarah. 2007. "Erlitou and the Formation of Chinese Civilization: Toward a New Paradigm." *Journal of Asian Studies* 66: 461–96.

———, ed. 2002. *The Formation of Chinese Civilization.* New Haven, Conn.: Yale University Press.

Allen, Thomas B. 1989. "Shaking Gold from China's Treetops." *International Wildlife* 19, 4: 34–36.

Allsen, Thomas. 1994. "The Rise of the Mongolian Empire and Mongolian Rule in North China." In *The Cambridge History of China,* Vol. 6, *Alien Regimes and Border States, 907–1368,* ed. Herbert Franke and Denis Twitchett. Cambridge: Cambridge University Press. 321–413.

———. 1997. *Commodity and Exchange in the Mongol Empire: A Cultural History of Islamic Textiles.* Cambridge Studies in Islamic Civilization. Cambridge: Cambridge University Press.

———. 2001. *Culture and Conquest in Mongol Eurasia.* Cambridge: Cambridge University Press.

———. 2006. *The Royal Hunt in Eurasian History.* Philadelphia: University of Pennsylvania Press.

———. 2009. "Mongols as Vectors for Cultural Transmission." In *The Cambridge History of Inner Asia: The Chinggisid Age,* ed. Nicola Di Cosmo, Allen. J. Frank, and Peter B. Golden. Cambridge: Cambridge University Press. 135–54.

Almond, Richard. 2003. *Medieval Hunting.* Stroud, Gloucestershire: Sutton.

Alter, Joseph S. 2008. "Rethinking the History of Medicine in Asia: Hakim Mohammed Said and the Society for the Promotion of Eastern Medicine." *Journal of Asian Studies* 67: 1165–86.

Alvard, Michael. 1995. "Interspecific Prey Choice by Amazonian Hunters." *Current Anthropology* 36: 789–818.

Alvard, Michael, and Lawrence Kuznar. 2001. "Deferred Harvests: The Transition from Hunting to Animal Husbandry." *American Anthropologist* 103: 295–311.

Ames, Roger. 1994. *The Art of Rulership: A Study of Ancient Chinese Political Thought*. Albany, N.Y.: SUNY Press.

Ammianus Marcellinus. 1939. *History*. Trans. J. C. Rolfe. Loeb Classical Library. Cambridge, Mass.: Harvard University Press.

Anderson, Danica M., Jan Salick, Robert K. Moseley, and Ou Xiaokun. 2005. "Conserving the Sacred Medicine Mountains: A Vegetation Analysis of Tibetan Sacred Sites in Northwest Yunnan." *Biodiversity and Conservation* 14: 3065–91.

Anderson, E. N. 1988. *The Food of China*. New Haven, Conn.: Yale University Press.

———. 1991. "Chinese Folk Classification of Food Plants." *Crossroads* 1, 2: 51–67.

———. 1996. *Ecologies of the Heart*. New York: Oxford University Press.

———. 2001. "Flowering Apricot: Environmental Practice, Folk Religion, and Daoism." In *Daoism and Ecology: Ways Within a Cosmic Landscape*, ed. N. J. Girardot, James Miller, and Liu Xiaogan. Cambridge, Mass.: Harvard University Press for Center for the Study of World Religions, Harvard Divinity School. 157–84.

———. 2005a. *Everyone Eats*. New York: New York University Press.

———. 2005b. "Lamb, Rice, and Hegemonic Decline: The Mongol Empire in the Fourteenth Century." In *The Historical Evolution of World-Systems*, ed. Christopher Chase-Dunn and E. N. Anderson. New York: Palgrave Macmillan. 113–21.

———. 2007. *Floating World Lost*. New Orleans: University Press of the South.

———. 2009a. "Indigenous Traditions: Asia." In *Berkshire Encyclopedia of Sustainability*, Vol. 1, *The Spirit of Sustainability*. Great Barrington, Mass.: Berkshire. 216–21.

———. 2009b. "Northwest Chinese Cuisine and the Central Asian Connection." In *Regionalism and Globalism in Chinese Culinary Culture*, ed. David Holm. Taipei: Foundation of Chinese Dietary Culture. 49–78.

———. 2010. "Ancient and Modern Foods from the Tarim Basin." *Expedition* 52, 3: 5–6.

———. 2011. "Agriculture." In *Ethnobiology*, ed. E. N. Anderson, Eugene Hunn, Deborah Pearsall, and Nancy Turner. New York: Wiley-Blackwell.

———. 2012. "Environmental Ruin: The Drag on China's Future." Paper, California Sociological Association, annual conference, Riverside, California.

Anderson, E. N., and Barbara A. Anderson. 2012. *Warning Signs of Genocide*. Lanham, Md.: Lexington Books.

Anderson, E. N., and Marja L. Anderson. 1973. *Mountains and Water: The Cultural Ecology of South Coastal China*. Taipei: Orient Cultural Service.

Anderson, E. N., and Christopher Chase-Dunn. 2005. "The Rise and Fall of Great Powers." In *The Historical Evolution of World-Systems*, ed. Christopher Chase-Dunn and E. N. Anderson. New York: Palgrave Macmillan.

Anderson, E. N., and Lisa Raphals. 2007. "Taoism and Animals." In *A Communion of Subjects: Animals in Religion, Science, and Ethics*, ed. Paul Waldau and Kimberley Patton. New York: Columbia University Press. 275–90.

Anderson, E. N., Teresa Wang, and Victor Mair. 2005. "Ni Zan, Cloud Forest Hall Collection of Rules for Drinking and Eating." In *Hawaiʻi Reader in Traditional Chinese Culture*, ed. Victor Mair, Nancy Steinhardt, and Paul R. Goldin. Honolulu: University of Hawai'i Press. 444–55.

Anderson, Perry. 1974. *Lineages of the Absolutist State*. London: NLB.

Andersson, J. G. 1934. *Children of the Yellow Earth*. London: Kegan Paul, Trench, Trubner.

———. 1943. *Researches into the Prehistory of the Chinese*. Bulletin 15. Stockholm: Museum of Far Eastern Antiquities.

Anthony, David W. 2007. *The Horse, the Wheel and Language: How Bronze-Age Riders from the Eurasian Steppes Shaped the Modern World*. Princeton, N.J.: Princeton University Press.

Archer, W. G. 1974. *The Hill of Flutes: Life, Love and Poetry in Tribal India: A Portrait of the Santals*. Pittsburgh: University of Pittsburgh Press.

Arseniev, V. K. 1996. *Dersu the Trapper (Dersu Uzala)*. Trans. Malcolm Burr. Russian original, early twentieth century, Kingston, N.Y.: McPherson.

Aslanian, Sebouh David. 2011. *From the Indian Ocean to the Mediterranean: The Global Trade Networks of Armenian Merchants from New Julfa*. Berkeley: University of California Press.

Asouti, Eleni, and Dorian Q. Fuller. 2013. "A Contextual Approach to the Emergence of Agriculture in Southwest Asia: Reconstructing Early Neolithic Plant-Food Production." *Current Anthropology* 54: 299–345.

Atleo, E. Richard. 2004. *Tsawalk: A Nuu-Chah-Nulth Worldview*. Vancouver: University of British Columbia Press.

Atran, Scott. 2002. *In Gods We Trust*. New York: Oxford University Press.

Bagley, Robert, ed. 2001. *Ancient Sichuan: Treasures from a Lost Civilization*. Seattle: Seattle Art Museum.

Baker, Hugh. 1989. Review of *The Food of China* by E. N. Anderson. *China Quarterly* 119: 661–62.

Barber, Elizabeth Wayland. 1999. *The Mummies of Ürümchi*. New York: Norton. <U with double acute accent>

Barbieri-Low, Anthony J. 2011. "Craftsman's Literacy: Uses of Writing by Male and Female Artisans in Qin and Han China." In *Writing and Literacy in Early China: Studies from the Columbia Early China Seminar*, ed. Li Feng and David Prager Branner. Seattle: University of Washington Press. 370–99.

Barfield, Thomas J. 1989. *The Perilous Frontier: Nomadic Empires and China, 221 BC to AD 1757*. Cambridge, Mass.: Blackwell.

———. 1993. *The Nomadic Alternative*. Englewood Cliffs, NJ: Prentice-Hall.

Barker, Graeme. 2006. *The Agricultural Revolution in Prehistory: Why Did Foragers Become Farmers?* Oxford: Oxford University Press.

Barnhill, David Landis. 2005. *Bashō's Journey*. Albany, N.Y.: SUNY Press.

Barthold, W. 1968 [1928]. *Turkestan Down to the Mongol Invasion*. 3rd ed. Gibb Memorial Series n.s. 5. London: Luzac.

Barton, Loukas, Seth D. Newsome, Fahu Chen, Hui Wang, and Robert L. Bettinger. 2008. "An Isotopic Evaluation of Early Agriculture at Dadiwan." Paper, Society for American Archaeology annual meeting, Vancouver.

Bar-Yosef, Ofer, and Youping Wang. 2012. "Paleolithic Anthropology in China." *Annual Review of Anthropology* 41: 319–35.

Batchelor, John. 1901. *The Ainu and Their Folk-Lore*. London: Religious Tract Society.

Beaujard, Philippe. 2009. *Les mondes de l'océan indien*. Vol. 1, *De la formation de l'état au premier système-monde afro-eurasien (4e millénaire av. J.-C.–6e siècle apr. J.-C.)*. Paris: Armand Colin.

———. 2010. "From Three Possible Iron-Age World Systems to a Single Afro-Eurasian World-System." *Journal of World History* 21: 1–43.

———. 2012. *Les mondes de l'océan indien.* Vol. 2, *L'océan indien, au coeur des globalisations de l'ancien monde du 7e au 15e siècle.* Paris: Armand Colin.

Beckerman, Stephen, Paul Valentine, and Elise Eller. 2002. "Conservation and Native Amazonians: Why Some Do and Some Don't." *Antropológica* 96: 31–51.

Beckford, George. 1972. *Persistent Poverty: Underdevelopment in Plantation Economies of the Third World.* Oxford: Oxford University Press.

Bellah, Robert N. 2011. *Religion in Human Evolution: From the Paleolithic to the Axial Age.* Cambridge, Mass.: Harvard University Press.

Bellwood, Peter. 1997. *Prehistory of the Indo-Malaysian Archipelago.* Honolulu: University of Hawai'i Press.

———. 2002. "Farmers, Foragers, Languages, Genes: The Genesis of Agricultural Societies." In *Examining the Farming/Language Dispersal Hypothesis*, ed. Peter Bellwood and Colin Renfrew. Cambridge: McDonald Institute for Archaeology. 17–28.

———. 2005. "Examining the Farming/Language Dispersal Hyothesis in the East Asian Context." In *The Peopling of East Asia: Putting Together Archaeology, Linguistics and Genetics*, ed. Laurent Sagart, Roger Blench, and Alicia Sanchez-Mazas. London: RoutledgeCurzon. 17–30.

———. 2009. "The Dispersals of Established Food-Producing Populations." *Current Anthropology* 50: 621–26.

Bellwood, Peter, and Colin Renfrew, eds. 2002. *Examining the Farming/Language Dispersal Hypothesis.* Cambridge: McDonald Institute for Archaeology.

Benedict, Carol. 1996. *Bubonic Plague in Nineteenth-Century China.* Stanford, Calif.: Stanford University Press.

Benedict, Paul K. 1975. *Austro-Tai Culture, with a Glossary of Roots.* New Haven, Conn.: HRAF Press.

Benn, James A. 2005. "Buddhism, Alcohol, and Tea in Medieval China." *Sterckx* 2005: 213–36.

Berger, Patricia. 1994. "The Ran Fangding." In *The Asian Art Museum of San Francisco: Selected Works*, ed. Asian Art Museum of San Francisco. Seattle: University of Washington Press. 86.

Berkes, Fikret. 2008. *Sacred Ecology.* 2nd ed. New York: Routledge.

Bettinger, Robert, Loukas Barton, Christopher Morgan, Fahu Chen, Hui Wang, Thomas P. Guilderson, Duxue Ji, and Dongju Zhang. 2010. "The Transition to Agriculture at Dadiwan, People's Republic of China." *Current Anthropology* 51: 703–14.

Billing, Jennifer, and Paul W. Sherman. 1998. "Antimicrobial Functions of Spices: Why Some Like It Hot." *Quarterly Review of Biology* 73: 3–49.

Biran, Michal. 2005. *The Empire of the Qara Khitai in Eurasian History: Between China and the Islamic World.* Cambridge: Cambridge University Press.

Birge, Bettine. 2002. *Women, Property, and Confucian Reaction in Sung and Yuan China (960–1368).* Cambridge: Cambridge University Press.

Birrell, Anne, trans. 1999. *The Classic of Mountains and Seas.* London: Penguin.

Blacker, Carmen. 1986. *The Catalpa Bow: A Study of Shamanism in Japan.* 2nd ed. London: Allen & Unwin.

Blench, Roger. 2005. "From the Mountains to the Valleys: Understanding Ethnolinguistic Geography in Southeast Asia." In *The Peopling of East Asia: Putting Together Archaeology, Linguistics and Genetics*, ed. Laurent Sagart, Roger Blench, and Alicia Sanchez-Mazas. London: RoutledgeCurzon. 31–50.

———. 2007. "Using Linguistics to Reconstruct African Subsistence Systems: Comparing Crop Names to Trees and Livestock." In *Rethinking Agriculture: Archaeological and Ethnoarchaeological Perspectives*, ed. Tim Denham, José Iriarte, and Luc Vrydaghs. Walnut Creek, Calif.: Left Coast Press. 408–38.

Bold, Sharav. 2009. *History and Development of Traditional Mongolian Medicine*. 2nd ed. Ulaanbaatar: Sharav Bold.

Bond, Michael, ed. 1986. *The Psychology of the Chinese People*. Oxford: Oxford University Press.

Bos, Gerrit. 2010. "Isaac Todros on Facial Paresis: Edition of the Hebrew Text with Introduction, English Translation and Glossary." *Korot* 20: 181–203.

Bosworth, C. E., and M. S. Asimov, eds. 2000. *History of Civilizations of Central Asia*. Vol. 4, *The Age of Achievement: A.D. 750 to the End of the Fifteenth Century*, Part 2, *The Achievements*. Paris: UNESCO.

Bouckaert, Remco, Philippe Lemey, Michael Dunn, Simon Greenhill, Alexander V. Alexeyenko, Alexei Drummond, Russell D. Gray, Mark A. Suchard, and Quentin D. Atkinson. 2012. "Mapping the Origins and Expansion of the Indo-European Language Family." *Science* 337: 957–60.

Branner, David Prager. 2011. "Phonology in the Chinese Script and Its Relationship to Early Chinese Literacy." In *Writing and Literacy in Early China: Studies from the Columbia Early China Seminar*, ed. Li Feng and David Prager Branner. Seattle: University of Washington Press. 85–137.

Brantingham, Jeffrey, and Gao Xing. 2006. "Peopling of the Northern Tibetan Plateau." *World Archaeology* 38: 387–414.

Bray, Francesca. 1984. *Science and Civilisation in China*. Vol. 6, *Biology and Biological Technology*, Part 2, *Agriculture*. Cambridge: Cambridge University Press.

Brite, Elizabeth Baker. 2011. "The Archaeology of the Aral Sea Crisis: Environmental Change and Human Adaptation in the Khorezm Region of Uzbekistan ca. AD 300–800." Ph.D. dissertation, Anthropology, UCLA.

Brite, Elizabeth B., and Ghairadin Khozhaniyazov. 2010. "Local and Global Patterns of Socio-Political Integration in Khorezm, Uzbekistan." Paper, Society for American Archaeology annual conference, St. Louis.

Brook, Timothy. 2010. *The Troubled Empire: China in the Yuan and Ming Dynasties*. Cambridge, Mass.: Harvard University Press.

Brown, Cecil. 2010. "Development of Agriculture in Prehistoric Mesoamerica: The Linguistic Evidence." In *Pre-Columbian Foodways: Interdisciplinary Approaches to Food, Culture, and Markets in Ancient Mesoamerica*, ed. John Staller and Michael Carrasco. New York: Springer. 71–108.

Buck, John Lossing. 1937. *Land Utilization in China*. Chicago: University of Chicago Press.

Budge, E. Wallis. 1913. *The Syriac Book of Medicines: Syrian Anatomy, Pathology and Therapeutics in the Early Middle Ages*. 2 vols. Oxford: Oxford University Press. Reprint Amsterdam: APA.-Philo Press, 1976.

———. 1928. *The Monks of Kublai Khan, Emperor of China*. London: Religious Tract Society.

Buell, Paul D. 2004. "Popoli e ciba della steppa." In *Atlante dell'alimentazione e della gastronomia*, ed. Massimo Montanari and Françoise Sabban. 2 vols. Torino: UTET. Vol. 1, 242–57.

———. 2012. "Qubilai and the Rats," *Sudhoffs Archiv* 96, 2 (December): 127–44.

Buell, Paul D., E. N. Anderson, and Charles Perry. 2010. *A Soup for the Qan*. 2nd ed. Leiden: Brill.

Buell, Paul D., and Ngan Le. 2006. "Globalization and Mongolia: Blessing or Curse?" In *Mongolian Culture and Society in the Age of Globalization*, ed. Henry G. Schwarz. Bellingham: Western Washington University Center for Asian Studies.

Callicott, J. Baird, and Roger T. Ames, eds. 1989. *Nature in Asian Traditions of Thought*. Albany, N.Y.: SUNY Press.

Campany, Robert. 2002. *To Live as Long as Heaven and Earth: A Translation and Study of Ge Hong's Traditions of Divine Transcendents*. Berkeley: University of California Press.

Campbell, Joseph. 1983. *The Way of the Animal Powers*. New York: Harper and Row.

Campbell, Roderick, Zhipeng Li, Yuling He, and Yuan Jing. 2011. "Consumption, Exchange, and Production at the Great Settlement Shang: Bone-working at Tiesanlu, Anyang." *Antiquity* 85: 1279–97.

Campbell, T. Colin with Thomas M. Campbell, II. 2005. *The China Study*. Dallas: Benbella Books.

Campbell, T. Colin, and Chen Junshi. 1994. "Diet and Chronic Degenerative Diseases: Perspectives from China." *American Journal of Clinical Nutrition* 59 (supplement): 1153S–61S.

Carneiro, Robert L. 1970. "A Theory of the Origin of the State." *Science* 169: 733–38.

———. 2012a. "Answers to Critiques." *Social Evolution and History* 11, 2: 131–90.

———. 2012b. "The Circumscription Theory: A Clarification, Amplification, and Reformulation." *Social Evolution and History* 11, 2: 5–30.

Carson, Rachel. 1962. *Silent Spring*. Boston: Houghton Mifflin.

Carswell, John. 2000. *Blue and White: Chinese Porcelain Around the World*. Chicago: Art Media Resources.

Carter, Thomas F. 1955. *The Invention of Printing in China and Its Spread Westward*. New York: Ronald Press.

Carver, Martin. 2011. "Editorial." *Antiquity* 239: 709–14.

Chandler, Paul. 1994. "*Shamu Jianzhong*: A Traditionally Derived Understanding of Agroforest Sustainability in China." *Journal of Sustainable Forestry* 1: 1–24.

Chang Chun-shu. 2007a. *The Rise of the Chinese Empire*. Vol. 1, *Nation, State, and Imperialism in Early China, ca. 1600 B.C.–A.D. 8*. Ann Arbor: University of Michigan Press.

———. 2007b. *The Rise of the Chinese Empire*. Vol. 2, *Frontier, Immigration, and Empire in Han China, 130 B.C.–157 A.D.* Ann Arbor: University of Michigan Press.

Chang, Kwang-chih. 1977. "Ancient China." In *Food in Chinese Culture*, ed. K.-C. Chang. New Haven, Conn.: Yale University Press. 23–52.

———. 1980. *Shang Civilization*. Cambridge, Mass.: Harvard University Press.

———. 1983. *Art, Myth, and Ritual: The Path to Political Authority in Ancient China*. Cambridge, Mass.: Harvard University Press.

———. 1999. "China on the Eve of the Historical Period." In *The Cambridge History of Ancient China*, ed. Michael Loewe and Edward Shaughnessy. Cambridge: Cambridge University Press. 37–73.

———. 2002a. "Epilogue 2." In *The Formation of Chinese Civilization: An Archaeological Perspective*, ed. Sarah Allan. New Haven, Conn.: Yale University Press. 289–94.

———. 2002b. "The Rise of Kings and the Formation of City-States." In *The Formation of Chinese Civilization: An Archaeological Perspective*, ed. Sarah Allan. New Haven, Conn.: Yale University Press. 125–40.

Chang, Kwang-chih, ed. 1977. *Food in Chinese Culture*. New Haven, Conn.: Yale University Press.

Chase-Dunn, Christopher, and E. N. Anderson, eds. 2005. *The Historical Development of World-Systems*. New York: Palgrave Macmillan.

Chase-Dunn, Christopher, Thomas Hall, and Peter Turchin. 2007. "World-Systems in the Biogeosphere: Urbanization, State Formation and Climate Change Since the Iron Age." In *The World*

System and the Earth System: Global Socioenvironmental Change and Sustainability Since the Neolithic, ed. Alf Hornborg and Carole Crumley. Walnut Creek, Calif.: Left Coast Press. 132–48.

Chaudhuri, K. N. 1985. Trade and Civilisation in the Indian Ocean: An Economic History from the Rise of Islam to 1750. Cambridge: Cambridge University Press.

Chen Junshi, T. Colin Campbell, Li Junyao, and Richard Peto. 1990. Diet, Life-Style, and Mortality in China: A Study of the Characteristics of 65 Chinese Counties. Ithaca, N.Y.: Cornell University Press.

Ch'en, Kuo-Tung. 1998. "Nonreclamation Deforestation in Taiwan, c. 1600–1976." In Sediments of Time: Environment and Society in Chinese History, ed. Mark Elvin and Liu Ts'ui-Jung. Cambridge: Cambridge University Press. 693–727.

Chen, Sanping. 2012. Multicultural China in the Early Middle Ages. Philadelphia: University of Pennsylvania Press.

Cheng, Libin. 1936. "Are the So-Called Poisonous Food Combinations Really Poisonous?" Contributions from the Biological Laboratory of the Science Society of China, Zoological Series 2, 9: 307–16.

Cheng Wing fun and Hervé Collet, eds. 1998. Dans la cuisine du poète taoïste. Millemont, France: Moundarren.

Cheung, Sidney, and Tan Chee-Beng. 2007. Food and Foodways in Asia: Resource, Tradition and Cooking. London: Routledge.

Chi, Zhang, and Hsiao-chun Hung. 2012. "Later Hunter-Gatherers in Southern China, 18,000–3000 BC." Antiquity 86: 11–29.

Chia, Lucille. 1996. "The Development of the Jianyang Book Trade, Song-Yuan." Late Imperial China 17:10–48.

———. 2002. Printing for Profit: The Commercial Publishers of Jianyang, Song-Ming. Cambridge, Mass.: Harvard University Press.

Childe, V. Gordon. 1954. What Happened in History. Harmondsworth: Penguin.

Chin, Tamara. 2010. "Defamiliarizing the Foreigner: Sima Qian's Ethnography and Han-Xiongnu Marriage Diplomacy." Harvard Journal of Asiatic Studies 70: 311–54.

Chindarsi, Nusit. 1975. The Religion of the Hmong Njua. Bangkok: Siam Society.

Chipman, Leigh. 2010. The World of Pharmacy and Pharmacists in Mamlūk Cairo. Leiden: Brill.

Chow, Kit, and Ione Kramer. 1990. All the Tea in China. San Francisco: China Books and Periodicals.

Christian, David. 2000. "Silk Roads or Steppe Roads?" Journal of World History 11: 1–26.

Clunas, Craig. 1996. Fruitful Sites: Garden Culture in Ming Dynasty China. Durham, N.C.: Duke University Press.

Cochran, Gregory, and Henry Harpending. 2009. The 10,000 Year Explosion: How Civilization Accelerated Human Evolution. New York: Basic Books.

Cohen, David Joel. 2011. "The Beginnings of Agriculture in China: A Multiregional View." Current Anthropology 52, Supplement 4: S273–S293.

Collins, Minta. 2000. Medieval Herbals: The Illustrative Traditions. London: British Library.

Conis, Elena. 2005. "White Tea Merits Further Research." Los Angeles Times, March 21, F3.

Conklin, Harold. 1957. Hanunoo Agriculture. Rome: FAO.

Craig, O. E., H. Saul, A Lucquin, Y. Nishida, K. Taché, L. Clarke, A. Thompson, D. T. Altoft, J. Uchiyama, M. Ajimoto, K. Gibbs, S. Isaksoon; C. P. Heron, and P. Jordan. 2013. "Earliest Evidence for the Use of Pottery." Nature 496: 351–54.

Crawford, Gary W. 2006. "East Asian Plant Domestication." In *Archaeology of Asia*, ed. Miriam T. Stark. Oxford: Blackwell. 77–95.

Crawford, Gary W., and Chen Shen. 1998. "The Origins of Rice Agriculture: Recent Progress in East Asia." *Antiquity* 72: 858–66.

Da Gen. 1988. "China's Oldest Dragon Figure." *China Reconstructs* (July): 48.

Dallal, Ahmad. 2010. *Islam, Science, and the Challenge of History*. New Haven, Conn.: Yale University Press.

Dalton, Rex. 2010. "Fossil Finger Points to New Human Species." *Nature* 464: 472–73.

Darlington, Susan M. 1998. "The Ordination of a Tree: The Buddhist Ecology Movement in Thailand." *Ethnology* 37: 1–15.

Davis, Richard L. 2009. "The Reign of Li-Tsung." In *The Cambridge History of China*, Vol. 5, *The Sung Dynasty and It Precursors, 907–1279*, ed. Denis Twitchett and Paul Jakov Smith. Cambridge: Cambridge University Press. 839–912.

Dawson, Christopher. 1955. *The Mongol Mission: Narratives and Letters of the Franciscan Missionaries in Mongolia and China in the Thirteenth and Fourteenth Centuries*. New York: Sheed and Ward.

De Rachewiltz, Igor. 2004. *The Secret History of the Mongols: A Mongolian Epic Chronicle of the Thirteenth Century*. Leiden: Brill.

Deng, Gang. 1997. *Chinese Maritime Activities and Socioeconomic Development c. 2100 B.C.-1900 A.D.* Westport, Conn.: Greenwood.

Deweese, Devin. 1994. *Islamization and Native Religion in the Golden Horde: Baba Tukles and Conversion to Islam in Historical and Epic Tradition*. State College: Pennsylvania State University Press.

Diamond, Jared. 1997. *Guns, Germs and Steel: The Fates of Human Societies*. New York: Norton.

———. 2005a. *Collapse: How Societies Choose to Fail or Succeed*. New York: Viking.

———. 2005b. "Geography and Skin Colour." *Nature* 435: 283–84.

Di Cosmo, Nicola. 1994. "Ancient Inner Asian Nomads: Their Economic Basis and Its Significance in Chinese History." *Journal of Asian Studies* 53: 1092–1126.

Di Cosmo, Nicola; Allen J. Frank; Peter B. Golden, eds.. 2009. *The Cambridge History of Inner Asia: The Chinggisid Age*. Cambridge: Cambridge University Press.

Dien, Albert. 2007. *Six Dynasties Civilization*. New Haven, Conn.: Yale University Press.

———. 2008. "The Tomb of the Sabao Wirkak." Talk, University of Washington-Seattle, April 24.

Dikötter, Frank, Lars Laamann, and Zhou Xun. 2002. *Narcotic Culture: A History of Drugs in China*. Chicago: University of Chicago Press.

Dols, Michael. l977. *The Black Death in the Middle East*. Princeton, N.J.: Princeton University Press.

———. 1984. *Medieval Islamic Medicine: Ibn Ridwān's Treatise "On the Prevention of Bodily Ills in Egypt."* Berkeley: University of California Press.

———. 1992. *Majnūn: The Madman in Medieval Islamic Society*. Oxford: Oxford University Press.

Donohue, Mark, and Tim Denham. 2010. "Farming and Language in Island Southeast Asia: Reframing Austroneisian History." *Current Anthropology* 51: 223–56.

Douglas, Mary. 1966. *Purity and Danger: An Analysis of Concepts of Purity and Taboo*. London: Routledge, Kegan Paul.

———. 1970. *Natural Symbols: Explorations in Cosmology*. New York: Pantheon.

Du Bois, Christine M., Chee-Beng Tan, and Sidney Mintz, eds. 2008. *The World of Soy*. Urbana: University of Illinois Press.

Dunstan, Helen. 1998. "Official Thinking on Environmental Issues and the State's Environmental Roles in Eighteenth-Century China." In *Sediments of Time: Environment and Society in Chinese History*, ed. Mark Elvin and Liu Ts'ui-Jung. Cambridge: Cambridge University Press. 585–614.

Durkheim, Emile. 1995 [1912]. *The Elementary Forms of Religious Life*. Trans. Karen E. Fields. New York: Free Press.

Ebrey, Patricia. 1978. *The Aristocratic Families of Early Imperial China: A Case Study of the Po-ling Ts'ui Family*. Cambridge: Cambridge University Press.

Elvin, Mark. 1973. *The Pattern of the Chinese Past*. Stanford, Calif.: Stanford University Press.

——. 2004a. *The Retreat of the Elephants: An Environmental History of China*. New Haven, Conn.: Yale University Press.

——. 2004b. "Vale Atque Ave." In *Science and Civilisation in China*, Vol. 7, part 2, *General Conclusions and Reflections*, ed. Joseph Needham et al. Cambridge: Cambridge University Press. xxiv–xliii.

Elvin, Mark, and Liu Ts'ui-Jung, eds. 1998. *Sediments of Time: Environment and Society in Chinese History*. Cambridge: Cambridge University Press.

Elvin, Mark, and Su Ninghu. 1998. "Action at a Distance: The Influence of the Yellow River on Hanzhou Bay Since A.D. 1000." In *Sediments of Time: Environment and Society in Chinese History*, ed. Mark Elvin and Liu Ts'ui-Jung. Cambridge: Cambridge University Press. 344–407.

Endicott-West, Elizabeth. 1994. "The Yuan Government and Society." In *The Cambridge History of China*, Vol. 6, *Alien Regimes and Border States, 907–1368*, ed. Herbert Franke and Denis Twitchett. Cambridge: Cambridge University Press. 587–615.

Engelhardt, Ute. 2001. "Dietetics in Tang China and the First Extant Works of *Materia dietetica*." In *Innovation in Chinese Medicine*, ed. Elisabeth Hsu. Cambridge: Cambridge University Press. 173–91.

Engelhardt, Ute, and Carl-Hermann Hempen. 1997. *Chinesische Diätetik*. Munich: Urban und Schwartzenberg.

Engels, Frederick. 1942 [1892]. *The Origin of the Family, Private Property and the State, in the Light of the Researches of Lewis H. Morgan*. New York: International.

Eren, Hasan. 1999. *Türk Dilinin Etimolojik Sözüğlü*. Ankara: Z. Baskı.

Falkenhausen, Lothar von. 1999. "The Waning of the Bronze Age." In *The Cambridge History of Ancient China*, ed. Michael Loewe and Edward Shaughnessy. Cambridge: Cambridge University Press. 450–544.

——. 2006. *Chinese Society in the Age of Confucius (1000–250 BC)*. Los Angeles: Cotsen Institute of Archaeology, University of California, Los Angeles.

——. 2011. "The Royal Audience and Its Reflections in Western Zhou Bronze Inscriptions." In *Writing and Literacy in Early China: Studies from the Columbia Early China Seminar*, ed. Li Feng and David Prager Branner. Seattle: University of Washington Press. 239–70.

Farquhar, Judith. 1993. *Knowing Practice: The Clinical Encounter of Chinese Medicine*. Boulder, Colo.: Westview.

Finnane, Antonia. 2004. *Speaking of Yangzhou: A Chinese City, 1550–1850*. Cambridge, Mass.: Harvard University Press.

Fischetti, Mark. 2006. "Protecting New Orleans." *Scientific American*, February, 65–71.

Fitzgerald, C. P. 1965. *Barbarian Beds: The Origin of the Chair in China*. South Brunswick, N.J.: A.S. Barnes.

Fitzhugh, William, and Chisato O. Dubreuil, eds. 1999. *Ainu: Spirit of a Northern People*. Washington, D.C.: Smithsonian Institution with University of Washington Press.

Flad, Rowan K. 2008. "Divination and Power: A Multiregional View of the Development of Oracle Bone Divination in Early China." *Current Anthropology* 49: 403–37.

Foucault, Michel. 2008. *The Birth of Biopolitics*. Ed. Michel Senellart, trans. Graham Burchell. New York: Palgrave MacMillan.

Frachetti, Michael D. 2008. *Pastoralist Landscapes and Social Interaction in Bronze Age Eurasia*. Berkeley: University of California Press.

———. 2012. "Multiregional Emergence of Mobile Pastoralism and Nonuniform Institutional Complexity Across Eurasia." *Current Anthropology* 53: 2–38.

Frachetti, Michael D., Robert N. Spengler, Gayle J. Fritz, and Alexei N. Mar'yashev. 2010. "Earliest Direct Evidence for Broomcorn Millet and Wheat in the Central Eurasian Steppe Region." *Antiquity* 84, 326: 993–1010.

Franke, Herbert, and Denis Twitchett, eds. 1994. *The Cambridge History of China*. Vol. 6, *Alien Regimes and Border States, 907–1368*. Cambridge: Cambridge University Press.

Freeman, Michael. 1977. "Sung." In *Food in Chinese Culture*, ed. K.-C. Chang. New Haven, Conn.: Yale University Press. 141–92.

Freyre, Gilberto. 1964. *The Masters and the Slaves (Casa Grande e Senzala): A Study in the Development of Brazilian Civilization*. Trans. Samuel Putnam. New York: Knopf.

Fried, Daniel. 2007. "A Never-Stable Word: Zhuangzi's *Zhiyan* and 'Tipping-Vessel' Irrigation" *Early China* 31: 145–70.

Fuller, Dorian Q., Ling Qin, Yunfei Sheng, Shijun Zhao, Xugao Chen, Leo Aoi Hosoya, and Guoping Sun. 2009. "The Domestication Process and Domestication Rate in Rice: Spikelet Bases from the Lower Yangtze." *Science* 323: 1607–10.

Furth, Charlotte. 1999. *A Flourishing Yin*. Berkeley: University of California Press.

Galen. 2003. *Galen on the Properties of Foodstuffs*. Trans. Owen Powell. Oxford: Oxford University Press.

Gamuyao, Rico, Joong Hyoun Chin, Juan Pariasca-Tanaka, Paolo Pesaresi, Sheryl Catausan, Cheryl Dalid, Inez Slamet-Loedin; Evelyn Mae Tecson-Mendoza; Matthias Wissuwa; Sigrid Heuer. 2012. "The Protein Kinase Pstol1 from Traditional Rice confers Tolerance of Phosphorus Deficiency." *Nature* 488: 535–39.

Gaukroger, Stephen. 2006. *The Emergence of a Scientific Culture: Science and the Shaping of Modernity 1210–1685*. Oxford: Oxford University Press.

Geddes, W. R. 1976. *Migrants of the Mountains: The Cultural Ecology of the Blue Miao (Hmong Njua) of Thailand*. Oxford: Oxford University Press.

Geertz, Clifford. 1963. *Agricultural Involution*. Berkeley: University of California Press.

Gibbons, Ann. 2000. "Chinese Stone Tools Reveal High-Tech *Homo erectus*." *Science* 287: 1566.

———. 2011a. "New View of the Birth of *Homo sapiens*." *Science* 331: 392–94.

———. 2011b. "Who Were the Denisovans?" *Science* 333: 1084–87.

Gignoux, Christopher, Brenna Henn, and Joanna Mountain. 2011. "Rapid, Global Demographic Expansions after the Origins of Agriculture." *Proceedings of the National Academy of Sciences* 108: 6044–49.

Giles, Herbert A. 1923. *Gems of Chinese Literature*. Shanghai: Kelly and Walsh.

Girardot, N. J., James Miller, and Liu Xiaogan, eds. 2001. *Daoism and Ecology: Ways Within a Cosmic Landscape*. Cambridge, Mass.: Harvard University Press.

Glover, Denise. 2005. "Up from the Roots: Contextualizing Medicinal Plant Classifications of Tibetan Doctors in Rgyalthang, PRC." Ph.D. dissertation, Department of Anthropology, University of Washington.

Golas, Peter J. 1999. *Science and Civilisation in China*. Vol. 5, *Chemistry and Chemical Technology*, Part 13, *Mining*. Cambridge: Cambridge University Press.

Golden, Peter B. 1994. "Chopsticks and Pasta in Medieval Turkic Cuisine." *Rocznik Orientalistyczny* 44: 73–82.

Gorshunova, Olga. 2012. "Pray, Howl and Take My Power: Sacred Images and Nature Cult in Central Asian Islam." Presentation, International Society for the Study of Religion, Nature and Culture, Malibu, California, August 9.

Graham, A. C. 1958. *Two Chinese Philosophers: Ch'eng Ming-tao and Ch'eng Yi-ch'uan*. London: Lund Humphries.

———. 1960. *The Book of Lieh-tzu*. London: John Murray.

———. 1981. *Chuang Tzu: The Inner Chapters*. London: Allen & Unwin.

———. 1989. *Disputers of the Tao*. La Salle, Ill.: Open Court.

GRAIN (Genetic Resources Action International). 2005. "Fiasco in the Field: An Update on Hybrid Rice in Asia." www.grain.org, January 13, 2013.

Gross, John. 1983. *The Oxford Book of Aphorisms*. Oxford: Oxford University Press.

Gunther, Robert T. 1934. *The Greek Herbal of Dioscorides*. Oxford: Oxford University Press.

Guo Xi. 2005. "Advice on Landscape." Trans. John Hay, Victor H. Mair, Susan Bush, and Hsio-yen Shih. *In Hawai'i Reader in Traditional Chinese Culture*, ed. Victor Mair, Nancy Steinhardt, and Paul R. Goldin. Honolulu: University of Hawai'i Press. 380–87.

Gwinner, Thomas. 1988. *Essen und Trinken: Die Klassischer Kochbuchliteratur Chinas*. Heidelberg: Haag und Herchen.

Hames, Raymond. 2007. "The Ecologically Noble Savage Debate." *Annual Review of Anthropology* 36: 177–90.

Hamilton, Roy W. 2003. *The Art of Rice: Spirit and Sustenance in Asia*. Los Angeles: UCLA Fowler Museum of Cultural History.

Hansen, Valerie. 2012. *Silk Road: A New History*. New York: Oxford University Press.

Harbsmeier, Christoph. 1998. *Science and Civilisation in China*, Vol. 7, part 1, *Language and Logic*. Cambridge: Cambridge University Press.

Harington, John, trans. 1966 [ca. 1600]. *The School of Salernum*. Salerno: Ente Provinciale per il Turismo.

Harmatta, Janos, B. N. Puri, and G. F. Etemadi, eds. 1994. *History of Civilizations of Central Asia*. Vol. 2, *The Development of Sedentary and Nomadic Civilizations: 700 BC to AD 250*. Paris: UNESCO.

Harper, Donald. 1998. *Early Chinese Medical Literature: The Mawangdui Manuscripts*. London: Kegan Paul International.

Harrell, Barbara B. 1981. "Lactation and Menstruation in Cultural Perspective." *American Anthropologist* 83: 796–823.

Harris, David R. 2010. *Origins of Agriculture in Western Central Asia: An Environmental-Archaeological Study*. Philadelphia: University of Pennsylvania Museum of Archaeology and Anthropology.

Hartwell, Robert. 1962. "A Revolution in the Chinese Iron and Coal Industries During the Northern Sung, 960–1126 A.D." *Journal of Asian Studies* 21: 153–62.

———. 1982. "Demographic, Political, and Social Transformations of China, 750–1550." *Harvard Journal of Asian Studies* 42: 365–442.

Harvey, Graham. 2006. *Animism: Respecting the Living World*. New York: Columbia University Press.

Haw, Stephen. 2006. *Marco Polo's China: A Venetian in the Realm of Khubilai Khan*. London: Routledge.

———. 2008. *The Mongol Unification of China*. London: Routledge.

Hayami, Yujiro, and Vernon Ruttan. 1985. *Agricultural Development*. 2nd ed. Baltimore: Johns Hopkins University Press.

Hayden, Brian, ed. 2001. *Feasts: Archaeological and Ethnological Perspectives on Food, Politics and Power*. Washington, D.C.: Smithsonian Institution Press.

Hennessey, William O. 1981. *Proclaiming Harmony*. Ann Arbor: Center for Chinese Studies, University of Michigan.

Henricks, Robert G. 1989. *Lao-Tzu Te-Tao Ching: A New Translation Based on the Recently Discovered Ma-wang-tui Texts*. New York: Ballantine.

Heritage Daily. 2012. "Archaeologists Uncover Paleolithic Ceramic Art." www.heritagedaily.com, July 26.

Higham, Charles, and Tracey L.-D. Lu. 1998. "The Origins and Dispersal of Rice Cultivation." *Antiquity* 72: 867–77.

Hill, D. R. 2000. "Physics and Mechanics: Civil and Hydraulic Engineering, Industrial Processes and Manufacturing, and Craft Activities." In *History of Civilizations of Central Asia*, Vol. 4, *The Age of Achievement: A.D. 750 to the End of the Fifteenth Century*, Part 2, *The Achievements*, ed. C. E. Bosworth and M. S. Asimov. Paris: UNESCO. 249–74.

Hill, John E. 2009. "Through the Jade Gate to Rome: A Study of the Silk Routes During the Later Han Dynasty, 1st to 2nd Centuries CE." N.p.: John E. Hill.

Hillman, Gordon. 2003. "Investigating the Start of Cultivation in Western Eurasia: Studies of Plant Remains from Abu Hureyra on the Euphrates." In *The Widening Harvest: The Neolithic Transition in Europe—Looking Back, Looking Forward*, ed. Albert J. Ammerman and Paolo Biagi. Boston: American Institute of Archaeology. 75–98.

Hippocrates, et al. 1978. *Hippocratic Writings*. London: Penguin.

Ho Ping-ti. 1955. "The Introduction of American Food Plants into China." *American Anthropologist* 57: 191–201.

Hohenegger, Beatrice, ed. 2009. *Steeped in History: The Art of Tea*. Los Angeles: Fowler Musuem at UCLA.

Hohenstaufen, Frederick, II. 1943. *The Art of Falconry*. Trans. Casey Wood and F. Marjorie Fyfe. Stanford, Calif.: Stanford University Press.

Holm, David. 1999. "Culinary Culture in Guangxi." Paper, Sixth Symposium on Chinese Dietary Culture, Fuzhou.

———, ed. 2009. *Regionalism and Globalism in Chinese Culinary Culture*. Taipei: Foundation of Chinese Dietary Culture.

Hommel, Rudolf. 1937. *China at Work*. New York: John Day.

Honeychurch, William, and Chunag Amartuvshin. 2006. "States on Horseback: The Rise of Inner Asian Confederations and Empires." In *Archaeology of Asia*, ed. Miriam Stark. Oxford: Blackwell. 255–78.

Hopkins, J. F. P. 1990. "Geographical and Navigational Literature." In *Religion, Learning and Science in the 'Abbasid Period*, ed. M. J. L. Young, J. D. Latham, and R. B. Serjeant. Cambridge: Cambridge University Press. 301–27.

Hotz, Robert Lee. 2000. "Stone Axes Suggest Diversity's Dawn." *Los Angeles Times*, March 3, A24.

Hsu, Cho-yun, and Kathryn Linduff. 1988. *Western Chou Civilization*. New Haven, Conn.: Yale University Press.

Hsu, Elisabeth. 1999. *The Transmission of Chinese Medicine*. Cambridge Studies in Medical Anthropology 7. Cambridge: Cambridge University Press.

———, ed. 2001. *Innovation in Chinese Medicine*. Cambridge: Cambridge University Press.

Hsu, Hong-yen, and William Peacher, trans. and eds. 1981. *Shang Han Lun, the Great Classic of Chinese Medicine*. Los Angeles: Oriental Healing Arts Institute.

Hsu Shin-Yi. 1969. "The Cultural Ecology of the Locust Cult in Traditional China." *Annals of the Association of American Geographers* 59: 731–52.

Hu Shiu-Ying. 2005. *Food Plants of China*. Hong Kong: Hong Kong University Press.

Huang, H. T. 2000. *Science and Civilisation in China*. Vol. 6, *Biology and Biological Technology*, Part 5, *Fermentations and Food Science*. Cambridge: Cambridge University Press.

Huang, Shih-shan Susan. 2012. *Picturing the True Form: Daoist Visual Culture in Traditional China*. Cambridge, Mass.: Harvard University Press.

Huang Shu-min. 2005. "The Articulation of Culture: Agriculture and the Environment of Chinese in Northern Thailand." *Ethnology* 44: 1–12.

Huang, Xuehui, Nori Kurata, Xinghua Wei, Zi-Xuan Wang, Ahong Wang, Qiang Zhao, Yan Zhao, Kunyan Liu, Hengyun Lu, Wenjun Li, Yunli Guo, Yiqi Lu, Congcong Zhou, Danlin Fan, Qijun Weng, Chanrang Zhu, Tao Huang, Lei Zhang, Yongchun Wang, Lei Feng, Hiroyasu Furuumi; Takahiko Kubo, Toshie Miyabayashi, Xiaoping Yuan, Qun Xu, Guojun Dong, Qilin Zhan; Canyang Li, Asao Fujiyama, Atsushi Toyoda, Tingting Lu; Qi Feng,Qian Qian, Hayang Li, and Bin Han. 2012. "A Map of Rice Genome Variation Reveals the Origin of Cultivated Rice." *Nature* 490: 497–501.

Huber, Toni. 1999. *The Cult of Pure Crystal Mountain*. New York: Oxford University Press.

Humphrey, Caroline, with Urgunge Onon. 1996. *Shamans and Elders: Experience, Knowledge, and Power Among the Daur Mongols*. Oxford: Oxford University Press.

Hunn, Eugene. 1990. *Nch'i-Wana, the Big River*. Seattle: University of Washington Press.

Hvistendahl, Mara. 2012. "Roots of Empire." *Science* 337: 1596–99.

Ibn Battuta. 1959. *The Travels of Ibn Battuta*. Vol. 2. Trans. Sir Hamilton Gibb. Hakluyt Society 2nd ser. 117. Cambridge: Cambridge University Press for Hakluyt Society.

Ibn Khaldun. 1958. *The Muqaddimah*. Trans. Franz Rosenthal. New York: Pantheon.

Idema, Wilt, and Beata Grant. 2004. *The Red Brush*. Cambridge, Mass.: Harvard University Press.

Itoh, Teiji. 1973. *Kura: Design and Tradition of the Japanese Storehouse*. Tokyo: Kodansha.

Jackson, Peter. 2005. *The Mongols and the West*. London: Pearson Education.

Jagchid, Sechin, and Van Jay Simons. 1989. *Peace, War, and Trade Along the Great Wall: Nomadic-Chinese Interaction Through Two Millennia*. Bloomington: Indiana University Press.

Jaramillo, Cleofas. 1981 [1942]. *The Genuine New Mexico Tasty Recipes*. Santa Fe: Ancient City Press.

Jia Ming. 1969. *Yinshi Xuzhi*. Taipei: Jin Guo Ming Da.

Jia, Peter Wei-Ming, Alison Betts, and Xinhua Wu. 2011. "New Evidence for Bronze Age Agricultural Settlements in the Zhunge'er (Jungfgar) Basin, China." *Journal of Field Archaeology* 36: 269–80.

Jiang, Leping, and Li Liu. 2006. "New Evidence for the Origins of Sedentism and Rice Domestication in the Lower Yangzi River, China." *Antiquity* 80: 355–61.

Jin Qicong. 1995. "Jurchen Literature Under the Chin." In *China Under Jurchen Rule: Essays on Chin Intellectual and Cultural History*. Albany, N.Y.: SUNY Press. 216–38.

Jing, Yuan, and Rod Campbell. 2009. "Recent Archaeometric Research on 'the Origins of Chinese Civilisation.'" *Antiquity* 83: 96–109.

Jing, Yuan, and Rowan K. Flad. 2002. "Pig Domestication in Ancient China." *Antiquity* 76: 724–32.

Johnson, David. 1977. *The Medieval Chinese Oligarchy*. Boulder, Colo.: Westview.

———. 2009. *Spectacle and Sacrifice: The Ritual Foundations of Village Life in North China*. Cambridge, Mass.: Harvard University Asia Center.

Juvaini, 'Ata-Malik. 1958. *The History of the World-Conqueror*. Trans. J. A. Boyle. 2 vols. Cambridge, Mass.: Harvard University Press.

Kadoi, Yuka. 2009. *Islamic Chinoiserie: The Art of Mongol Iran*. Edinburgh: Edinburgh University Press.

Kahneman, Daniel. 2011. *Thinking, Fast and Slow*. New York: Farrar, Straus.

Karlgren, Bernhard. 1950. *The Book of Odes*. Stockholm: Museum of Far Eastern Antiquities.

Kasai, N., and S. Natsagdorj. 1998. "Socio-Economic Development: Food and Clothing in Eastern Iran and Central Asia." In *History of Civilizations of Central Asia*, Vol. 4, *The Age of Achievement: A.D. 750 to the End of the Fifteenth Century*, Part 1, *The Historical, Social and Economic Setting*, ed. M. S. Asimov and C. E. Bosworth. Paris: UNESCO. 381–90.

Kay, Charles E., and Randy T. Simmons, eds. 2002. *Wilderness and Political Ecology: Aboriginal Influences and the Original State of Nature*. Salt Lake City: University of Utah Press.

Kearney, Michael. 1984. *Worldview*. Novato, Calif.: Chandler and Sharp.

Keightley, David. 1999. "The Shang: China's First Historical Dynasty." In *The Cambridge History of Ancient China*, ed. Michael Loewe and Edward Shaughnessy. Cambridge: Cambridge University Press. 232–91.

———. 2000. *The Ancestral Landscape: Time, Space, and Community in Late Shang China (ca. 1200–1045 B.C.)*. Berkeley: University of California Press.

———. 2006. "Marks and Labels: Early Writing in Neolithic and Shang China." In *Archaeology of Asia*, ed. Miriam Stark. Oxford: Blackwell. 177–201.

Kendall, Laurel. 1985. *Shamans, Housewives, and Other Restless Spirits: Women in Korean Ritual Life*. Honolulu: University of Hawai'i Press.

Kenin-Lopsan, Mongush B. 1997. *Shamanic Songs and Myths of Tuva*. Ed. and trans. Mihály Hoppál. Budapest: Akadémiai Kiadó.

Kerr, Rose, and Nigel Wood. 2004. *Science and Civilisation in China*. Vol. 5, *Chemistry and Chemical Technology*. Part 12, *Ceramic Technology*. Cambridge: Cambridge University Press.

Khamsi, Roxanne. 2004. "Prehistoric Dregs Pack a Punch." *Nature* online, December 6.

Kazanov, A. M. 1984. *Nomads and the Outside World*. 2nd ed. Trans. Julia Crookenden. Cambridge: Cambridge University Press.

Kieschnick, John. 2005. "Buddhist Vegetarianism in China." *Sterckx 2005*: 186–213.

Kim Bok-rae. 2009. "Chinese Cuisine in Korean Dining-Out Culture." In *Regionalism and Globalism in Chinese Culinary Culture*, ed. David Holm. Taipei: Foundation of Chinese Dietary Culture. 285–398.

Kim Chun Ho. 1999. "On the Exchange and Comparison of the Confucian Dietary Culture Between Korea, China and Japan." Paper, Sixth Symposium on Chinese Dietary Culture, Fuzhou.

Kim, Kijeung, Charles H. Brenner, Victor Mair, et al. 2010. "A Western Eurasian Male Is Found in 2000-Year-Old Elite Xiongnu Cemetery in Northeast Mongolia." *American Journal of Physical Anthropology* 142, 3: 429–40.

Kim, Seung-Ok. 1994. "Burials, Pigs, and Political Prestige in Neolithic China." *Current Anthropology* 35: 119–41.

Kimata, Mikio. 2012. "Domestication of *Panicum miliaceum* L." Poster presentation, International Society of Ethnobiology Conference, Montpellier, France.

King, F. H. 1911. *Farmers of Forty Centuries*. New York: Mrs. F. H. King.

Kitayama, Shinobu, and Dov Cohen, eds. 2007. *Handbook of Cultural Psychology*. New York: Guilford.

Klee, Gary, ed. 1980. *World Systems of Traditional Resource Management*. New York: V.H. Winston.

Kleinman, Arthur, Peter Kunstadter, E. Russell Alexander, and James E. Gale, eds. 1975. *Medicine in Chinese Cultures*. Washington, D.C.: U.S. Dept. of Health, Education and Welfare.

Knauer, Elfriede Regia. 1998. *The Camel's Load in Life and Death: Iconography and Ideology of Chinese Pottery Figurines from Han to Tang and Their Relevance to Trade Along the Silk Routes*. Zürich: Akanthus Verlag für Archäologie.

Knechtges, David R. 1986. "A Literary Feast: Food in Early Chinese Literature." *Journal of the American Oriental Society* 106: 49–63.

Kochian, Leon V. 2012. "Rooting for More Phosphorus." *Nature* 488: 466–67.

Kohl, Philip L. 2007. *The Making of Bronze Age Eurasia*. Cambridge: Cambridge University Press.

Kohn, Livia. 2005. *Health and Long Life*. Cambridge, Mass.: Three Pines Press.

Komaroff, Linda, ed. 2006. *Beyond the Legacy of Genghis Khan*. Leiden: Brill.

Komaroff, Linda, and Stefano Carboni. 2002. *The Legacy of Genghis Khan: Courtly Art and Culture in Western Asia, 1256–1353*. New York: Metropolitan Museum of Art.

Kong, Y. C., ed. 1996. *Huihui Yaofang*. Hong Kong: Y. C. Kong.

Kong, Y. C., and D. S. Chen. 1996. "Elucidation of Islamic Drugs in Hui Hui Yao Fang: A Linguistic and Pharmaceutical Approach." *Journal of Ethnopharmacology* 54: 85–102; reprinted in *Huihui Yaofang*, ed. Y. C. Kong. Hong Kong: Chinese University of Hong Kong Press.

Kong, Y. C., P. S. Kwan, P. H. But, A. Ulubelen, and Y. Aneychi. 1996. "A Botanical and Pharmacognostic Account of *Hui Hui Yao Fang*, the Islamic Formulary." In *Huihui Yaofang*, ed. Y. C. Kong. Hong Kong: Chinese University of Hong Kong Press. Reprinted from *Hamdard* 31, 1 (1988): 3–34.

Kouymjian, Dickran. 2006. "Chinese Motifs in Thirteenth-Century Armenian Art: The Mongol Connection." In *Beyond the Legacy of Genghis Khan*, ed. Linda Komaroff. Leiden: Brill. 303–24.

Krause, Johannes, Quiaomei Fu, Jeffrey M. Good, Bence Viola, Michael V. Shunkov, Anatoli P. Derevianko, and Svante Pääbo. 2010. "The Complete Mitochondrial DNA Genome of an Unknown Hominin from Southern Siberia." *Nature* 464: 894–89.

Kuhn, Dieter. 2009. *The Age of Confucian Rule: The Song Transformation of China*. Cambridge, Mass.: Harvard University Press.

Kuhn, Thomas. 1962. *The Structure of Scientific Revolutions*. Chicago: University of Chicago Press.

Kuzmin, Yaroslav. 2008a. "Lord Avebury's Virtual Journey Through Time." *Review of Archaeology* 28: 72–83.

———. 2008b. "Pottery and Agriculture in the Terminal Pleistocene-Middle Holocene of Northeast Asia; Peculiarities of Spatial-Temporal Relationship." Paper, Society for American Archaeology annual meeting, Vancouver.

Kuzmin, Yaroslav, Charles T. Keally, A. J. Timothy Jull, George S. Burr, and Nikolai A. Klyuev. 2012. "The Earliest Surviving Textiles in East Asia from Chertovy Vorota Cave, Primorye Province, Russian Far East." *Antiquity* 86: 325–37.

Lamouroux, Christian. 1998. "From the Yellow River to the Huai." In *Sediments of Time: Environment and Society in Chinese History*, ed. Mark Elvin and Liu Ts'ui-Jung. Cambridge: Cambridge University Press. 545–84.

Lane, George. 2003. *Early Mongol Rule in Thirteenth Century Iran*. London: RoutledgeCurzon.

———. 2006. *Daily Life in the Mongol Period*. Westport, Conn.: Greenwood.

Langham, Nigel. 1980. "Breeding Biology of the Edible-Nest Swiftlet *Aerodramus fuciphagus*." *Ibis* 122: 447–61.

Larson, Gregor, Ranran Liu, Xingobo Zhao, Jing Yuan, Dorian Fuller, Loukas Barton, Keith Dobney, et al. 2010. "Patterns of East Asian Pig Domestication, Migration, and Turnover Revealed by Modern and Ancient DNA." *Proceedings of the National Academy of Sciences* 107: 7686–91.

Lattimore, Owen. 1940. *Inner Asian Frontiers of China*. New York: American Geographical Society.

Laufer, Berthold. 1919. *Sino-Iranica*. Chicago: Field Museum.

Lawler, Andrew. 2009. "Beyond the Yellow River: How China Became China." *Science* 325: 930–43.

———. 2012. "Persians Made the Afghan Desert Bloom." *Science* 337: 289.

Lee, Gyoung-Ah. 2007. "Crop Evolution, Human-Environment Interactions, and Politics of Food in Early East Asia." Talk, February 27, University of Washington, Seattle.

Lee, Gyoung-Ah, Li Liu, Gary Crawford, and Xingcan Chen. 2008. "Origins of Soybean in East Asia: Comparative, Interdisciplinary Perspectives." Paper, Society for American Archaeology annual meeting, Vancouver.

Legge, James, trans. and ed.. 2008 [1885]. *The Li Chi, or Book of Rites*. 2 vols. (author wrongly given on title page as "K'ung-fu [sic] Tzu"). Hong Kong: Forgotten Books.

Lerro, Bruce. 2000. *From Earth Spirits to Sky Gods: The Socioecological Origins of Monotheism, Individualism, and Hyperabstract Reasoning from the Stone Age to the Axial Iron Age*. Lanham, Md.: Lexington Books.

Lev, Eraim, and Zohar Amar. 2008. *Practical Materia Medica of the Medieval Eastern Mediterranean According to the Cairo Genizah*. Leiden: Brill.

Levey, Martin. 1966. *The Medical Formulary or Aqrābādhīn of Al-Kindī*. Madison: University of Wisconsin Press.

Levey, Martin, and Noury Al-Khaledy. 1967. *The Medical Formulary of Al-Samarqandī*. Philadelphia: University of Pennsylvania Press.

Levin, Theodore. 1996. *The One Hundred Thousand Fools of God*. Bloomington: Indiana University Press.

Levine, Ari Daniel. 2009. "The Reigns of Hui-tsung (1100–1126) and Ch'in-tsung (1126–1127) and the Fall of Northern Sung." In *The Cambridge History of China*, Vol. 5, *The Sung Dynasty and It Precursors, 907–1279*, ed. Denis Twitchett and Paul Jakov Smith. Cambridge: Cambridge University Press.

Levine, Marsha, Colin Renfrew, and Katie Boyle, eds. 2003. *Prehistoric Steppe Adaptations and the Horse*. Cambridge: McDonald Institute for Archaeological Research.

Lewis, Mark Edward. 2006. *The Construction of Space in Early China*. Albany, N.Y.: SUNY Press.

———. 2007. *The Early Chinese Empires: Qin and Han*. Cambridge, Mass.: Harvard University Press.

———. 2009a. *China Between Empires: The Northern and Southern Dynasties*. Cambridge, Mass.: Harvard University Press.

———. 2009b. *China's Cosmopolitan Empire: The Tang Dynasty*. Cambridge, Mass.: Harvard University Press.

Li Bozhong. 1998. *Agricultural Development in Jiangnan, 1620–1850*. New York: St. Martin's.

———. 2003. "Was There a 'Fourteenth-Century Turning Point?'" In *The Song-Yuan-Ming Transition in Chinese History*, ed. Paul Jakov Smith and Richard von Glahn. Cambridge, Mass.: Harvard University Asia Center. 135–75.

Li Feng. 2006. *Landscape and Power in Early China: The Crisis and Fall of the Western Zhou, 1045–771 BC*. Cambridge: Cambridge University Press.

———. 2008. *Bureaucracy and the State in Early China: Governing the Western Zhou*. Cambridge: Cambridge University Press.

Li Feng, and David Prager Branner. 2011. *Writing and Literacy in early China: Studies from the Columbia Early China Seminar*. Seattle: University of Washington Press.

Li Feng, Xing Gao, Fuyou Chen, Shuwen Pei, Yue Zhang, Xiaoling Zhang, Decheng Liu, Shuangquan Zhang, Ying Guan, Huimin Wang, and Steven L. Kuhn. 2013. "The Development of Upper Palaeolithic China: New Results from the Shuidonggou Site." *Antiquity* 87, 336: 368–83.

Li Hui-Lin. 1977. "Hallucinogenic Plants in Chinese Herbals." Harvard Botanical Museum Leaflets 25, 6: 161–81.

———. 1979. *Nan-fang Tsao-mu Chuang, A Fourth Century Flora of Southeast Asia*. Hong Kong: Chinese University of Hong Kong.

Li, Jun Z., Devin M. Absher, Hua Tang, Audrey M. Southwick, Amanda M. Casto, Sohini Ramachandran, Howard M. Cann, Gregory S. Barsh, Marcus Feldman, Luigi L. Cavalli-Sforza, and Richard M. Myers. 2008. "Worldwide Human Relationships Inferred from Genome-Wide Patterns of Variation." *Science* 319: 1100–1104.

Li, Lillian. 2007. *Fighting Famine in North China: State, Market, and Environmental Decline, 1690s-1990s*. Stanford, Calif.: Stanford University Press.

Li Linna, chief ed. 2007. *Treasures from the Museum of the Nanyue King*. Guangzhou: comp. Museum of the Nanyue King, published by Cultural Relics Press.

Li Min. 2012. "Storytellers in Bronze Age China." Talk, UCLA, January 7.

Li Shizhen. 2003 [1593]. *Compendium of Materia Medica (Bencao Gangmu)*. Beijing: Foreign Language Press.

Li, Wenjun, and Lynn Huntsinger. 2011. "China's Grassland Contract Policy and Its Impacts on Herder Ability to Benefit in Inner Mongolia: Tragic Feedbacks." *Ecology and Society* 16, 2, article 1.

Li, Xiaoqiang, Nan Sun, John Dodson, Zinying Zhou, and Keliang Zhao. 2013. "Vegetation Characteristics in the Western Loess Plateau Between 5200 and 4300 cal. B.P. Based on Fossil Charcoal Records." *Vegetation History and Archaeobotany* 22: 61–70.

Lieberman, Victor. 2003. *Strange Parallels: Southeast Asia in Global Context, c. 800–1830*. Vol. 1: *Integration on the Mainland*. Cambridge: Cambridge University Press.

———. 2009. *Strange Parallels: Southeast Aisa in Global Context, c. 800–1830*. Vol 2: *Mainland Mirrors: Europe, Japan, China, South Asia, and the Islands*. Cambridge: Cambridge University Press.

Liu An. 2010. *Huainanzi*. Trans. and ed. John Major, Sarah Queen, Andrew Seth Mayer, and Harold D. Roth. New York: Columbia University Press.

Liu Li. 2004. *The Chinese Neolithic*. Cambridge: Cambridge University Press.

———. 2012. "Archaeology Under the Microscope." Lecture, Fowler Museum of UCLA, January 6.

Liu, Li, Sheahan Bestel, Jinmin Shi, Yanhua Song, and Xingcan Shen. 2013. "Paleolithic Human Exploitation of Plant Foods During the Last Glacial Maximum in North China." *Proceedings of the National Academy of Sciences* 110: 5380–85.

Liu, Li, Judith Field, Richard Fullagar, Sheahan Bestel, Xingcan Chen, and Xiaolin Ma. 2010. "What Did Grinding Stones Grind? New Light on Early Neolithic Subsistence Economy in the Middle Yellow River Valley, China." *Antiquity* 84: 816–33.

Liu, Shu-fen. 2006. "Between Self-cultivation and the Monastic Code: Tea and Medicinal Soup in

Tang and Song Monastic Life." *Bulletin of the Institute of History and Philology, Academia Sinica* (Taiwan), September.

Liu, Xinru, and Lynda Norene Shaffer. 2007. *Connections Across Eurasia: Transportation, Communication, and Cultural Exchange on the Silk Route.* Boston: McGraw-Hill.

Liu, Xinyi, Harriet V. Hunt, and Martin K. Jones. 2009. "River Valleys and Foothills: Changing Archaeological Perceptions of North China's Earliest Farms." *Antiquity* 83: 82–95.

Lloyd, Geoffrey. 1996. *Adversaries and Authorities.* Cambridge: Cambridge University Press.

———. 2002. *The Ambitions of Curiosity: Understanding the World in Ancient Greece and China.* Cambridge: Cambridge University Press.

———. 2007. *Cognitive Variations: Reflections on the Unity and Diversity of the Human Mind.* Oxford: Oxford University Press.

Lo, Vivienne. 2001. "The Influence of Nurturing Life Culture on the Development of Western Han Acumoxa Therapy." In *Innovation in Chinese Medicine*, ed. Elizabeth Hsu. Cambridge: Cambridge University Press. 19–50.

———. 2005. "Pleasure, Prohibition, and Pain: Food and Medicine in Traditional China." *Sterckx* 2005: 163–85.

Lo, Vivienne, and Jenny Lo. 2003. *Secrets from a Chinese Kitchen.* London: Pavilion Books.

Lü Buwei. 2000. *The Annals of Lü Buwei.* Trans. John Knoblock and Jeffrey Riegel. Stanford, Calif.: Stanford University Press.

Lu, Houyuan, Xiaoyan Yang, Maolin Ye, Kam-Biu Liu, Zhengkai Xia, Xiaoyan Ren, Linhai Cai, Naiqin Wu, and Tung-Sheng Liu. 2005. "Millet Noodles in Late Neolithic China." *Nature* 437: 967.

Lu Liancheng and Yan Wenming. 2002. "Society During the Three Dynasties." In *The Formation of Chinese Civilization: An Archaeological Perspective*, ed. Sarah Allan. New Haven, Conn.: Yale University Press. 141–202.

Lu, Tracey. 2005. "The Origin and Dispersal of Agriculture and Human Diaspora in East Asia." In *The Peopling of East Asia: Putting Together Archaeology, Linguistics and Genetics*, ed. Laurent Sagart, Roger Blench, and Alicia Sanchez-Mazas. London: RoutledgeCurzon. 51–62.

———. 2011. "Prehistoric Migration, Historic War, and the Occurrence of Rice Farming and Consumption in South China." Proceedings, 12th Conference of the Foundation for Chinese Dietary Culture, Okinawa. 239–51.

Luo Feng. 2008. "A History of the Production and Consumption of Milk Products in the North of China: an Archaeological and Ethnological Enquiry." *Journal of Chinese Dietary Culture* 4: 115–78.

———. 2012. "Liquor Still and Milk-Wine Distilling Technology in the Mongol-Yuan period." In *Chinese Scholars on Inner Asia*, ed. Luo Xin and Roger Covey. Bloomington: Indiana University, Sinor Research Institute for Inner Asian Studies. 487–518.

Ma Lie. 2010. "2,400-Year-Old Soup Found in NW China." *China Daily* online, December 13.

MacNeish, Richard S., and Jane G. Libby. 1995. *Origins of Rice Agriculture: The Preliminary Report of the Sino-American Jiangxi (PRC) Project SAJOR.* University of Texas at El Paso Publications in Anthropology 13. El Paso: El Paso Centennial Museum.

Maenchen-Helfen, Otto. 1973. *The World of the Huns.* Berkeley: University of California Press.

Mair, Victor. 1998. *Canine Conundrums: Eurasian Dog Ancestor Myths in Historical and Ethnic Perspective.* Sino-Platonic Papers 87. Philadelphia: University of Pennsylvania, Department of Asian and Middle Eastern Studies.

———. 2005. "The Northwest(ern) Peoples and the Recurrent Origins of the 'Chinese' State." In *The*

Teleology of the Modern Nation-State: Japan and China, ed. Joshua Fogel. Philadelphia: University of Pennsylvania Press. 46–86.

———, ed. 2006. *Contact and Exchange in the Ancient World*. Honolulu: University of Hawai'i Press.

Mallory, J. P., and Victor H. Mair. 2000. *The Tarim Mummies: Ancient China and the Mystery of the Earliest Peoples from the West*. London: Thames and Hudson.

Mallory, Walter H. 1926. *China, Land of Famine*. Special Publication 6. New York: American Geographical Society.

Mann, Charles C., photographs by Vincent J. Musi. 2011. "The Birth of Religion." *National Geographic*, June, 34–59.

Marks, Robert B. 1996. "Commercialization Without Capitalism: Processes of Environmental Change in South China, 1550–1850." *Environmental History* 1: 56–82.

———. 1998. *Tigers, Rice, Silk, and Silt: Environment and Economy in Late Imperial South China*. New York: Cambridge University Press.

———. 2009. "Geography Is Not Destiny: Historical Contingency and the Making of the Pearl River Delta. In *Good Earths: Regional and Historical Insights into China's Environment*, ed. Ken-Ichi Abe and James E. Nickum. Kyoto: Kyoto University Press. 1–28.

———. 2012. *China: Its Environment and History*. Lanham, Md.: Rowman and Littlefield.

Marmé, Michael. 2005. *Suzhou: Where the Goods of All the Province Converge*. Stanford, Calif.: Stanford University Press.

Marozzi, Justin. 2004. *Tamerlane: Sword of Islam, Conqueror of the World*. London: Da Capo.

Martinez, Arsenio Peter. 2009. "Institutional Development, Revenues and Trade." In *The Cambridge History of Inner Asia: The Chinggisid Age*, ed. Nicola Di Cosmo, Allen J. Frank, and Peter B. Golden. Cambridge: Cambridge University Press. 89–108.

Maugh, Thomas H., II, and Karen Kaplan. 2005. "Neolithic Chinese Used Their Noodles." *Los Angeles Times*, October 13, 1, 25.

May, Timothy. 2007. *The Mongol Art of War*. Yardley, Pa.: Westholme.

———. 2012. *The Mongol Conquests in World History*. London: Reaktion Books.

Mazumdar, Sucheta. 1998. *Sugar and Society in China: Peasants, Technology, and the World Market*. Cambridge, Mass.: Harvard University Press.

———. 1999. "The Impact of New World Food Crops on the Diet and Economy of China and India, 1600–1900." In *Food in Global History*, ed. Raymond Grew. Boulder, Colo.: Westview.

McGovern, Patrick E. 2003. *Ancient Wine: The Search for the Origins of Viniculture*. Princeton, N.J.: Princeton University Press.

———. 2009. *Uncorking the Past: The Quest for Wine, Beer, and Other Alcoholic Beverages*. Berkeley: University of California Press.

McNeill, J. R. 1998. "China's Environmental History in World Perspective." In *Sediments of Time*, ed. Mark Elvin and Liu Ts'ui-jung. Cambridge: Cambridge University Press. 31–49.

Mencius. 1970. *Mencius*. Trans. D. C. Lau. Harmondsworth: Penguin.

Menzies, Nicholas. 1988. "Taungya: A Sustainable System of Forestry in South China." *Human Ecology* 16, 4: 361–74.

———. 1994. *Forest and Land Management in Imperial China*. New York: St. Martin's.

Métailié, Georges. 1989. "Histoire naturelle et humanisme en Chine et en Europe au XVIe siècle: Li Shizhen et Jacques Dalechamp." *Revue de l'Histoire des Sciences* 42: 353–74.

Metzo, Katherine. 2005. "Articulating a Baikal Environmental Ethic." *Anthropology and Humanism* 30: 39–54.

Meyer, Andrew. 2011. "The Alters of the Soil and Grain and Closer Than Kin: The Qi Model of In-
    tellectual Participation and the Jixzia Patronage Community." *Early China* 33–34 (2010–2011):
    37–99.
Meyer, Rachel, Kenneth Karol, Damon Little, Michael Nee, and Amy Litt. 2012. "Phylogeographic
    Relationships Among Asian Eggplants and New Perspectives on Eggplant Domestication." *Mo-
    lecular Phylogenetics and Evolution* 63: 685–701.
Mintz, Sidney. 1985. *Sweetness and Power: The Place of Sugar in Modern History*. New York: Penguin.
Mirbabaev, A. K., P. Zieme, and Wang Furen. 2000. "The Development of Education: *Maktab,
    Madrasa*, Science and Pedagogy." In *History of Civilizations of Central Asia*, Vol. 4, *The Age of
    Achievement: A.D. 750 to the End of the Fifteenth Century*, Part 2, *The Achievements*, ed. C. E.
    Bosworth and M. S. Asimov. Paris: UNESCO. 31–59.
Mithen, Stephen. 2006. *The Singing Neanderthals: The Origins of Music, Language, Mind, and Body*.
    Cambridge, Mass.: Harvard University Press.
Mithen, Steven J., Bill Finlayson, Sam Smith, Emma Jenkins, Mohammed Najjar, and Darko
    Maričević. 2011. "An 11,600 Year-old Communal Structure from the Neolithic of Southern Jor-
    dan." *Antiquity* 85: 350–64.
Moerman, Daniel E. 1998. *Native American Ethnobotany*. Portland, Ore.: Timber Press.
Molina, Jeanmaire, Martin Sikora, Nandita Garud, Jonathan M. Flowers, Samara Rubinstein, Andy
    Reynolds, Pu Huang, Scott Jackson,Barbara A. Schaal, Carlos D. Bustamante, Adam R. Boyko,
    and Michael D. Purugganana. 2011. "Molecular Evidence for a Single Evolutionary Origin of
    Domesticated Rice." *Proceedings of the National Academy of Sciences* (May 2).
Morgan, David. 2006. "The Mongol Empire in World History." In *Beyond the Legacy of Genghis
    Khan*, ed. Linda Komaroff. Leiden: Brill. 425–37.
Morris, Ian. 2010. *Why the West Rules—For Now: The Patterns of History, and What They Reveal
    about the Future*. New York: Farrar, Straus and Giroux.
Mote, Frederick. 1994. "Chinese Society Under Mongol Rule, 1215–1368." In *The Cambridge History
    of China*, Vol. 6, *Alien Regimes and Border States, 907–1368*, ed. Herbert Franke and Denis
    Twitchett,. Cambridge: Cambridge University Press. 616–64.
———. 1999. *Imperial China 900–1800*. Cambridge, Mass.: Harvard University Press.
Mote, Frederick, and Denis Twitchett, eds. 1988. *The Cambridge History of China: The Ming Dynasty*.
    2 vols. Cambridge: Cambridge University Press.
Mukhamedjanov, A. R. 1994. "Economy and Social System in Central Asia." In *History of Civiliza-
    tions of Central Asia*, Vol. 2, *The Development of Sedentary and Nomadic Civilizations: 700BC
    to AD 250*, ed. Janos Harmatta, B. N. Puri, and G. F. Etemadi. Paris: UNESCO. 265–90.
Nadkarni, K. M. 1976. *Indian Materia Medica*. Rev. and enlarged A. K. Nadkarni. Bombay: Popular
    Prakashan.
Nappi, Carla. 2009. *The Monkey and the Inkpot: Natural History and Its Transformations in Early
    Modern China*. Cambridge, Mass.: Harvard University Press.
Needham, Joseph, with Lu Gwei-djen. 2000. *Science and Civilisation in China*. Vol. 6, *Biology and
    Biological Technology*, Part 6, *Medicine*, ed. Nathan Sivin. Cambridge: Cambridge University
    Press.
Needham, Joseph, Lu Gwei-Djen, and Ling Wang. 1971. *Science and Civilisation in China*, Vol. 4,
    Physics and Physical Technology, Pt. 3, *Civil Engineering and Nautics*. Cambridge: Cambridge
    University Press.
Nelson, Sarah M. 1993. *The Prehistory of Korea*. Cambridge: Cambridge University Press.

——. 1994. *The Development of Complexity in Prehistoric North China*. Sino-Platonic Papers. Philadelphia: University of Pennsylvania, Department of Asian and Middle Eastern Studies.

——, ed. 1995. *The Archaeology of Northeast China: Beyond the Great Wall*. London: Routledge.

——, ed. 1998. *Ancestors for the Pigs: Pigs in Prehistory*. Philadelphia: University of Pennsylvania Museum.

——. 1999. "Megalithic Monuments and the Introduction of Rice into Korea." In *The Prehistory of Food: Appetites for Change*, ed. Chris Gosden and Jon Hather. London: Routledge. 147–65.

Newman, Jacqueline M., and Roberta Halporn, eds. 2004. *Chinese Cuisine, American Palate: An Anthology*. New York: Center for Thanatology Research and Education.

Nisbett, Richard E. 2003. *The Geography of Thought: How Asians and Westerners Think Differently . . . and Why*. New York: Free Press.

Nisbett, Richard E., K. Peng, I. Choi, and Ara Norenzayan. 2001. "Culture and Systems of Thought: Holistic Versus Analytic Cognition." *Psychological Review* 108: 291–310.

Nowak, Margaret, and Stephen Durrant. 1977. *The Tale of the Nišan Shamaness: A Manchu Folk Epic*. Seattle: University of Washington Press.

Nuijten, Edwin, Robbert van Treueren, Paul Struik, Alfred Mokuwa, Florent Okry, Bela Teeken, and Paul Richards. 2009. "Evidence for the Emergence of New Rice Types of Interspecific Hybrid Origin in West African Farmers' Fields." PLoS One 4(10) e7335. doi 10:1371/journal.pone 0007335.

Ohnishi, Ohmi. 1998. "Search for the Wild Ancestor of Buckwheat III: The Wild Ancestor of Cultivated Common Buckwheat, and of Tatary Buckwheat." *Economic Botany* 52: 123–33.

Olsen, Stanley J. 1993. "Evidence of Early Domestication of the Water Buffalo in China." In *Skeletons in Her Cupboard*, ed. Anneke Clason, Sebastian Payne, and Hans-Peter Uerpmann. Oxford: Oxbow Monographs. 151–56.

Oppenheimer, Stephen, and Martin Richards. 2002. "Polynesians: Devolved Taiwanese Rice Farmers or Wallacean Maritime Traders with Fishing, Foraging and Horticultural Skills?" In *Examining the Farming / Language Dispersal Hypothesis*, ed. Peter Bellwood and Colin Renfrew. Cambridge: McDonald Institute for Archaeology. 287–97.

Ouyang Xiu. 2004. *Historical Records of the Five Dynasties*. Trans. Richard Davis. New York: Columbia University Press.

Pagel, Mark, Quentin D. Atkinson, Andreea Calude, and Andrew Meade. 2013. "Ultraconserved Words Point to Deep Linguistic Unity Across Eurasia." *Proceedings of the National Academy of Sciences* 110: 8471–76.

Pages 2k Consortium. 2013. "Continental-Scale Temperature Variability During the Past Two Millennia." *Nature Geoscience* 6: 339–46.

Palandri, Angela Jung. 1977. *Yüan Chen*. New York: Twayne.

Park, Jang-Sik, William Honeychurch, and Amartuvshin Chunag. 2011. "Ancient Bronze Technology and Nomadic Communities of the Inner Gobi Desert, Mongolia." *Journal of Archaeological Sciences* 38: 805–17.

Pascal, Blaise. 2005. *Pensées*. Ed. and trans. Roger Ariew. Indianapolis: Hackett.

Paz, Victor. 2002. "Island Southeast Asia: Spread or Friction Zone?" In *Examing the Farming / Language Dispersal Hypothesis*, ed. Peter Bellwood and Colin Renfrew. Cambridge: McDonald Institute for Archaeology. 275–85.

Pechenkina, Ekaterina, and Xiaolin Ma. 2008. "Trajectories of Health in Early Farming Communities of East Asia. Paper, Society for American Archaeology, annual meeting, Vancouver.

Pemberton, Robert W. "The Use of the Thai Giant Waterbug, *Lethocerus indicus* (Hemiptera: Belostomatidae), as Human Food in California." *Pan-Pacific Entomologist* 64: 81–82.

Peterson, Christian, Xueming Lu, Robert D. Drennan, and Da Zhu. 2010. "Hongshan Chiefly Communities in Neolithic Northeastern China." *Proceedings of the National Academy of Sciences* 107: 5756–61.

Peterson, Christian, and Gideon Shelach. 2010. "The Evolution of Early Yangshao Period Village Organization in the Middle Reaches of Northern China's Yellow River Valley." In *Becoming Villagers: Comparing Early Village Societies*, ed. Matthew Bandy and Jake Fox. Tucson: University of Arizona Press. 246–75.

———. 2012. "Jiangzhai: Social and Economic Organization of a Middle Neolithic Chinese Village." *Journal of Anthropological Archaeology* 31: 265–301.

Philippi, Donald. 1982. *Songs of Gods, Songs of Humans: The Epic Tradition of the Ainu*. San Francisco: North Point Press.

Pierotti, Raymond. 2011. *Indigenous Knowledge, Ecology, and Evolutionary Biology*. New York: Routledge.

Pines, Yuri. 2009. *Envisioning Eternal Empire: Chinese Political Thought of the Warring States Era*. Honolulu: University of Hawai'i Press.

Pinkaew Laungaramsri. 2001. *Redefining Nature: Karen Ecological Knowledge and the Challenge to the Modern Conservation Paradigm*. Chennai, India: Earthworm Books.

Pinker, Stephen. 2011. *The Better Angels of Our Nature: Why Violence Has Declined*. New York: Viking.

Polo, Marco. 1927. *The Book of Ser Marco Polo the Venetian*. Trans. Henry Yule, ed. George Parks. New York: Macmillan.

Pomeranz, Kenneth. 2000. *The Great Divergence: China, Europe, and the Making of the Modern World Economy*. Princeton, N.J.: Princeton University Press.

Porkert, Manfred. 1974. *Theoretical Foundations of Chinese Medicine*. Cambridge, Mass.: MIT Press.

Ptak, Roderich. 2011. *Birds and Beasts in Chinese Texts and Trade: Lectures Related to South China and the Overseas World*. Wiesbaden: Harrassowitz.

Rall, Jutta. 1970. *Die vier grossen Medizinschulen der Mongolenzeit: Stand und Entwicklung der chinesische Medezin in der Chin- und Yüan-Zeit*. Wiesbaden.

Raphals, Lisa. 1998. *Sharing the Light: Representations of Women and Virtue in Early China*. Albany, N.Y.: SUNY Press.

Ratchnevsky, Paul. 1991. *Genghis Khan: His Life and Legacy*. Oxford: Blackwell.

Read, Bernard E. 1946. *Famine Foods Listed in the Chiu Huang Pen Ts'ao*. Shanghai: Henry Lester Institute of Medical Research.

Redford, Kent. 1990. "The Ecologically Noble Savage." *Orion Nature Quarterly* 9: 25–29.

Reich, David, et al. 2010. "Genetic History of an Archaic Hominin Group from Denisova Cave in Siberia." *Nature* 468: 1053–60.

Reich, David, Kumarasamy Thangaraj, Nick Patterson, Alkes L. Price, and Lalji Singh. 2009. "Reconstructing Indian Population History." *Nature* 461: 489–94.

Rice, Patricia C. 2005. "Recent Finds, Paleoanthropology 2005." *General Anthropology* 11, 2: 11–15.

Richardson, S. D. 1990. *Forests and Forestry in China*. Washington, D.C.: Island Press.

Richter-Bernburg, L., and H. M. Said. 2000. "Medical and Veterinary Sciences." In *History of Civilizations of Central Asia*, Vol. 4, *The Age of Achievement: A.D. 750 to the End of the Fifteenth Century*, Part 2, *The Achievements*, ed. C. E. Bosworth and M. S. Asimov. Paris: UNESCO. 299–322.

Rickett, W. Allyn. 1965. *Kuan-Tzu*. Vol. 1. Hong Kong: Hong Kong University Press.

———. 1985. *Guanzi: Political, Economic, and Philosophical Essays from Early China*. Vol. 1. Princeton, N.J.: Princeton University Press.

———. 1998. *Guanzi: Political, Economic, and Philosophical Essays from Early China*. Vol. 2. Princeton, N.J.: Princeton University Press.

Riddle, John. 1985. *Dioscorides on Pharmacy and Medicine*. Austin: University of Texas Press.

Robinson, Cyril D. 1998. "The Bagel and Its Origins—Mythical, Hypothetical and Undiscovered." *Petits Propos Culinaires* 58: 42–46.

Rodinson, Maxime, A. J. Arberry, and Charles Perry. 2001. *Medieval Arab Cookery*. Totnes, Devon: Prospect Books.

Rogers, David. 2007. "The Contingencies of State Formation in Eastern Inner Asia." *Asian Perspectives* 46: 249–74.

Rossabi, Morris. 1988. *Khubilai Khan: His Life and Times*. Berkeley: University of California Press.

———. 1992. *Voyager from Xanadu: Rabban Sauma and the First Journey from China to the West*. Tokyo: Kodansha International.

———. 1994. "The Reign of Khubilai Khan." In *Cambridge History of China*, Vol. 6, *Alien Regimes and Border States, 907–1368*, ed. Herbert Franke, Denis Twitchett and Nicola di Cosmo. Cambridge: Cambridge University Press. 414–89.

Roux, Jean-Paul. 1966. *Faune et flore sacrées dans les sociétés altaïques*. Paris: A. Maisonneuve.

———. 1984. *Religion des Turcs et des Mongols*. Paris: Payot.

Rozin, Elisabeth. 1983. *Ethnic Cuisine: The Flavor Principle Cookbook*. Lexington, Mass.: Stephen Greene Press.

Ruddle, Kenneth, and Tomoya Akimichi, eds. 1984. *Maritime Institutions in the Western Pacific*. Senri Ethnological Studies 17. Osaka: National Museum of Ethnology.

Ruddle, Kenneth, and Gongfu Zhong. 1988. *Integrated Agriculture-Aquaculture in South China: The Dike-Pond System of the Zhujiang Delta*. Cambridge: Cambridge University Press.

Rummel, Rudolph. 1998. *Statistics of Democide*. Munich: LIT.

Sabban, Françoise. 1986. "Un savoir-faire oublié: le travail du lait en Chine ancienne." *Zibun: Memoirs of the Research Institute for Humanistic Studies* 21: 31–65.

———. 1993. "La viande en Chine: Imaginaire et usages culinaires." *Anthropozoologica* 18:79–90.

———. 1997. "La diète parfaite d'un lettré retiré sous les Song du Sud." *Études Chinoises* 16: 7–57.

———. 1999. "Chinese Regional Cuisine: The Genesis of a Concept." Paper, Sixth Symposium on Chinese Dietary Culture, Fuzhou.

———. 2009. "Forms and Evolution of Chinese Cuisine in France." In *Regionalism and Globalism in Chinese Culinary Culture*, ed. David Holm. Taipei: Foundation of Chinese Dietary Culture. 369–80.

Saferi, Helen. 1986. *Noshe Djan: Afghan Food and Cookery*. Totnes, Devon: Prospect Books.

Sagart, Laurent, Roger Blench, and Alicia Sanchez-Mazas, eds. 2005. *The Peopling of East Asia: Putting Together Archaeology, Linguistics and Genetics*. New York: RoutledgeCurzon.

Said, Hakim Mohammed. 1990. "Some Common Herbal Drugs Used in Chinese and Greco-Arab Medicine." Paper presented at the Sixth International Conference on the History of Science in China, Cambridge, England.

———. 1997. *Hamdard Pharmacopoeia of Eastern Medicine*. Karachi: Hamdard Foundation.

Salick, Jan, Yang Yongping, and Anthony Amend. 2005. "Tibetan Land Use and Change near Khawa Karpo, Eastern Himalayas." *Economic Botany* 59: 312–25.

Sanders, Alan, and Jantsangiin Bata-Ireedüi. 1999. *Colloquial Mongolian*. London: Routledge.

Sanft, Charles. 2009. "Edict of Monthly Ordinances for the Four Seasons in Fifty Articles from 5 C.E.: Introduction to the Wall Inscription Discovered at Xuanquanzhi, with Annotated Translation." *Early China* 32: 125–208.

Santangelo, Paolo. 1998. "Ecologism Versus Moralism: Conceptions of Nature in Some Literary Texts of Ming-Qing Times." In *Sediments of Time: Environment and Society in Chinese History*, ed. Mark Elvin and Liu Ts'ui-Jung. Cambridge: Cambridge University Press. 617–56.

Sauer, Carl. 1952. *Agricultural Origins and Dispersals*. Berkeley: University of California Press.

Savage-Smith, Emilie, F. Klein-Franke, and Ming Zhu. 2011. "Medicine." In *Food Culture and Health in Pre-Modern Islamic Societies*, ed. David Waines. Leiden: Brill. 207–17.

Schäfer, Dagmar. 2010. *The Crafting of the 10,000 Things: Knowledge and Technology in Seventeenth-Century China*. Chicago: University of Chicago Press.

Schafer, Edward. 1963. *The Golden Peaches of Samarkand*. Berkeley: University of California Press.

———. 1967. *The Vermilion Bird*. Berkeley: University of California Press.

Scheid, Volker, Dan Bensky, Andrew Ellis, and Randall Barolet. 2009. *Chinese Herbal Medicine: Formulas and Strategies*. Seattle: Eastland Press.

Schlosser, Eric. 2002. *Fast Food Nation*. New York: Perennial.

Schmitt, Edwin. 2012. "The Unintended Consequences of De-Swiddening in Western China." Manuscript.

Schneewind, Sarah. 2006. *A Tale of Two Melons: Emperor and Subject in Ming China*. Indianapolis: Hackett.

Schoppa, Keith. 2002. *Song Full of Tears: Nine Centuries of Chinese Life Around Xiang Lake*. Boulder, Colo.: Westview.

Scott, James C. 2009. *The Art of Not Being Governed: An Anarchist History of Upland Southeast Asia*. New Haven, Conn.: Yale University Press.

Sen, Tansen. 2003. *Buddhism, Diplomacy, and Trade: The Realignment of Sino-Indian Relations, 600–1400*. Honolulu: Association of Asian Studies and University of Hawai'i Press.

Serventi, Silvano, and Françoise Sabban. 2002. *Pasta: The Story of a Universal Food*. New York: Columbia University Press.

Shao Wangping. 2002. "The Formation of Civilization: The Interaction Sphere of the Longshan Period." In *The Formation of Chinese Civilization: An Archaeological Perspective*, ed. Sarah Allan. New Haven, Conn.: Yale University Press. 85–124.

Shelach, Gideon. 2012. "On the Invention of Pottery." *Science* 336: 1644–45.

Shelach, Gideon, and Leore Grosman. 2008. "From the Younger Dryas to the Yellow River." Paper, Society for American Archaeology, annual meeting, Vancouver.

Shelach, Gideon, Kate Raphael, and Yitzhak Jaffe. 2011. "Sanzuodian: The Structure, Function and Social Significance of the Earliest Stone Fortified Sites in China." *Antiquity* 85: 11–26.

Sherratt, Andrew. 1981. "Plough and Pastoralism: Aspects of the Secondary Products Revolution." In *Pattern of the Past: Studies in Honour of David Clarke*, ed. Ian Hodder, Glynn Isaac, and Norman Hammond. Cambridge: Cambridge University Press. 261–305.

———. 2006. "The Trans-Eurasian Exchange: The Prehistory of Chinese Relations with the West." In *Contact and Exchange in the Ancient World*, ed. Victor Mair. Honolulu: University of Hawai'i Press. 30–62.

Shi, Tian. 2010. *Sustainable Ecological Agriculture in China: Bridging the Gap Between Theory and Practice*. Amherst, N.Y.: Cambria Press.

Shih Sheng-Han. 1973. *On "Fan Sheng-chih Shu," an Agriculturist Book of China Written in the First Century B.C.* Peking: Science Press.

———. 1974. *A Preliminary Survey of the Book Ch'i Min Yao Shu, an Agricultural Encyclopaedia of the 6th Century.* 2nd ed. Peking: Science Press.

Shutova, Nadezhda. 2006. "Trees in Udmurt Religion." *Antiquity* 80: 318–27.

Silverstein, Todd. 2007. "Religion: Islamic Science Fading Before Colonialism." *Nature* 448: 864.

Simmons, Richard VanNess. 2011. "Hangzhou Storytelling and Songs." In *The Columbia Anthology of Chinese Folk and Popular Literature*, ed. Victor H. Mair and Mark Bender. New York: Columbia University Press. 472–78.

Simoons, Frederick J. 1991. *Food in China: A Cultural and Historical Inquiry.* Boca Raton, Fla.: CRC Press.

Sinoda, Osamu. 1977. "The History of Chinese Food and Diet." *Progress in Food and Nutritional Science* 2: 483–97.

Sinor, Denis. 1998. In *History of Civilizations of Central Asia.* Vol. 4, *The Age of Achievement: A.D. 750 to the End of the Fifteenth Century*, Part 1, *The Historical, Social and Economic Setting*, ed. M. S. Asimov and C. E. Bosworth. Paris: UNESCO. 227–42.

Sivin, Nathan. 2000. Introduction. In Joseph Needham with Lu Gwei-djen, *Science and Civilisation in China.* Vol. 6, *Biology and Biological Technology*, Part 6, *Medicine*, ed. Nathan Sivin. Cambridge: Cambridge University Press.

Skinner, G. William, ed. 1977. *The City in Late Imperial China.* Stanford, Calif.: Stanford University Press.

———. 2001. *Marketing and Social Structure in China.* Ann Arbor, Mich.: Association for Asian Studies.

Smil, Vaclav. 2000. *Feeding the World.* Cambridge, Mass.: MIT Press.

———. 2004. *China's Past, China's Future: Energy, Food, Environment.* New York: RoutledgeCurzon.

Smith, Adam. 1910 [1776]. *The Wealth of Nations.* London: J. M. Dent.

Smith, Paul Jakov. 1991. *Taxing Heaven's Storehouse.* Cambridge, Mass.: Harvard University Press.

———. 2003. "Introduction: Problematizing the Song-Yuan-Ming Transition." In *The Song-Yuan-Ming Transition in Chinese History*, ed. Paul Jakov Smith and Richard von Glahn. Cambridge, Mass.: Harvard University Asia Center. 1–34.

Smith, Paul Jakov, and Richard von Glahn, eds. 2003. *The Song-Yuan-Ming Transition in Chinese History.* Cambridge, Mass.: Harvard University Asia Center.

Smith, Robert L. 2003. "On the Scent." *Natural History* (March): 60–62.

So, Yan-kit. 1992. *Classic Food of China.* London: Macmillan.

Song Xian. 2000. *Huihui Yaofang.* Beijing: Chinese Arts Press.

Spence, Jonathan D. 1974. *Emperor of China: Self-Portrait of K'ang-Hsi.* New York: Knopf.

Spencer, J. E. 1966. *Shifting Agriculture in Southeast Asia.* Berkeley: University of California Press.

Standen, Naomi. 2011. *Unbounded Loyalty: Frontier Crossing in Liao China.* Honolulu: University of Hawai'i Press.

Stearns, Justin K. 2011. *Infectious Ideas: Contagion in Premodern Islamic and Christian Thought in the Western Mediterranean.* Baltimore: Johns Hopkins University Press.

Stein, Rolf A. 1990 [1987]. *The World in Miniature: Container Gardens and Dwellings in Far Eastern Religious Thought.* Trans. Phyllis Brooks. Stanford, Calif.: Stanford University Press.

Steinhardt, Nancy Shatzman. 1998. "Liao Archaeology: Tombs and Ideology Along the Northern Frontier of China." *Asian Perspectives* 37: 224–44.

Sterckx, Roel. 2002. *The Animal and the Daemon in Early China*. Albany, NY: SUNY Press.

———, ed. 2005. *Of Tripod and Palate: Food, Politics, and Religion in Traditional China*. New York: Palgrave Macmillan.

———. 2011. *Food, Sacrifice and Sagehood in Early China*. Cambridge: Cambridge University Press.

Sternberg, Tony. 2012. "Piospheres and Pastoralists: Vegetation and Degradation in Steppe Grasslands." *Human Ecology* 40: 811–20.

Stone, Richard. 2008. "Three Gorges Dam: Into the Unknown." *Science* 321: 628–32.

———. 2012. "Despite Gains, Malnutrition Among China's Rural Poor Sparks Concern." *Science* 336: 402.

Strassberg, Richard. 1994. *Inscribed Landscapes: Travel Writing from Imperial China*. Berkeley: University of California Press.

Sturgeon, Janet. 2005. *Border Landscapes: The Politics of Akha Land Use in China and Thailand*. Seattle: University of Washington Press.

Su Heng-an. 2004. *Culinary Arts in Late Ming China: Refinement, Secularization and Nourishment: A Study on Gao Lian's Discourse on Food and Drink*. Taipei: SMC Publishing.

Sukhu, Gopal. 2012. *The Shaman and the Heresiarch: A New Interpretation of the Li Sao*. Albany, N.Y.: SUNY Press.

Sun Guangren, Liu Zhaochun, Li Hongho, Yang Suqin, and Chong Guipin. 1990. *Health Preservation and Rehabilitation*. Shanghai: Publishing House of the Shanghai College of Traditional Chinese Medicine.

Sun Simiao. 2007. *Recipes Worth a Thousand Gold*. Trans. Sumei Yi, ed. E. N. Anderson. www.krazykioti.com.

Sung Ying-hsing. 1966. *T'ien-kung K'ai-wu: Chinese Technology in the Seventeenth Century*. Trans. and annotated E-Tu Zen Sun and Shiou-Chuan Sun. University Park: Pennsylvania State University Press.

Tacuinum Sanitatis: The Medical Health Handbook. 1976. Ed. and trans. Luisa Cogliati Arano. New York: Braziller.

Tan Ta Sen. 2009. *Cheng Ho and Islam in Southeast Asia*. Singapore: Institute of Southeast Asian Studies.

Tao, Jing-Shen. 1976. *The Jurchen in Twelfth-Century China*. Seattle: University of Washington Press.

Theophrastus. 1926. *Enquiry into Plants*. Trans. A. F. Hort. 2 vols. Loeb Classical Library. Cambridge, Mass.: Harvard University Press.

Thick, Malcolm. 2010. *Sir Hugh Plat: The Search for Useful Knowledge in Early Modern London*. Totnes, Devon: Prospect Books.

Tillman, Hoyt, and Stephen H. West, eds. 1995. *China Under Jurchen Rule: Essays on Chin Intellectual and Cultural History*. Albany, N.Y.: SUNY Press.

Tilt, Bryan. 2009. *The Struggle for Sustainability in Rural China*. New York: Columbia University Press.

Tjan Tjoe Som. 1949. *Po Hu T'ung, The Comprehensive Discussions in the White Tiger Hall*. 2 vols. Leiden: Brill.

Tooker, Deborah. 2012. *Space and the Production of Cultural Difference Among the Akha Prior to Globalization: Channeling the Flow of Life*. Amsterdam: Amsterdam University Press.

Totman, Conrad. 1989. *The Green Archipelago: Forestry in Preindustrial Japan*. Berkeley: University of California Press.

———. 1995. *The Lumber Industry in Early Modern Japan*. Honolulu: University of Hawai'i Press.

Trombert, Eric. 2009. "Between Harvesting and Cooking: Grain Processing in Dunhuang, a Qualitative and Quantitative Survey." In *Regionalism and Globalism in Chinese Culinary Culture*, ed. David Holm. Taiwan: Foundation of Chinese Dietary Culture. 147–79.

Tsang, Cheng-Hwa. 2005. "Recent Discoveries at the Tapenkeng Culture Sites in Taiwan: Implications for the Problem of Austronesian Origins." In *The Peopling of East Asia: Putting Together Archaeology, Linguistics and Genetics*, ed. Laurent Sagart, Roger Blench, and Alicia Sanchez-Mazas. London: RoutledgeCurzon. 63–74.

Tsien, Tsuen-Hsuin. 1985. *Science and Civilisation in China*. Vol. 5, *Chemistry and Chemical Technology*. Part 1, *Paper and Printing*. Cambridge: Cambridge University Press.

Tuan, Yi-Fu. 1968. "Discrepancies Between Environmental Attitudes and Behavior: Examples from Europe and China." *Canadian Geographer* 12: 176–91.

———. 1969. *China*. Chicago: Aldine.

Tuchman, Barbara. 1978. *A Distant Mirror: The Calamitous Fourteenth Century*. New York: Knopf.

Tucker, Mary Evelyn, and John Berthrong. 1998. *Confucianism and Ecology: The Interrelation of Heaven, Earth, and Humans*. Cambridge, Mass.: Harvard University Press for Harvard University Center for the Study of World Religions.

Tucker, Mary Evelyn, and Duncan R. Williams, eds. 1997. *Buddhism and Ecology: The Interaction of Dharma and Deeds*. Cambridge, Mass.: Harvard University Press for Center for the Study of World Religions.

Tuite, Kevin. 1994. *An Anthology of Georgian Folk Poetry*. Cranbury, N.J.: Associated University Presses.

Twitchett, Denis, ed. 1979. *The Cambridge History of China*. Vol. 3, *Sui and T'ang China, 589–906*. Cambridge: Cambridge University Press.

———, ed. 2001. *The Cambridge History of China: The Ch'ing Dynasty*. 2 vols. Cambridge: Cambridge University Press.

Twitchett, Denis, and Paul Jakov Smith. 2009. *The Cambridge History of China*. Vol. 5, *The Sung Dynasty and Its Precursors, 907–1279*. Cambridge: Cambridge University Press.

Tylor, Edward. 1871. *Primitive Culture*. London: John Murray.

Underhill, Anne P., and Junko Habu. 2006. "Early Communities in East Asia: Economic and Sociopolitical Organization at the Local and Regional Levels." In *Archaeology of Asia*, ed. Miriam T. Stark. Oxford: Blackwell. 121–48.

Unschuld, Paul U. 1985. *Medicine in China: A History of Ideas*. Berkeley: University of California Press.

———. 1986. *Medicine in China: A History of Pharmaceutics*. Berkeley: University of California Press.

———. 2003. *Huang Di Nei Jing Su Wen. Huang Di's Inner Classic. Basic Questions. Nature, Knowledge, Imagery in an Ancient Chinese Medical Text*. Appendix assisted by Zheng Jinsheng and Hermann Tessenow. Berkeley: University of California Press.

———. 2009. *What Is Medicine? Western and Eastern Approaches to Healing*. Berkeley: University of California Press.

Vainstein, Sevyan. 1980 [1972]. *Nomads of South Siberia: The Pastoral Economies of Tuva*. Cambridge. Ed. Caroline Humphrey, trans. Michael Colenso. Studies in Social Anthropology 25. London: Cambridge University Press. [Russian].

Vaissière, Étienne de la. 2005a. "Huns et Xiongnu." *Central Asiatic Journal* 49: 3–26.

———. 2005b. *Sogdian Traders: A History*. Trans. James Ward. Leiden: Brill.

Van de Mieroop, Marc. 2008. *A History of the Ancient Near East ca. 3000–323 B.C.* Oxford: Black-well.

Van Driem, George. 1999. "Neolithic Correlates of Ancient Tibeto-Burman Migrations." In *Archaeology and Language II*, ed. by Roger Blench and M. Spriggs. London: Routledge. 67–102.

———. 2002. "Tibeto-Burman Phylogeny and Prehistory: Languages, Material Culture and Genes." In *Examining the Farming/Language Dispersal Hypothesis*, ed. Peter Bellwood and Colin Renfrew. Cambridge: McDonald Institute for Archaeology. 233–49.

Vermeer, Eduard B. 1998. "Population and Ecology Along the Frontier in Qing China." In *Sediments of Time: Environment and Society in Chinese History*, ed. Mark Elvin and Liu Ts'ui-Jung. Cambridge: Cambridge University Press. 235–79.

Vico, Giambattista. 1999. *New Science: Principles of the New Science Concerning the Common Nature of Nations*. Trans. David Marsh. New York: Penguin.

Virmani, S. S. 1994. *Heterosis and Hybrid Rice Breeding*. FAO Monographs in Theoretical and Applied Genetics 22. Berlin: Springer-Verlag.

Visson, Lynn. 1999. *The Art of Uzbek Cooking*. New York: Hippocrene Books.

Vogel, Hans Ulrich. 2009. "Salt and Chinese Culture: Some Comparative Aspects." In *Regionalism and Globalism in Chinese Culinary Culture*, ed. David Holm. Taipei: Foundation of Chinese Dietary Culture. 181–248.

Von Glahn, Richard. 2003a. "Imagining Pre-modern China." In *The Song-Yuan-Ming Transition in Chinese History*, ed. Paul Jakov Smith and Richard von Glahn. Cambridge, Mass.: Harvard University Asia Center. 35–70.

———. 2003b. "Towns and Temples: Urban Growth and Decline in the Yangzi Delta, 1100–1400." In *The Song-Yuan-Ming Transition in Chinese History*, ed. Paul Jakov Smith and Richard von Glahn. Cambridge, Mass.: Harvard University Asia Center. 176–211.

Vovin, Alexander. 2005. "The End of the Altaic Controversy: In Memory of Gerhard Doerfer." *Central Asiatic Journal* 49: 71–132.

Wade, Geoff, and Sun Laichen, eds. 2010. *Southeast Asia in the Fifteenth Century: The China Factor*. Singapore: National University of Singapore Press.

Wagner, Donald. 2008. *Science and Civilisation in China*. Vol. 5, *Chemistry and Chemical Technology*. Part 11, *Ferrous Metallurgy*. Cambridge: Cambridge University Press.

Waley, Arthur. 1939. *Three Ways of Thought in Ancient China*. New York: Macmillan.

———. .1946. *Chinese Poems*. London: Allen and Unwin.

———. .1955. *The Nine Songs: A Study of Shamanism in Ancient China*. London: Allen and Unwin.

Waley-Cohen, Joanna. 2007. "The Quest for Perfect Balance." In *Food: The History of Taste*, ed. Paul Freedman. Berkeley: University of California Press. 99–134.

Walker, Anthony R. 1986. *The Toda of South India: A New Look*. Delhi: Hindustan.

———, ed. 1995. *Mvuh Hpa Mi Hpa: Creating Heaven, Creating Earth: An Epic Myth of the Lahu People in Yunnan*. Trans. Shi Kun. Chiang Mai: Silkworm Books.

Wallerstein, Immanuel. 1976. *The Modern World-System: Capitalist Agriculture and the Origins of the European World-Economy in the Sixteenth Century*. New York: Academic Press.

Wallis, Faith. 2010. *Medieval Medicine: A Reader*. Toronto: University of Toronto Press.

Wang Ch'ung. 1907. *Lun-Heng*. Trans. Alfred Forke. Leipzig: Otto Harrassowitz; London: Luzac; Shanghai: Kelly and Walsh.

Wang, Di. 2008. *The Teahouse: Small Business, Everyday Culture, and Public Politics in Chengdu, 1900–1950*. Stanford, Calif.: Stanford University Press.

Wang Jianhua "Ayoe." 2007. "Landscapes and Natural Resource Management of Akha People in Xishuangbanna, Southwestern China." Paper, Society of Ethnobiology, annual meeting, Berkeley, California.

———. 2008. "Cultural Adaptation and Sustainability: Political Adaptation of Akha People in Xishuangbanna, Southwestern China." Final Report to Sumernet Foundation, Bangkok.

———. 2013. "Sacred and Contested Landscapes." Ph.D. dissertation, Anthropology, University of California, Riverside.

Wang Zhongshu. 1982. *Han Civilization*. Trans. K. C. Chang. New Haven, Conn.: Yale University Press.

Ware, James R. 1966. *Alchemy, Medicine and Religion in the China of A.D. 320: The Nei P'ien of Ko Hung*. New York: Dover.

Watson, James L., ed. 1997. *Golden Arches East: McDonald's in East Asia*. Stanford, Calif. Stanford University Press.

Watson, James L., and Rubie S. Watson. 2004. *Village Life in Hong Kong: Politics, Gender, and Ritual in the New Territories*. Hong Kong: Chinese University Press.

Watson, Oliver. 2006. "Pottery Under the Mongols." In *Beyond the Legacy of Genghis Khan*, ed. Linda Komaroff. Leiden: Brill. 346–54.

Weatherford, Jack. 2004. *Genghis Khan and the Making of the Modern World*. New York: Three Rivers Press.

Weber, Max. 1946. *From Max Weber: Essays in Sociology*. Ed. and trans. Hans Gerth and C. Wright Mills. New York: Oxford University Press.

Weeks, Martha E. 2004. "Cuisine of Dungan (Hui) People." *Flavor and Fortune* 11, 2: 9–11, 28.

———. 2005. *Kyrgyz Cooking*. Northampton, Mass.: Martha E. Weeks.

Weiner, Steve, Qinqi Xu, Paul Goldberg, Jinyi Liu, and Ofer Bar-Yosef. 1998. "Evidence for the Use of Fire at Zhoukoudian, China." *Science* 281: 251–53.

Wen Duzhong and David Pimentel. 1986a. "Seventeenth Century Organic Agriculture in China, Part I: Cropping Systems in Jiaxing Region." *Human Ecology* 14, 1: 1–14.

———. 1986b. "Seventeenth Century Organic Agriculture in China, Part II: Energy Flows Through an Agrosystem in Jiaxing Region." *Human Ecology* 14, 1: 15–28.

West, Barbara, and Ben-Xiong Zhou. 1988. "Did Chickens Go North? New Evidence for Domestication." *Journal of Archaeological Science* 15: 515–34.

West, Paige. 2012. *From Modern Production to Imagined Primitive: The Social World of Coffee from Papua-New Guinea*. Durham, N.C.: Duke University Press.

West, Stephen H. 1987. "Cilia, Scale and Bristle: The Consumption of Fish and Shellfish in the Eastern Capital of the Northern Song." *Harvard Journal of Asian Studies* 47: 595–634.

Wheatley, Paul. 1965. "A Note on the Extension of Milking Practices into Southeast Asia in the First Millennium AD." *Anthropos* 60: 577–90.

Widmer, Ellen. 2006. *The Beauty and the Book: Women and Fiction in Nineteenth-Century China*. Cambridge, Mass.: Harvard University Asia Center.

Wiens, Herold. 1954. *China's March Toward the Tropics*. New York: Shoe String Press.

Will, Pierre-Étienne. 1990 [1980]. *Bureaucracy and Famine in Eighteenth-Century China*. Trans. Elborg Forster. Stanford, Calif.: Stanford University Press.

Will, Pierre-Étienne, and R. Bin Wong, with James Lee. 1991. *Nourish the People: The State Civilian Granary System in China, 1650–1850*. Ann Arbor: University of Michigan Press.

Willcox, George, and Danielle Stordeur. 2012. "Large-Scale Cereal Processing Before Domestication During the Tenth Millennium cal BC in Northern Syria." *Antiquity* 86: 99–114.

Willerslev, Rane. 2007. *Soul Hunter: Hunting, Animism, and Personhood Among the Siberian Yuk-aghirs*. Berkeley: University of California Press.

Williams, Dee Mack. 1996a. "The Barbed Walls of China: A Contemporary Grassland Drama." *Journal of Asian Studies* 55: 665–91.

———. 1996b. "Grassland Enclosure: Catalyst of Land Degradation in Inner Mongolia." *Human Organization* 55: 307–13.

———. 2000. "Representations of Nature on the Mongolian Steppe: An Investigation of Scientific Knowledge Construction." *American Anthropologist* 102: 503–19.

———. 2002. *Beyond Great Walls: Environment, Identity and Development on the Chinese Grasslands of Inner Mongolia*. Stanford, Calif.: Stanford University Press.

Wilms, Sabine. 2002. "The Female Body in Medieval China." Ph.D. dissertation, East Asian Studies, University of Arizona, Tucson.

Wink, Andre. 2002. *Al-Hind: The Making of the Indo-Islamic World*. Leiden: Brill.

Witzel, Michael. 2006. "Early Loan Words in Western Central Asia: Indicators of Substrate Popula-tions, Migrations, and Trade Relations." In *Contact and Exchange in the Ancient World*, ed. Victor Mair. Honolulu: University of Hawai'i Press. 158–90.

Wolpert, Lewis. 1993. *The Unnatural Nature of Science*. Cambridge, Mass.: Harvard University Press.

Wong, R. Bin. 1997. *China Transformed: Historical Change and the Limits of European Experience*. Ithaca, N.Y.: Cornell University Press.

Wright, Arthur. 1978. *The Sui Dynasty*. New York: Knopf.

Wu Jing-Nuan, ed. and trans. 1993. *Ling Shu, or the Spiritual Pivot*. Washington, D.C.: Taoist Center.

Wu, Xiaolong. 2013. "Cultural Hybridity and Social Status: Elite Tombs on China's Northern Fron-tier During the Third Century BC." *Antiquity* 87: 121–36.

Wu, Xiaolong, Chi Zhang, Paul Goldberg, David Cohen, Yan Pan, Trina Arpin, and Ofer Bar-Yosef. 2012. "Early Pottery at 20,000 Years Ago in Xianrendong Cave, China." *Science* 336: 1696–1700.

Wu, Xu. 2011. *Farming, Cooking, and Eating Practices in the Central China Highland: How Hezha Foods Function to Establish Ethnic Identity*. New York: Edwin Mellen.

Wu, Yi-Li. 2010. *Reproducing Women: Medicine, Metaphor, and Childbirth in Late Imperial China*. Berkeley: University of California Press.

———. 2011. "Body, Gender, and Disease: The Female Breast in Late Imperial Chinese Medicine." *Late Imperial China* 32: 83–128.

Xie, Jian, Liangliang Hu, Jianjun Tang, Xue Wu, Nana Li, Yongge Yuan, Haishue Yang, Jiaen Zhang, Shimin Luo, and Xin Chen. 2011. "Ecological Mechanisms Underlying the Sustainability of the Agricultural Heritage Rice-Fish Coculture System." *Proceedings of the National Academy of Sciences*, online, November 14.

Xu, Jianchu, Erzi T. Ma, Duojie Tashi, Yongshou Fu, Zhi Lu, and David Melick. 2005. "Integrating Sacred Knowledge for Conservation: Cultures and Landscapes in Southwest China." *Ecology and Society* 10, 2, article 7.

Xu Pingfang. 2002. "The Formation of the Empire by the Qin and Han Dynasties and the Unifica-tion of China." In *The Formation of Chinese Civilization: An Archaeological Perspective*, ed. Sarah Allan. New Haven, Conn.: Yale University Press. 249–82.

Xuanzang. 1996. *The Great Tang Dynasty Record of the Western Regions*, edited by Xuanzang's fol-lowers from his writings, ca. 700 CE. Ed. and trans. Li Rongxi. Berkeley, Calif.: Mnumata Center for Buddhist Translation and Research.

Xunzi. 1999. *Xunzi*. Trans. John Knoblock. Changsha and Beijing: Hunan People's Publishing House and Foreign Language Press.

Yan Wenming. 2002. "The Beginning of Farming." In *The Formation of Chinese Civilization: An Archaeological Perspective*, ed. Sarah Allan. New Haven, Conn.: Yale University Press. 26–41.

Yang Xiaoneng. 1999. *The Golden Age of Chinese Archaeology: Celebrated Discoveries from the People's Republic of China*. Washington, D.C.: National Gallery of Art.

Yang, Xiaoyan, Zhiwei Wan, Linda Perry, Houyuan Lu, Qiang Wang, Chaohong Zhao, Jun Li, Fei Xie, Jincheng Yu, Tianxing Cui, Tao Wang, Mingqi Li, and Quansheng Ge. 2012. *Proceedings of the National Academy of Sciences* 109: 3726–30.

Yao, Alice, and Jiang Zhilong. 2012. "Rediscovering the Settlement System of the 'Dian' Kingdom, in Bronze Age Southern China." *Antiquity* 86: 353–67.

Yates, Robin. 1997. *Five Lost Classics*. New York: Ballantine.

———. 2011. "Soldiers, Scribes, and Women: Literacy Among the Lower Orders in Early China." In *Writing and Literacy in Early China: Studies from the Columbia Early China Seminar*, ed. Li Feng and David Prager Branner. Seattle: University of Washington Press. 339–69.

Yi Jianping. 2012. "Circumscription Theory and the Political Evolution in Prehistoric China." *Social Evolution and History* 11, 2: 120–30.

Yin Shaoting. 2001. *People and Forests: Yunnan Swidden Agriculture in Human-Ecological Perspective*. Trans. Marcus Fiskejo. Kunming: Yunnan Educational Publishing House.

Yuan Jing, Rowan Flad, and Luo Yunbing. 2008. "Meat-Acquisition Patterns in the Neolithic Yangzi River Valley, China." *Antiquity* 82: 351–66.

Yuan Longping. 2002. "The Second Generation of Hybrid Rice in China." Presentation, 20th annual FAO International Rice Commission meeting, Bangkok. Retrieved from FAO website January 13, 2013.

Yuan Mei. 1997. *I Don't Bow to Buddhas: Selected Poems of Yuan Mei*. Trans. J. P. Seaton. Port Townsend, Wash.: Copper Canyon Press.

Zeder, Melinda. 2012. "The Domestication of Animals." *Journal of Anthropological Research* 68: 161–90.

Zeitlin, Judith. 1991. "The Petrified Heart: Obsession in Chinese Literature." *Late Imperial China* 12: 1–26.

Zhang Chi and Hsiao-chun Hung. 2013. "Jiahu 1: Earliest Farmers Beyond the Yangtze River." *Antiquity* 87: 46–63.

Zhang He. 2011. "Is *Shuma* the Chinese Analog of *Soma/Haoma*? A Study of Early Contacts Between Early Iranians and Chinese." Sino-Platonic Papers 216. Philadelphia: University of Pennsylvania, Department of Asian and Middle Eastern Studies.

Zhang Jinghong. 2010. "Multiple Visions of Authenticity: Pure Tea Consumption in Yunnan and Other Places." *Journal of Chinese Dietary Culture* 6: 63–105.

Zhang Juzhong and Lee Yun Kuen. 2005. "The Magic Flutes." *Natural History* (September): 43–47.

Zhang Liangren. 2011. "Soviet Inspiration in Chinese Archaeology." *Antiquity* 85: 1049–59.

Zhang, Pingszhong, Hai Cheng, R. Lawrence Edwards, Fahu Chen, Yongjin Wang, Xulin Yang, Jian Liu, Ming Tan, Xianfeng Wang, Jinghua Liu, Chunlei An, Zhibo Dai, Jing Zhou, Dezhong Zhang, Jihong Jia, Liya Jin, and Kathleen R. Johnson. 2008. "A Test of Climate, Sun, and Culture Relationships from an 1810-Year Chinese Cave Record." *Science* 322: 940–42.

Zhang Wengao, Jia Wencheng, Li Shupei, Zhang Jing, Ou Yangbing, and Xu Xuelan. 1990. *Chinese Medicated Diet*. Shanghai: Publishing House of the Shanghai College of Traditional Chinese Medicine.

Zhang Zhongpei. 2002. "The Yangshao Period." In *The Formation of Chinese Civilization: An Archaeological Perspective*, ed. Sarah Allan. New Haven, Conn.: Yale University Press. 42–83.

Zhang Zhongqing. 1987. *Synopsis of Prescriptions of the Golden Chamber: A Classic of Traditional
Chinese Medicine*. 2nd century A.D. Trans. and ed. Luo Xiwen. Beijing: New World Press.

———. 1993. *Treatise on Febrile Diseases Caused by Cold, with 500 Cases*. 2nd century A.D. Trans.
and ed. Luo Xiwen. Beijing: New World Press.

Zhao Zhijun. 2011. "New Archaeobotanic Data for the Study of the Origins of Agriculture in China."
Current Anthropology 52, S4: S295–S306.

Zheng Yunfei, Sun Guoping, Qin Ling, Li Chunhai, Wu Xianhong, and Chen Xugao. 2010. "Rice
Fields and Modes of Rice Cultivation Between 5000 and 2500 BC in East China." *Journal of
Archaeological Science* 36: 2609–16.

Zhou, Xinyue, Lingnan He, Qing Yang, Junpeng Lao, and Roy F. Baumeister. 2012. "Control Depri-
vation and Styles of Thinking." *Journal of Personality and Social Psychology* 102: 460–78.

Zhou, Yichun. 2013. "*Honglou Meng* and Agrarian Values." *Late Imperial China* 34: 28–66.

Zhuschchikhovskaya, Irina. 1997. "On Early Pottery-Making in the Russian Far East." *Asian Perspectives* 36: 159–74.

Ziegler, Alan D., Ross H. Andrews, Carl Grundy-Warr, Paiboon Sithithaworn, and Trevor N. Petney.
2011. "Fighting Liverflukes with Food Safety Education." *Science* 331: 282–83.

INDEX